The Exemplary Sidney and the Elizabethan Sonneteer

Sir Philip Sidney. From Thomas Lant, *Sequitur celebritas & pompa funebris* (1587). By permission of the British Library CC20f12, plate 1, detail.

The Exemplary Sidney and the Elizabethan Sonneteer

Lisa M. Klein

Newark: University of Delaware Press
London: Associated University Presses

Associated University Presses
440 Forsgate Drive
Cranbury, NJ 08512

Associated University Presses
16 Barter Street
London WC1A 2AH, England

Associated University Presses
P.O. Box 338, Port Credit
Mississauga, Ontario
Canada L5G 4L8

The paper used in this publication meets the requirements of the American National Standard for Permanence of Paper for Printed Library Materials Z39.48–1984.

Library of Congress Cataloging-in-Publication Data

Klein, Lisa M., 1958-
The exemplary Sidney and the Elizabethan sonneteer / Lisa M. Klein.
p. cm.
Includes bibliographical references and index.
ISBN 0-87413-624-5 (alk. paper)
1. Sidney, Philip, Sir, 1554–1586—Criticism and interpretation. 2. Literature and history—England—History—16th century. 3. Great Britain—History—Elizabeth, 1558–1603. 4. Petrarca, Francesco, 1304–1374—Influence. 5. Sonnets, English—History and criticism. 6. English poetry—Italian influences. 7. Renaissance—England. I. Title.
PR2343.K56 1998
821'.3—dc21 96–45480
CIP

PRINTED IN THE UNITED STATES OF AMERICA

Follow the direction of your most loving brother. . . . Imitate his virtues, exercises, studies and actions; he is a rare ornament of this age, the very formular that all the well-disposed young gentlemen of our Court do form also their manners and life by. In truth I speak it without flattery of him or of myself: he hath the most rare virtues that ever I found in any man. . . . Once again I say, imitate him.

—Sir Henry Sidney to Robert Sidney

Contents

Acknowledgements

I am grateful to Judith H. Anderson for her guidance on this project from its earliest incarnation. She taught me to read Elizabethan poetry for its nuances, and she challenged me at every turn with her incisive comments on my work. Ohio State University has provided support in the form of leave time to attend to the writing of this book. Frank Donoghue, David Frantz, Margaret Hannay, John King, Jeredith Merrin, John Norman, Ann Lake Prescott, and Luke Wilson have read all or a part of the manuscript. Their comments and suggestions have helped me to improve the book, though of course any remaining errors or omissions are my own responsibility. I am grateful to Barbara Brumbaugh and Nancy Miller for their painstaking research assistance. I offer special thanks to Alan Hager for his generosity and his advice in shaping the opening chapters. For their moral support and scholarly advice, I am grateful to Chris Highley and Janine Reed. Portions of chapters 5 and 6 appeared in *Sidney Newsletter and Journal* 12 (1993) and in *Spenser Studies* 10 (1992), and I thank Gerald Rubio and AMS Press for permission to use this material. I also wish to acknowledge the readers, editors, and staff of the University of Delaware Press and Associated University Presses for their responsiveness and assistance in the publication of this book. Finally, my profoundest thanks go to my husband, Rob Reed, for his patience and love; he is the coauthor of my best and, I pray, most enduring works: our sons, David and Adam.

The Exemplary Sidney and the Elizabethan Sonneteer

Introduction: The Exemplary Sir Philip Sidney

The Sidney Legend

On 17 February 1587, the city of London, from its commonest citizens to its highest nobility, beheld an event it would not soon forget. A funeral cortege wound its way along the chief streets of the city to St. Paul's Cathedral. It was headed by thirty-two of the poor, signifying the age of the deceased, followed by soldiers, family servants, friends, and kindred, to the number of about two hundred twenty. A footman led the field horse caparisoned in rich embroidery and ridden by a page trailing a broken lance; another led a horse in cloth of gold, its page carrying a battle-ax, head down. One observer, moved at the vivid reminder that the deceased had fallen in battle, "markt his stately Horse, how they hong downe their head, / As if they mourned for their Knight that followed after dead."[1] At the center of the procession, fourteen yeomen and four friends (including Fulke Greville) bore the funeral bier of Sir Philip Sidney, lord governor of Flushing in the Low Countries, who had died the previous 17 October of a musket wound to his thigh, inflicted at the battle of Zutphen. His near kinsmen carried banners, and the chief mourner, Robert Sidney, followed with various gentlemen, male relatives, and noblemen, "who fixt their eyes upon the ground, which now must howse their Knight."[2] Black-robed representatives of the states of Holland, city officials in their purple gowns, including the lord mayor, and 120 members of the grocer's company in their livery followed, bringing the total procession to some four hundred mourners. Behind them marched the citizens of London, led by their captains and bearing pikes, halberds, and muskets, with fifes and drums adding their lilting but solemn notes. This entire procession was rendered in exquisite detail in a series of thirty engravings, *Sequitur & pompa funebris*. Also known as *Lant's Roll*, the pictorial representation of Sidney's funeral was the work of Thomas Lant, a member of the Sidney household who accompanied him to the Low Countries. Besides representing and naming all the formal participants, Lant gives the impression of a groundswell of public affection and grief for Sidney. The streets along the route to St. Paul's, he reports,

> were so thronged with people, that ye mourners had scarcely rome to pass. the houses likewise weare as full as they might be of which great multitude ther wear few or none that shed not some tears as the corps passed by them. Of the mourners every Gent had a man, every knight 2, some Noblemen 12, some more, some less as also sundry Englishe Captaynes of the low Countrie with divers other Gent. that came voluntary and are not in this woorke expressed, so that the whole nomber were about 700 persons.[3]

Following the sermon and burial, the troops fired their weapons, as Bernard Whetstone relates: "two volley of brave shot, they thundred in the skies, / And thus his funerall did ende with many weeping eies."[4] This event, publicized and commemorated, inaugurated the posthumous cult of Sidney, who shortly came to occupy a significant place in the collective memory of Elizabethan culture. His priority as a poet and statesman was acknowledged by all who took up their pens in his wake, among them the poets of my study: Fulke Greville, Samuel Daniel, and Edmund Spenser.

The response to Sidney's death was immediate and widespread, and his appeal was strong in all levels of society. In the month after his death, an epitaph authorized by the archbishop was registered and printed. Within ten days of his funeral, three accounts of his death and funeral were registered. Elegies by George Whetstone, Angel Day, John Phillips, Thomas Churchyard, and Lodowick Bryskett appeared in 1587. Copies of these survive, but many other broadside ballads and elegies were lost. So numerous were the tributes to Sidney that Thomas Churchyard found himself coming too late to an already harvested field where "there is left no Seede nor Graine to no such an infortunate Gleaner as myself." He turned the situation to his advantage by claiming to speak for everyone: "[T]he generall consent of many multitudes procured my Pen to set forth this work."[5] The universities of Oxford and Cambridge also rushed to praise Sidney, issuing three volumes of Latin memorial verse; the first was addressed to Leicester on the day of Sidney's funeral.[6] The University of Leiden also issued a collection.[7] As many critics have pointed out, this efflorescence of elegiac verse was unprecedented; before this moment, there had been virtually no vernacular tradition of funeral elegy, nor were academic collections common.[8] Sidney's death, displayed in public ritual and published in verses and visual images, was an event made available to all; nobles, poets, and the illiterate participated in and shaped the meaning of Sidney's life and death.[9]

The celebration of Sidney was impelled by more than grief for a fallen hero. From its origin in the funeral, the development of the Sidney legend evinced motives of political or poetic gain. The very funeral pageantry disguised behind-the-scenes struggles for control over Sidney's image. Elaborate funerals were the order of the day for members of the aristocracy, but such a display was unprecedented for one of Sidney's rank, a mere knight. Sidney had not been among Queen Elizabeth's favorites, and she did not finance or attend his funeral. She seemed determined to control the event, however, refusing offers from the states of Holland to bury his body at their expense.[10] In the end, the staggering expenses were borne by Sidney's father-in-law, Sir Francis Walsingham, who, according to Lant, "spared not any coste to have this funerall well performed," to his own financial ruin.[11] Sidney's body had reached England on 5 November 1586, but the funeral was not held until mid-February 1587, a delay no one has satisfactorily accounted for. Walsingham may simply have been struggling to settle Sidney's estate in order to fund the funeral, but some biographers suggest a more Machiavellian subterfuge: that Elizabeth allowed the elaborate funeral and postponed its date in order to divert the populace from the execution of Mary, queen of Scots, which occurred just eight days before Sidney's funeral.[12] Though financially strapped, Walsingham produced a blockbuster funeral, perhaps hoping to rally support for the political cause for which Sidney had died: the defense of Protestantism in the Low Countries. (Walsingham and Sidney's uncles encouraged a reluctant Elizabeth actively to support this cause, a war also likely to be unpopular with her subjects.)[13]

Walsingham not only staged the elaborate funeral but also patronized the work which portrayed its splendor and asserted a symbolic status for Sidney far beyond his actual rank. It was Walsingham who brought together Thomas Lant and the Dutch engraver Theodoor de Brij. Their frieze-like rendering of the funeral procession, consisting of thirty-two plates, was a genre unknown in England, but it was used on the Continent to depict funeral processions of royalty, most recently that of William of Orange; this Protestant leader, assassinated in

Detail of Sir Philip Sidney's Funeral Procession.
From Thomas Lant's *Sequitur celebritas & pompa funebris* (1587).
By permission of the British Library CC20f12, plate 16.

1584, had been an ally of the Leicester-Walsingham faction at court and a personal friend to Sidney.[14] There was some danger in supervising a work which symbolically linked Sidney to continental royalty, but there was a possible payoff, too, if citizens could be inspired to follow Sidney's example and fight Spain in the Netherlands. Significantly, almost a third of the plates depict foot soldiers with their harquebuses, halberds, and pikes; moreover, the work records that commoners swelled the ranks to seven hundred, suggesting that the various estates were unified in their grief and wholehearted support for Sidney. Thus, even Sidney's allies were not above using his death for propaganda purposes, making of his funeral a public occasion (and publication event) that expressed and sought to affect the social and political order.[15]

Lant was one of the first to benefit measurably from commemorating Sidney. His work was evidently pleasing to Sidney's allies, for Leicester and Walsingham obtained for him a position in the College of Arms in 1588.[16] In fact, the celebration of Sidney's virtues was for many a gesture of political allegiance to the Leicester-Walsingham faction and their activist Protestant agenda. The Oxford *Exequiae* and the Cambridge *Lachrymae* were dedicated to Leicester, and Oxford's *Peplus* was dedicated to the earl of Pembroke, who had married Sidney's sister, Mary.[17] Arthur Golding dedicated his completion of Sidney's translation of the Protestant Philippe de Mornay's *A Woorke Concerning the Trewnesse of the Christian Religion* (1587) to Leicester. John Phillips's elegy was offered to Essex, Leicester's stepson and inheritor of Sidney's best sword (as well as of his wife). George Whetstone's elegy was addressed to Warwick, and Angel Day's to Walsingham; Robert Waldegrave, a radical Protestant publisher, issued both Day's and Phillips's elegies.[18]

The origin of the Sidney legend in this world of Protestant politicking is, however, often obscured by the idealizing verses of admiring poets. Enabled by the conventions of epideictic verse, Sidney's first memorial poets lifted him from the mire of history to the realm of eternal and sacred virtue.[19] Phillips denies that "sweet *Sidney* was ever touched with one spot of disloyaltie"; he possessed "a cleare conscience, & a mind garnished with innocencie." He is a type of Christ who triumphs over death and sin: "But is *Sidney* deade, no he liveth, his virtues in this life have made a conquest of death" and placed him in the company of saints.[20] In his dedication to Leicester, Golding also praises conventional virtues of piety and patriotism in Sidney:

> [T]his comfort remayneth, that he dyed not languishing in ydlenesse ryot and excesse . . . but of manly wounds received in service of his Prince, in defence of persons oppressed, in maintenance of the only true Catholick & Christian Religion . . . the honorablest death that could be desired, and best beseeming a Christian Knight. . . .[21]

For Golding, Sidney's death in the service of his country sanctified him and removed from him any taint of worldliness. This same idealizing impulse is exhibited by those who recount scenes of Sidney's deathbed renunciation, hinted at in the early elegies but lavishly expanded in later prose accounts. Chief among these is *The Manner of Sir Philip Sidney's Death*, possibly written by the minister George Gifford, which recounts Sidney's deathbed behavior as a model of holy dying. Featured are his acts of prayer, repentance, reading of Scripture, confession of his "vanity" (loving Lady Rich), the ensuing comfort, and finally, a joyful embrace of the life to come.[22] For Sidney's life to become exemplary, it must be shown to culminate in a godly death, which crowns its virtues and absolves its indiscretions.

Death, burial, and poetic eulogies mark only the beginning of the Sidney legend, the collective (and selective) remembrance of Sidney. With the publication of *Arcadia* in 1590 and *Astrophil and Stella* in 1591, poetic fame was added to Sidney's reputation for military heroism.[23] His sonnets not only helped launch the career of Samuel Daniel, whose own poems were appended to the pirated 1591 volume, but also legitimized, even inspired, the writing and publication of dozens of sonnet sequences before the decade ended. Sonneteers from the anonymous author of *Zepheria* (1594) to the ambitious Michael Drayton, author of *Ideas Mirrour* (1594), hailed Sidney as "high mus'd Astrophil" and "Divine Syr *Phillip*." Long after the sonnet vogue had passed, Sidney's niece, Lady Mary Wroth, published a sonnet sequence, *Pamphilia to Amphilanthus*, appended to a romance, *The Countess of Montgomery's Urania*; the gesture of compliment and debt to her uncle is obvious. Nor did the lamentation over Sidney's death cease soon after his burial. *The Phoenix Nest* (1593) featured elegies by Matthew Roydon, Walter Ralegh, and Edward Dyer; these were reprinted with Spenser's *Astrophel* and several new elegies in 1595. Fifteen years after Sidney's death, Francis Davison's *A Poetical Rapsody* (1602) contained several elegies on Sidney. The countess of Pembroke began her poetic career lamenting her brother's loss, composing original poems of mourning, completing his Psalm translations, editing the *Arcadia*, and patronizing works that glorified his image.[24]

From the beginning, however, the poetic impulse to idealize and imitate Sidney was paired with a baser motive of self-promotion. One example is Arthur Golding, whose completion of Sidney's translation of Philippe de Mornay was entered on the Stationer's Register on 7 November, a mere five days after news of Sidney's death reached London. When Sidney exchanges his pen for a pike, Golding picks up the fallen pen, performing *his* service to the country. By claiming to fulfill Sidney's will, Golding identifies with his godly model of Christian service:

> [I]t was his pleasure to commit the performance of this peece of service which he had intended to the Muses or rather to Christes Church and his native Countrie, unto my charge. . . . In his name therefore & as an executor of his will in that behalf, I humbly offer this excellent worke unto your good Lordship, as his and not myne.[25]

The language is both self-effacing and self-promoting. A cynic might see in the timing of the publication and its dedication a self-serving effort to capitalize on the event of Sidney's death. Indeed, Sidney's close friend, Fulke Greville, called it a "mercenary book."[26]

John Phillips's elegy also shapes an image of Sidney that serves to fashion and promote its own author, in part by openly urging the generosity of patrons. Exemplifying Sidney's populist appeal, Phillips presents Sidney as a model of piety, courtesy, and love of country for all to emulate. The poem is dedicated to the earl of Essex, Leicester's stepson, to whom Sidney had just bequeathed his best sword (and who would soon marry his widow):

> This *Phenix* sweet *Sidney* was the flower of curtesie, who in his life time gave a perfect light in his conversation to leade men to virtue, the fruits wherof so glistered in the eies of mortall creatures, that by his example they might both learne to feare God, to glory in sincerity, to abound in loyalty, & to become carefull lovers of their native countrie.[27]

Phillips continues to characterize Sidney's generous spirit of *noblesse oblige*, providing a model not only for his inferiors but also for his peers:

> [T]his most worthy Knight passing his pilgrimage in this terrestriall vale. . . . to the poore he was mercifull, to the learned liberall, to Sutors a great comfort, to the fatherlesse favourable, to the widdowes, helpfull. . . . (ibid.)

Like Chaucer's Knight, whose worthiness rebukes the unworthy, Sidney's generosity sets an example for all nobles to emulate, specifically Phillips's anticipated patron. The elegy itself is spoken by Sidney's ghost, in the tradition of Churchyard's *Mirror for Magistrates*. There is a moment of uncanny ventriloquism that assists the poet's appeal for patronage when the voice of Sidney's ghost addresses Essex, the patron that Phillips seeks:

> My Devorax, my deare, my joy, my friend,
> of *Essex* Earle ten thousand times adue,
> to God with hart I humblie thee commend,
> hoping in heaven thee face to face to view,
> Mourne not for me, though death my life subdue,
> I live to die, and die to live in deed . . . (ibid.)

For the reader (certainly if he is Essex), this is a disruptive moment in the poem, for we suddenly hear not only Sidney's ghostly voice but also the live voice of the poet addressing his patron. This strange moment reminds us that it is Sidney who (in his death) gives poetic voice to John Phillips—or does Phillips give voice to Sidney? In a kind of literary symbiosis, the elegiac poet helps to fashion Sidney's posthumous image, then draws upon it for self-justification as a poet and patronage-seeker. Phillips's maneuver will be executed with more subtlety in *Delia*, as Daniel recommends himself to the countess of Pembroke by complimenting Sidney and emulating his voice.

Examining the origins of the Sidney legend should convince us that the poetic response to Sidney is not a disinterested aesthetic act but a self-authorizing and sometimes critical gesture inseparable from the matrix of literary and social acts that begot Sidney's reputation. These include dedications to Sidney, elegies, and the funeral and its representations. This cultural matrix also consists of Sidney's own works, the *Defence of Poetry*, *Arcadia*, and *Astrophil and Stella*, read both in manuscript and in print. In the latter form, Sidney's works, especially *Astrophil and Stella*, helped to overcome the "stigma of print" and to unleash the sonnets, elegies, and romances that continued to pay tribute to Sidney's powerful example and to promote their own writers.[28] Yet even as they praised and imitated him, writing voluminous sonnets and other tributes, contemporary poets recognized and shared Sidney's ambivalent views about the poetic vocation, aware that the age, with some reason, placed a higher value on action and public service than on poetry and loving. What makes Sidney a characteristic and exemplary figure is that his life exhibits and his writings explore the tension between civic obligation and scholarly retirement, between a man's high aspirations and his limited capabilities. It is this conflicted figure, the alternately confident and sorry maker and defender of fictions, to which poets respond as they struggle for legitimation in his wake. All the poets I study—Fulke Greville, Samuel Daniel, and Edmund Spenser—initially draw on the example of Sidney to justify their own profession of poetry, to define and authorize themselves, so powerful is his presence as a cultural forebear, but their writings ultimately contest and variously modify Sidney's heroic image. In his sonnets, each poet appropriates and refashions Sidney's example; the sonnet sequence thereby becomes a locus of literary change, a forum in which these writers fashion themselves as poets and engage issues central to Sidney's humanist and Protestant legacy.

Sidney's Exemplarity

The hindsight of literary history has made Shakespeare and Spenser the giants of the age, but it was Sidney who was most often cited, admired, and remembered by his contemporaries and seventeenth-century descendants.[29] Those who wrote in his wake often invoke him directly as their model or inspiration, but even writers who never knew Sidney or who lived after him express a sense of loss. Dudley Digges, writing in 1604, laments that "though he lived an age before me, I yet honor, I love his memorie."[30] Praising "Divine Sidney . . . deceas'd ere I begun," George Wither regrets that "I have oft sighed, and bewail'd my *Fate*, / That brought me foorth so many yeeres too late / To view that *worthy*."[31]

John Aubrey, the antiquary and biographer, testifies to Sidney's enduring example in the following century. True or not, his story of the meeting of Sidney and Spenser conveys an important perception that Sidney was the literary master of the age. According to Aubrey, Spenser brought his *Faerie Queene* to Sidney, who first dismissed him but then read his work with delight, sought him out, gave him gold, and remained his lifelong friend.[32] Aubrey himself has a vivid memory of Sidney's image:

> When I was a boy 9 years old, I was with my father at one Mr. Singleton's an Alderman and Wollen-draper in Glocester, who had in his parlour over the

> Chimney, the whole description of the Funerall, engraved and printed on papers pasted together, which at length was, I beleeve, the length of the room at least; but he had contrived it to be turned upon two Pinnes, that turning one of them made the figures march all in order. It did make such a strong impression on my tender Phantasy that I remember it as if it were but yesterday.[33]

In 1635, a copy of *Lant's Roll* mounted in a draper's shop in Gloucester exerted a hold on the imagination of the nine-year-old John Aubrey. This is not hard to imagine, for unrolled, the engravings stretched thirty-eight feet in length.[34] In the fifty years since Sidney's death, it must have been seen and remembered by thousands of people.

Aubrey's account of Sidney is an example of the production of collective memory, defined by Pierre Nora as "what remains of the past in the lived reality of groups, or what these groups make of the past."[35] Truly, Sidney assumed an importance in the collective memory that belied his relative historical insignificance as a coterie writer and a minor courtier who met an untimely death in a foreign war. In fact, one might say that the memory of Sidney—contained and conveyed in manuscripts and in printed works by and about him—eclipsed his own history. Nora's thoughts help to illuminate the vitality of the Sidney legend as a construction of memories rather than of history:

> Memory is life . . . vulnerable to manipulation and appropriation, susceptible to being long dormant and periodically revived. History, on the other hand, is the reconstruction, always problematic and incomplete, of what is no longer. Memory is a perpetually actual phenomenon, a bond tying us to the eternal present; history is a representation of the past.[36]

Aubrey's memory of Sidney's funeral roll exhibits this tension; viewing a historical artifact, a printed text, places him in a kind of eternal present, reveling in the memory itself: "I remember it as if it were but yesterday." My attempt to recover the memory of Sidney and to claim it as a potent cultural force participates in the history of *mentalité*, an inquiry into the attitudes, forms of behavior, and collective representations, conscious or unconscious, of this period of the English Renaissance.[37] Thus I am concerned not with poetic influence but with the construction of poetic reputation, deserved or not. Sidney's reputation is fashioned from memories, individual and collective, stored for the most part in written texts. It is created by writers who are sometimes but not always fully conscious of their intentions as they variously fashion, contest, appropriate, and bequeath to their successors Sidney's image as a hero and poet.

Sidney's exemplarity signals a shift in his humanist culture, which was dedicated to the revival of the classical models of its past.[38] What makes Sidney atypical and hence significant is that he is a contemporary model—one who, moreover, lays claim to the authority usually vested in ancients, in effect superseding them. Lodowick Bryskett's elegy "The Mourning Muse of Thestylis," published with Spenser's *Astrophel* (1595), envisions Sidney in heaven, where Venus, Apollo, and Mars revere him and "even they that boast / Themselves of ancient fame, as *Pirrhus, Hanniball, / Scipio* and *Caesar* . . . high thy glorie do admire." In the same volume, Ralegh praises Sidney as the "*Scipio, Cicero,* and *Petrarch* of our time,"[39] one who combines the virtues of a Roman general, a classical orator, and a vernacular poet—all, of course, authors and authorities. George Whetstone likened Sidney's early death to that of Alexander, who died at the age of twenty-four. In the seventeenth century, Anne Bradstreet continues this vein of praise, even alluding to Spenser's collection. She imagines Sidney at Zutphen as "Brave Hector by the walls of Troy" and, like Ralegh, designates him "our noble Scipio." Her epitaph hails him as "Philip and Alexander, both in one; / Heir to the Muses, the son of Mars in truth."[40]

When Sidney endorsed classical heroes as models in the *Defence of Poetry*, he surely never expected to join their ranks. Men delight, he wrote, "to hear the tales of Hercules, Achilles, Cyrus, Aeneas; and, hearing them, must needs hear the right description of wisdom, valour, and justice."[41] After his death, however, he displaced these heroes, becoming himself the exemplary image of valor. Greville relates a story, apocryphal but nonetheless significant, in which Sidney, bleeding profusely, asks for water; then, before he drinks, he passes the bottle to a poor man with the words, "Thy necessity is yet greater than mine."[42] This story may allude to a similar incident in the life of Alexander.[43] Either Greville makes the association or Sidney recalls it in his action. In turn, this incident in Sidney's life (or legend) becomes the inspiration for Sir Walter Ralegh's display of *sprezzatura* on his way to the scaffold. He offers a poor man his nightcap, echoing Sidney by saying, "for thou hast more need of it now than I."[44]

Importantly, when a figure like Sidney embodies the qualities usually associated with exemplary heroes or writers of the past, the authority of the past is paradoxically both confirmed and subtly undermined; the authority of the present replaces that of the classical exemplar. (Ralegh's heroic gesture recalls Sidney, not Alexander.)[45] Moreover, when the classical model is superseded by an English model, a significant claim for the native land and its military or literary achievements is implied. As an apologist for poetry and as an example of literary achievement, Sidney is the key figure in the development of a nationalist poetics. The important "digression" in his *Defence of Poetry* is really central, for it establishes a canon that includes Chaucer's *Troilus and Criseyde*, the *Mirror of Magistrates*, the lyrics of the earl of Surrey (and Sir Thomas Wyatt), *The Shepheardes Calender*, and *Gorboduc* in order to promote the excellence of the English tongue for poetry.[46] The Englishing of exemplary authors becomes an important trope in the praise of Sidney. John Harington calls him "our English Petrarke," and Gabriel Harvey recommends that "if Homer be not at hand . . . you may read his furious Iliads, & cunning Odysses in the brave adventures of Pyrocles, and Musidorus,"[47] implying that Sidney is England's own epic poet. For Harvey, Sidney's life and fictions are themselves sources of authoritative models: "What should I speake of the two brave Knightes, Musidorus, and Pyrocles, combined in one excellent Knight, Sir Philip Sidney" (51).

One characteristic of the exemplary figure that has hitherto escaped comment is its instability, a Janus-like ability to present opposing faces. The exemplar's excellent features can be cited for imitation and its counterimage suppressed until a chance evocation or intended allusion undermines the positive image. As the next chapters will illustrate, this dynamic is central to Sidney's self-presentation in the *Defence of Poetry* and *Astrophil and Stella* in terms of conflicted exemplars: David was a divine poet *and* a sinner, Epaminondas a general and a street cleaner. Mars was a warrior and Hercules an orator, yet both were shamed by their sexual escapades. These figures are appropriate and perhaps intentional self-images of Sidney, conscious as he was of man's simultaneous erected wit and infected will.

As a military hero and committed Protestant who spent a good deal of his time in the idle pursuit of poetry, Sidney, too, was an equivocal model. Many of Sidney's greatest admirers betray a divided response to him. For instance, Fulke Greville's entire oeuvre can be seen as a coming-to-terms with his ambivalence towards his friend, a fellow Protestant whose most enduring legacy, his amatory fiction and poetry, smacked of immorality. Perhaps Sidney's contemporaneity made his authority more tenuous and open to criticism.[48] Anthony Stafford's ambivalent response to Sidney is clear from his address to the reader of his *The Guide of Honor* (1634?), in which he admits that Sidney's achievements are not universally admired:

> These severe Judges will have a man as serious in his first Booke as his last Will. Some of them lately have not spared even *Apollo's* first-borne, incomparable, and inimitable Sir *Phillip Sydney*, whose *Arcadia* they confine onely to the reading of Chambermaids. . . .[49]

Stafford's response is to defend Sidney as king material, "a man deserving both the Lawrels, and the Crowne to boote," possessing "all the requisits of a King but the Title." He further exhorts the reader:

> [T]he Guide I have given you, is also the Champion of Honor and of her sacred seed. . . . Are you enflamed with a Desire of Domesticall Glory? Imitate the truly great *Sydney*, whose onely Example is far above all my Precepts. . . . emulate the ever famous, everblessed *Sydney*, who is as far above the Envy, as the Understanding of his Detracters, more capable of a Bastinado then an Apology.

Stafford's defense of Sidney as a guide and model of virtue reveals and confronts the darker side of his image, defaced by envy and detraction. He counters Sidney's critics not by defending his literary activity but by asserting his fitness to be a ruler. Indirectly, he valorizes the face of the statesman over that of the poet and expresses persistent cultural doubts about the possibility of reconciling poetry and public action. This complex and ambivalent response to Sidney is typical, suggesting that undecidability is an essential feature of Sidney's exemplary image.

In sum, the importance of exemplary figures in the Renaissance is not merely that they express, enable, or constrain certain behaviors but that they are themselves unstable and malleable, both reflecting and producing changes in the figuration of selfhood and in literary forms. As Timothy Hampton writes:

> Changes in representations of exemplary figures can be seen as symptoms of political and ideological struggles that demand new figurations of the self. These figurations, embodied in the heroic model held up as an image to the reader, in turn act dialectically to produce new discursive modes for representing virtue and, ultimately, new literary forms. . . . It is through developing interplay between the literary representation of historical exemplars and the sphere of public action that the evolution of literary forms in early modernity can be understood.[50]

The case of Sidney confirms Hampton's observation that the interplay of literature and the sphere of public action pressures literary forms and modes of representation. Sidney's life and works generate heroic fictions that serve as exemplary models, enabling admirers like Ralegh to fashion themselves anew, writers to legitimate English romance as a heroic genre, and sonneteers to publish their private amours. Specifically, Sidney's imaginative occupation of the persona of the poet-lover in *Astrophil and Stella* enables successive poets to envision new possibilities for the sonnet—beyond Neoplatonic idealism or Petrarchan imitation—as a means of engagement with culturally central issues of humanist activism, scholarship, and the soul's salvation. But what makes Sidney truly exemplary are the conflicts his image expresses and uneasily reconciles. The contradictions in the heroic facade—between the love poet and the military hero, for instance—make him a complex and equivocal example, such that writers do not simply emulate, but wrestle with and refashion, his figure. This conflicted exemplarity and the ways in which poets accentuate or efface it as they struggle for legitimation in Sidney's wake—this is the burden of my study.

Sidney, the English Petrarch

Ralegh's praise of Sidney as the "Petrarch of our time" introduces an important but complex aspect of Sidney's exemplarity: his relation to Petrarch, himself an exemplary vernacular poet and humanist scholar.[51] Petrarch was an appropriate alter ego for the age's premier love poet, for besides certain of the *Rime sparse* (his love lyrics), his four *Trionfi* were known in translation, and Petrarch's beloved, Laura, figures prominently in all these works.[52] Never mind that most English poets had probably never read an Italian sonnet of Petrarch; their knowledge of him was secondhand, via the translations of Wyatt, Surrey, and Watson, or the French poets Ronsard, DuBellay, and Desportes. Though Bishop Hall would charge that Elizabethan poets filched "whole Pages at a clap for need / From honest *Petrarch*, clad in English weed,"[53] the defining characteristic of English Petrarchism was hardly fidelity to the master's works. The conventions inherited by Elizabethan poets were an amalgam of native and Continental practices, mingling Petrarch with Provençal lyricism, Ovidian eroticism, and a moralistic English strain.[54] Hence I use the term "Petrarchism" loosely, to designate a mode for exploring unrequited passion between a confessed inferior (social or otherwise) and a dominating, somewhat distant mistress and for exhibiting self-conscious artistry by exploiting the tension between established conceits and individual expression of ideas and feeling. The aristocratic culture in which Sidney, Greville, Daniel, and Spenser participated was saturated with Petrarchism, both literary and ideological; as a courtly ideology, it provided a set of beliefs and practices, social and poetic, which helped to perpetuate the Elizabethan hierarchy and informed the individual's very perception of the world.[55]

Self-aware Petrarchism was a feature of the Elizabethan court and its poets. The queen herself, familiar with both Machiavelli and Petrarch, helped to construct her identity as a Petrarchan lady and used it to her own advantage in encounters both amorous and political.[56] She uses Petrarchan rhetoric in a sonnet thought to be a response to the departure of the duke of Alençon after it became clear that their long, politicized courtship would not culminate in marriage. The poem captures the tension of courtly politics and exhibits the ability of Petrarchan rhetoric to express conflict both personal and political:

> I grieve, and dare not show my discontent,
> I love and yet am forced to seem to hate,
> I do, yet dare not say I ever meant,
> I seem stark mute, but inwardly do prate.
> I am and am not, I freeze and yet am burned,
> Since from myself, another self I turned.[57]

The use of oxymoron expresses the tension between her two bodies; though privately she may have wished to marry the duke, the interests of her body politic might be compromised by such a marriage.[58]

Sir John Harington, an assiduous courtier and godson to the queen, also imagined their relationship in Petrarchan terms:

> The Queene stoode up, and bade me reache forthe my arme to reste her thereon. Oh, what swete burden to my nexte songe!—Petrarcke shall eke out good matter for this businesse.[59]

Harington's ecstatic moment of favor with the queen and his instant resolve to render it in Petrarchan song shows him acting within and sustaining the ideological framework. With its configuration of domineering mistress and subordinated poet-lover, Petrarchism helped to render meaningful the peculiar situation of a female monarch who controlled and dispensed political power to male subordinates. Petrarchan language enabled the expression of courtly power relations and one's position within them, whether queen or suitor.

If the unattainable and virtuous beloved was one alter ego of the virgin queen, Petrarch was the legitimizing figure for the courtly poet and lover. George Gascoigne realizes this as he offers his *Tale of Hemetes the Hermit* to Elizabeth with this wish: "YF god wolde deigne to make, a *Petrarks* heire of me / the coomlyest Queene that ever was, my *Lawra* nedes must be."[60] Here and in Ralegh's praise of Spenser in a sonnet prefixed to *The Faerie Queene*, the likeness to Petrarch effectively exalts the poet:

> Me thought I saw the grave, where *Laura* lay
> . . . .
> All suddeinly I saw the Faery Queene:
> At whose approch the soule of *Petrarke* wept,
> And from thenceforth those graces were not seene.
> For they this Queene attended, in whose steed
> Oblivion laid him downe on *Lauras* herse.[61]

Even the praise of the Faerie Queene, an Elizabeth figure, contributes to the elevation of the poet, for if she outshines and outlives Laura, her poet must be Petrarch's superior. Gabriel Harvey, in *Pierces Supererogation*, offers Petrarch as a model for the poet of honorable and witty love:

> Petrarck was a delicate man, and with an elegant judgement gratiously confined Love within the limits of Honour. . . . All posterity honour Petrarck, that was the harmony of heaven; the lyfe of Poetry; the grace of Arte; a precious tablet of rare conceits, & a curious frame of exquisite workemanship; nothing but neate Witt, and refined eloquence.[62]

The comparison to Petrarch was especially apropos to writers of sonnet collections. A commendatory sonnet to Thomas Watson's sequence, *Hecatompathia or Passionate Century of Love* (1582), suggests that Watson and his lady deserve equal praise to Petrarch and Laura and may surpass them. Sidney, above his other contemporaries, was honored as Petrarch's rival. He was dubbed "our English Petrarke" by John Harington and the "Petrarch of our time" by Ralegh. Thomas Churchyard and Barnabe Barnes considered him England's laureate poet.[63]

Sidney's own invocations of Petrarch, however, exhibit a tension between identification with and distinction from his predecessor. Though many poets undoubtedly welcomed the flattering comparison to Petrarch, Sidney, as Astrophil, rejects the association, even the name poet ("I sweare, I wish not there should be / Graved in mine Epitaph a Poet's name").[64] In his sonnets, he is generally aware of Petrarch's priority, but he does not directly imitate or borrow from the *Rime sparse*. Sidney can seem blithely dismissive of derivative Petrarchism while using a Petrarchan gambit to authorize himself, as in this sonnet from *Astrophil and Stella*:

You that poore *Petrarch's* long deceased woes,
With new-borne sighes and denisend wit do sing;
You take wrong waies, those far-fet helpes be such,
As do bewray a want of inward tuch:
And sure at length stolne goods do come to light.
But if (both for your love and skill) your name
You seeke to nurse at fullest breasts of Fame,
Stella behold, and then begin to endite.

(*AS* 15:7–14)

This gesture of renunciation is also one of imitation and substitution; Stella displaces Laura and Sidney, Petrarch. Sidney, moreover, commits the very offense he mocks, singing Petrarch's woes with "new-borne sighes and denisend wit," reviving love poetry and advancing the vernacular, as Petrarch had done before him.[65] As a self-authorizing gesture, however, it signals a renunciation of sociopolitical Petrarchism. Astrophil refuses to play the role of subordinate suitor, even to the point of stealing a kiss from Stella (*AS* song 2) and fantasizing a rape (*AS* song 10). In the end, however, like Petrarch turning to the queen of heaven in the final poem of his *Rime sparse*, he submits completely to Stella's sovereign will. The English Petrarch simultaneously invokes and defies his Italian forebear.

The attempts of Sidney and his fellow poets to authorize themselves in the wake of precursors like Petrarch involve them in what John Guillory calls the "maneuvers of invocation and recognition by which an author becomes an *auctor*."[66] Indeed, the achievement of poetic authority in the Renaissance involves a complex negotiation with prior authorities—literary, political, even divine. Something like a Bloomean "anxiety of influence" pervades the work of English sonneteers, who authorize themselves by acts of poetic misprision (that is, misreading), driven in some cases by anxiety about the precursor, in other cases by a conscious desire to revise or surpass him.[67] To begin with, Wyatt and Surrey creatively and deliberately misread Petrarch.[68] Then, not only Petrarch but Sidney became the prior poet upon whom Spenser, Daniel, and Greville committed their acts of willful misreading, correcting, completing, or rejecting the example of the master.[69] A good example of this complex negotiation with poetic authorities is Drayton's dedication of his sonnet sequence, *Ideas Mirrour* (1594), to Anthony Cooke:

> Yet these mine owne, I wrong not other men,
> Nor trafique further then thys happy Clyme,
> Nor filch from *Portes* nor from *Petrarcks* pen,
> A fault too common in thys latter tyme,
> Divine Syr *Phillip*, I avouch thy writ,
> I am no Pickpurse of anothers wit.[70]

Drayton boldly confronts prior poets, but his claim of originality is undermined by the perfect echo of *AS* 74: 7–8 ("And this I swear, by blackest brook of hell, / I am no pick-purse of another's wit"). Occupying the same poem as Desportes and Petrarch, Sidney is clearly the more immediate and powerful authority for Drayton.

Anxieties about poetic priority and authority are always culturally embedded, hence the limited usefulness of Bloom's post-Romantic taxonomy. Sidney, Spenser, Daniel, and Greville were aware that to invoke Petrarch was potentially to allude to a realm of sociopolitical relationships involving power and sexuality.[71] For poets who also courted the queen's favor, the sonnet mistress was potentially an Elizabeth figure. By his attitude of worshipful submission or hostility toward the lady, the poet either affirmed or challenged the sexual-political hierarchy for which Petrarchism was a metaphor. Likeness to Petrarch was a way of asserting authority and proclaiming laureate ambitions while remaining within the safe bounds of social and poetic convention. (Daniel's poetic "courtship" of the countess of Pembroke's patronage is a case in point.) Accordingly, an anti-Petrarchan stance could suggest a critique of Elizabethan hierarchy (as in Sidney's *Astrophil and Stella*) or a rejection and redefinition of laureate poetics (as in Spenser's *Amoretti*). In sum, in the poetry of those imbued with the Renaissance courtly ethos (and that includes Sidney, Spenser, Daniel, and Greville), literary Petrarchism becomes a means of negotiating their subjection to various cultural authorities.

A profound cultural authority that affects the reception of Petrarchism in Elizabethan England is Protestantism. Against the courtly ethos that made poetry a necessary accomplishment of the courtier, the Protestant belief in the depravity of the human mind and will contributed to a disdain for amorous songs and sonnets, the toys of a wayward poet's youth. Preachers excoriated poets for their "foul and corrupt ballads" and urged them to learn and sing the Psalms of David instead.[72] Indeed, Giles Fletcher observed in the dedication to his sonnet sequence *Licia* (1593) that "our English Genevan Purity hath quite debarred us of honest recreation" and put a damper on the writing of poems and sonnets.[73] Sidney's own Calvinism disposed him to disparage poetry even as he defends it, and to bemoan the misuse of sonnets, which should sing God's immortal praises rather than a mistress's beauty (*Defence* 69). At the time of his death, he was attempting a poetic self-reformation by translating the Psalms, and legend reports that he consigned his looser works to the flames.

Yet Protestantism also dovetailed with certain Petrarchan attitudes; lovers and sinners alike experience fluctuations of hope and despair. Moreover, the utter helplessness of the poet-lover before his mistress is analogous to the reliance of the sinner on the grace of God.[74] The Petrarchan language can express the vagaries of spiritual experience as well as the conflicts of love. It may be no coincidence that the Petrarchan poem most frequently invoked by English Renaissance poets (including the queen) is *Pace non trovo* (*Rime* 134), translated by Wyatt as "I find no peace and all my war is done. / I fear and hope, I burn and freeze like ice."[75] Sidney's formulation of the simultaneously exalted and debased human condition reinscribes the kind of paradox which was so characteristic of English Petrarchism: our "erected wit maketh us know what perfection is, and yet our infected will keepeth us from reaching unto it" (*Defence* 25).[76] Sidney, Greville, and Spenser all express the limited potential for poetry or any other human action to lift man from the mire, and they call for ultimate reliance on theological grace. The greatest limitation on poetic self-fashioning is not without but within the Protestant poet; it is the self-awareness of sin that subdues the Petrarchan poetic ego.[77]

Protestantism, actively professed by Sidney, Greville, and Spenser, assisted the revision of Petrarchism and the English sonnet. All the poets attempt to redirect their earthly love heavenward, as did Petrarch in the final poem of the *Rime sparse*, which is addressed to the Virgin Mary as an act of repentance and renunciation.[78] The move towards renunciation and transcendence is not easily achieved by English sonneteers, however. Sidney acknowledges that much love poetry is vain and scurrilous and that the "lyric is larded with passionate sonnets" (*Defence* 54). His Astrophil assays the voice of the repentant psalmist but remains mired in the clichés of love poetry. The speaker in Greville's *Caelica* associates vain love with religious error and yearns for apocalyptic purgation: "sweet *Jesus*, fill up time and come, / To yeeld the sinne her everlasting doome" (*C* 109).[79] Only Spenser's lover successfully turns from selfish and sterile Petrarchism to mutual love that looks heavenward, as he exhorts the lady, "Let us love, deare love, lyke as we ought, / Love is the lesson which the Lord us taught" (*Amoretti* 68:13–14).[80]

Cultural and Historical Approaches to the Sonnet

The sonnet sequence is one arena where engagement with Sidney's example was inevitable, given the priority and popularity of *Astrophil and Stella*. Thus my focus on the construction of the Sidney legend aims to redirect and revitalize criticism of the Elizabethan sonnet and the Petrarchan poetic tradition generally. Hitherto, sonnets have been deemed derivative and somewhat peripheral to the great achievements of Renaissance literature.[81] In the nineteenth and early twentieth centuries, sonnets as biographical narratives interested critics. Then C. S. Lewis made his stern pronouncement that a sonnet sequence "is not a way of telling a story" but "exists for the sake of prolonged lyrical meditation, chiefly on love," shifting interest to literary and formalist concerns.[82] Modernists have tended to focus on the sonnets' meditative, even tormented, persona, evaluating the poet's sincerity and originality. These elements are obviously in tension with sonnet conventions, rooted in custom and culture, which have accordingly—and mistakenly—been undervalued.[83]

Lately, however, "new historicist" critics who profess the dynamic and reciprocal relation of text and context, literature, and history, offer a fresh way to assess the embeddedness of Renaissance poetry.[84] Aspects of culture, including the poet's biography, are not simply mirrored by texts but are complexly inscribed within and often transformed by them. Poets and readers (indeed all subjects) engage in symbolic activities that constitute themselves and construct culture. Compatible with these tenets of the cultural poetics practiced by literary critics are the insights of the "new" history, practiced and theorized by the likes of Jacques LeGoff and Pierre Nora. It seeks a basis for history in collective memory, which is constructed less in single events than over the long period. It also renounces linear temporality for time as experienced "at the levels where the individual takes root in the social and collective."[85] The very concept of a poet's life-and-works is expanded to incorporate aspects of *mentalité*, that is, individual and collective attitudes, anxieties, and representations. In the new history, one's view of originary events is altered as study reveals "the manipulation by collective memory of a historical phenomenon [in this case, Sidney's life, death, and works] which up to this point only traditional history [or literary criticism] has studied."[86] My own study of the poetic construction of and response to Sidney's heroic image is a literary critical narrative, albeit one informed by new historicist assumptions and by the "new" history.

Being a literary critic, not a historian, I prioritize texts (of greater and lesser fame and "literariness") as mediators of cultural forms and vessels of collective memory. The "new" history usually seeks to recover cultural traces less in printed texts than "in the spoken word, images, gestures, rituals and festivals."[87] Admittedly, the collective memory of Sidney is primarily textual. Yet, these nontextual experiences—speech, gestures, and rituals—are in fact mediated by published works such as *Lant's Roll*, Greville's biography of Sidney, and commemorative elegies and imitative sonnets, all of which are repositories of the remembered image of Sidney. These printed works also testify to Sidney's exemplarity, to his status as an acknowledged model for imitation; thus, the choice of Sidney as an illustrative exemplar is not arbitrary or contrived (a charge often leveled against new historicist practice) but essential to our understanding of changing cultural perceptions of poetry, heroism, and humanism.[88] Since these are my concerns, I make few claims about the implications of Sidney's exemplarity for our understanding of Elizabethan politics. Admittedly, Sidney's career must be seen in light of his political ambitions, especially with regard to the Low Countries, and the careers of Daniel and Greville are inextricable from patronage networks, while Spenser's writings negotiate the tensions of the Elizabethan court of the 1590s. Unlike many new historicists, though, I am concerned less with hegemonic political power and courtly strategizing, "the forms of power," than with the "power of forms," that is, the authority of literary convention, humanist values, poetic precursors, and heroic exemplars, and the ways in which these various and sometimes conflicting authorities are mediated, affirmed, or reimagined in literary texts, specifically sonnets.

As a reconstructed formalist, I believe that only close, careful reading can release the nuances of a written work.[89] Suspicious of the totalizing interpretations of "new criticism" (which emphasizes artistic unity) and "new historicism" (which finds hegemonic power),

I listen for the dissonant voices within a text, evidence of Sidney's conflicted image or of a divided response to him. Dissonant voices also enable a text such as the sonnet to speak simultaneously within and against convention. For example, English sonneteers may reiterate Petrarchan commonplaces, but they reject Petrarch's otherworldliness, ultimately participating in the construction of a poetics more in line with Protestant, humanist values exemplified in a model like Sidney. Thus, the containment of subversion by poetic and/or political authority (the dominant new historicist paradigm) does not justly describe the complex poetic and social negotiations occurring in sonnets and other writings.

Obviously a deterministic view of poets and culture will not work; even if poets doubt the value of their poetry or its efficacy, the collective fashioning of Sidney's reputation is evidence that poets affirm, contest, subvert, and even recreate the authority of culture residing in legends, political institutions, and the written word. But what is the nature of the power that Sidney or any poet exercises? Sidney's political power was negligible; he was a bit player in the dramas of Elizabeth's domestic and foreign policy. His authority as an exemplary figure of the committed poet and public servant, however, was considerable, and, importantly, it was available to be criticized, contested, and shaped. Following Greenblatt, we may think of this power as "social energy" encoded in texts and circulating throughout society.[90] This concept resembles Foucauldian relational power, a reciprocal force generated in all encounters: between a poet and any element of his culture—a poem, a prior tradition, a religious doctrine, a cultural exemplar such as Sidney—or between individuals such as Aubrey and his draper, Sidney and his queen.[91] Such an understanding of power avoids the trap of thinking in terms of hegemonic power structures and institutions that make individual self-fashioning an illusion.[92]

In response to the materialist bias of much recent work, a call has been sounded—by anthropologists, philosophers, and literary critics—to restore human agency and intentionality to the study of culture.[93] This study heeds that call, proposing Sidney and his fellow poets as intentional subjects who construct and manipulate poetic models and thus initiate literary change; they are cultural actors who create collective memory.[94] This is not to celebrate unfettered subjectivity, however; one irony inherent in the model that makes actors' intentions central is that change usually results as an *unintended* consequence of action.[95] "To say that society and history are products of human action is true, but only in a certain ironic sense.

They are rarely the products the actors themselves set out to make."[96] What Renaissance actors thought they were doing, even when such intentions are recoverable, is not the end of the story. For example, the simple aim of elegies, dedications, and sonnets floating in Sidney's wake—to honor him—is complicated by our retrospective recognition of a host of additional and competing motivations: the desire to benefit materially from Sidney's reputation or to earn fame, the need to justify one's own poetry or to promote political causes, the impulse to question the basis of Sidney's heroism. Renaissance poets, including Greville, Daniel, and Spenser, might not have been aware of just how conflicted were their responses to Sidney's posthumous reputation or to the power structures that Petrarchism expressed and reinforced. Nor could they know the authority that their printed works and exemplary deeds would have or how they would be received, emulated, and criticized. But LeGoff reminds us that the workings of memory are usually unconscious, that memory not only manipulates the past but is itself subject to manipulation by time and social forces.[97]

The sonnet is a form surprisingly amenable to cultural studies and questions of poetic agency. For a number of reasons, the sonnet sequence proves an ideal arena in which to promote and contest Sidney's exemplarity. An epideictic lyric, the sonnet is capable of expressing praise and also blame. An important feature of Petrarchan rhetoric is the oxymoron, which conveys experience in terms of intense, even paradoxical, conflict: simultaneous freezing and burning, hope and despair. Whether comprised of octave and sestet or quatrains and a couplet, the sonnet is able to turn against itself, allowing for the expression and exploration of conflict and its resolution. The rigid rhyme scheme and concise fourteen lines contain the conflict within the poem's borders. In a sonnet sequence, however, resolution and containment are often only temporary, for the conflict is reiterated or refigured in successive poems. With its insistent protagonist, the sonnet highlights issues of agency and subjectivity, which is created in the clash with authority: that of the powerful and denying mistress and the traditions embodied in the sonnet's formal conventions. An English sonneteer has many powerful precursors, including Petrarch and Sidney, in relation to whom he defines himself by repeated acts of imitation and individuation. A sonnet sequence is, therefore, a good place to search for evidence of both continuity and change. Repetition, coupled with the need to avoid sameness, forces the writer of a sonnet sequence (if he is better than a hack) to register subtle changes between poems, even producing "new discursive modes"

(Hampton's term). The apparent rhetorical function of sonnets—to persuade a mistress to grant favors—disposes them to effect change rather than to maintain stasis. Not only its privileged place as a courtly genre, then, but also the characteristics of the form itself enable the sonnet sequence to register a poet's changing or conflicted relationship to authorities and not only to express, but also to transform, his experience.[98]

It should, therefore, not be surprising that a conventional form like the Elizabethan Petrarchan sonnet can do so much to register and occasion changes in literary and cultural perceptions and practice.[99] Literary conventions are like ideologies, for they derive authority from and lend it to poetic and social practice. They signal cultural consensus about the forms of expression and representation available to poets. They govern poetic representation but in turn are pressured by poetic practice. Greville, Daniel, and Spenser, though they share a profound sense of human limitation, nonetheless demonstrate, in their responses to Sidney's exemplarity, the authority of the individual poet pressuring conventional forms. While Spenser was the only poet of the four to attain "laureate" status, Greville and Daniel also proved adept at manipulating the literary system, poetic conventions, and their relationship to Sidney for the purpose of self-presentation.[100] They call on his example variously for self-justification (Greville), self-promotion (Daniel), and self-questioning (Spenser), at once creating and contesting Sidney's cultural authority, revealing human agency in the production of culture and collective memory.

In sum, Sidney's exemplarity, forged by his fellow poets, expresses the values of their shared humanist culture. Like the Elizabethan sonnet, it registers the tensions of Petrarchism and Protestant humanism, the conflicts between authority and submission and between man's exalted aspirations and his limited achievements. In the next chapter, I detail how Sidney's legendary image becomes a site where Mars competes with the Muses, heroic activity with the pursuit of poetry and love-in-idleness. Indeed, for Sidney, the roles of soldier and scholar-poet often conflict. My reading of the *Defence of Poetry* thus stresses its simultaneous and contrary goals: defending poetry and promoting public action. The work displays Sidney's struggle to justify poetic making as a route to virtuous action, but it also reveals the sense of shame and failure that haunts his efforts to be a right poet. *Astrophil and Stella*, discussed in chapter 2, is a Petrarchan performance of the conflict central to the *Defence*, where Astrophil's discourse of desire brilliantly refigures but poorly substitutes for the more activist course Sidney preferred. Astrophil is

Sidney's self-image, a model of the aspirations, anxieties, and ultimate limitations of the right poet who seeks through language to empower himself and move others to virtue.

Ironically, Sidney's failures are part of his enduring success. The conflicts are essential to his exemplarity, which is created and contested by poets who similarly struggled with the issues that his image mediates: the role of poetry in the attainment of public and private virtue and in the authorization of the self. In chapter 3, I show how Fulke Greville, Sidney's friend and first biographer, shaped him as an image of virtue, suppressing his failures; Greville then fashioned himself in that ideal image of the Protestant statesman and moral poet. In his theories of learning, he intensifies Sidney's fallen poetics, and in his semi-allegorical *Caelica*, he overshoots the more morally ambiguous *Astrophil and Stella*, attacking Petrarchan poetics with a vengeance and exploring the profound social and political effects of earthly love, conceived of as sexual sin.

Samuel Daniel, by contrast, cheerfully affirms the sociopolitical reference of Petrarchism on which his own future depends. His sonnet sequence, *Delia*, discussed in chapter 4, instantly capitalizes on the popularity of *Astrophil and Stella* in order to win recognition from Sidney's sister, the countess of Pembroke. Daniel succeeds brilliantly in materially affecting the social order with his poetry; he gains a patron, advances his career, and contributes to Sidney's burgeoning reputation. Yet his later works, *Musophilus* and *A Defence of Ryme*, express growing doubts about the efficacy of poetry; while seeming to defend learning and poetry, like Sidney, he articulates activist political values that supersede them.

The final chapters trace Spenser's participation in the creation and contestation of the Sidney legend. His career begins in worshipful admiration of the prior poet, but with *Astrophel* (1595), Spenser interrogates the values embodied in Sidney, the shepherd-knight, and expresses despair at the failure of Sidney's humanist poetics, the belief that poetry enables virtuous action. In his sonnet sequence, *Amoretti*, he pressures the conventions associated with *Astrophil and Stella*. He transforms Petrarchism with a Protestant ideal of chaste married love that is, moreover, personally and socially redeeming. With his marriage volume, Spenser comes closest to attaining the ideal of right poesy Sidney had envisioned for the love sonnet in his *Defence of Poetry*. My conclusion glances at the fortunes of Sidneian poetics in the seventeenth century, considering how George Herbert, Lady Mary Wroth, and Thomas Carew extend Spenser's critique of Petrarchism and disengage further from the humanist concerns of

Elizabethan poets, valorizing private virtue over public involvement. Like their predecessors, these poets meditate upon the authority of culture, including Sidney's legendary priority, the system of courtly patronage, and the sonnet tradition, and they attempt to refashion those authorities to serve their poetic ambitions.

1

"Mars and the Muses meete": The Divided Aims of Sidney's *Defence of Poetry*

A recurring feature of the Sidney legend propounded by elegists was the compelling image of Sidney as the scholar and soldier, a seeming happy union of opposites. This is the theme of one of the first elegies to be issued after Sidney's burial, George Whetstone's "Sir Phillip Sidney, his honorable life, his valiant death, and true vertues." The title page proclaims his subject to be an exemplary model, a "perfect Myrror for the followers both of *Mars* and *Mercury*." In Sidney, "Mars and the Muses meete," that is, the patrons of soldiery and those of scholarship.[1] To some, including Greville, Sidney achieved an ideal balance between the exercise of warfare and the pursuit of wisdom, between action and contemplation. For others, such as Spenser, Sidney's exaggerated allegiance to the pursuits of Mars compromised his devotion to the Muses and hence his exemplary status. Sidney's image became one locus of the contemporary struggle to balance the often competing values of *otium* and *negotium*, a struggle singly manifested in critical studies of Sidney's life and works. While modern critics usually seek to heal or transcend the division by either valorizing the poet over the Protestant man of action or, in the case of new historicists, the reverse, I maintain that the unresolved tension between these roles is essential to understanding the dynamism of Sidney's example. In particular, critics have read the *Defence of Poetry* either as a poetic manifesto in which Sidney embraces his literary career or as a disguised apology for Protestant activism. I argue, however, that the work maintains contrary and simultaneous goals: defending poetry and promoting public action. Sidney presents himself in terms of various and conflicting exemplars, such as David and Mars, expressing the difficulty of combining poetic making with heroic action. The aspiring Davidic poet acknowledges his weakness and questions his ability to incite an audience to virtue; the would-be Mars is shamed by his dalliance with the Muses, that is, with poetry and the attendant *otium* of love. My interpretation of Sidney's *Defence* highlights the twin struggles to reconcile soldiery and scholarship and to succeed as a right poet in a Protestant world of limitations and inevitable failure.

Mars versus the Muses

On the surface, Whetstone's elegy celebrates Sidney's successful embodiment of activity (Mars) and contemplation (the Muses). The oppositions united within Sidney are expressed by the alliterative yoking of the laurels of poetry and the lance of warfare, both means to honor: "And evermore, the Lawrell with the Launce: He exerside [sic] his Honour to advaunce." Whetstone imagines Sidney on his bier, a figure of triumph both poetic and military: "About his Healme, a Lawrell wreath is brayde. / And by his swoord a Silver penne is layd."[2] In this couplet, the images of a helmet and laurels, sword and pen, are woven together visually and poetically to express the essential unity of Sidney's activities. Like Whetstone, Arthur Golding represents Sidney as conjoining disparate virtues of Mars and the Muses:

> [H]e willingly passed for a tyme from the companie of the Muses to the Campe of Mars, there to make tryall as well of the Pyke as he had done of his Pen, after the example of the valiant Julius Caesar. . . .[3]

For Golding, Sidney's writing, like his military duty, served his church and his country; there is no divided allegiance to the "companie of the Muses" and the "Campe of Mars." Both writers achieve this reconciliation of the poet and the warrior by means of rhetoric, linking opposed qualities in alliterative phrases.

This image of Sidney as a happy union of opposites is sanctioned by no less an authority than Fulke Greville, Sidney's lifelong friend and biographer, who describes the Sidney he desires to imitate: "[T]hat exact image of quiet, and action: happily united in him . . .

made me thinke it no small degree of honour to imitate, or tread in the steps of such a Leader."[4] George Peele, in his *Polyhymnia*, calls him "Sweete Sydney, fairest shepheard of our greene, / Well-lettred Warriour."[5] Finally, Ralegh's famous epitaph succinctly summarizes this conception of Sidney as man of letters and man of action; he calls him the "*Scipio*, *Cicero*, and *Petrarch* of our time."[6]

Often, however, Sidney's yoking of Mars and the Muses is strained, and writers betray a more ambivalent tone towards him. For example, though Whetstone glories in Sidney's reconciliation of the laurels and the lance, upon a closer reading, his elegy betrays some anxiety about the courtier's profession of poetry:

> In Court he liv'de, not like a Carpet knight,
> Whose glory is in garments, and his tongue:
> If men but knew the halfe that he did write,
> Enough to tyre, a memory so young.
> Needes must they say the Muses in him sounge
> His *Archadia*, unmacht for sweete devise:
> Where skill doth judge, is held in Soveraigne price.
>
> What else he wrote, his will was to suppresse . . .[7]

Whetstone goes on to attribute *The Shepheardes Calender* to Sidney, his ignorance revealing that Sidney's suppression of his poetic identity was largely successful. This stanza uneasily yokes Sidney's courtly service and his literary output, the awkward transition revealing a significant disjunction in the image of Sidney that Whetstone has crafted. The assertion that Sidney is not like a carpet knight is awkward, given the circumstances in which Sidney's knighthood was conferred. (Surely the well-informed Whetstone knew that Sidney was knighted in order to stand as the proxy at Prince Casimir's inauguration to the Order of the Garter, not as a reward for his own merit or service.) The denial that Sidney's glory was in his tongue is contradicted by the immediate reference to him as a writer and the rhyme with "the Muses in him sounge," making Sidney look a lot like those courtiers who write verses simply because it is the fashion or to gain patronage ("sweete devise . . . is held in Soveraigne price"). Despite the compliment to the *Arcadia*, Whetstone seems reluctant to endorse writing and singing as proper forms of courtly service. He is more comfortable praising Sidney's translation of du Plessis Mornay's *De la verite de la religion Chrestienne*, "A Learned worke, more pretious farre then Gold. / Worthy his paynes" (B3r).

Sometimes the opposition between Sidney's roles of poet and military hero is underscored rather than reconciled. Arthur Gorges, for example, a contemporary of Sidney and a fellow courtier, depicts a violent clash between these roles:

> Mars and the Muses weare att mortall stryfe
> which of them had in Sydney grettest parte
> the one layde clayme unto his valyaunt harte
> The other to his mynde in knowledge ryfe.[8]

Gorges may be imitating the opening lines of *Astrophil and Stella* 52, "A strife is growne betweene *Vertue* and *Love*, / While each pretends that *Stella* must be his." In Gorges's poem, envious death settles the strife by seizing Sidney. In Bryskett's "The Mourning Muse of Thestylis," Mars actually deserts Sidney; the speaker laments, "Ah dreadfull *Mars* why didst thou not thy knight defend?" and suggests that Mars was angry, perhaps over England's military commitment to the Netherlands.[9] (Mars turned a deaf ear to the cry of "woful England" and to "*Zeland's* piteous plaint" and to Holland's torn hair.) The elegy that most interrogates Sidney's heroic image, decisively disrupting the union of Mars and the Muses, is Spenser's *Astrophel*, which criticizes the myth of Sidney as military hero and even questions whether the pursuit of poetry can be reconciled with heroic action.

This theme of the contest between Mars and the Muses does not originate with the Sidney elegies, but the elegies themselves participate in the contemporary debate about the relative values of arms and letters to the courtier. One locus of the debate is courtesy literature, specifically Castiglione's *The Book of the Courtier*, translated by Sir Thomas Hoby in 1561 and by Sidney's day a staple of courtly culture, and George Pettie's introduction to his translation of Stefano Guazzo's *Civile Conversation*, published in 1581. In Castiglione's work, the discussion of arms and letters occasions lively disagreement. Count Lodovico, delineating the courtier, promotes learning as an incentive to heroic action, much as Sidney will do in the *Defence*:

> And every man may conceive it to be true glory, that is stored up in the holy treasure of letters. . . . What minde is so fainte, so bashfull, and of so base a courage, that in reading the actes and greatnes of Cesar, Alexander, Scipio, Annibal, and so many other, is not incensed with a most fervent longing to be like them. . . .[10]

Though learning provides exemplary models for action, letters are ultimately subordinate to arms and serve them; the courtier must show "armes to bee his principall profession, and all the other good qualities for an ornament thereof" (72). Pietro Bembo disagrees, arguing that letters "are in dignitie so much above armes, as the mind is above the bodie," to which the Count answers that "the practising of arms belongeth as well to the minde as to the bodie," (72) dismissing Bembo, the scholar and poet, as a biased judge. For the count—presumably the normative voice—the use of learning is to praise "great men and glorious acts" (73) and hence to make men hungry for glory. If the courtier does not achieve such perfection in his writings (or his behavior), however, he ought to "bee circumspect in keeping them close, least he make other men to laugh at him. Onely hee may shew them to a friende whom he may trust" (71). Surely Sidney (and other courtier-poets) had Castiglione in mind as they wrote prose and verse and sheltered their works from mocking readers, protecting themselves from scorn by a studied *sprezzatura*. A similar undercurrent of shame runs through the *Defence*, the fear of scorn and the awareness of not measuring up to the perfection of a Homer or an Alexander.

Pettie's defense of learning positions itself against the Italian work by defending his decision to publish, rather than to hide, the fruits of his learning and by revealing the hypocrisy of *sprezzatura*, criticizing those

> curious Gentlemen, who thynke it most commendable in a Gentleman, to cloake his art and skill in every thyng . . . [who] make protestation that they are no Schollers: whereas notwithstanding they have spent all theyr tyme in studie.[11]

A one-time soldier himself, Pettie rescues learning from the mockery of ignorant soldiers. Still, he stresses learning's utilitarian function; one simply cannot be a courtier or a gentleman without it:

> Alas you wyll be but ungentle Gentlemen, yf you be no Schollers: you wyll doo your Prince but simple service, you wyll stande your Countrey but in slender steade, you wyll bryng your selves but to small preferment, yf you be no Schollers. . . . To come lower, can you discourse with Strangers, inquire the state of forraine Countries, geve entertainement to Ambassadours, being no Schollers? . . . To come lowerst of all, Can you so much as tell your Mistresse a fine tale, or delight her with pleasant device, beyng unlearned? (8)

At the very least, learning should enable one to write a love sonnet; at the very most, learning exalts one to the company of heroic, highborn men:

> You knowe Caesar was a brave Gentleman, but yet he was a Scholler. . . . Marcus Aurelius was an Emperour, but he was learned. . . . Therefore (Gentlemen) never deny your selves to be Schollers, never be ashamed to shewe your learnyng, confesse it, professe it, imbrace it, honor it: for it is it which honoureth you . . . it is only it which maketh you Gentlemen. (10)

Castiglione also said that learning makes men desire to emulate glorious leaders, while conceding that poetry often serves the less exalted ends of pleasing oneself and the ladies:

> Let him much exercise him selfe in Poets, and no lesse in Oratours and Historiographers, and also in writing both rime and prose, and especially in this our vulgar tongue. For beside the contentation that hee shall receive thereby him selfe, hee shall by this meanes never want pleasant intertainements with women which ordinarily love such matters. (71)

Interestingly, Sidney's *Defence of Poetry* performs a similar downward turn, setting forth poetry's exalted purpose, namely, building virtuous heroes and statesmen, but admitting its diminished reality: poets use sonnets to flatter ladies, not to praise God or heroic men. In fact, for Sidney and his contemporaries, poetic activity—following the Muse—was often a mark of their exclusion from the more rewarded and desirable public activity—the pursuits of Mars.

With sound reason, critics and biographers have interpreted Sidney's life and works in terms of the contemporary tension between *negotium* and *otium*, active engagement in the world and the pursuit of love or poetry in retirement.[12] Biographers tend to favor a unified subject who exhibits an "ability to encompass and balance contradictions,"[13] while literary critics often infer from Sidney's conflicted protagonists his own divided self.[14] Turning to his works, however, critics of both kinds agree that their aesthetic dimension reconciles elements of Sidney's divided personality and experience. In traditional readings of *Astrophil and Stella*, for instance, Sidney abandons public life and internalizes its conflicts, which find expression in the persona of Astrophil, who lives only for loving Stella.[15] Most critics find Sidney the artist firmly in control of his art and his personae, creating from his political disappointments or from his unrequited love of Penelope Rich a golden poetic world. The

Defence is viewed in similar terms; according to Katherine Duncan-Jones, it records Sidney's "deliberate decision to seek in literature . . . the fulfillment and autonomy that were lacking elsewhere," that is, in political life.[16] Belief in Sidney's conscious, controlled artistry was boosted when Kenneth Myrick discovered that the *Defence* exhibits the structure of a classical oration and contended that a studied *sprezzatura* accounts for Sidney's disparaging attitude towards his literary vocation.[17] Critics usually concur that the *Defence* is a sublime literary artifact and a sincere, largely unproblematic profession of Sidney's beliefs about poetry.[18] The view that Sidney abandoned his political ambitions to embrace literature, where he is able to maintain control, falsely simplifies the complexity of his attitudes towards these vocations.

Other readers, many with affinities to the new historicism, find the conflicts of Sidney's public life reenacted and problematized, not lessened, reconciled, or celebrated, in his works.[19] They often rely on analogies between courtly arts and poetic arts, looking for similar patterns of experience and expression.[20] Common to these critics is the conviction that lyric poetry cannot be disentangled from the actions of poets as social beings. In its extreme version, such criticism sees literature as merely serving ideological agendas; Alan Sinfield, for example, argues that Sidney's *Defence* appropriates literature to promote earnest Protestant activism.[21] Margaret Ferguson, on the other hand, seeks to reintegrate the personal and political dimensions of Sidney's work; her poet is a master of "deep dissimulation," whose *Defence* is a project of self-defense and self-promotion of poets.[22] Even cultural critics, however, sometimes give in to the temptation to empower the poet-figure to resolve conflicts. For Sinfield, the *Defence* is a "triumphant merger" of Protestant and humanist conceptions of poetry, while Maureen Quilligan celebrates Sidney's "self-creation as a poet-lover," and Ferguson's Sidney emphasizes poetry's mediating, conciliatory function.[23]

In sum, Sidney studies are animated by representations of Sidney or his writing as a site where Mars and the Muses meet or compete, where ambition struggles with submission, and aesthetics with ideology. Still, however, Sidney's success is measured by his ability (or that of his critics) to transcend or to reconcile these conflicts in his writing, creating himself as a successful poet. I doubt, however, that golden poetry so handily defeats brazen history, and I allege that the unresolved competition of Mars and the Muses is productive of Sidney's exemplarity.

My own reading of the *Defence*, accordingly, glories in its divided aims and questions the success of Sidney's poetic self-creation. Sidney may promote poetry as a spur to virtue and the recovery of the golden world (ambiguously paradise or the Elysium of Elizabeth's court), but he is always aware of how far he is from occupying either of these golden worlds. The question is not only whether poetry is worthwhile and conducive to virtue but whether poetry is a worthy imitation of heroic action, a way of being virtuous. Alone among critics, I believe Sidney would answer "no" to both queries. Though he is surely sincere about the desirability of poetry's exalted goals, he is equally convinced that poets—including himself—fail to attain these goals. Finding himself "sick among the rest" with the "common infection grown among the most part of writers" (*Defence* 72), he pens the *Defence*, imagines Astrophil, and shields his *Arcadia* from all but his closest friends. With its many ironic rhetorical maneuvers and its conflicted exemplary figures, who function as self-images of the poet, the *Defence* negotiates Sidney's experiences of shame at his poetic vocation and the failure of his political career, rationalizing these losses in terms of Protestant beliefs about human nature. While the rhetorical brilliance of the *Defence* is a product of its maker's intentions, the failure of the argument is both inevitable and willed. Aware of his shortcomings—one of which is a weakness for profane poetizing—the poetic maker determines his own failure to be a divine poet. This failure, though, has its own function: it enables him to preempt criticism of his poetic efforts and to maintain humility in the face of his fallen humanity, avoiding the hubris of rivaling the divine maker.

Protestant Poetics: Fashioning the Right Poet and His Reader

In a nutshell, the argument of the *Defence of Poetry* is that poetic fictions (weighed against the limitations of examples from philosophy and history) are best able to move men to right action. Thus it would seem that, for Sidney, poetry is the means to unite scholarship and soldiery and transcend the division between Mars and the Muses. But Sidney, acknowledging human frailty and limitation, formulates a rather more modest and instrumental aim for poets:

> This purifying of wit—this enriching of memory, enabling of judgement, and enlarging of conceit—which commonly we call learning . . . the final end is

> to lead and draw us to as high a perfection as our degenerate souls, made worse by their clayey lodgings, can be capable of. . . . the ending end of all earthly learning [is] virtuous action. . . . (28–29)

Given our "degenerate souls" in their "clayey lodgings," the ambitious goal of perfecting the soul gives way to the more modest goal of acting virtuously in the world. The poet's exalted humanist goals are frustrated by the frailty and failure that touches every area of human striving.[24] In Sidney's words, to cite them again, "our erected wit maketh us know what perfection is, and yet our infected will keepeth us from reaching unto it. But these arguments will by few be understood, and by fewer granted" (25). Articulating a deep conviction of human sinfulness, Sidney is hardly sanguine about the possibility of being a successful poet or finding a receptive reader.[25] Still, he maintains that poetry is the best means of self-improvement, for it not only teaches but also moves the will to embrace virtue. The right poet's modest and moral goal is to "imitate both to delight and teach; and delight, to move men to take that goodness in hand, which without delight they would fly as from a stranger . . ." (27). By enticement of the wary reader, the poet is able to win "the mind from wickedness to virtue—even as the child is often brought to take most wholesome things by hiding them in such other as have a pleasant taste . . ." (40). That is, the poet's success depends partly upon his persuasive skills and moral force, partly upon the disposition of his reluctant, resisting child-reader.

One model for the right poet and aspiring courtier who pursues both Mars and the Muses is David, the biblical soldier and poet-figure. A lowly shepherd who became a talented musician, David was also a military hero who gained King Saul's favor but later aroused his jealousy ("Saul hath slaine his thousand, and David his ten thousand" [1 Sam. 18:7]). Among Protestants, David was also known as a figure of the repentant sinner; after he became king, he fell in love with Bathsheba, murdered her husband, and was brought to repentance by Nathan the prophet (2 Sam. 11–12). To his credit, Sidney avoided this scenario in his desire for Penelope Rich, though he must have had the conflicted David in mind as a figure for Astrophil. In the *Defence*, Sidney emphasizes that it is Nathan's feigned discourse that makes David recognize his wrongs and ask for God's mercy (42). Here Nathan takes the role of poet-as-courtier, working as God's instrument to bring kings to virtue, and even David, the poet who became king, is in need of redemption through poetry.[26]

Though Sidney places David in the distinct category of divine poet, or *vates* (22), he is familiar with traditions in which the psalmist is also a right poet who imitates invisible excellence and creates lively, moving images that teach goodness.[27] Sidney describes David's psalms as "heavenly poesy, wherein almost he showeth himself a passionate lover of that unspeakable and everlasting beauty to be seen by the eyes of the mind, only cleared by faith" (22). What distinguishes a right poet from a divine one is the latter's faith, which clears his imagination and judgment. David's "heavenly poesy" and his passionate love of God make him a divine sonneteer. By contrast, the fallen Sidney is conscious of his own failure to use poetry rightly.

In the sixteenth century, David was held up as a model by reformers eager to put lyric poetry to godly use. Thomas Becon exhorts:

> Let all mynstrels gyve place to this our Mynstrel. . . . Let all songes be banyshed, whan Davids Psalmes be songe. For what so ever David syngethe, it is excellent & incomparable. He [with] his songes exciteth, provoketh & enflameth ye myndes of the faythefull & diligent hearers unto the love & desyre not of transitory but of heavenly thynges.[28]

Miles Coverdale hopes that his translation of the Psalms will "give our youth of England some occasion to change their foul and corrupt ballads into sweet songs and spiritual hymns of God's honor."[29] Sidney's yearning to be a Davidic poet is indebted to such thinking and expressed in his vision of what sonnets ought to achieve. In the *Defence*, he bewails the waste of wit on "that lyrical kind of songs and sonnets," even as he was most likely writing love sonnets himself, aware of his failure to live up to the promise of his erected wit.

> Lord, if He gave us so good minds, how well it might be employed, and with how heavenly fruit, both private and public, in singing the praises of the immortal beauty: the immortal goodness of that God who giveth us hands to write and wits to conceive. . . . But truly many of such writings as come under the banner of unresistible love, if I were a mistress, would never persuade me they were in love: so coldly they apply fiery speeches. . . . But let this be a sufficient though short note, that *we miss the right use of the material point of poesy*. (69–70; emphasis added)

Sidney begins by expressing the ideal of the divine sonneteer, a psalmist praising God the Maker and immortal source of inspiration. In the next sentence, this superego slips to reveal the baser poetic ego that bemoans poets' failure to achieve a different—and degraded—

purpose, persuading a mistress.[30] By the end of the passage, the right poet reasserts control with his moral message that love sonnets are a misuse, if not abuse, of poetry. To write them abrogates the duty to be a right poet, a designation that shifts towards that of divine poet, despite Sidney's attempts to distinguish them.

The self-disparaging tone that creeps into Sidney's *Defence* and his other writing, variously seen as conventional or self-protective *sprezzatura*, can perhaps be better understood in terms of his desire to shape a poetic career according to the example of David, the reformed sinner. Claiming that he has "slipped into the title of a poet" and has been "provoked to say something unto you in the defence of that my unelected vocation" (18), he reveals self-disparagement that resonates with Protestant beliefs about the will's unfreedom. Later he also explains: "[A]s I never desired the title [of poet], so have I neglected the means to come by it. Only, overmastered by some thoughts, I yielded an inky tribute unto them" (63).[31] With the choice of words suggesting unfreedom ("provoked," "unelected," "never desired," "overmastered") and passivity ("idleness," "neglected"), he makes it clear that he has not chosen his vocation as a poet but has been called and therefore must submit. In this case, the ironic resemblance to the calling of the unwilling poet-prophet only underscores Sidney's distance from the divine poet, or *vates*. Perhaps by beginning his translation of the Psalms as he passed his thirtieth year, Sidney hoped to model himself more closely in the image of David, repenting his lusty youth (the Astrophil persona) and singing of God's goodness.

Upon this pretext of being called to be a poet, Sidney becomes poetry's enthusiastic apologist. His image of the poet as a god-like figure whose wit exhibits creative and possibly redemptive powers seems a paean to poetic invention:

> Only the poet, disdaining to be tied to any such subjection, lifted up with the vigour of his own invention, doth grow in effect another nature, in making things either better than nature bringeth forth, or quite anew, forms such as never were in nature, as the Heroes, Demigods, Cyclops, Chimeras, Furies, and such like: so as he goeth hand in hand with nature, not enclosed within the narrow warrant of her gifts, but freely ranging only within the zodiac of his own wit. Nature never set forth the earth in so rich tapestry as divers poets have done; neither with so pleasant rivers, fruitful trees, sweet-smelling flowers, nor whatsoever else may make the too much loved earth more lovely. Her world is brazen, the poets only deliver a golden.

> But let those things alone, and go to man . . . and know whether she have brought forth so true a lover as Theagenes, so constant a friend as Pylades, so valiant a man as Orlando, so right a prince as Xenophon's Cyrus.. . . (23–24)

This imaginative act of invention reenacts God's creation of paradise and the perfect man. Andrew Weiner exults that Sidney is "declaring poetry's lack of complicity in that corruption of nature."[32] According to William Craft, Sidney believes that in such acts of invention, the poet achieves his fullest humanity and emulates the divine Creator.[33] I would emphasize, however, that this imitation of God's action involves the poet in a demonstration of overweening pride; "disdaining . . . subjection," flying on wings of his own invention, he overreaches nature itself. His creation of unnatural beasts, Cyclops and Chimeras, testifies to poets' fallen imaginations, which produce fantastic images versus merely icastic ones, the former images "infect[ing] the fancy with unworthy objects," the latter "figuring forth good things" (54).[34] Surely Sidney is aware of the dangerous paradox of poetic invention, namely, that which links poetry to divine creation also makes it most susceptible to evil: it is an art not tied to nature.

Importantly, this portrait of the creative poet outdoing God and nature precedes Sidney's introduction of right poets, whose reach is more circumscribed; they

> do imitate to teach and delight, and to imitate borrow nothing of what is, hath been, or shall be, but range, only reined with learned discretion, into the divine consideration of what may be and should be. (26)

Despite its Platonic ring, this passage actually affirms that what right poets do is still imitation. Even Platonic poets always *only* imitate truth but never attain it.[35] A right poet is not a *vates*, or prophet, with access to divine truth. Still, "reined with learned discretion," he does his best to align his mimesis with God's truth. Sidney believes that poetry is rightly *functional*, its goodness conditional, not absolute. Rightly used, poetry moves men to good and virtuous action; abused, it is an example of and incentive to transgression.

The right poet's modest and functional aim (moving the reader to embrace goodness) is always being complicated by his pride that disdains the subjection of mimesis and desires to rival the creator. Sidney does try to rein in the wit that ranges too freely in the above passage, urging that poets

> give right honour to the heavenly Maker of that maker [the Poet] who having made man to His own likeness, set him beyond and over all the works of that second nature: which in nothing he showeth so much as in poetry, when with the force of a divine breath he bringeth things forth surpassing her doings—with no small arguments to the credulous of that first accursed fall of Adam, since our erected wit maketh us know what perfection is, and yet our infected will keepeth us from reaching unto it. (25)

In his homage to the "heavenly Maker of that maker," Sidney is torn between submission and exaltation of the poet-maker. He might do well simply to acknowledge that God's creation of man in his own image was an act of (self-)imitation that ennobles mimesis, but his egoistic persona is bent on claiming for the poet God's *creative* capacity, "the force of a divine breath." In Platonic terms, however, the poet can only be a secondhand maker of images, not of realities. The analogy to God collapses, then, with the sudden remembrance of Adam's "accursed fall," which infects the poet's will and hinders his achievement. Unlike Craft, I find that Sidney struggles against identifying the poet with God, recognizing the vanity of such a likeness.

In suggesting that the poet's endeavors are inevitably tainted by the sin of pride, Sidney tips the delicate balance of humanism and Protestantism, for the pull of man's "erected wit" towards virtue is countered by the stronger tug of his "infected will" away from it. For Victoria Kahn, Sidney's work is located at an important crossroads, where sixteenth-century humanism encounters skepticism about its claims to persuade the will:

> In early humanism, dialogue and other instances of deliberative rhetoric are encomia of the will: the very fact of written debate is taken to be evidence of the reader's ability to respond, and thus of the existence of free will and the genuine possibility of rhetorical persuasion. In later humanist-influenced works, dialogue turns in on itself and the encomium of the will becomes paradoxical. . . . Skepticism, in short, is no longer compatible with rhetorical persuasion; instead, it takes the possibility of persuasion itself as its object.[36]

The many readings of the *Defence* as an ironic work or as a mere disputation *in utramque partem*, as an exercise in impersonation or as a more serious abuse of logic and reason, all point to this crisis in humanism that Kahn identifies.[37]

Exposing the infection of the poet, the *Defence* calls into question the entire humanist project of fashioning a virtuous reader. Given the poet's infected will *and* wit, how can his poetry be good and how can it benefit the reader? The burden of goodness shifts to the reader, who must penetrate the bad poet's deceits and perceive correctly the right poet's meanings. But the reader, of course, shares the "common infection" of humanity with the poet. (Sidney imagines this reader as a recalcitrant child who must be tricked into taking the poet's medicine, and he fears being misunderstood by his readers.) For Sidney, though, the reader must be worse off than the poet, hence the need for poetry. In the *Defence*, he employs a strategy for delighting and instructing the reader, whose weaknesses he shares and therefore understands: enacting a humanist-Protestant tension, he enlists the reader simultaneously on the level of his erected wit and that of his infected will, appealing both to his better judgment and to his baser desires.[38]

The work's exordium and peroration illustrate this divided strategy at work. The example of Pugliano, the Italian horseman who praises the horse as "a peerless beast . . . the only serviceable courtier without flattery," brings Sidney's wry comment that "if I had not been a piece of a logician before I came to him, I think he would have persuaded me to have wished myself a horse" (17). While disarming and softening the lighter reader, this introductory story alerts the careful reader to the ironic parallels between the persuasive Pugliano and the poet, between their "exalted" subjects, the horse and poetry, and between the gullible speaker and the reader he addresses. The reader or auditor is warned to be attentive and logical, not to fall into the trap that the speaker escaped only by being something of a logician himself.[39] He even gives this moral: "that self-love is better than any gilding to make that seem gorgeous wherein ourselves be parties" (17). That is, human weakness will predispose the reader to desire praise and hence to identify with the object of praise. Yet it is precisely this weakness to which the speaker, a devilish alter ego of the right poet, appeals in his peroration, flattering the reader and inviting him into a select fellowship of lovers and patrons of poetry. Like a magician, he conjures the reader

> to believe, with me, that there are many mysteries contained in poetry, which of purpose were written darkly, lest by profane wits it should be abused . . . to believe [poets] when they tell you they will make you immortal by their verses. Thus doing, your name shall flourish in the printers' shops . . . you shall be most fair, most rich, most wise, most all . . . you shall suddenly grow *Herculea proles* [offspring of Hercules]. (75)

The misuse of poetry is mutual, as poets deceive and flatter readers, who, in turn, support poetry out of their vain desires for fame and status. The high moral purpose of poetry, the original ground for its defensibility, gives way to baser practical motives: persuading for dubious claims, gaining patronage, or angling for immortality. Sites such as these remind us that the poet's erected wit, as well as the reader's, is always tainted by the "sin of self-love."

One then-contemporary reader of Sidney's *Defence* unwittingly reveals his self-interested motives in pursuing poetry. Thomas Churchyard, whose 1587 elegy had commemorated Sidney in his public role of governor of Flushing, issued *A Praise of Poetry* in 1595, on the heels of Sidney's newly published *Defence*. On one level, Churchyard is a right reader; he endorses Sidney's moral intent and reiterates his call for divine poetry:

He cals them Poets that embrace
True vertue in hir kinde
And do not run with rimes at bace
With wanton blotted minde.
. . . .
Of heavens and the highest throne
Where God himselfe doth sit
Good poets still should treat alone
To showe their flowing wit.[40]

Yet Churchyard is much taken with Sidney's image of the godlike poet creating a golden world; he exults that Sidney enabled wit "Not to give counsell nor to teach / But to write fancies new" (33). Like Sidney in the peroration, he mystifies the poet's superior knowledge: "A poet is no common man / He lookes with Argoes eyes" (40). He even buys the notion of poetic immortality: "For by his works who notes them well / In world he lives againe" (43). The uncertain referent of "he" together with the many current meanings of "note" allow the suggestion that many profit, and in various ways, from Sidney's works. One who "notes" Sidney's works—that is, marks, annotates, copies, makes use of them, or sets them to music—lives again (gains a livelihood perhaps) or resurrects Sidney.[41]

Churchyard reserves particular praise for the *Defence*, a work that authorizes and validates his own lifetime of poetic activity:[42]

Which booke deckt up in trim attire
Of authors wise and grave

In matters of mine owne desire
Great light to poetrie gave.

And made me write of poets praise
Thus so to starrie skie
My Sidneies honor heere I raise
As far as fame can flie.

(43)

Churchyard clearly sees himself as one of Sidney's careful readers, able to perceive—and worthy to enhance—Sidney's immortality. Embracing and promoting what he sees as Sidney's poetics of transcendence, he expects to share in the glory he claims for Sidney.

Ironically, though Churchyard apprehends the moral seriousness in Sidney's treatise, he falls prey to the very trap Sidney sets for his light reader: self-love. As the Pugliano anecdote advises and the peroration reiterates, we should always be suspicious of the orator's powers of persuasion, especially when he praises a subject such as poetry, which *can* be dangerous if abused, and especially because his appeal preys upon our weak minds and wills, always predisposed to self-interested judgments.

The issue of critical judgment is specifically raised when Sidney embarks upon his refutation of poetry's critics, who are figured, in a complex allusion, by King Midas. At this point in his *Defence*, Sidney invites consideration of his work within the traditions of the mock encomium and the rhetorical paradox. The possibilities for irony that immediately surface necessitate the reader's use of judgment in evaluating both the poet and his work.[43] As Erasmus was "merry . . . in the commending of folly" and Agrippa exercised his "playing wit" in praising "the discretion of an ass" (49), Sidney can be merry in his praise of poetry, but with a serious, ulterior aim the discerning reader will detect. Aware that his work is more like a joke than a heroic Iliad, but defending it nonetheless, Sidney may have in mind Persius's Satire I:

vidi, vidi ipse, libelle: *auriculas asini quis non habet?* hoc ego opertum, hoc ridere meum, tam nil, nulla tibi vendo Iliade.

[I have seen the truth; I have seen it with my owne eyes, O my book: *Who is there who has not the ears of an ass?* this dead secret of mine, this poor little joke, I will not sell for all your Iliads!][44]

King Midas, in Ovid's *Metamorphoses*, had the ears of an ass, which he used to judge the contest between Pan and Apollo. Alone in deeming Pan the better musician, he was punished—indeed, shamed—with a set of ass's ears for his lack of discrimination.[45] Sidney uses Midas as a figure for the reader, especially the critical one, as he embarks upon the refutation of poetry's critics: "[B]ecause we have ears as well as tongues . . . let us hear, and . . . ponder what objections can be made against this art" of poesy (49). As he prepares to be the sole defender of poetry against its detractors, he also risks the ignominy that Midas suffered. On the other hand, while Midas was unqualified to judge a musical contest, Sidney, because he is a poet, is uniquely qualified to judge critics of poetry. Still, in his position as poet and judge, he is vulnerable to shame. Again in the peroration, the "ass's ears of Midas" (75) refers to the fate of the ignorant judge of poetry, whom Sidney attempts to exclude from the fellowship of fame and eternity. Thus, Midas also figures the bind of the reader, called upon to make a critical judgment but subject to ridicule if his judgment is unfavorable to the poet.

Though Midas with his donkey's ears is a figure for the ignorant critic or unfavorable reader, poetry itself may be implicated as well.[46] Shortly after the mention of Agrippa's ass in the *Defence*, the ass metaphor recurs in direct association with poetry. The speaker affirms that "poesy must not be drawn by the ears; it must be gently led, or rather it must lead—which was partly the cause that made the ancient-learned affirm it was a divine gift . . ." (63). The images first of a stubborn donkey ("drawn by the ears"), then of a more noble beast ("gently led"), are evoked to aid his point that "a poet no industry can make, if his own genius be not carried into it" (63). (That is, poesy "must lead" instead of being led, like an unwilling beast.) Perhaps Sidney also has in mind Psalm 32, in which David is a kind of divine Orpheus:

> I wil instruct thee, & teache thee in the way, that thou shalt go. . . . Be ye not like an horse, or like a mule, which understand not: whose mouthes thou doest binde with bit and bridel.

The association with divine poetry is fleeting, undermined by the scatalogical implications of the ass/horse metaphor; in the next paragraph, he confesses "that as the fertilest ground must be manured, so must the highest-flying wit have a Daedalus to guide him . . . that is, art, imitation, and exercise" (63). As the Midas-ass allusion deteriorates (or escapes Sidney's control), the image of the poet shifts to

Icarus. The irony is that Icarus, the son of Daedalus, refused to be guided by his father, flew too close to the sun, and perished with the very wings his father had fashioned.[47] Sidney can simultaneously jest with the reader and remind him, using the mocking self-image of Midas, the ironic one of Icarus, and a veiled allusion to David, of the dangers to himself of defending poetry and of the limitations of human striving.[48]

Sidney's witty and fallible persona provides for the reader a lesson in reading and the exercise of good judgment, furthering the work's serious moral aim. For Kahn, Sidney emphasizes the reader's role in bridging rhetoric and prudential action, recognizing that "the power of poetry to persuade to right action depends on the reader's . . . access to a standard of judgment that would enable him to make an appropriate interpretation of and response to the text."[49] For instance, a well-equipped reader of Sidney's *Defence* would surely be conversant with Ciceronian oratory; familiar with Ovid's *Metamorphoses*, he might be able to follow Sidney's fugue upon the Midas theme. One reader, in fact, did respond with appropriate judgment and skepticism to Sidney's *Defence*: William Temple, Sidney's personal secretary and a noted logician, wrote a response in which he summarized, praised, and openly criticized the work. His commentary exposes inconsistencies in the argument for the superiority of poetry over history and philosophy, disagreeing that the philosopher provides only abstract precepts with no examples and that moving is of a higher order than teaching. Temple's analysis is often pedantic, as befits the moral philosopher whom Sidney caricatures, but it confirms that Sidney's arguments and assumptions did not go unquestioned by his contemporary readers.[50] In his *Defence of Poetry*, Sidney demonstrates that rhetoric, well-used or abused, ultimately serves a moral end, teaching the reader how to read rightly. He sets forth the ideal of the right poet but, pleading human weakness, virtually begs not to be held to too high a standard of perfection. One would hope that the *Defence* found some ideal readers who would be as astute as Temple but less self-interested than Churchyard, while also being moved to grant the moral value of poetry and to imitate its divine potential.

The Defence of Public Action

Sidney's argument in the *Defence of Poetry* is really quite a modest one. It is that poetry, rightly used, can move one to virtuous action;

then, and only then, can poetry claim to be the highest form of learning. Poetry, or any form of study, must serve the ultimate goal of learning, that is, ethical action. For Sidney and men of his class, this meant public service, preferably military service—the surest, if the most perilous, route to honor.[51] These values inform Sidney's *Defence*; indeed, the treatise on poetry is really a call to action, even to arms.[52] The ironic elements of the *Defence*—for instance, the poet's critical self-images of Midas and Icarus—encourage the reader's own critical engagement with the models proposed as exemplars. Irony also, however, disables belief in the possibility of effective action.[53] In this section, I focus on Sidney's self-images of Mars and Epaminondas, ironic models for the poet-as-warrior, and on Sidney's quarrel with Gosson in order to demonstrate how the defender of poetry is ultimately committed to heroic action but conscious of shame and failure on both fronts.[54]

The expectation that the pursuit of learning is properly directed towards action of a military nature is also articulated in Sidney's oft-quoted letter to his friend, Edward Denny.[55] He advises that "since the unnoble constitution of our tyme, doth keepe us from fitte imployments, you doe yet keepe your selfe awake, with the delight of knowledge. . . ." He recommends a course of study with a double aim: self-knowledge and the "outward application of our selves." For the former aim, he advises that "holy scriptures, if not the only, are certainly the incomperable lanterne in this fleshly darkness of ours." His friend should then proceed to works of moral philosophy and history. For the second part, "to you that with good reason bend your selfe to souldiery," he advises practical study of geography, cartography, "books of the Art of Souldiery," and the "practise of Arithmetike." Like the *Defence*, the letter to Denny sets forth the value of action, for which the pursuit of poetry can be a preparation but never a substitute.

In this letter, indeed in all of his extant correspondence, there is virtually no mention of Sidney's writing.[56] The letters between Sidney and Hubert Languet, ranging over Sidney's entire educational program, never mention poetry, though Languet encourages Sidney to read moral philosophy and history.[57] Of course, poetry was not likely to be a subject of correspondence between gentlemen, given that their culture dictated a formal disdain or dismissal of poetry. At best, it was deemed useful for teaching children or, as Castiglione suggested, pleasing the ladies. Sir Thomas Elyot's program of instruction includes poetry in the child's early years, but after age thirteen he should progress to logic, rhetoric, cosmography, history,

Enea Vico, after Parmigiano, *Venus and Mars Embracing with Vulcan at His Forge* (1543). Reprinted with permission of the Board of Trustees, National Gallery of Art, Washington, D.C.

and moral philosophy, the subjects Sidney recommends to Edward Denny and to his brother, Robert.[58] Poetry was considered a kind of cultural baby food, a form of moral instruction pleasant and easily digestible. In the *Defence*, Sidney calls it "the first light-giver to ignorance, and first nurse, whose milk by little and little enabled them to feed afterwards of tougher knowledges" (18), that is, philosophy and history. Indeed, Sidney's writings of the period associate poetry with childish dependency and insignificant play. When he refers—surely with some irony—to his *Arcadia* as a "toyfull booke," Sidney reinscribes himself as a child and his poetic activity as boyish play. In his sonnets, his persona is alternately maternal, struggling to give birth, and infantile, desiring food from his nurse or from Stella.[59]

This pattern of reference linking poetry and childhood not only reflects cultural attitudes towards poetry but also incorporates elements of Sidney's own experience. It may suggest unresolved pre-Oedipal conflicts; more prosaically, it may allude to Sidney's immediate environment. Sidney's sister, Mary Sidney Herbert, gave birth to her first son at Wilton in April 1580, while Sidney was also in a kind of confinement there, writing. He thus found himself literally returned to the society of women and children, like a prerational boy. (Elyot advises, in book 1, chapter 6, that once a boy turns seven, he should be taken from the company of women and turned over to a tutor.) He may also be identifying closely with his sister's travail when he imagines himself fathering his works in the opening sonnet of *Astrophil and Stella.*[60] Here the analogy with Sidney's experience enhances the convention of speaking of ones poems as offspring. Again, in the *Defence*, Sidney asks, "why England, the mother of so excellent minds, should be grown so hard a stepmother to poets" (61), accusing England and, shall we add, Elizabeth of being stingy to her foster children.[61] Possibly Sidney also felt himself to be like a child in his continual dependence on the queen's vacillating favor; as he bided his time, writing in defense of the child's play of poetry, he waited for the summons to a man's life of soldiery.[62]

The tensions of trivial poetry versus heroic action are evident in the following passage of the *Defence*. Complaining that England is a harsh stepmother to poets, he laments the lack of patronage and, more to the point, the lack of subject matter for heroic poetry. He observes that

> heretofore poets have in England also flourished, and, which is to be noted, even in those times when the trumpet of Mars did sound loudest. And now that an overfaint quietness should seem to strew the house for poets, they are

> almost in as good reputation as the mountebanks at Venice. Truly even that, as of the one side it giveth great praise to poesy, which like Venus (but to better purpose) had rather be troubled in the net with Mars than enjoy the homely quiet of Vulcan: so serves it for a piece of a reason why they are less grateful to idle England, which now can scarce endure the pain of a pen. (62)

The Elizabethan peace was a boon neither for aspiring soldiers nor for poets, who have descended to the level of Venetian mountebanks, that is, itinerant entertainers and quacks. If poets are in disgrace, Sidney intimates, it is because there are no opportunities for heroic action, the subject of epic poesy. Thus, the poetic crisis alludes to a wider crisis: the lack of opportunity for men of Sidney's class.

The image of poetry as Venus revealed in flagrante delicto with Mars does little to exalt poetry, but it confirms Sidney's unease with domestic quiet. In book 4 of the *Metamorphoses*, when Vulcan discovers his wife, Venus, in the act of adultery with Mars, he forges a net to catch them, and the gods laugh at the helplessly entangled lovers, whose shame is emphasized. One unusually explicit sixteenth-century print depicts Vulcan at his forge while a naked Venus cavorts in bed with Mars, who is helmeted but bare from the waist down, a faintly ridiculous figure. In the pictorial tradition, Venus's dalliance with Mars detains him from his business as a warrior. Curiously, Sidney defends Venus, casting her in the role of poetry desiring to embrace Mars, that is, to tell of martial exploits, rather than to sit quietly at home with Vulcan. It is impossible, however, to dismiss the prevailing interpretation that a warrior dallying with Venus, whether she represents love or poetry, is a shameful sight. For Sidney, however, it may be Mars's desire to disrupt the domestic quietude of poesy's life with Vulcan that draws him to the tale.

The "overfaint quietness" on the home front and the lack of "fit employment" clearly galled Sidney, who was forced to bide his time studying and, as we know, writing poetry. As he complained to Languet in 1578:

> The use of the pen, as you may perceive, has plainly fallen from me; and my mind itself, if it was ever active in anything, is now beginning, by reason of my indolent ease, imperceptibly to lose its strength. . . . For to what purpose should our thoughts be directed to various kinds of knowledge, unless room be afforded for putting it into practice, so that public advantage may be the result, which in a corrupt age we cannot hope for?[63]

The problem is that writing and learning are not viable substitutes for action, especially for a young man eager to make his mark on the world. With his image of the pen falling from his hand and a reference to his weakening mind, Sidney betrays a fear of physical and mental debility as well as moral weakness ("indolent ease") brought on by too much study.[64]

Indeed, Sidney's idleness during the years he penned his major works invites comparisons with the tale of Mars lured into dalliance with Venusian poetry. Thomas Moffet, in his panegyric biography of Sidney, decried the abysmal state of the military at the time Sidney accepted his commission at Flushing:

> [O]ne was horrified to observe that many youths sprung from the rank of nobles were—what shall I say?—sons of Mars? Nay, rather nephews of Venus! So unmanned were they by ease, delicacies, drunkenness, and sensual pleasure that they preferred to pursue their debaucheries at home . . . instead of to cross the sea for the sake of the commonwealth. . . . Then, also, some veteran soldiers objected, and perhaps justly, that greater rewards are paid daily, and publicly, to flute players, singers, and musicians than to those who by their wounds and blood maintained for us the commonwealth in life and safety.[65]

For Moffet, the decline of manliness and military preparedness accords with a resurgence of trivial arts. Similarly, Sidney's already-cited criticism that "idle England . . . can scarce endure the pain of a pen" implies not only that England is unreceptive to poetry but that she has gone soft militarily; where she was used to bearing the brunt of a sword, she now cringes at a pen prick. This pen, in turn, is metonymically related to the woman's weak instrument, her needle ("Truly a needle cannot do much hurt, and . . . it cannot do much good" [*Defence* 55]); both are counterparts of the man's sword. Through the interstices of Sidney's language in the *Defence* and in his letters can be glimpsed his real concern: that England provides her gentlemen and noblemen no "fit employment," that is, no opportunities for military service.

The courtier's desire for public achievement and his sense that his abilities are wasted in shameful, nonmilitary, activity are conveyed in the *Defence* by this exemplum, which follows Sidney's criticism of "idle England, which can scarce endure the pain of a pen":

> And so as Epaminondas is said with the honour of his virtue to have made an office, by his exercising it, which before was contemptible, to become highly respected; so these men [servile wits], no more but setting their names to it, by their own disgracefulness disgrace the most graceful poesy. . . . But I that, before even I durst aspire unto the dignity, am admitted into the company of the paper-blurrers, do find the very true cause of our wanting estimation is want of desert—taking upon us to be poets in despite of Pallas. (62–63)

Epaminondas, as Elyot reminds us, was the tutor to King Philip, father of Alexander; he was

> a noble and valiant captain; of whom he [Philip] received such learning, as well in acts martial as in other liberal sciences, that he excelled all other kings that were before his time in Greece, and finally, as well by wisdom as prowess, subdued all that country.[66]

Obviously, Elyot's Epaminondas would be a model of humanist success for Sidney as well, but it is clearly Plutarch whom Sidney echoes in the *Defence*. In the *Moralia*, Plutarch relates the "fall" of this learned teacher, statesman, and general:

> [W]hen through envy and as an insult he had been appointed *telmarch* by the Thebans, he did not neglect his duties, but saying that *not only does the office distinguish the man, but also the man the office*, he advanced the telmarchy to a position of great consideration and dignity, though previously it had been nothing but a sort of supervision of the alleys for the removal of dung and the draining off of water in the streets. (emphasis added)[67]

Though one could hardly imagine a more contemptible occupation than street cleaner, Epaminondas is an appropriate self-image for Sidney, an out-of-work statesman now dignifying the unesteemed office of poet. But Sidney does not develop this analogy between the men who ennoble humble occupations; indeed, our expectations for meaning are repeatedly confounded in this passage. Given its structure ("so as Epaminondas . . . so these men. . . . But I"), we expect "these men" to resemble the respected Epaminondas; instead, they turn out to be men who disgrace poetry, and the analogy fails. Then, rather than distinguishing himself from these base men, Sidney admits himself to "the company of the paper-blurrers" and continues with an unrelated observation. In short, he misses the opportunity to defend his role as a poet with the analogy of Epaminondas, as if resisting the recognition of himself in the demoted Theban.

Sidney also misses an opportunity to defend his pursuit of poetry in a time of quietude by citing David, who successfully combined the roles of soldier and scholar. In his 1573 apology for poetry, Richard Willes had praised David, who "when he had escaped from battles and dangers, and was enjoying the most profound peace and joy . . . composed hymns to God in a variety of metres."[68] Sidney, more concerned with political preeminence than with moral stature, here overlooks the possible contributions of a Davidic poet to reversing England's moral decline. Instead of pursuing these appropriate and self-searching analogies, he locates blame externally: "But I . . . do find the very true cause of our wanting estimation is want of desert—taking upon us to be poets in despite of Pallas." Sidney suggests that poets are unesteemed both because they are undeserving and because they lack reward (from Elizabeth, as Pallas/Minerva), in spite of which (or whom) they undertake poetry.[69] Still, his references to Epaminondas and the self-image of Mars embracing Venusian poetry, together with the omission of David, betray an inarticulate ambivalence about his vocation as a poet, a defensiveness mingled with a sense of shame and failure.

Surprisingly, poetry's most famous detractor in the period, Stephen Gosson, agreed with its defender, Sidney, that the state of poetry reflected a wider cultural crisis, namely a lack of military preparedness. Sidney's *Defence* may or may not be a direct answer to Gosson's *Schoole of Abuse* (1579), which was dedicated to Sidney, but what is often overlooked in this controversy is the common ground shared by the two men, both stern moralists who viewed poetry as functional and educative.[70] One important mutual subtext is the relation between the abuses of poetry and the decline of heroic action in England. Sidney denies that poetry "abuseth men's wit, training it to wanton sinfulness and lustful love" (54), affirming that poetry "is the companion of camps" and incites men to perform brave deeds; from Homer, "active men received their first motions of courage" (56). Even Gosson admitted (following Plato) that "[t]he right use of auncient Poetrie was to have the notable exploytes of worthy Captaines . . . set downe in numbers" (A7v).[71] Sidney's ambition was to be a soldier; Gosson would encourage the profession of soldiery with a meritocracy based on military service:

> I coulde wish it in Englande . . . that our lawes were directed to rewarding of those, whose lives are the first, that must be hazarded to maineteyne the liberty of the lawes . . . [that] none but they might be suffered to drinke out of plate, that have in skirmish slain one of her maiesties enimies. . . . (D7–D7v)

He expresses a common sense of uneasiness over the possibility of England's political decline: "It were not good for us to flatter our selves with these golden dayes . . . never Monarch so mighty but he might be weakened; never Realme so large, but it mighte bee lessened" (E1). Like Sidney, he also believes that learning is no good unless it leads to virtuous action: "I cannot but blame those . . . which sit concluding of Sillogismes in a corner, in a close studye in the Universitye . . . and professe nothing. The bell is knowen by his sounde . . . the tree by the fruite, a man by his woorkes" (E2–E2v). Taken out of context, Gosson's criticism may seem, in Sidney's words, "a chainshot against all learning" (*Defence* 56), but his target is those who fail to put their knowledge into practice. Nervous about the long peace and the decline of soldiery in England, Gosson cautions, "[S]tudie with a booke in one hand, a darte in the other: enjoy peace, with provision for warre" (D8v), advice Sidney himself lived by. Like Sidney, Gosson is engaged in a project of self-defense; he had been a poet and playwright. In the *Schoole of Abuse*, he likens himself to a wayward child who has disobeyed the mother-queen. He characterizes himself among Elizabeth's subjects as "degenerate children of so good a mother, unthankful subjects of so loving a prince, [who] wound her swete hart with abusing her lenitie . . ." (C5v-C6). This abuse involves transgressing apparel laws and restrictions on the theaters; Gosson defends himself by citing several worthy plays, including one of his own and another that decries sedition.[72]

Both Sidney and Gosson, then, combine self-defense with a critique of learning and a call to public service. Both are deeply concerned with the possibility of England's demise and express fundamental fears of military weakness and the moral dangers of prolonged idleness. Though one attacks and the other defends, both betray ambivalence regarding the pursuit of poetry and learning. It is possible that Sidney never read Gosson's work but felt honor-bound to reply because it was dedicated to him. Indeed, he need not have read beyond the title page to feel a defense was in order, for Gosson aims his "invective against Poets, Pipers, Plaiers, Justers, and such like Caterpillers of a Comonwelth" engaged in "mischievous exercise." Given Sidney's commitment to serving the state and his sensitivity about being known as a poet, a work linking his name with the abuse of poetry and the decay of the commonwealth would understandably incite a response.[73] Most likely Gosson expected to find a sympathetic ear and hence a patron, but he badly miscalculated his move, to the ultimate benefit of posterity and the delight and confusion of Sidney scholars.

Sidney the defender of poetry echoes the concerns of Gosson its detractor; for both of them, more than poetry is at stake in the debate over learning. Sidney's *Defence*, written probably in 1580, reiterates his commitment to public action—not his retreat from it—at a time when his hopes in that direction seemed most remote. The years preceding this work and *Astrophil and Stella* were ones of continual frustration for Sidney. The great expectations of his first diplomatic mission came to naught, for Elizabeth dropped her plans for a league of Protestant states late in 1577. His father was out of favor with the queen over matters in Ireland, and in 1578 he was recalled, his health severely weakened. The family fortunes were in decline, and Sidney was perpetually debt ridden. Political appointments were repeatedly rumored and proposed, only to fall through, for he was too young for a major post. Eager for action, he contemplated exploits abroad; financially strapped, he invested in Frobisher's vain expeditions for gold. During most of the year 1581, his energies were dissipated in merely formal tasks, among them escorting the claimant to the Portuguese throne, Don Antonio, and occupying a seat in Parliament. In 1582, he had the galling task of escorting the duke of Anjou, Elizabeth's sometime suitor, to the Netherlands, where he was installed as duke of Brabant. To Sidney, the queen's entente with the French, designed to curb Spanish aggression, meant that there would be no immediate opportunity for military prowess in the Netherlands.[74] Hence he looked for other fields of action. Ironically, by the time he received his commission in Flushing, he was more interested in confronting Spain by direct attack and by establishing English colonies in the New World.[75]

Something of the boredom, restlessness, and powerlessness Sidney experienced during these years is conveyed in his extensive correspondence with his mentor, Languet. In March 1578, Sidney expresses frustration with his "indolent ease" and lack of opportunity to put his knowledge into practice in this "corrupt age." He goes on to complain, "There is no news here, except that it is a novel and almost unheard-of circumstance in government, that nothing novel has occurred. Frobisher's gold is now melted. . . ."[76] Later that month, he writes of his regret that the queen has rejected the activist course of Leicester and Walsingham: "For my own part, unless God powerfully counteract it, I seem to myself to see our cause withering away, and am now meditating with myself some Indian project."[77] Sidney's retirement at Wilton worried Languet, who relied on the younger Englishman to effect his own political goal of establishing a Protestant league. In a letter that dates from 1578, he chastises Sidney for desiring "to fly from the light of your court . . . to the privacy of secluded places to escape the tempest of affairs by which statesmen are generally harassed."[78] For the next few years, he is concerned that Sidney is wasting the flower of his life and neglecting his public responsibilities, but he is cheered by news of his quarrel with the earl of Oxford, whose "arrogance and insolence . . . have roused you from your trance. . . ."[79] This famous tennis-court confrontation with Oxford, who supported the queen's proposed French marriage while Sidney opposed it, expresses a pugnacity possibly related to his political impotence.[80] Indeed, Greville's account of this incident highlights Sidney's sensitivity to his subordinate and powerless status, as he talks back both to Oxford and to the queen, asserting his own rights as a member of the gentry. Sidney's own boredom and frustration are also evident in another letter to his brother, Robert, which dates from October 1580:

> Sir, for news, I refer myself to this bearer, he can tell you how idle we look on at our neighbours' fires, and nothing is happened notable at home, save only Drake's return . . . and rich he is returned. Portugal we say is lost: and to conclude, my eyes are almost closed up, overwatched with tedious business.[81]

Thrice Sidney writes of his inaction and boredom, relieved only by news or dreams of expeditions to the New World, a new arena promising both political and economic opportunities.

Perhaps to compensate for his social and political impotence, Sidney fantasizes, in the *Defence,* a poet with the power to determine the affairs of state. He peoples his golden world with "so true a lover as Theagenes, so constant a friend as Pylades, so valiant a man as Orlando, so right a prince as Xenophon's Cyrus" (24), all ideal types that might inhabit a prelapsarian Elizabethan court, along with Sidney himself. In defiance of history, which often rewards evil, the poet, "having all, from Dante's heaven to his hell, under the authority of his pen" (37), enacts the justice belonging to God or an anointed king. So powerful and righteous is poetry that it "deviseth new punishments in hell for tyrants . . . [who] speed well enough in their abominable injustice of usurpation" (38). One of the uses of tragedy is that it "maketh kings fear to be tyrants . . . [it] teacheth the uncertainty of this world, upon how weak foundations gilden roofs are builded" (45). Sidney here anticipates the argument of Percy Bysshe Shelley, his literary descendant, who claimed in his own *Defence of Poetry* (1821) that "poets are the unacknowledged legislators of the world."[82] The successful right poet would occupy the center of power as a trusted adviser to the prince, like Nathan to David. There he has a chance to fashion the most exalted reader, his monarch. Not content with that position, however, Sidney would claim for the poet a crown. The poet is the "monarch" of all sciences (*Defence* 39), and his poetry is most "princely" in moving the mind towards virtue (42). Its excellence "setteth the laurel crown upon the poets as victorious" over the philosopher and the historian (38), the crown of poetic laurels also suggestive of military and political preeminence.[83]

As a military leader in the Netherlands, Sidney had his chance to fulfill this vision of the princely poet. His ambitions and failures are conveyed in a revealing letter to Sir Francis Walsingham, his intermediary with the queen, in which complaints about Elizabeth's parsimony mingle with professions of belief in their shared higher cause:

> If her Majesty wear the fowntain I woold fear considring what I daily fynd that we shold wax dry, but she is but a means whom God useth . . . I am faithfully persuaded that if she shold withdraw her self other springes woold ryse to help this action.[84]

Sidney sees himself as an important actor in this cosmic drama: "[M]e thinkes I see the great work indeed in hand, against the abusers of the world, wherein it is no greater fault to have confidence in mans power, than it is to hastily to despair of Gods work." As in Sidney's defense of poetic making, man's powers work in accord with God's but in uneasy submission to them. Personally committed to a holy war, Sidney is frustrated by the queen's failure to provide for her troops and accordingly defensive about his own impotence as a leader:

> If the queen pai not her souldiours she must loos her garrisons there is no doubt thereof.
>
> But no man living shall be hable to sai the fault is in me. . . . I am sure no creature shall be hable to lai injustice to my charge.

He goes on to lament a misunderstanding concerning a house he favored: "[C]onsidering how apt the Queen is to interpret every thing to my disadvantage, I have resigned it to my Lord Willowghby. . . ." Feeling somewhat beleaguered, he continues, "I understand I am called very ambitious and prowd at home, but certainly if thei knew my ha[rt] thei woold not altogether so judg me." He considers that this misunderstanding may be due to some letters that went astray. What is remarkable and somewhat pathetic about this letter is Sidney's virtual helplessness; he is hamstrung by circumstance, Elizabeth's parsimony, and bad mail service. The poet, now on the stage of history, finds himself unable to bring about right action in God's cause. His epistolary pleas for assistance and understanding falling on deaf ears, it would seem that his real-life project of fashioning a right reader must be deemed a failure.

For Sidney, the purpose of poetic making was not to transcend nature or repudiate history but to control and fashion them. This fantasy of the poet's omnipotence, the *Defence of Poetry*, is on one level a successful fiction that disguises Sidney's own failure, a triumph of the wit that is simultaneously the ultimate expression of sinful, self-serving love. Importantly, however, Sidney's idealized view of the princely poet who recreates a golden world represents not his defeated retreat from public action into *otium* but his unwavering endorsement of *negotium*. Poetry—allegiance to the Muses—can never substitute for virtuous action—the pursuits of Mars. Nor does mastery of it qualify one for public service, as it should. During Sidney's life, his poetry won him neither public acclaim nor the queen's favor; rather, it was shielded to protect him from ridicule. After his death, however, the reverse occurred; his perceived heroic action eventually won him fame as a poet. Indeed, Sidney, Gosson, and Castiglione agreed that heroic action affords the most appropriate subject matter for poetry, providing models of virtue for admiration and imitation. This is confirmed by Sidney's own death and the subsequent poetic creation of his legend. He was glorified as England's own Scipio and Petrarch, both soldier and scholar, by those who used his example to authorize their own poetic making. His reputation secured, his poetry garnered the acclaim it deserved; poets could freely admire and emulate his verses.

In an irony hitherto unremarked, it is Sidney's ordinary humanity, nothing truly extraordinary, that enabled his exemplary heroism: that thigh wound, suppurating with infection that would eventually kill him, symbolizes Sidney's own fleshly desires and inescapable mortality, out of which potent fictions were made, guaranteeing him an immortality transcending his earthly limitations.

2
Astrophil and Stella and the Failure of the Right Poet

Sidney's activities as a poet and as an aspiring statesman in Elizabeth's court often involve him in what I term "Petrarchan performances"; that is, he assumes the role of subordinate to a powerful authority, figured as a Petrarchan mistress who both inspires and impedes his erotic or political ambitions and his mastery as a right poet. This Petrarchan configuration shapes his experiences as an Elizabethan ambassador, marriage suitor, author of and participant in court entertainments, letter writer to the queen, and sonneteer to Stella. This chapter will explore the resemblances between Sidney's courtly and literary performances, beginning with a discussion of his 1577 embassy and ending with *Astrophil and Stella*, a Petrarchan sonnet sequence that enacts the fantasies of power and failures of influence rehearsed in the *Defence of Poetry.* Literary performances such as *Astrophil and Stella* transform Sidney's experiences of erotic or political ambition into the language of desire central to Petrarchan poetics; this discourse of desire substitutes for the more activist course Sidney preferred. A case in point is Astrophil, for whom desire issues only in unworthy action, the attempted poetic seduction of Stella. Sidney's sonnet persona is a self-image, a model of the aspirations, anxieties, and ultimate limitations of the right poet who seeks through language to empower himself and to move others to virtue.

Sidney and Petrarchan Politics

When he was barely twenty-three years old, Sidney was granted his first opportunity to play the right poet on the stage of history. He was already deemed a rising star in Elizabeth's court when, in 1577, she sent him to the Continent to convey her condolences on the death of the Emperor Maximilian and to discern relations between various Catholic and Protestant princes. The young statesman duly carried out his mission, reporting his actions, speeches, and impressions in a lengthy letter to Sir Francis Walsingham.[1] He made his family proud as well; Walsingham wrote to Henry Sidney that his son "handled [his service] with great judgment and discretion, and [he] hath been honoured abroad in all the Princes' courts with much extraordinary favour."[2] Yet this mission involved Sidney in secretive negotiations that demonstrate the Petrarchan nature of Elizabethan politics, as he sought to effect an alliance of Protestant states and enhance his own status via marriage.

In negotiating these matters, Sidney appears to have taken considerable license with his instructions from the queen. Greville, who accompanied Sidney on this mission, tells us that Sidney,

> to improve that journey, and make it a real service to his Soveraign, procure[d] an Article to be added to his Instructions, which gave him scope . . . to salute such *German* Princes, as were interested in the cause of our Religion, or their own native liberty.[3]

No evidence of such an article exists; probably such sensitive political business was not authorized by the queen.[4] The letters of Sidney and Languet following his return are, however, full of cryptic allusions to less official matters discussed between Sidney and William of Orange. Languet had observed that Sidney "was burning to be presented to Orange, and form an acquaintance with him."[5] He recalls his pleasure that Sidney was directed to visit the Prince,

> for by this means, without any risk to yourself, your wish might be satisfied, and that it will be more honourable to you to go thither in the discharge of a public duty, than as a private person, as you had intended.[6]

Towards the end of this same letter, Languet reminds Sidney, with a touch of exasperation: "See that you do not forget what I said to you at the mouth of the Main, and write about it as soon as you can, as you have more than once promised me." A month later he prods Sidney to a more definite reply to his proposal, which Sidney favored but "could not come to any determination on the subject until [he] had consulted those who had a control over [him],"[7] possibly his uncles or even the queen. When Sidney finally responds in a letter dated 1 October 1577, he is encouraging. He speaks of his eagerness for the "formation of this new commonwealth," expresses regard for the Prince of Orange, and predicts that

> the leaning of our minds is such at this present time, that (should the wars be continued in Flanders) I am in some hope that the prediction which you formerly uttered respecting me at Vienna, will have a happy fulfillment.[8]

Sidney's biographers agree that he refers here to negotiations for his own marriage either to William of Orange's daughter, Marie of Nassau, or to a German princess.[9] The Spanish ambassador, Mendoza, reported to his king in April 1578 the rumors of marriage between Sidney and the willing Dutch princess, who "promises as a dowry to make him lord of Holland and Zealand."[10] The proposed marriage would have been a means to an important political end, a treaty establishing a Protestant league. Of course, Sidney's social status and political clout would be tremendously enhanced as well.

Sidney's initial enthusiasm for this proposal, which must have fueled his desire for greatness, seems to have waned by the time he writes again to Languet in March 1578, five months later. Sidney's letter seems to beg his mentor's indulgence while betraying an irritation at his persistence, even his hypocrisy, in the matter:

> But I wonder, my very dear Hubert, what has come into your mind, that, when I have not as yet done anything worthy of me, you would have me bound in the chains of matrimony; and yet without pointing out any individual lady, but rather seeming to extol the state itself, which, however, you have not as yet sanctioned by your own example. Respecting her of whom I readily acknowledge how unworthy I am, I have written you my reasons long since, briefly indeed, but yet as well as I was able.[11]

Considering his social status, Sidney may have honestly felt unworthy of the princess. Possibly he wished to resist becoming a pawn of Languet and Orange. Surely he was also aware that the prospect of personal gain must be weighed against the risk of damaging his career by negotiating such a marriage without the queen's prior consent. Indeed, the queen mistrusted Sidney's motives in negotiating with

William of Orange; as she wrote to Daniel Rogers, on 22 June 1578, regarding the proposed treaty:

> [W]e could not like that any forreyn prince should enter into any such secreat combination with our President of Wales or Deputye of Ireland or any other governor under us, which might any waye estraunge him from th'obedience he oweth us.[12]

One of his biographers suggests that Elizabeth was afraid of Sidney emerging as a leader on whom the Dutch might bestow sovereignty and possibly as the Dudley candidate for her own throne.[13] At the very least, the alliance would obligate her to support Orange and the Dutch revolt, a commitment she was unwilling to make.

The significance of Sidney's role in this abortive marriage scheme has not been given much consideration, but I believe that the experience was crucial, for Sidney learned firsthand the complexity and inevitable political nature of erotic attachments and the necessity of his own subjection. Plans for a wedding involved Sidney in a profound dilemma: marrying Orange's daughter would make him a prince, but it would also make him a pawn of Languet and Orange and an enemy of the queen; by not marrying her, he would remain a lowly yet loyal servant of the queen. His duty to Elizabeth deprived him of genuine choice in the matter, and he remained subject to her. Then, cruelly, this powerful, denying mistress rejected his proposed treaty. On all counts, Sidney failed to achieve the influence he desired with this premier mission.

Besides the Marie of Nassau alliance, Sidney's other unsuccessful liaisons accentuated his unworthiness and social inferiority. In 1569, at the age of 15, he became engaged to Anne Cecil, daughter of William Cecil, Lord Burghley, quite a match for a mere gentleman from a struggling family. In 1571, however, Anne married the earl of Oxford, who was rich, showy, and able to bestow upon a wife the title of countess. Whether or not Sidney loved Anne Cecil, this marriage must have galled him and contributed to the animosity between him and Oxford, which erupted openly in their famous tennis-court quarrel of 1579.[14] Of course, Sidney's most famed beloved, Penelope Devereux, was also his social superior, married to Lord Rich, and unattainable in more ways than one. In matters political and amorous, Sidney often found himself playing the role of lowly and rejected suitor. (His eventual marriage, in 1583, to Frances, daughter and heir of statesman Sir Francis Walsingham, while not a love match, was politically and financially advantageous to Sidney.)

Following his embassage to the continent, a further attempt to fill the role of right poet at the center of public life was Sidney's pastoral entertainment, *The Lady of May* (1578). This fiction, performed before the queen at the Wanstead estate of his uncle, the earl of Leicester, attempted to fashion her response to matters of foreign policy and marriage. The left-wing Protestants, among them Leicester and Sidney, were urging a policy of direct aid to the Protestant rebels in the Netherlands. Indeed, Sidney may have shortly expected a commission to head English troops there.[15] Elizabeth's Netherlands policy was linked to her renewed marital and diplomatic courtship of the duke of Alençon, a form of entente with the French that foreclosed the possibility of more direct action against the Spanish; additionally, the prospect of a Catholic regent worried English Protestants.[16] During this time, Leicester himself was a suitor for the queen's hand in marriage—a possible alliance that must have fueled Sidney's ambition, for if the queen married Leicester but remained childless, Sidney would be in the position of a prince and possible heir to the throne.[17]

Within these contexts, Sidney's entertainment presented the queen with an important political choice disguised in a pastoral love debate. The debate seems designed to encourage the May Lady to choose "the well deserving and painefull *Therion*," a huntsman and representative of the active life, apparently the Leicester figure, over the "idle *Espilus*," a retiring shepherd.[18] But the queen proves to be a clever reader, not an easily persuaded one, and she imposes her own meaning on the event; her choice of Espilus at once rebukes Leicester's amorous and political ambitions and acknowledges the traditional hero of pastoral.[19] The strongest evidence that Elizabeth made a choice unintended by the writers is in the final songs.[20] Espilus inappropriately sings of the forester who rejoices that he "[a]t length obtained the point of his desire"; presumably the two players, probably in some confusion after the queen's surprising judgment, hastily exchanged parts. Sidney does not say why the queen confounded his carefully wrought drama, reporting only that "it pleased her Majesty to judge that Espilus did the better deserve her; but what words, what reasons she used for it, this paper, which carrieth so base names, is not worthy to contain."[21] The queen's inexplicable response to his drama signals the poet's failure to fashion and persuade his reader.

Because his own political ambitions and religious convictions were at stake, it was particularly hard for Sidney to remain silent on the subject of the queen's marriage, especially the proposed Alençon match. Sidney's *Letter to Queen Elizabeth touching her marriage with Monsieur* (1579) is another of Sidney's courtly performances; here the posture of a plain-speaking, devoted lover helps to justify his harsh message while flattering Elizabeth in her favored role as Petrarchan beloved. He approaches the queen

> carying no other olive branches of intercession, but the lying myself at your feete, nor no other insinuacion either for attention or pardon but the *true* vowed sacrifice of *unfeined* love, I will in simple and direct termes . . . sett down the over flowing of my minde in this most important matter importing as I think, the continewance of your safety, & as I know the joyes of my life. (emphasis added)[22]

In the opening sonnet of *Astrophil and Stella,* Astrophil will assume the same posture, employing similar language—"Loving in *truth*, and *faine* in verse my love to show"—but he will find himself less easily unburdened of words. Sidney's criticism flows easily; he calls Alençon "the sonne of that Jezabel of our age" (*Letter,* 52) and charges him with some responsibility for the St. Bartholomew's Day Massacre of 1572. He is concerned with maintaining the integrity and autonomy of the English body politic, "those buildinges being most ever strongly durable which leaning upon no other remaine firme upon their owne foundacion . . ." (*Letter,* 55). He uses a revealing image of a baby experiencing a sudden loss of security: "[I]n so lineal a monarchie where even the Infantes sucke the love of their rightfull Prince, who would leave the beames of so feare [sic] a Sunne for the dreadfull expectacion of a devided companie of starres[?]" (*Letter,* 58). Like the Petrarchan lover, the role of infant conveys submission and dependence, not to mention a primal fear of abandonment. Not surprisingly, the queen was displeased with Sidney's presumption; surprisingly, however, she did not discipline him so rigorously that posterity has recorded it. His return to court was occasioned by a gesture ripe with significance; at the New Year, 1581, he gave the queen a gift of a whip garnished with small diamonds. The token charges her with cruelty but invites her to curb his aggressive devotion. Sidney, rather than Spenser, might have written these lines to enclose with the gift: "But since ye are my scourge I will intreat, / that for my faults ye will me gently beat."[23] In this affair, Sidney's self-presentation is as varied and complex as that of Astrophil, for he is lover, courtier, and unruly child all at once.

In 1581, Sidney again registered his opposition to the still-pending French marriage by participating in *The Fortress of Perfect Beauty*, an entertainment with the familiar Petrarchan configuration of abject lover and powerful, denying mistress. In this work, the conventional siege motif of courtly literature is easily adaptable to the performance of Petrarchan desire. Again Sidney played the roles of lover and delinquent child by appearing as one of the Four Foster Children of Desire (signifying the French delegation), upstart suitors who lay siege to the Fortress of Perfect Beauty (Elizabeth). The Fortress proves impregnable and the suitors retire, acknowledging "this Fortresse to be reserved for the eye of the whole worlde."[24] Considering that the language and themes of the entertainment resonate with his other literary performances of this period, it is likely that Sidney was closely involved in its authorship. The suitors are infantile, "long haples, now hopeful, fostered children of Desire . . . nourished up with that infective milke" (*Fortress,* 67), and prone to violence to obtain their ends. The assault is hardly threatening, however. Two cannons shoot sweet powder and sweet water, accompanied by music, while footmen throw "Flowers and such fancies" against the walls (*Fortress,* 73). Of course, the two dozen or more defenders easily repulse the foster children; Beauty's virtue is never seriously threatened.

The paradox of Desire is articulated by one of Beauty's defenders: "[N]o soner hath desire what he desireth, but that he dieth presently: so that when Bewtie yeeldeth once to desire, then can she never vaunt to be desired againe" (*Fortress,* 79–80). On the second day, the weary challengers admit defeat, acknowledging that "Desire received his beginning and nourishment of this Fortresse" and pledging to be her slaves forever (*Fortress,* 84). The praise is not without blame. At first it is simply Desire that nurses the overreaching foster children. Then Beauty, Queen Elizabeth, is identified as the source and nurse of the Desire that drives and destroys the men who pursue her. Even the frozen knight, Beauty's defender, was dissolving into drops from beholding the Sun until he pulled himself together to come to her aid. He counsels the foster children to "content your selves with the sunnes indifferent succor . . . claime no prerogative where the sun grauntes no priviledge" (*Fortress,* 75). The prospects for Beauty's favor are bleak, her kindness absent, and Desire is always debilitating, always unsatisfied. The message to Alençon is clear: the English queen is not available. For Sidney, participation in this entertainment allows him to express the frustration of unrewarded service, as he acts out the metaphorical aggression against the Fortress of Beauty, then retires in submission before the queen, on whom he depends for his livelihood.[25] He subsides into the Petrarchan role of distant worshipper, like the Adam and Eve knights who pledge to "take heede to taste of the forbidden fruite, contented to beholde, not coveting to take holde" (*Fortress,* 76).

The Poetics of Desire in *Astrophil and Stella*

Beauty's defender aptly articulated the paradox of desire so central to Petrarchan poetics: "No sooner hath Desire what he desireth, but that he dieth presently. . . . it is convenient for Desire ever to wish; necessary also that he always want" (*Fortress,* 79–80). The nature of desire is to be unfulfilled and unending; thus a sonnet sequence, in which the poet rehearses, in poem upon poem, his attempts to win the disdainful lady, is a perfect vehicle for exploring and perpetuating desire. Unfulfilled desire is also essential to the Petrarchan poet's art. Once desire is satiated, its expression ceases, and the poet's voice must fall silent. The achievement of desire also presents another conundrum: attaining the heights of virtue occupied by the beloved implies an unimaginable human perfection, while the gratification of lesser desire compromises the virtue of the lady and her lover. The poet must content himself with loss, and his desire sustains itself in sonnet after Petrarchan sonnet. Twinned with desire, loss is also necessary to poetry; it is the lack which language fills and transforms into poetic gain.

Astrophil and Stella explores desire for and loss of the desired object, not only or primarily Lady Rich/Stella but also political preeminence, royal favor, and right poetry. As the Foster Children and the May Lady's suitors make clear, amorous desire can figure political ambition; in the right context, Petrarchism has inescapable political reference. I contend that Astrophil's unsuccessful courtship of Stella crowns and expresses for Sidney a pattern of desire and loss, beginning with his foregone marriage opportunity in 1576 and his failures to capitalize on his early diplomatic success, and including his performances designed to influence the queen. Most recently, of course, Sidney had lost his position as Leicester's heir and the status and influence it promised. William Camden relates how, at a tilt in 1581, shortly after Leicester produced a son, Sidney appeared at a tilt with his device altered to "~~SPERAVI~~, thus dashed through to shew his hope therein was dashed."[26] Sidney's fantasies of power and his failures of influence find expression in his writings of this period, in the poet-statesman of the *Defence*, whose infected will impedes his erected wit, and in the poet-lover, Astrophil, whose desire for Stella hinders (rather than assists) his attainment of virtue.

In *Astrophil and Stella*, the energy of unfulfilled ambition is redirected onto language, producing what I term a "poetics of desire" that characterizes Sidney's literary performances. Let me illustrate this poetics of desire with an example from book 2 of Sidney's revised *Arcadia*, where the continuance of the narrative itself depends on the repression and redirection of Pyrocles' ambition, expressed as sexual desire for the princess Philoclea. Zelmane, the disguised Pyrocles, fired with lust at the sight of Philoclea bathing, becomes a parody of the prophet-poet "taking up the lute . . . with a divine fury inspired," for the blason he sings begins and ends in sexual double entendre: "What tongue can her perfections tell, / In whose each part all pens may dwell?"(287). Pyrocles must necessarily repress his desire, but it finds expression in the suggestion that his penis desires to dwell where only his pen can venture. Later, when Pyrocles and Philoclea become engaged, he longs to seal the bargain "with the chief arms of his desire" (331); to prevent him, Philoclea begs him to continue with his story. Pyrocles "knew this discourse was to entertain him from a more straight parley, yet he durst not but kiss his rod" and, sighing, he continues his story (ibid.). The indirection of discourse contrasts the "straight parley" of lovemaking preferred by the aroused Pyrocles. Soon thereafter, Philoclea is moved at Pyrocles' story, and she kisses him, "which had almost brought Pyrocles into another discourse, but that she with so sweet a rigour forbade him that he durst not rebel" (357), and she commands him again to continue his story. Here, "discourse" is a transparent metaphor for sexual activity; the lady's refusal allows the other discourse, the story, to continue. Ironically, Pyrocles' story treats his heroic exploits, reminding us that courtship, with its language of "arms," "straight parley," and rebellion, is itself a redirection of heroic, military action. Once more the story is interrupted as Pyrocles begs Philoclea to be gracious to him. Philoclea refuses and

> with a sweetly disobeying grace, desired him that her desire, once for ever, might serve, that no spot might disgrace that love which shortly she hoped should be to the world warrantable. Fain he would not have heard, till she threatened anger; and then the poor lover durst not, because he durst not. (375)

Though he subsides, moments later he "rebel[s] so far as to kiss her . . . while she spake, he kissed, and it seemed he fed upon her words." She resists, asking, "How will you have your discourse . . . without you let my lips alone?" (376). Again, the speech of the virtuous Philoclea controls Pyrocles' desire, which, acted upon, would compromise her virtue. This scene, for all its charm, dramatizes the complex dynamic informing verbal discourse and the physical "discourse" of desire for which it substitutes and on which it depends.[27]

This dynamic of desire sheds light on Sidney's performance as Astrophil in a poetic discourse that substitutes for and alludes to a more active course. As Sidney could not be silenced on the matter of the French marriage, and as Pyrocles tries time and again to kiss Philoclea, so the irrepressible Astrophil employs various strategies, verbal and physical, to win over the virtuous and resisting Stella. In each case of Sidney's writing, verbal discourse (letter, court drama, narrative, or sonnet) replaces, while also urging, a more active course. Sidney's personae, all foster children of desire, alternate between the desire for autonomy and the need for dependency, between rebellion and submission. *Astrophil and Stella* is, like Pyrocles' lengthy, oft-interrupted narration of his heroic past and like Sidney's role playing as an aggressive lover of Elizabeth, a discourse of frustrated desires—including erotic love, religious devotion, political ambition, and poetic aspiration—for which the idiom of unfulfilled Petrarchan love is perfectly suited.

This approach assumes some correspondence between Sidney and his sonnet persona that Sidney himself invites, in part by the self-allusive name Astro*phil* and the puns on "rich."[28] Moreover, the sonnets frequently engage issues that concerned Sidney and experiences very close to his own. Sonnet 18, for instance, reflects upon the proper function of learning for one obligated by birthright to a life of public service:

> With what sharp checkes I in my self am shent,
> When into Reason's audite I do go:
> And by just counts my selfe a banckrout know
> Of all those goods, which heav'n to me hath lent:
> Unable quite to pay even Nature's rent,
> Which unto it by birthright I do ow:
> And which is worse, no good excuse can show,
> But that my wealth I have most idly spent.
> My youth doth waste, my knowledge brings forth toyes,
> My wit doth strive those passions to defend,
> Which for reward spoile it with vaine annoyes.
> I see my course to lose my selfe doth bend:
> I see and yet no greater sorow take
> Then that I lose no more for *Stella's* sake.

The bankruptcy metaphor alludes to Sidney's own disastrous financial situation as well as to his youthful squandering of nature's gifts. The sense of shame at failing to live up to his birthright (l. 6) borders on self-loathing. In the sestet, Sidney turns from his wasted wealth to his wasted knowledge, which has brought forth not action but "toyes," that is, his writings. (He called his *Defence* an "ink-wasting toy" and the *Arcadia* an "idle work" and a "trifle.") The rhyme with "vaine annoyes" is suggestive of the speaker's irritation at his own penchant for these useless toys. He is annoyed that he spends (uses and depletes) his wit defending passions (love and poetry) whose only reward is vanity. The loss of self he anticipates in line 12 is a parody of Christian self-abnegation, even a suggestion of his own damnation. The couplet is an instance (the first in the sequence) of Sidney's practice of throwing his sonnet into reverse gear, as he triumphantly opposes Stella to the entire set of values unfolded by the poem. This couplet, however, is not a ringing affirmation of love for Stella. The use of a negative in each line ("no greater sorow take . . . lose no more for *Stella's* sake") makes the speaker sound as if he is trying to summon up more sorrow and hold down his losses. The introduction of Stella in the last line in no way compensates for the self-laceration of the preceding thirteen lines.[29]

In the *Defence*, Sidney struggled to demonstrate that his evident love of poetry assisted, rather than impeded, his obligation to live an active life in the service of the state. In the sonnets, however, loving Stella is clearly an impediment to Astrophil's achievement of similar goals, but it is one that he embraces despite his awareness of what he has failed to achieve—morally, politically, and intellectually. Sonnet 21 dramatizes this all-for-love choice, as Astrophil admits to his scolding friend that his "young mind [is] marde" and that his writings "show / My wits, quicke in vaine thoughts, in vertue lame" (ll. 3–4). Astrophil, like Sidney, is aware that

> to my birth I owe
> Nobler desires, least else that friendly foe,
> Great expectation, wear a traine of shame.
> For since mad March great promise made of me,
> If now the May of my years much decline,
> What can be hoped my harvest time will be?
>
> (*AS* 21:6–11)

Languet reflects in one of his last letters to Sidney on how he admired his "mental endowments, splendour of birth, majesty of person, the expectation of great wealth . . . and all those other . . . gifts of fortune." He reminds Sidney of the success of his first embassy in 1577 (the "mad March" of his life), when he "carried away the admiration of all men" and won "the good-will of her most gracious Majesty" and the admiration of his father. But now, in September 1580 (the May of Sidney's years), Languet finds "a sort of cloud over your fortunes" and attempts to rouse him to action, questioning whether it is "honourable . . . to lurk where you are, whilst your country is imploring the aid and support of her sons."[30] The friend in the sonnet goes on to encourage Astrophil, "your wisdome's golden mine / Dig deep with learning's spade," to which he replies, "now tell me this, / Hath this world ought so faire as *Stella* is?" Astrophil's reply is something of a non sequitur; he is clearly not listening to his friend's advice.

While Astrophil is a self-image for Sidney (albeit a sometimes ironic one), Stella is not simply referential. She unfolds the complexity and variety of Sidney's desires for social status, royal favor, and poetic mastery. She occasionally signifies, in both veiled and explicit ways, the poet's nonfictional Petrarchan mistresses who often denied his desires: the queen and Penelope Rich. Stella emerges as a rival to the queen, especially in sonnets that allude to a courtly milieu. In one of these, the curious court wits attempt to locate Astrophil's pensiveness and melancholy in his studies or his attempts to redress "state errours" (*AS* 23:8). Other envious detractors "judge ambition's rage, / Scourge of it selfe, still climing slipprie place, / Holds my young braine captiv'd in golden cage" (*AS* 23:9–11). Elizabeth's court was indeed a slippery place, a golden cage to captivate a young courtier's mind. (The image of ambition scourging itself also brings to mind Sidney's New Year's gift to the queen in 1581, the diamond-studded whip.) Astrophil, characteristically, denies his courtly ambitions and claims that Stella is his cynosure: "O fooles, or over-wise, alas the race / Of all my thoughts hath neither stop nor start, / But only *Stella's* eyes and *Stella's* hart" (*AS* 23:12–14).[31] In sonnet 22, Stella challenges the sun, which progresses like a monarch through the sky. The sun, suggestive of the queen, is forced to kiss Stella, an act implying her submission to the superior beauty. In the tournament sonnets, it is Stella, not the queen, who spurs Astrophil's achievements (*AS* 41) or causes him shame before the court (*AS* 53). In sonnet 9, the Petrarchan blason of Stella both invokes and usurps the image of the Tudor queen as the union of Lancastrian red rose and Yorkist white: In "Queene *Vertue's* court, which some call *Stella's* face / . . . . Marble mixt red and white do enterlace" her cheeks (*AS* 9:1, 8). Given that the identity of a Petrarchan mistress is a well-known aspect of Elizabeth's personal mythology, a poet's praises of his lady's beauty and his expressions of sexual desire or complaints against her cruelty could include Elizabeth while protecting the poet in the safety net of convention.[32] Similarly, Sidney's wordplay on "rich" identifies a historical woman he may have loved and lost; furthermore, it makes of her a metaphor ironically appropriate for a sonnet speaker reflecting on his impoverished wit and purse.[33]

Astrophil and Stella takes Sidney's experiences of loss—of royal favor, social status, and Stella's love—and transforms them to poetic gain; he fills a lack with language. The speaker of the *Defence* negotiated his failure as a statesman by striving for success as a poet. Similarly, Sidney as Astrophil redefines himself as a love poet to seek the fame that has eluded him: "long needy Fame / Doth even grow rich, naming my *Stella's* name" (*AS* 35:10–11). As Sidney's oration defended poor poetry, Astrophil's sonnets defend his much-criticized love for Stella. To his accusing friend, who says that desire leads him into sin and ruin, he responds by converting the criticism to praise: "If that be sinne which in fixt hearts doth breed / A loathing of all loose unchastitie, / Then Love is sinne, and let me sinfull be" (*AS* 14:12–14). *Astrophil and Stella* becomes, like the *Defence*, something of a paradoxical encomium requiring a good deal of wit. The defense of the indefensible involves him in some clever but dubious maneuvers, when virtue and love, like plaintiffs in a courtroom, vie for Stella. The poet negotiates: "Well *Love,* since this demurre our sute doth stay, / Let *Vertue* have that *Stella's* selfe; yet thus, / That *Vertue* but that body graunt to us" (*AS* 52:12–14). Astrophil, whisking Stella away from Virtue's claim, is like the defender of poetry who mediates between history and philosophy and claims from both the prize.[34] Both defend, even exalt, their much-maligned pursuits: making love and making poetry.

It is Stella's virtuous denial of Astrophil, like Philoclea's denial of Pyrocles, that forces him back onto the resources of language; discourse replaces, while urging, the acting out of desire. Stella reminds him that his desire degrades him, while hers is ennobling, "a Love not blind, / Which would not let me, whom she loved, decline / From nobler course, fit for my birth and mind" (*AS* 62:6–8).[35] Astrophil, unheeding, pleads, "Deare, love me not, that you may love me more" (*AS* 62:14), a paradox that hinges on two meanings of love, his activist and hers idealist. In the next sonnet, Astrophil's desire is insistent and frankly sexual: "with heart most high, with eyes most low, / I crav'd the thing which ever she denies" (*AS* 63:5–6). Her repeated refusal, "No, No," Astrophil turns into his cheapest conquest, invoking the rules of grammar: "For Grammer sayes . . . / That in one speech two Negatives affirme" (*AS* 63:13–14). Again in the fourth song, Astrophil, under cover of moonlight, attempts to seduce Stella, who responds with the resolute refrain, "'No, no, no, no, my Deare, let be.'" In the last stanza, however, her words take on a different, encouraging meaning when Astrophil changes his tactic from hopeful pleading to despairing: "Soone with my death I will please thee. / 'No, no, no, no, my Deare, let be'" (*AS* song 4:53–54). Stella's words have not changed, but Astrophil has been able to manipulate their meaning so that what Stella refuses is not her body but her lover's death. In the face of persistent frustration and denial, Astrophil's only triumph occurs in language.

Another strategy employed by Astrophil to negotiate the desire aroused by Stella is to assume a boyish persona, one function of which is to defuse the sexual threat of his desire. In the first sonnet, he is a self-punishing errant schoolboy, "Biting my trewand pen, beating my selfe for spite" (*AS* 1:13). Early in the sequence, he is a student unapt for complex learning, satisfied with copying what Nature writes in Stella (*AS* 3:10–14). Elsewhere, he identifies with the boyish Cupid who flits throught the sonnets, reflecting "I perhaps am somewhat kinne to thee / . . . . Thou bear'st the arrow, I the arrow head" (*AS* 65:12, 14). Both Cupid and Astrophil are tyrannized by Stella; both "from booke myche to desire" (*AS* 46:13), that is, play truant from the school of virtue, giving themselves to desire.[36] Love can also be a superficial schoolboy enjoying a picture book, unable to apprehend its serious matter,

like a child, that some faire booke doth find,
With guilded leaves or colourd Velume playes,
Or at the most on some fine picture stayes,
But never heeds the fruit of writer's mind.

(*AS* 11:5–8)

Astrophil also takes the role of errant schoolboy unable to learn the most evident lessons from Nature's book, Stella:

Who will in fairest booke of Nature know,
How Vertue may best lodg'd in beautie be,
Let him but learne of *Love* to read in thee,
Stella, those faire lines, which true goodnesse show.

(*AS* 71:1–4)

Here Love is the schoolmaster and Stella the textbook of Nature, whose lines convey goodness, virtue, and reason; more importantly, she also moves all minds to seek virtue. Thus she is, ideally, the poet and the poetic image both: "So while thy beautie drawes the heart to love, / As fast thy Vertue bends that love to good: / 'But ah', Desire still cries, 'give me some food'" (*AS* 71:12–14). Just as his will is being moved to do good, Astrophil's fallen appetite, appropriately represented as a baby crying for food, interrupts. We are reminded of Sidney as the Foster Child, nursed by Desire and weaned by Despair, and of Pyrocles, whose discourse of desire always interrupts Philoclea's discourse of virtue. In this justly famed sonnet, Sidney's high hopes for poetry are expressed in the image of Stella as the right poet moving the beholder to virtuous action; her failure and his despair are uttered in desire's cry for food.[37]

At this point, an unlicensed action disrupts the discourse; unable to banish desire, Astrophil steals a kiss from Stella. The kiss is an appropriate synecdoche for the oral satisfaction craved by the baby of sonnet 71. As he hovers over the sleeping Stella, he is driven by lust and sheer boyish cussedness:

> Yet those lips so sweetly swelling,
> Do invite a stealing kisse:
> Now will I but venture this,
> Who will read must first learne spelling.
>
> (*AS* song 2:21–24)

As she wakes, he flees, cursing himself as a "Foole, more foole, for no more taking," for not taking more kisses or more *than* a kiss (*AS* song 2:28). Stealing the kiss, however, is more than a witty prank; it signifies a transgressive act akin to Pyrocles' attempted assaults on Philoclea. In book 4 of *The Courtier*, Bembo issues this caution to lovers:

> For since a kisse is a knitting together both of bodie and soule, it is to bee feared, lest the sensuall lover will be more enclined to the part of the bodie, than of the soule: but the reasonable lover woteth well, that . . . the mouth . . . is an issue for the wordes, that be the interpreters of the soule.[38]

Astrophil knows that taking the kiss is serious business; later, he rhapsodizes: "O kisse, which soules, even soules together ties / By linkes of *Love*" (*AS* 81:5), but he behaves more like a sensual than a rational lover.

Astrophil resorts to his boyish persona to diminish the importance of the stolen kiss, which he equates with the sugar water given to pacify hungry babies:

> *Love* still a boy, and oft a wanton is,
> School'd onely by his mother's tender eye:
> What wonder then if he his lesson misse,
> When for so soft a rod deare play he try?
>   And yet my Starre, because a sugred kisse
> In sport I suckt, while she asleepe did lie,
> Doth lowre, nay, chide; nay, threat for only this:
> Sweet, it was saucie *Love*, not humble I.
>
> (73:1–8)

The dynamics are complex here, suggesting an Astrophil-Cupid simultaneously childish and precociously sexual and a Stella both maternal and erotic. Love is the child of a doting mother whose easy punishment ("soft rod") is worth a missed lesson. Astrophil's transgression, however much he tries to equate it with Cupid's play, is more serious: he sucks a sugared kiss from Stella while she sleeps. This action suggests nursing, but Stella is not his mother, as Venus is Love's mother. Hence, sucking a kiss can only be a sexual advance. In retrospect then, Love's "soft rod" also looks less innocent, and Astrophil's advance can be seen as a definite attempt to arouse himself (and Stella from sleep). After Astrophil steals the kiss, he exults in terms similarly ripe with sexual ambiguity. Using no less than thirteen metaphors in one sonnet, he praises the kiss as

> Neast of young joyes, schoolmaster of delight,
>   Teaching the meane, at once to take and give
> The friendly fray, where blowes both wound and heale,
>   The prettie death, while each in other live.
>
> (*AS* 79:8–11)

Here the persona is first babyish, playing in a nest, then schoolboyish, then suddenly manly. Delight accompanies teaching, but the golden mean of reciprocal kissing is hardly a lesson in virtue for a young student or a courtly lover. The "friendly fray" is a clever transitory phrase, suggesting both schoolyard roughhousing and amorous tangling, but the "prettie death, while each in other live" denotes sexual union. As in sonnet 73, Astrophil displays a boyish charm to disguise his coercive sexual poetics.[39]

This persona of the irrepressible but well-meaning boy may be one that Sidney employed to his advantage in dealing with his queen; if so, it provides another link between his political and literary performances. In the Alençon affair, for example, Sidney seems to have escaped censure for his *Letter to Queen Elizabeth* while the publisher John Stubbs lost his right hand for advancing similar arguments against the French marriage in his "Discovery of a Gaping Gulf." Granted, Sidney did not publish his letter, but a score of manuscript copies still exist, so it must have circulated widely.[40] It is generally believed that Sidney wrote the letter at the instigation of Leicester and Walsingham, whose strategy then resembles that of Shakespeare's Worcester, who incited Hotspur to rebellion, reasoning, "My nephew's trespass may be well forgot, / It hath the excuse of youth and heat of blood, / And an adopted name of privilege."[41] Like Astrophil, Sidney could pretend that youth and innocent love excuse the offense or that he was put up to it: "Sweet, it was saucie *Love*, not humble I."

The post-kiss sonnets manage to contain the poet's desire within language, but in the tenth song, desire escapes the discipline of the sonnet form, finding expression in Astrophil's fantasies of sexual and political mastery. He sends his thoughts to ravish Stella:

> Thinke of my most Princely power,
> When I blessed shall devower,
> With my greedy licorous sences,
> Beauty, musicke, sweetnesse, love
> While she doth against me prove
> Her strong darts, but weake defences.
>
> (*AS* song 10:31–36)

The use of the word "devower," with its likeness to "deflower," strengthens the sexual connotations of Astrophil's imagined assault. Having stormed the citadel, he imagines enjoying her wholly: eyes and heart, body and soul. This "rape" of Stella recalls the assault on the Fortress of Perfect Beauty, with Astrophil as one of the Foster Children of Desire. While they admitted their defeat, Astrophil only temporarily assuages his desires: "Thinke no more but die in me, / Till thou shalt revived be, / At her lips my Nectar drinking" (*AS* song 10:46–48). As his language indicates, the hope of sexual gratification and power over Stella is not abandoned. This familiar convention of the love assault as a military conquest suggests Astrophil's grievous misapplication of the duty to perform heroic action. The fantasy of raping Stella also turns Petrarchan order on its head; it debases the language of service and shows how far Astrophil is from his goal of being a right poet.[42]

The Failure of Astrophil as a Right Poet

Unable either to control or to satisfy his desires, Astrophil is self-condemned to loss: of Stella's grace and of the virtue that attends worthy achievement. Sonnet 71 dramatizes Astrophil's intransigence, for even Stella, the very speaking picture of virtue, cannot move Astrophil to goodness. (Neither, fortunately, can Astrophil's poetry move Stella to sleep with him.) As a desiring poet-lover, Astrophil is a carefully crafted counterimage to the divine sonneteer imagined in the *Defence*, but he is also a self-image of Sidney in his struggles to authorize himself in the face of powerful, denying authorities. In Astrophil's poetic method, Sidney conveys his anxieties about feigning images and being unable to move an audience. The exemplary figure against which he measures himself is Hercules, a hero also known for his powers as an orator. In the striving and failure of Astrophil's art, Sidney brilliantly figures the scarce possibility for poetic or public achievement in a fallen world.

From the beginning, Astrophil's poetic practice invites consideration in terms of the strategy of right poets, who

> make to imitate, and imitate both to delight and teach; and delight, to move men to take that goodness in hand, which without delight they would fly as from a stranger; and teach, to make them know that goodness whereunto they are moved. . . . (*Defence* 27)

Similarly using *gradatio*, the initial sonnet of *Astrophil and Stella* echoes this passage, as Astrophil presents himself

> Loving in truth, and faine in verse my love to show,
> That the deare She might take some pleasure of my paine:
> Pleasure might cause her reade, reading might make her know,
> Knowledge might pitie winne, and pitie grace obtaine,
>   I sought fit words to paint the blackest face of woe.
>
> (*AS* 1:1–5)

Astrophil's mimesis aims first to delight, then to instruct, then to move the "deare She" to the action of bestowing her grace. His motives not yet suspect, his plan seems logical and "right," but it does not work. This is apparent by sonnet 44. The poem's use of *gradatio* recalls sonnet 1:

My words I know do well set forth my mind,
    My mind bemones his sense of inward smart;
    Such smart may pitie claime of any hart,
Her heart, sweete heart, is of no Tygre's kind:
And yet she heares, yet I no pitty find;
    But more I crie, lesse grace she doth impart.

(*AS* 44:1–6)

Astrophil's words not only do not move Stella, but they have the reverse of their intended effect and instead harden her heart: the "*more* I crie, *lesse* grace she doth impart." Stella is no fool; surely by now she knows the kind of knowledge, pleasure, and grace Astrophil desires—erotic, not innocent.

In retrospect, however, even the ambiguous first line of sonnet 1, with its complex pun on "faine" and "feign," suggests something morally suspect about Astrophil's mimesis. The speaker, "faine in verse [his] love to show," is both obligated and pleased to express his love by writing verses. The pun on "feign" reminds us that the verse presents only a fictive image of his love. This is hardly problematic, for in the *Defence*, Sidney defines poetry as "feigning notable images of virtues and vices" (27) and adduces the superior moving and teaching abilities of the feigned images of poetry over the true images of history (36). An additional possibility, that Astrophil's love itself is a pretense, is, however, problematic, for it denies the speaker's claim that he loves in truth.[43] To complicate the issue, in sonnet 5, loving Stella is opposed to all the higher truths in Astrophil's canon:

    True, that true Beautie Vertue is indeed,
Whereof this Beautie can be but a shade,
Which elements with mortall mixture breed:
True, that on earth we are but pilgrims made,
    And should in soule up to our countrey move:
    True, and yet true that I must *Stella* love.

(*AS* 5:9–14)

In the last line, with its characteristic Sidneian reversal, the speaker's progress is arrested; the sonnet admits that Astrophil's feigned/fained love of Stella carries him away from higher, religious truth.

For Sidney, feigning is a political strategy as well as a poetic necessity, and *Astrophil and Stella* is implicated in both activities. Puttenham, in his *Arte of English Poesie*, also agrees that dissimulation is essential to poets and courtiers. He calls allegory the "figure of false semblant or dissimulation . . . the chief ringleader and captaine of all other figures" without which no one, from the "common Courtier" to the "gravest Counsellour, yea and the most noble and wisest Prince" can persuade.[44] In the *Defence*, Sidney's discussion of the merits of feigned versus true images, like Puttenham's discussion of allegory, is placed in a political context. Interestingly, it includes the same homonymic pun on "feign" and "fain" as the first line of *Astrophil and Stella*:

> For that a feigned example hath as much force to teach as a true example. . . . Herodotus and Justin do both testify that Zopyrus, King Darius' faithful servant . . . *feigned* himself in extreme disgrace of his king: for verifying of which, he caused his own nose and ears to be cut off, and so flying to the Babylonians, was received, and for his known valour so sure credited, that he did find means to deliver them over to Darius. . . . Xenophon excellently *feigneth* such another stratagem performed by Abradatas in Cyrus' behalf. Now would I *fain* know, if occasion be presented unto you to serve your prince by such an honest dissimulation, why you do not as well learn it of Xenophon's fiction as of the other's verity; and truly so much the better, as you shall save your nose by the bargain. (36–37; emphasis added)

In Sidney's first (historical) example, the one who feigns loses his nose and ears. In the second (poetic) example, in which the author and subject both feign, Abradatas keeps his appendages. This outcome, rather than the greater moving or teaching ability of Xenophon, recommends the poet over the historian! Sidney includes himself among the counterfeiters with his own pun on "fain," inviting the reader to imagine himself a courtier with the opportunity to serve the prince "by such an honest dissimulation." With his obvious suggestion that any wise person would choose to learn from Xenophon's example, Sidney implies that only a fool would sacrifice his ears and nose, even to serve his prince. The defense of poetry has become a lesson in Machiavellian statecraft. Abradatas and Zopyrus are both courtiers (not poets) who advance through feigning. To their company we may add Sidney, who offered his queen the "*true* vowed sacrifice of *unfained* love" in his letter, and who fashions in Astrophil another suitor hoping to flourish by "honest dissimulation" (a most courtly oxymoron), by feigning his love in language.

In addition to its poetic and political utility, feigning also implies a dramatic posturing that goes along with Sidney's other Petrarchan performances. Astrophil even resorts to complex role playing when he discovers that fiction is more persuasive than truth.[45] The "blackest face of woe," a mask Astrophil tried to paint in the first sonnet, is now fully displayed for Stella, but the picture fails to persuade as it should:

> *STELLA* oft sees the verie face of wo
> Painted in my beclowded stormie face:
> But cannot skill to pitie my disgrace,
> Not though thereof the cause her selfe she know:
> Yet hearing late a fable, which did show
> Of Lovers never knowne, a grievous case,
> Pitie thereof gate in her breast such place
> That, from that sea deriv'd, teares' spring did flow.
> Alas, if Fancy drawne by imag'd things,
> Though false, yet with free scope more grace doth breed
> Then servant's wracke, where new doubts honor brings;
> Then thinke my deare, that you in me do reed
> Of Lover's ruine some sad Tragedie:
> I am not I, pitie the tale of me.
>
> (*AS* 45)

Clearly the program of the first sonnet has failed. Astrophil shows his woe, and Stella knows its cause, but the expected pity and grace are not forthcoming. Instead, a feigned example, a tale of "Lovers never knowne," moves her to tears of pity. Unfairly, though not surprisingly (considering Sidney's promotion of poetry over history in the *Defence*), the feigned image of woe is more effective in moving Stella. Doubting the value of loving in truth, Astrophil gives himself over to feigning, asking to be read as a tragedy and denying the "I" who loves in truth: "I am not I, pitie the tale of me." Here Sidney toys with the very fictionality of his poetry by having his fictitious persona wish himself a fiction. Astrophil immediately betrays that fiction with a characteristic bawdy pun on "tale" and "tail." Through the multiple levels of feigning emerges the truth, and it is no greater a truth than Astrophil's lust for Stella.

As Astrophil struggles to legitimate himself as a poet, a feigner of images, his main challenge is not to portray or to praise Stella; it is to move her. Stella is not, however, the compliant reader Astrophil desires but a resisting one. Moreover, she usurps the role of poet from Astrophil. He sends Stella some poems, hoping that her soul will be "pierc'd with sharpnesse of the mone," but this plan backfires:

She heard my plaints, and did not o
But them (so sweete is she) most swe
With that faire breast making woe's da
A prety case! I hoped her to bring
To feele my griefes, and she with face and voice
So sweets my paines that my paines me rejoyce.

(*AS* 57:8, 9–14)

Stella transforms his words of woe into joyful words, defeating their original purpose. Like the May Lady, Stella is a Petrarchan mistress who not only denies the lover's desire and misreads his intention but generates her own, contrary meaning.[46]

Stella's refusal to read rightly precipitates a crisis for Astrophil and a demonstration of his oratorical and rhetorical prowess. Sonnet 58 enacts the ideal of the orator-poet as cultural hero, adumbrated in Sidney's *Defence* and other Renaissance texts and expressed in the exemplary figure of Hercules.

Doubt there hath bene, when with his golden chaine
The Oratour so farre men's harts doth bind,
That no pace else their guided steps can find,
But as he them more short or slacke doth raine,
Whether with words this soveraignty he gaine,
Cloth'd with fine tropes, with strongest reasons lin'd,
Or else pronouncing grace, wherewith his mind
Prints his owne lively forme in rudest braine.
Now judge by this: in piercing phrases late,
Th'anatomy of all my woes I wrate,
Stella's sweete breath the same to me did reed.
O voice, ô face, maugre my speeche's might
Which wooed wo, most ravishing delight
Even those sad words even in sad me did breed.

(*AS* 58)

The audience is witness to the debate, the issue being whether Astrophil or Stella is the more convincing orator. In the question Astrophil poses, whether the orator gains his sovereignty with "words . . . fine tropes . . . [and] strongest reasons" (his own forte) or "pronouncing grace" (Stella's advantage), the decision is not difficult. Both tradition, including Cicero and Quintilian, and Stella support the latter. Cicero, in *De Oratore*, affirms that delivery is the dominant factor in oratory and relates that "when Demosthenes was asked what is the first thing in speaking, he assigned the first role to delivery, and also the second, and also the third."[47] It would seem Stella has been the more effective orator, printing her "lively forme" in Astrophil's "rudest braine." Sovereignty, too, belongs to Stella, for her victory in the prior sonnet confirms that she possesses the creative and transforming power the poet usually exercises.

Upon further consideration, however, the victory has to go to Astrophil and hence to Sidney, who composed the sonnet as a masterful piece of oratory. The octave is a single prose period, the strongly accented opening clause seizing our attention but suspending satisfaction. Frequent enjambment (ll. 1, 3, 7, 12, and 13) makes the verse tend towards prose. The phrasing is rounded and full, rather than lyrical and end-stopped. The poet engages the audience with direct address, "Now judge by this." The command becomes ambiguous if "this" is taken to refer not only to the example of the prior sonnet, which established Stella's mastery, but also to the poem itself, which demonstrates Astrophil's oratorical powers. The use of apostrophe in line 12 ("O voice, ô face") raises the tone. Repetition of verbs in the emphatic position at the end of the line occurs no less than eight times (ll. 2–6, 10–11, 14), lending strength and conviction. Repetition also adds sonority to the final line: "most ravishing delight / Even those sad words even in sad me did breed." While we hear of Stella's prowess, we actually witness Astrophil's. He converts Stella's coup into his own poetic victory, demonstrating his ultimate control over the language.[48]

When Sidney assumes the mantle of orator, both in the *Defence* and in sonnet 58, he aspires to the orator's power, which is expressed in his rapprochement of heroism and scholarship, works and words. Thomas Wilson, in his *Arte of Rhetorique* (1560), praises the orator Cineas, who

> through the eloquence of his tongue, wanne mo Cities unto him, then ever himself should els have beene able by force to subdue. . . . [W]hat worthier thing can there bee, then with a word to winne Cities and whole Countries? . . . What greater delite . . . then to see a whole multitude, with the onely talke of man, ravished and drawne which way he liketh best to have them?[49]

The orator is a figure of the right poet whose powers of moving put him at the center of political life, guiding the outcome of events. A symbol of the orator's power over his listeners is the golden chain to which Sidney alludes in sonnet 58. In an emblem from Cristoforo Giarda's *Icones symbolicae* (1628), the figure of rhetoric has three chains (symbolizing low, medium, and high styles of discourse) streaming from her mouth and encircling the necks of beasts at her feet. In her right hand she bears the caduceus of Mercury, the herald of the gods associated with eloquence. As Mercury's wand reconciled the opposing serpents now entwined as figures of concord, the orator's art reconciles conflicting arguments.[50]

This figure of eloquence is sometimes conflated with Hercules, the mighty hero, perhaps because of their shared forcefulness. Alciati's *Emblemata* (1574) also depicts Hercules leading crowds by golden chains issuing from his mouth. Puttenham, recounting the tale of an orator so persuasive that (like Spenser's Despair) he persuaded many to end their lives violently, recalls a portrait of Hercules described to him:

Hercules as a figure for eloquence. Alciata, *Emblemata* (1574). By permission of The Ohio State University Libraries, Rare Books and Manuscripts.

> [T]hey had figured a lustie old man with a long chayne tyed by one end at his tong, by the other end at the peoples eares, who stood a farre of and seemed to be drawen to him by the force of that chayne fastned to his tong, as who would say, by force of his perswasions.[51]

It is not hard to see why Hercules would be an appropriate figure for Sidney's struggling poet. Hercules was a moral hero for Renaissance humanists, not primarily for his feats of strength but for the familiar legend in which he is shown deliberately choosing the kind of life he will lead.[52] In this legend, familiar from Xenophon's *Memorabilia*, the young Hercules sits at a fork in the road, contemplating his course of life, when he is greeted by two women, Pleasure and Virtue. After listening to their persuasions, he chooses

The Choice of Hercules. From George Wither, *A Collection of Emblems* (1635). By permission of the Bodleian Library (Mason.E.105).

the difficult path of Virtue. He thus presents a picture of the hero facing a moral dilemma and exhibiting the strength of mind to conquer the desire for idleness and pleasure. He was also enlisted in the humanist debate over the virtues of the active versus the solitary life. Cicero, in *De Officiis*, recommends that it is better "to emulate the great Hercules and undergo the greatest toil and trouble for the sake of aiding or saving the world, if possible, than to live in seclusion . . . revelling in pleasures. . . ."[53] Petrarch also cites Hercules, along with Achilles, as his model:

> We read that Achilles learned in solitude what soon made him terrible in the cities of Asia and famous in those of Greece. Hercules too attained in solitude that wholesome plan of life . . . and marching indefatigably along its course he was raised not only to the apex of human glory but to a reputation of divinity.[54]

Astrophil is aware that he is no Hercules, having chosen instead the path of pleasure. He dismisses those who continue to rebuke his "straying wayes": "find some *Hercules* to beare, in steed / Of *Atlas* tyr'd, your wisedome's heav'nly sway" (*AS* 51:11, 7–8). Sidney, writing love sonnets in retirement at Wilton, was surely aware that he was not on the path of virtue, public service, and eventual glory.

Hercules is, however, a Janus-faced exemplar. An episode that figured prominently in Elizabethan allusions to his legend was his humiliating enslavement to Omphale. In *The Faerie Queene*, Spenser's Artegall, captured by the Amazonian Radigund, is forced to don women's clothes and take up spinning. This incident occasions Spenser's condemnation of women rulers, carefully exempting Elizabeth. In the *Defence*, Sidney cites Hercules spinning at Omphale's commandment as an example that "breedeth both delight and laughter . . . [at] the scornfulness of the action" (68). In the *Arcadia*, Pyrocles' transformation into the Amazon Zelmane occasions Musidorus's fervent diatribe against such degradation and "bastard love . . . engendered betwixt lust and idleness" (133). Pyrocles' mantle is fastened with a jewel bearing the device of Hercules with a distaff and the inscription "Never more valiant" (131). This phrase perfectly captures the ambiguity of such heroism: Is Hercules-(or Pyrocles)-in-love at the apogee or the perigee of his heroism? These incidents conflate Hercules' defeat of the Amazons and his enslavement to Omphale, as does Greville's praise of Sidney's Herculean political virtue: he

> did generally adde reputation to his Prince, and Country, by restoring amongst us the ancient Majestie of noble, and true dealing: As a manly wisdome, that can no more be weighed down, by any effeminate craft, than *Hercules* could be overcome by that contemptible Army of Dwarfs.[55]

Greville's praise of Sidney as Hercules is shadowed by allusions to two of its most threatening, emasculating events: Hercules' encounter with the man-hating Amazons and his pursuit of the "effeminate craft" of weaving under Omphale. Yet these aspects of the Hercules legend increased its appropriateness for Elizabethan males, ruled as they were by a domineering queen.

The allusion to Hercules in the orator sonnet invites us to measure Astrophil, and ultimately Sidney, against the cultural hero who was also an ambivalent exemplar. He was known variously for his heroic exploits, his enslavement to and triumph over women, his choice of the virtuous life, and his association with eloquence. The conflation of orator and hero in the Hercules legend recalls the yoking of opposites in the construction of Sidney's mythic image, in which Mars and the Muses likewise meet. Astrophil's failure, seen in terms of the Hercules model, is more than just a moral one; it is a failure of virtue conceived in heroic, activist terms—the collapse of the ideal of the courtier-poet at the center of public life.

Astrophil's submission of his wit and will to Stella in the penultimate sonnet also suggests the failure of the right poet to command the stage of history:

> And as a Queene, who from her presence sends
> Whom she imployes, dismisse from thee my wit,
> Till it have wrought what thy owne will attends.
> On servants' shame oft Maister's blame doth sit;
> O let not fooles in me thy workes reprove,
> And scorning say, 'See what it is to love.'
>
> (*AS* 107:9–14)[56]

Here Stella is the superior poet, for her "workes," the desires she has wrought in Astrophil, prevail, to his shame and scorn. Aside from the slight rebuke to Stella, this sonnet resembles the gestures of other courtier-poets before the queen. To Spenser, she is his "most peereles Prince, most peereles Poetresse," and Puttenham calls her "of any that I know in our time, the most excellent Poet."[57] In this sonnet, Astrophil's failures as a lover gesture towards the wider context of Sidney's courtly performances. Ironically, Astrophil proves poetry not the monarch of the sciences, as Sidney envisioned, but a mere "serving science" (*Defence*, 31).

Astrophil as Repentant David

In loving Stella, Astrophil—unlike Hercules—chooses the easy path of pleasure over the hard one of virtue. He also fails as an orator, for his "fine tropes," "strongest reasons," and "piercing phrases" all fail to move her. Moreover, by employing sonnets to seduce her, he scorns the right use of poetry. While the skill of his sonnets testifies to Sidney's erected wit, on a metapoetic level, Astrophil's failure to love Stella virtuously manifests Sidney's belief in man's infected nature. *Astrophil and Stella* muses on the inevitability of transgression, the easy choice for pleasure, and their aftermath. Astrophil is an everyman—the lover as sinner—whose infected will impedes the promise of his erected wit. He knows the truths towards which he should strive. He knows that love "An image is, which for our selves we carve; / And, fooles, adore in temple of our hart" (*AS* 5:6–7), but he still makes Stella his idol. Following the stolen kiss, sonnet 82 finds Astrophil in a garden, craving forbidden fruit and reenacting a sexual Fall. He begs the "Sweet gard'n Nymph, which keepes the Cherrie tree,"

> do not alas,
> From comming neare those Cherries banish me:
> For though *full of desire, emptie of wit,*
> Admitted late by your best-graced grace,
> I caught at one of them a hungrie bit;
> Pardon that fault, once more graunt me the place.
>
> (*AS* 82:5, 7–12; emphasis added)

The sonnet employs Sidney's favorite opposition: Astrophil is *will*ful and *wit*less, helpless but self-aware. His will disordered, his wit produces clichéd Petrarchisms. For example, thrown out of Stella's heaven, he begs "some good body tell me how I do, / Whose presence, absence, absence presence is; / Blist in my curse, and cursed in my blisse" (*AS* 60:12–14). These almost meaningless oxymora do, however, manage to convey something of the suffering of a cursed sinner, exiled forever from the bliss of heaven. Imprisoned in the clichés of love poetry, idolizing Stella, Astrophil is a far cry from the divine sonneteer Sidney envisioned in the *Defence*, "singing the praises of the immortal beauty: the immortal goodness of that God who giveth us hands to write and wits to conceive" (69).

Sidney explores Astrophil's transgression from within the twin paradigms of Petrarchism and Protestantism, using the language of love poetry to convey profound spiritual alienation and despair.[58] Absence from the beloved, one of the standard sonnet motifs, resonates with Christian despair at being exiled, through sin, from the source of goodness. Following the rape fantasy of the tenth song, the speaker berates himself for some unspecified wrong against Stella, perhaps the sinning-in-thought of the prior song:

> O fate, o fault, o curse, child of my blisse,
> What sobs can give words grace my griefe to show?
> What inke is blacke inough to paint my wo?
>
> (*AS* 93:1–3)

The grace that would redress his fault is both inexpressible and unobtainable through poetry. Astrophil is unable to paint the "blackest face of woe" he assayed in the first sonnet, a face now made darker still by sin. He recognizes that he cannot be saved by his wit, that its cleverness in fact infects language.

> Witnesse with me, that my foule stumbling so,
> From carelesnesse did in no maner grow,
> But wit confus'd with too much care did misse.
> And do I then my selfe this vaine scuse give?
> I have (live I and know this) harmed thee,
> Tho worlds quite me, shall I my selfe forgive?
>
> (*AS* 93:6–11)

Only by experiencing Stella's suffering in a kind of *imitatio Christi* can he atone:

> Only with paines my paines thus eased be,
> That all thy hurts in my hart's wracke I reede;
> I cry thy sighs; my deere, thy teares I bleede.
>
> (*AS* 93:12–14)

The poem expresses with forceful plainness Astrophil's helpless awareness of his offense and the need for repentance.

Ironically, it is as a sinner that Astrophil most resembles David, for the divine poet was also an important model of repentance for Renaissance Protestants. Both David and Astrophil are brought down by sexual sin (though Astrophil is only a would-be adulterer) and express in verse their painful alienation from the source of grace. David's seven penitential psalms were popular in the sixteenth century as subjects for paraphrase and meditation. Wyatt, following Aretino, even expanded his paraphrases with a narrative of David's sorrow for his wrongs against Bathsheba and her husband, Uriah.[59] I suggest that Sidney's portrayal of Astrophil's quasi-spiritual torment following his transgression against Stella originates in the popular image of the penitent David. In Astrophil, Sidney tentatively assays the voice of the psalmist in his repentant mode, but his full identification with David is limited by the form and conventions of the Petrarchan sonnet sequence.[60]

Several of the last sonnets of *Astrophil and Stella* meditate upon themes of the seven penitential psalms. In Psalms 32, 38, 102, and 143, David presents himself as cast down, sick to death in flesh and soul, lying in darkness and beseeching the Lord to deliver him. Sonnets 93 and 94 are Sidney's portrayal of Astrophil as an abject sinner, a "wretch" and "caitife worthy so to die" (*AS* 94:14, 10). His understanding is so clouded by sin that he lives in darkness. His "poore soule . . . now that sicknesse tries, / Which even to sence, sence of it selfe denies, / Though harbengers of death lodge there his traine" (*AS* 94:6–8). Night, the time of a lover's sleeplessness and desiring thoughts, is the sinner's time of despairing self-reflection. In sonnet 96, the speaker, barred from his sun, identifies with Night and weeps: "Thy teares expresse night's native moisture right. / In both a mazefull solitarinesse" (*AS* 96:8–9). In the next sonnet, he identifies with Dian, the moon, "in love with *Phoebus'* light, / And endlesly dispairing of his grace" (*AS* 97:5–6).[61] David, like Astrophil, spends sleepless nights shedding tears: "I fainted in my mourning: I cause my bed every night to swimme, & watter my couche with my teares" (Ps. 6:6).[62] Though he resembles the prototypical afflicted lover, David bemoans instead his separation from God and longs for God's mercy.

Surely Sidney was familiar with the popular Psalm 130, *De profundis*, which David utters from the depths of grief: "Out of the depe places have I called unto thee, o Lord. Lord, heare my voyce. . . . My soule waiteth on the Lord more then the morning watche watcheth for the morning" (Ps. 130:1, 6). In the manner of the looser meditations upon the psalms (such as Wyatt's and Hunnis's), Sidney expands upon the image of the despairing sinner awaiting the morning. Astrophil lies awake one night, contemplating the darkness within and without:

With windowes ope then most my mind doth lie,
Viewing the shape of darknesse and delight,
Takes in that sad hue, which with th'inward night
Of his mazde powers keepes perfit harmony.
But when birds charme, and that sweete aire, which is
Morne's messenger, with rose enameld skies
Cals each wight to salute the floure of blisse;
In tombe of lids then buried are mine eyes,
Forst by their Lord, who is asham'd to find
Such light in sense, with such a darkned mind.

(*AS* 99:5–14)

The psalmist longs for the Lord as a sleepless man awaits the morning. Sidney intensifies this sense of anticipation, for Astrophil's innocent expectation of waking confronts his profound dread of final judgment. So deep is the metaphorical night of his mind that the darkness does not lift with daylight. With this sonnet, Sidney measures his distance from David while demonstrating his poetic skill, feigning vivid and moving images.

When Sidney imagines Astrophil's separation from Stella in terms of imprisonment, he may be echoing David's alienation from God, also figured as imprisonment. David prays "Hearken unto my crye, for I am broght verie lowe: deliver me from my persecuters . . . / Bring my soule out of prison, that I maie praise thy Name" (Ps. 142:6–7). The Geneva commentators remark that the imprisonment is metaphorical here. Astrophil also complains that he is far from Stella in "this dungeon darke, / Where rigrows exile lockes up all my sense" (*AS* 104:6–8). This dungeon is a metaphor for his own body, and the exile is spiritual. This image of the soul in captivity is intensified in the final poem of the sequence:

When sorrow (using mine owne fier's might)
Melts downe his lead into my boyling brest,
Through that darke fornace to my hart opprest,
There shines a joy from thee my only light;
But soone as thought of thee breeds my delight,
And my yong soule flutters to thee his nest,
Most rude dispaire my daily unbidden guest,
Clips streight my wings, streight wraps me in his night,
And makes me then bow downe my head, and say,
Ah what doth *Phoebus*' gold that wretch availe,
Whom iron doores do keepe from use of day?

(*AS* 108:1–11)

The speaker is trapped by iron doors within his own hell, suggested by the dark furnace of his breast, producing heat but no light. While Astrophil never escapes his prison, the faithful psalmist can expect deliverance: "They, that dwell in darkenes and in the shadowe of death, being bounde in miserie and yron, / Because they rebelled against the wordes of the Lord" were brought low, but "then they cryed unto the Lord in their trouble, *and* he delivered them from their distres." Praise is due God, "[f]or he hathe broken ye gates of brasse, and brast the barres of yron a sundre" (Ps. 107:10–11, 13, 16). Astrophil's language retains its courtliness, but his suffering approximates David's spiritual torment more closely than it does that of the Petrarchan lover imprisoned by his lady's charms, a theme wittily treated in earlier sonnets.[63]

In sonnet 107, Sidney fashions a sonnet persona who resembles the David of Psalm 51. As the headnote in the Geneva Bible informs the reader, this psalm recounts David's repentance after Nathan rebukes him for his affair with Bathsheba. David prays:

> Create in me a cleane hart, ô God . . . / Cast me not awaie from thy presence / . . . / Restore to me the joye of thy salvacion / . . . / *Then* shal I teache thy waies unto the wicked. . . . Open thou my lippes, ô Lord, and my mouth shal shewe forthe thy praise / . . . The sacrifices of God are a contrite spirit, a contrite & a broken heart, ô God, thou wilt not despise. (Ps. 51:10–13, 15, 17)

Though Astrophil addresses his lady love, not God, she is here lordly, the "Princesse . . . / Of all the powers which life bestowes on me" (*AS* 107:1–2). He is, like David, contrite and compliant. He is learning a new art, one of submission to Stella's will, but it is hard to forget the old passion, the lover's broken heart: "Sweete, for a while give respite to my hart, / Which pants as though it still should leape to thee" (AS 107:5–6). Like David, he is anxious to be in the royal presence and to that end promises to employ his art in her service:

> And on my thoughts give thy Lieftenancy
> To this great cause, which needs both use and art,
> And as a Queene, who from her presence sends
> Whom she imployes, dismisse from thee my wit,
> Till it have wrought what thy owne will attends.
> On servants' shame oft Maister's blame doth sit;
> O let not fooles in me thy workes reprove,
> And scorning say, 'See what it is to love.'
>
> (*AS* 107:7–14)

The fools who scorn Astrophil's service to his queen resemble David's enemies who persecute him for loving goodness (Ps. 38) and rejoice in his affliction (Ps. 6). Of course, Astrophil's friend also rebuked his love of Stella (in *AS* 14 and 21), as Nathan rebuked David for his adulterous love. This incident Sidney alleges in his *Defence*, with the penitential psalm specifically in mind:

> Nathan the prophet, who, when the holy David had so far forsaken God as to confirm adultery with murder . . . [did] the tenderest office of a friend in laying his own shame before his eyes . . . which made David . . . as in a glass see his own filthiness, as that heavenly psalm of mercy well testifieth. (42)[64]

Though Astrophil addresses Stella, not God, in sonnet 107, he exhibits the contrition of David and the desire to submit his will to another's; the sonneteer is in transition, becoming the reformed, Davidic poet whose verses serve a higher master.

The last breath of the seventh penitential psalm shows David in complete submission to God: "Teache me to do thy wil, for thou art my God. . . . I am thy servant" (Ps. 143:10, 12). The final note of Sidney's sequence is also one of resignation, as Astrophil submits to his sovereign Stella. But why did Sidney not have Astrophil more closely resemble David by turning to God? Why did he not end *Astrophil and Stella,* as many editors do, with the sonnet that begins: "Leave me o Love, which reachest but to dust, / And thou my mind aspire to higher things" and ends, "Eternall Love maintaine thy life in me"?[65] My answer is that Astrophil is, first and finally, a Petrarchan sonneteer and a sinner, with all the limitations implied by these roles; he is not David, and *Astrophil and Stella* is an amorous sonnet sequence, not divine poetry. Hence, the submission to Stella is matched by the bow to conventional sonnet language, as Astrophil admits: "in my woes for thee [Stella] thou art my joy, / And in my joyes for thee my only annoy" (*AS* 108:13–14). Astrophil remains in the prisonhouse of Petrarchan language, worshiping Stella, while Sidney goes on to pen metrical psalms praising "God our *only starr.*"[66]

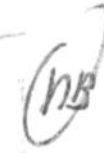

In the *Defence* and in his sonnets, Sidney questioned his ability as a poet to recover or create a golden world, to effect heroic or virtuous action in the service of his queen and his God. The final goal of learning, "to know, and by knowledge to lift up the mind from the dungeon of the body to the enjoying his own divine essence" (*Defence* 28), is denied Astrophil, as his bird-soul attempts flight in the final sonnet. Human limitations are indeed insuperable. Astrophil is literally the *Defence*'s comic astronomer, who "looking to the stars . . . fall[s] in a ditch" (28), a metonym of desire and loss.[67] His ambitions are Herculean and so are his failures. In the descent of Astrophil from promising young courtier to obsessive lover imprisoned in Petrarchan clichés, Sidney expresses and seeks to account for his own perceived failures as a statesman and divine poet. As a penitent poet-lover, however, Astrophil ironically yet fittingly resembles David, suggesting Sidney's persistent hopes for right poetry but his awareness that its triumph must occur outside the amorous sonnet sequence. *Astrophil and Stella* reflects upon the inevitability of human failure within the conventional paradigms of Protestantism and Petrarchism. Transgression and woe are inevitable and self-help impossible, yet the desire for goodness and the hope of grace are indefatigable.

3
Trophaeum Peccati: Fulke Greville's Monuments to Sidney

Inscribed on the tomb of Fulke Greville is this epitaph, chosen by him: "FULKE GREVILL/SERVANT TO QUEENE ELIZABETH/CONCELLOR TO KING JAMES/AND FREND TO SIR PHILIP SIDNEY/TROPHAEUM PECCATI."[1] The association with royalty elevates Greville and his friend, Sidney (a mere gentleman), but the tributes are muted by Greville's choice of the Latin motto TROPHAEUM PECCATI, which designates the foregoing epitaph, the tomb, and the flesh within as monuments to sin, one and all. It is a humbling conclusion to his list of proud associations. Moreover, the connotations of victory in "trophaeum" are ironic, for the monument records not its maker's victory but that of death empowered by human sin. The ambivalent testimonial also serves as a comment on Greville's life and works, possibly condemning his whole earthly career as a trophy of sin.[2] His works, even while they pay tribute to Sidney and their shared experiences and beliefs, ultimately reinforce this reading of the epitaph: that all human achievements, including learning, writing, and loving, are trophies of error.

Occupying the emphatic final place, the phrase "Frend to Sir Philip Sidney" suggests that this relationship—not his service to reigning monarchs—is the highest achievement of his life. Greville's epitaph on Sidney also extols their friendship above all: "[F]arewel friendships sacred league, uniting minds of worth. / . . . *Phillip*, the cause of all this woe, my lives content, farewell." He dispatches his rhymes to Sidney's tomb: "Go seeke that haples tombe, which if ye hap to finde, / Salute the stones, that keep the lims, that held so good a mind."[3] In a letter to the Scottish ambassador, Archibald Douglas,

Greville also mourns Sidney's death, lamenting "him, the name of whose friendship carried me above my own worth, and I fear hath left me to play the ill poet in my own part. Well, my Lord," he concludes, "divide me not from him, but love his memory, and me in it."[4] Greville even planned a vault to house his and Sidney's bodies. It was to be located in St. Paul's and to consist of two stones (the upper for Sidney, the lower for himself) borne up by four pillars, a symbolic eternal union of the two friends in a shared tomb.[5]

Though the plans for this monument were never realized, in accord with Greville's wishes, his own reputation has been indivisible from Sidney's memory; indeed, Greville has been largely responsible for our memory of Sidney. He arranged for the publication, from his personal copy, of the revised *Arcadia* in an attempt to defend and enhance Sidney's reputation as a serious, moral writer and perhaps to promote himself by virtue of his privileged association with Sidney.[6] Moreover, his *Life of Sidney*, originally conceived as a dedicatory introduction to his own collected works, helped to sustain well into the seventeenth century the legend that sprang up following Sidney's untimely death. In Greville's retrospective interpretation, Sidney incarnates the ideals of Christian chivalry; he possesses the valor and faith of the Redcrosse knight together with the *sprezzatura* of Castiglione's courtier. He is the chosen exemplar for Greville and his contemporaries who practiced poetry and statecraft, for he excels both in soldiery and in scholarship.

It is in his *Life of Sidney*, I argue, that Greville constructs this heroic and godly image of his friend, an image that served to sanction Greville's own poetic and political activity, much as Sidney's earliest memorializers, Arthur Golding and John Phillips, drew authority from Sidney's example. Not even Greville, however, is able to escape the contradictions of Sidney's exemplary status, for he shares Sidney's conviction that poetry can be a vain occupation. Greville even intensifies Sidney's Protestant poetics; his sonnet sequence, *Caelica*, meditates upon the debilitating personal, social, and political effects of sinful Petrarchan loving. Reforming the poet-lover's sinful imagination and redirecting his desire heavenward, Greville aims for the right use of poetry envisioned by Sidney in the *Defence of Poetry*. Though the publication of Greville's works postdates that of Daniel and Spenser (*Caelica* was first published in 1633), I have considered him first because he is Sidney's exact contemporary and intimate friend. Moreover, many of the *Caelica* poems are contemporary with Sidney's own sonnets, though the composition and arrangement of the sequence may span Greville's lifetime, registering change in the literary climate as well as Greville's deepening convictions about the errors of amorous sonnet writing. He unequivocally condemns the tradition of the amorous sonnet sequence as a trophy of sin; in *Caelica*, the poet-lover's desire is a sinful and subversive force and the sonnet mistress a figure of political tyranny and religious error. Greville was more zealous, if less subtle, than Sidney in exploring the baseness of man's infected will and the misuses of his erected wit.

Friend to Sir Philip Sidney

In their complex and symbiotic literary relationship, Sidney is both the model whose example legitimized Greville's own writing and, importantly, the creation of Greville's pen. Greville's *Life of Sidney* underscores the extent to which Sidney's posthumous identity is a literary and cultural construct serving a variety of ends. Originally conceived as a prose dedication for Greville's works on politics and government, it developed into a panegyric history of Queen Elizabeth and a criticism of King James, and it included reflections on Greville's own exclusion from office.[7] My interest, of course, is in Greville's construction of Sidney as the exemplary Elizabethan poet and courtier. The themes of Sidney as patron of learning and heroic soldier, servant of the queen, and godly Christian had emerged early. Greville's biographical account, composed between 1604 and 1614 and first published in 1652, issues from an individual's memory but imparts a collective image of Sidney.[8] Biographers in this period, Judith Anderson has argued, were becoming increasingly aware of the fictional nature of their enterprise.[9] Greville reveals this awareness as he crafts Sidney's exemplary image and claims authority as a chronicler of his life and times. Jonathan Crewe's description of Cavendish, the biographer of Cardinal Wolsey, could apply to Greville:

> The spectatorial dependent as privileged witness becomes profoundly complicit in the circulation of power and pleasure. In doing so, he emerges as a type of the Renaissance author. . . . [who] acquires the power at least of retroactive determination and reconstruction.[10]

This describes well the authority claimed by Greville's work. A closer look at the *Life*, however, reveals a more complex relation to his friend and subject. As a participant in the life he describes, Greville is unable to separate his own interests from his narrative. Christopher Martin observes, and I concur, that the "truth" of Greville's biography relies upon "the author's participatory presence in a life that was itself a kind of witness to its time," and he proposes that Greville recounted his intimacy with the great national figure as a means of self-promotion.[11] Clearly Greville's case exemplifies the complexity Greenblatt describes, when self-fashioning "crosses the boundaries between the creation of literary characters, the shaping of one's own identity, the experience of being molded by forces outside one's control, the attempt to fashion other selves."[12] The boundaries between Greville and his subject are fluid, for the shaping forces they exert on each other are mutual. Greville not only constructs but is constructed by the exemplary Sir Philip Sidney.

Greville's Sidney is primarily a soldier and man of action, not the defender and author of poetry. His scholarship, affirmed Greville, was secondary and instrumental to the goals of an active life:

> [H]is end was not writing, even while he wrote; nor his knowledge moulded for tables, or schooles; but both his wit, and understanding bent upon his heart, to make himself, and others, not in words or opinion, but in life, and action, good and great. (*Life* 21)

Still, however, Sidney mingles the achievements of the soldier and the virtues of a scholar. He is esteemed "a generall *Mecaenas* of Learning" to whom university scholars dedicated their books; at the same time, "Souldiers honoured him, and were so honoured by him, as no man thought he marched under the true Banner of *Mars*, that had not obtained Sir *Philip Sidney's* approbation" (*Life* 38–39). Greville takes pains to establish that his own high esteem and emulation of Sidney are shared by other men, testifying to the general fact of his exemplarity:

> [I]t will be confessed by all men, that this one mans example, and personall respect, did not onely encourage Learning, and Honour in the Schooles, but brought the affection, and true use therof both into the Court, and Camp. Nay more, even many Gentlemen excellently learned amongst us will not deny, but that they affected to row, and steer their course in his wake. (*Life* 40)[13]

With more alacrity than nonchalance, Greville steered his own boat directly in Sidney's wake. His life and ambitions paralleled Sidney's closely; born in the same year, the two boys entered Shrewsbury grammar school together in October 1564. Like Sidney, he was educated to be a servant of the state. He accompanied Sidney on his diplomatic mission to the Low Countries and Germany in 1577. He and Sidney were two of the Four Foster Children of Desire who challenged the Fortress of Perfect Beauty in the 1581 entertainment before Elizabeth. Like others of his class denied participation in important affairs of state during the 1580s, he was forced into a kind of domestic servitude:

> I found reason to contract my thoughts from those larger, but wandring *Horizons*, of the world abroad, and bound my prospect within the safe limits of duty, in such home services, as were acceptable to my Soveraigne.
>
> In which retired view, Sir *Philip Sidney*, that exact image of quiet, and action: happily united in him . . . being ever in mine eyes, made me thinke it no small degree of honour to imitate, or tread in the steps of such a Leader . . . to saile by his Compasse. (*Life* 171–72)

With Sidney's precedent before him, he took up writing in his spare time, producing poetry, treatises, and drama. Like Sidney, he published nothing in his lifetime, though he was known to be a poet.[14] Finally, Greville's role as pallbearer in Sidney's funeral procession testifies to their lifelong intimacy, as does his almost morbid desire to lie in the same tomb.

Greville was, however, acutely aware of his own distance from Sidney's greatness. The following passage from the *Life* shows Greville imitating Sidney and defending him, while justifying his own failures to live up to his model:

> But besides this self-respect of Dedication, the debt I acknowledge to that Gentleman is farre greater . . . in whom the life it self of true worth, did (by way of example) far exceed the pictures of it in any moral Precepts. So that (if my creation had been equal) it would have proved as easie for me, to have followed his patern, in the practice of reall vertue, as to engage my self into this *Characteristicall* kind of Poesie: in defence whereof he hath written so much. . . . For that this representing of vertues, vices, humours, counsells, and actions of men . . . is an inabling of free born spirits to the greatest affaires of States: he himself hath left such an instance in the too short scene of his life. . . . (*Life* 3)

Greville's little apology alludes ironically to Sidney's apology for poetry, also a kind of self-defense. First, he privileges history (Sidney's "life itself of true worth") over philosophy ("pictures . . .

in any moral Precepts") and poetry, which Greville claims he took up because of his inability to emulate the "reall vertue" of Sidney's life. He goes on to cite Sidney as evidence that poetry equips one for important public action, though Sidney was hardly privy to the "greatest affaires of States." Elsewhere Greville admits that Sidney "never was Magistrate, nor possessed of any fit stage for eminence to act upon" (*Life* 45). He regrets that Sidney's talents remained mostly buried, that in him were "sparkes of extraordinary greatnesse . . . which for want of clear vent lay concealed, and in a manner smothered up" (*Life* 12). If Sidney failed to achieve his promised greatness, Greville implies, the fault was not his own.

Aware of Sidney's shortcomings, Greville compensates by creating the imperfect Sidney as an image of virtue—an appropriate exercise of Sidneian poetic license. The quality he most admires is Sidney's honesty, a politic virtue he redefines in religious terms. He praises Sidney for adding to the reputation of his country and prince

> by restoring amongst us the ancient Majestie of noble, and true dealing. . . . I mean that his heart and tongue went both one way, and so with every one that went with the Truth; as knowing no other kindred, partie, or end.
>
> Above all, he made the Religion he professed, the firm Basis of his life: For this was his judgement (as he often told me) that our true-heartedness to the Reformed Religion in the beginning, brought Peace, Safetie, and Freedome to us. (*Life* 41)

Greville presents Sidney not only as a model courtier but, more importantly, as a model *Protestant* courtier. Possibly alluding to Scripture,[15] Greville asserts that Sidney's devotion to the truth set him free in a number of dangerous situations. One example Greville cites is Sidney's *Letter to Queen Elizabeth* concerning the proposed French marriage. He takes great pains to demonstrate how Sidney's criticism sprang from his justified conviction that England would lose her sovereignty and her religion by such a match. Though Greville allows that it might be considered "an error, and a dangerous one, for Sir *Philip* being neither Magistrate nor Counsellor, to oppose himself against his Soveraigns pleasure," he answers that "his worth, truth, favour, and sincerity of heart" were Sidney's privileges (*Life* 71). Greville also sweetens the surely bitter aftermath of this event. Though Sidney "found a sweet stream of Soveraign humors in that well-tempered Lady, to run against him, yet he found safety in her self . . ."

(*Life* 72), and his rustication at Wilton was not forced: "So that howsoever he seemed to stand alone, yet he stood upright; kept his access to her Majesty as before . . ." (*Life* 74).[16] Greville comments that "[t]his constant tenor of truth he took upon him . . . protected this Gentleman (though he obeyed not) from the displeasure of his Soveraign" (*Life* 81). Greville's defensive praise of his friend often supports the opposite conclusion: that Sidney's sometimes impolitic honesty caused him trouble and may actually have prevented him from being a more effective advocate for the Protestant cause.[17]

Greville's almost reverential regard for his friend is tinged with an awareness of Sidney's shortcomings, even failures, as a poet and statesman; though he seldom makes his criticisms explicit, he is unable to cloak them entirely. One example of Greville's technique of indirect criticism is his account of Sidney's plan to accompany Sir Francis Drake to the West Indies. Though designed to challenge Spanish hegemony in the New World, it was ultimately a rash and self-serving scheme. According to Greville, it was "an expedition of his own projecting; wherein he fashioned the whole body, with purpose to become head of it himself" (*Life* 81–82). Sidney's involvement was to be kept secret until they had departed England, and when the mission was completed, its "success would put envy and all her agents to silence" (*Life* 83). Greville explains Sidney's deception as necessitated by the queen's overprotectiveness of the valued young courtier, a generous interpretation given that she angrily commanded him to return, then sent him into a war zone as governor of Flushing. Greville was to accompany Sidney on the West Indies voyage, selected "to be his loving, and beloved *Achates* in this journey." At the time, he expressed his doubts about this expedition, noting particularly Drake's "discountenance and depression" upon Sidney's arrival. Sidney, however, shrugged off the fears of his loyal counselor; his "ingenuous spirit . . . made him suspend his own, & labor to change . . . my judgement" (*Life* 86). By alluding to his role as the cautious adviser in this miscarried expedition, Greville suggests his own, better judgment.[18] Still, by casting himself in the role of the faithful friend, Achates, he reinscribes the rash Sidney as a heroic, adventuring Aeneas.

Besides suggesting Sidney's impulsive judgment, Greville also seems to have felt that his friend's fictional writings lacked a requisite moral seriousness. In a letter to Walsingham, dated November 1586, Greville intimated his desire to oversee publication of Sidney's religious writings, a project which never materialized. Instead, he brought Sidney's revised, heroic *Arcadia* to print, successfully repressing the earlier, romantic version.[19] In his *Life*, he defends the *Arcadia* in somewhat ambiguous terms:

> [H]is end in them was not vanishing pleasure alone, but morall Images, and Examples . . . to guide every man through the confused *Labyrinth* of his own desires, and life: So that howsoever I liked them not too well (even in that unperfected shape they were) to condescend that such delicate (though inferior) Pictures of himselfe, should be suppressed; yet I do wish that work may be the last in this kind, presuming no man that followes can ever reach, much lesse go beyond that excellent intended patterne of his.
>
> For my own part, I found my creeping Genius more fixed upon the Images of Life than the Images of Wit. . . . (*Life* 245 [253])[20]

The vacillating tone of this passage conveys something of Greville's complex and mixed response to Sidney's work. He asserts that Sidney's purpose in writing the *Arcadia* was moral, yet he dislikes its imperfect images. Perhaps Greville viewed Pyrocles and Musidorus, the princes detained from their heroic exploits by love, as somewhat shameful "pictures of himself," that is, of Sidney. While Greville won't presume to suppress *Arcadia*, he ardently wishes "that work may be the last in this kind," ostensibly because no one can approach or exceed Sidney's mark. But this implies a perfection he denied by excusing the "unperfected shape" of its images. Though he praises "that excellent intended patterne" of the uncompleted *Arcadia*, ultimately Greville suspects it is not a moral work. Thus, he departs from Sidney and, becoming more sage and serious as he ages, fixes his own "creeping Genius" upon "the Images of Life," not the "Images of Wit." Most critics cite this passage as evidence that Greville cultivated a plain, didactic style as a revolt against Sidney's ornate and witty style, overlooking the shared political, religious, and aesthetic beliefs that inform their lives and works.[21]

Greville's compensatory creation of Sidney's image as a godly hero is most evident in his account of Sidney's behavior on the battlefield at Zutphen and on his deathbed, events Greville did not witness. It is a fact that Sidney went into battle without his thigh armor and thus received the leg wound from which he died three weeks later. No Christian knight goes to battle without his metaphoric armor, but Greville does not take occasion to rebuke his friend's careless haste or moral failing. Instead he explains that "meeting the Marshall of the Camp lightly armed . . . the unspotted emulation of his heart, to venture without any inequalitie, made him cast off his Cuisses" (*Life* 147). This interpretation is not corroborated by eyewitnesses, who assign to the gesture motivations other than spontaneous gallantry.[22] Greville's model for Sidney is the self-sacrificing leader who puts the suffering of others before his own; he relates the apocryphal story that Sidney, though bleeding and thirsty, first offered his water bottle to a poor soldier with the words "Thy necessity is yet greater than mine" (*Life* 147).

Greville's shaping hand is also evident as he describes Sidney's calm awareness of and preparations for his own impending death. In the "last scene of this Tragedy," the parting of the brothers, Sidney takes his leave of his younger brother with these words: "[A]bove all, govern your Will, and Affections, by the Will and Word of your Creator; in me, beholding the end of this World, with all her Vanities" (*Life* 160). In narrating Sidney's death, he fashions the event to accord with the movement of the final poem of Sidney's *Certaine Sonnets*, a renunciation of earthly for heavenly love. The sonnet begins, "Leave me o Love, which reachest but to dust" and concludes, "farewell world, thy uttermost I see, / Eternall Love maintaine thy life in me." By having Sidney renounce vain love, Greville completes Sidney's exemplary Christian life with an exemplary death, authoring and authorizing an interpretation of Sidney's life as an epitome of godliness: "Thus you see how it pleased God to show forth, and then suddenly withdraw, this precious light of our sky . . ." (*Life* 160).

Narrating and shaping the tragedy of his friend's life, Greville is a poet-maker who both engages and evades the issues of poetry's purpose raised by Sidney in his *Defence of Poetry*. When Greville writes that poetry "is an enabling of free born spirits to the greatest affaires of States," he clearly echoes Sidney's own high hopes for poetry. But if the writer of poetry is not thereby enabled to serve the state, indeed dies in the attempt, has his poetry then failed? How can it (and the poet) be defended? Greville's response to these implicit, though unarticulated, concerns is a poet's response. He makes fiction. Here Greville's use of dramatic metaphors is significant. Sidney's life is a "too short scene" (*Life* 3) upon an "unfit stage" (*Life* 45), a tragedy without decorum or proper closure. Greville takes the role of dramatist, shaping his hero's life, concealing its compromising flaws, and crafting an appropriate ending. At one point in his narrative, he calls attention to this role as maker: that "the abruptness of this Treatise may suit more equally with his fortune, I will cut off his Actions, as God did his Life, in the midst" (*Life* 142 [146]). Greville is not only the dramatist but also an actor, for he participated in Sidney's life and afterwards created himself in Sidney's image. So much depends on the success of this self-image that Greville hesitates to face his fears that writing may not be efficacious after all, that the ideal relationship of writing and public service he (and Sidney) envisioned may finally be unattainable.[23] But he eludes the despair attending poetic and political failure by incorporating Sidney's failures within a framework of Christian otherworldliness, thereby refashioning the fallen soldier of Zutphen as a Protestant martyr who renounces worldly fame as vanity.

Greville's Fallen Poetics

Greville's appreciation of Sidney as a Protestant hero more than a champion of poetry is reflected in his own Calvinist epistemology, which emphasizes the power of the "infected will" over the possibility of the "erected wit" in all areas of human endeavor. In his *Treatise of Religion*, a late work, he writes eloquently of man as a "painted tombe" whose "darckninge shadowes of his witte / Hid[e] his staines from all the world."[24] Greville's views on poetry and learning are expressed in his *Treatie on Humane Learning*, which ponders, from an Augustinian perspective, the infection of all human knowledge following the primal fall from grace. Properly beyond human comprehension, knowledge is "the same *forbidden tree*, / Which man lusts after to be made his Maker."[25] Sexual desire springs from this original sin and clouds the judgment; "Lust, our *Centaure*-like Affection. . . . / So add[s] to originall defection, / As no man knowes his owne unknowing minde" (*THL* 4). Sense, man's first instructor, now deceives him "And from this false root that mistaking growes, / Which truth in human knowledges hath lost" (*THL* 6). Sidney's belief that the end of learning is to "lift up the mind from the dungeon of the body to the enjoying his own divine essence" (*Defence* 28) looks increasingly to Greville like a vain delusion.[26] Books of philosophy and poetry are

> Farre more delightfull than they fruitfull be,
> Witty apparance, Guile that is beguil'd;
> Corrupting minds much rather than directing,
> The allay of Duty, and our Prides erecting.
>
> (*THL* 29)

For Greville, all knowledge is implicated in corruption. In the last line, erected pride is not only sinful but possibly sexual as well, given the available connotations of pride and Greville's frequent association of language and seduction.[27] Later in the treatise, for example, Greville complains that truth has been turned into rhetoric, a siren, "Captiving reason, with the painted skinne / Of many words, with empty sounds misleading / Us to false ends" (*THL* 107).[28] Like Sidney's "honey-flowing matron Eloquence . . . disguised in a courtesan-like painted affectation" (*Defence* 70), Rhetoric is represented as a false mistress, prefiguring the inconstant ladies of *Caelica.*

Not surprisingly, poetry does not make men more virtuous; it "Can move, but not remove, or make impression / . . . to enrich the Wit, / Or, which is lesse, to mend our states by it" (*THL* 111). Though poetry cannot mend the human condition, it has a place, conditionally,

> if to describe, or praise
> Goodnesse, or God she her *Ideas* frame,
> And like a Maker, her creations raise
> On lines of truth, it beautifies the same;
> And while it seemeth onely but to please,
> Teacheth us order under pleasures name;
> Which in a glasse, shows Nature how to fashion
> Her selfe againe, by ballancing of passion.
>
> (*THL* 114)

Greville still ascribes to key features of Sidney's poetics: the right poet imitates truth and uses lyric poetry to praise "the immortal goodness of that God who giveth us hands to write and wits to conceive" (*Defence* 69). Poetry delights in order to teach; it can restore order in nature, though not recapture Eden.[29] It remains what Sidney dismissively called a "serving science"; poetry (along with music) "Teaches, and makes, but hath no power to binde: / *Both, ornaments to life and other Arts / Whiles they doe serve, and not possesse our hearts*" (*THL* 115).

Greville's favorite metaphor for expressing the errors of learning or sinful pride is the Tower of Babel. Genesis 11 tells the story of the descendants of Ham, Noah's son, who propose to build "a citie and a tower, whose toppe may reach unto the heaven" (Gen. 11:4). God descends, scatters them, and as punishment "confounde[s] their language" (Gen. 11:7). The Geneva Bible gloss informs the reader, "By this great plague of the confusion of tongues, appeareth Gods horrible judgment against mans pride and vaine glorie." Greville, a committed reformer, knew his Geneva Bible well, as his allusions to Babel suggest. In the *Treatie of Humane Learning*, he expresses his conviction that all human knowledge and works are but a monument to sin:

> For if Mans wisedomes, lawes, arts, legends, schooles,
> Be built upon the knowledge of the evill;
> And if these Trophies be the onely tooles,
> Which doe maintaine the kingdome of the Divell;
>   If all these *Babels* had the curse of tongues,
>   So as confusions still to them belongs:
>
> Then can these moulds never containe their Maker
> . . . .
>   *These Arts, moulds, workes can but expresse the sinne,*
>   *whence by mans follie, his fall did beginne.*
>
> (*THL* 46–47)[30]

Not only a monument to man's pride and vainglory, Babel also signifies for Protestants the antithesis of the true church and, specifically, Rome. The preacher George Gifford explains the origin of the association of Babylon with Rome, using the logic of allegory:

> [B]ycause that citie in time past being most mightie and most proude, first was a rebell against God, when as that tower was buylded after which folowed the confusion of tongues, afterward it was the first citie, which exercised tyrannie upon men, which being begunne by Nymrod, continued even unto Nabuchadnezar . . . therefore the tyrannie, Idolatrie, pride and ungodliness of the citie of Rome, is signified under the figure of Babylon.[31]

Luther also identifies the inhabitants of Babel with the papists, confident that God will confound the pope, as he did the "tyrants and proud builders" of Babylon.[32] In the *Treatie*, Greville uses Babel to allude to the false church, "the kingdome of the Divell," and warns that "we must not . . . build up *Babels* for the Divels elect" (*THL* 147). In *Caelica*, he returns to the Babylon myth to explore the speaker's idolatrous lust for his ladies. Like Gifford, he finds the exemplum of Babel appropriate to express the confusion and tyranny resulting from sin. These passages from his *Treatie*, together with the Genesis myth of Babel, provide an apt gloss on Greville's own funeral monument and an introduction to his poetry: all works devised by humans are trophies of error, expressions of pride and vainglory.

Greville's grim epistemology and poetics suggest that he held little faith in the possibility of cultivating moral virtue through learning and poetry. Hence, he was not likely to be convinced by Sidney's extravagant claims for poetry.[33] Surely he recognized in the *Defence* Sidney's witty rhetorical display and the elements of a paradoxical encomium, no more taken by its fabulous claims for poetry than Sidney himself was by Pugliano's praise of the horse as the perfect courtier. Along with William Temple, this friend from grammar school to the grave was the kind of discerning reader Sidney envisioned for his writing. While he may have admired Sidney's virtuosity and his vision of redeemed and redeeming poetry, Greville shared a deeper distrust in the moral value and efficacy of poetry, an "idle mans profession," after all.

Caelica: Love as Sin

Given Greville's view of poetry and learning as "moulds [that] . . . can but express . . . sin," he was unlikely to write poetry that reveled in amorous experience. Additionally, Greville's probable homosexuality did not dispose him to celebrate heterosexual passion in the guise of a sonnet lover. He never married, and biographers concede that his most satisfying relationships were with male friends, Sidney in particular.[34] His sonnets were begun in 1577–80, the years of his association with Sidney and Edward Dyer, a trio of poets bound in a fast brotherhood, which Sidney celebrated as a "happy blessed Trinity; / As three most joyntly set, / In firmest band of Unitie." Together they share "one Minde in Bodies three," a communion like that of lovers or spouses.[35] "Striving with my mates in song,"[36] Sidney, Dyer, and Greville exemplify Wendy Wall's observation that the community of males fashions itself by writing, and that the "woman is used as a trope for solidifying male homosocial bonds."[37] This describes well the friendship and gentle rivalry out of which *Caelica* issued. Moreover, Greville's sequence is characterized by an unsubtle misogyny; the mistress is personified—even demonized—as sin, enabling the speaker's renunciation of erotic, heterosexual love for sacred union with the male image of Christ.

Given this context, *Caelica* has a complex, even antithetical, relation to the sonnet tradition generally and to *Astrophil and Stella* in particular. The poems were written over many years (between 1577 and Greville's death in 1628), not dashed off and published during the height of the sonnet craze in the 1590s.[38] Greville clearly admired and imitated Sidney's skill; many of his sonnets echo *Astrophil and Stella* in tone, imagery, and phrasing.[39] Like Sidney, he names a celestial mistress, one signifying all the heavens, not a single star. Despite the obvious debt to Sidney, however, *Caelica* reveals Greville's continual refashioning of Sidney's Petrarchan and Protestant legacy. To use Roland Greene's phrase, he both imitated and "innovated against" his master.[40] With its 109 sonnets, one more than *Astrophil and Stella*, Greville's *Caelica* modestly overshoots Sidney's sequence or, as Roche would have it, completes Sidney's "drama of the two loves," sacred and secular.[41] But *Caelica*, despite its name, does not celebrate earthly love and beauty as types of heavenly love and beauty, nor does it merely renounce the former for the latter. The poet-lover is enthralled by his lust and mired in religious error. The deceitful and inconstant ladies, Myra, Cynthia, and Caelica, who are elevated as saints by the idolatrous lover, are types of the false church, Rome as Babylon. In the quasi-allegorical *Caelica*, Greville wrenches the conventions of Petrarchan loving to metaphorize primal sin and the resultant social, political, and personal disorder in which the poet is enmeshed.

The Augustinian association of sin and sexual love profoundly colors Greville's representation of sonnet lovers whose enactment of desire nearly violates the decorum of Petrarchan poetry. In *The City of God*, Augustine contends that sexual desire arose in man as a result of the original sin of disobedience; henceforth the uncontrollable libido manifests the triumph of passion.[42] Greville's desiring speaker describes an encounter with Caelica in which he has enjoyed her favors to the full:

> *Caelica*, I overnight was finely used,
> Lodg'd in the midst of paradise, your Heart:
> Kind thoughts had charge I might not be refused,
> Of every fruit and flower I had part.
>
> (*C* 37:1–4)

After gaining this "knowledge," he is inexplicably rejected: "I from my paradise was straight forbidden,"

> And glassy Honour, tender of Disgrace,
> Stands *Ceraphim* to see I come not there;
> While that fine soyle, which all these joyes did yeeld,
> By broken fence is prov'd a common field.
>
> (*C* 37:8, 11–14)

The Fall has been reenacted, and Caelica is no longer the enclosed garden of virginal virtue but a "common field" with a "broken fence," a fallen woman or whore. Greville's language, laden with scriptural allusions, condemns amorous Petrarchan experience. Sexual love is sin, and with each transgression the primal loss of innocence is reenacted.

The erotic suggestions of man's sinfully erected, Babel-like pride in the *Treatie of Humane Learning* are given full rein in *Caelica*. The speaker's sexual transgression of sonnet 37 is appropriately explored in terms of Greville's favored tale of Babylon. "The pride of Flesh by reach of humane wit, / Did purpose once to over-reach the skye" (*C* 38:1–2) and thus built Babylon. Greville adds an erotic dimension to this exemplum of overweening ambition. While the "pride of Flesh" suggests generic human weakness, the likeness to a tower encroaching on the sky (that is, Caelica) adds a sexual double entendre. The speaker, perhaps unnecessarily, makes the connection more explicit, even using "babylon" as a euphemistic verb:

So I that heavenly peace would comprehend,
In mortall feat of *Caelica's* faire heart,
To babylon my selfe there, did intend,
With naturall kindnesse, and with passions art:
    But when I though[t] my selfe of her selfe free;
    All's chang'd: she understands all men but me.

(*C* 38:9–14)

Given the Protestant association of Babylon with Rome, the speaker's lust "to babylon" himself suggests as well the blasphemy in his desire for Caelica. The linguistic confusion sown in the wake of Babylon's destruction is in this poem represented by the discord between the lovers. The result of this misunderstanding is that Caelica disdains the speaker and promiscuously grants her favors to other men.[43] Lo and behold, the ideal, virginal sonnet mistress becomes the whore of Babylon.

A similar inversion of values occurs here, as the speaker laments his distance from Caelica:

And since my fall, though I now onely see
Your backe, while all the world beholds your face;
This shadow still shewes miracles to me,
And still I thinke your heart a heavenly place:
    For what before was fil'd by me alone,
    I now discerne hath roome for every one.

(*C* 63:9–14)

Despite his apparently serious tone, the speaker mocks heaven by comparing it to Caelica's false heart. He attempts to turn from his obsession with Caelica to a reflection on the true heaven, which is both like Caelica (it excludes him) and unlike her (it selectively admits men). His fallen imagination produces a metaphor verging on blasphemy but (perhaps unwittingly) expressing a deeper spiritual concern. As he was closed out of Caelica's heart—or because he desired no higher heaven than Caelica's heart—he may be excluded from the true heaven, which "hath roome for every one," that is, everyone except him. As Greville's speaker encroaches on his false heaven, Caelica, the discourses of Petrarchism and Protestantism clash, effectively reinforcing the Babel motif.

Expressing desire that is simultaneously (and by turns) spiritual and erotic, Greville enriches and ironizes the language of love poetry and reveals the error of his idolatrous poet-lover. In the pseudo-religious context of Greville's love sonnets, the lady's grace parodies divine grace—especially when it isn't forthcoming and the lover is closed out of her heart, his heaven.

Greville's frequent use of the rhyme "election/affection," juxtaposing religious and amorous language, also contributes to his critique of sinful loving, as in this sonnet:

And thou o *Love*, which in these eyes
Hast married *Reason* with *Affection*,
And made them Saints of beauties skyes,
Where joyes are shadowes of perfection,
Lend me thy wings that I may rise
Up not by worth but thy election.

(*C* 4:9–14)

The theological connotation of "election" in line 14 undermines the Neoplatonic optimism that the speaker can rise to heaven by contemplating the lady's perfection. Douglas Peterson calls this poem a deliberate religious parody,[44] but I detect a prayerful tone, a sincere desire for humility, and a hint of despair. The lover admits the corruption of his reason (married to affection), recognizes his own powerlessness, and fears his exclusion from human and divine grace.[45] Usually Greville's juxtaposition of these terms, "election" and "affection," underscores the speaker's error, ignorance, or confusion, as in this sonnet:

Poore fooles, why strive you then since all hearts feele
That idle *Chance* so governes in affection,

As *Cupid* cannot turne his fatall wheele,
Nor in his owne orbe banish her election?
Then teach Desire hope; not rage, feare, griefe,
Powers as unapt to take, as give reliefe.

(*C* 53:13–18)

The clashing images of Cupid, Fortune's wheel, and Protestant election show poetic traditions in awkward syncretism. In this poem, they also dramatize the speaker's inability to control his clashing passions of rage, fear, and grief. The jumble of forces aptly expresses the speaker's confused grasp of the mechanism of his own destiny. (Does Cupid, Fortune, or divine election rule him?) When Caelica tells Philocell to follow her no longer but to "Wake your selfe from Passions-traunce, / And let Reason guide affection, / From despaire to new election" (*C* 75:105–7), the rhyme is ironic, for she is telling him to choose (elect) another lover. Philocell is obsessed with Caelica, however, and will abandon her neither for

scornes of his affection,
Nor despaire in his election,
Nor his faith damn'd for obeying,
Nor her change, his hopes betraying.

(*C* 75:214–17)

It is precisely his disordered affections that compromise his election to divine grace.

When its metaphors of worship become literalized and informed by Protestant theology, Greville's poetic language mocks the idolatrous lover who employs it and, indeed, the whole Petrarchan tradition. The comparisons of heaven and his lady's false heart (*C* 63), the suggestion that his mistress is the whore of Babylon, and the repeated juxtaposition of election and affection underscore the speaker's blindness and error in aspiring to a false incarnation of the divine. Greville further condemns idolatry and vain love by his use of the Anacreontic and Ovidian Cupid, by now native to the sonnet tradition.[46] Like Sidney, Greville associates Cupid with the desire that blinds reason, making the man susceptible to the whims and appetites of a child.[47] Cupid is not simply a wayward boy, however, but a figure of religious error, a "faithless boy" who "doth aspire / To be God of desire" (*C* 28:7–8). He is yet another image of Babylonian pride:

Mercurie, Cupid, Mars, they be no Gods,
But humane Idols, built up by desire,

Fruit of our boughs, whence heaven maketh rods,
And babyes too for child-thoughts that aspire.

(*C* 61:19–22)

In making Cupid a self-created (and self-punishing) idol, Greville follows Sidney, who in sonnet 5 of *Astrophil and Stella* cites all the truths superceded by his love of Stella. Among them is the truism that

what we call *Cupid's* dart,
An image is, which for our selves we carve;
And, fooles, adore in temple of our hart,
Till that good God make Church and Churchman starve.

(*AS* 5:5–8)

Greville's treatment of Cupid as a false, created idol, however, is more sustained and serious than Sidney's, underscoring the complete inversion of moral values in *Caelica*. Specifically, the interaction of Cupid and Myra-as-Venus presents a parodic image of the relationship of the Virgin Mary and the Christ child. "Myra" is an anagram for Mary, and Myra is the mistress with whom Greville's Cupid is most often depicted.[48] Cupid at first settles in Myra's eyes, for the speaker has shown him "the birth, the fatall tombe and story" of love (*C* 15:8) in her, phrasing which brings to mind Mary's participation in the life and passion of her son. Myra, tyrannizing even Cupid, becomes an image of the denying mother and mistress both. When the speaker tries to determine the cause of Cupid's crying, he asks, "would they have thee from sweet *Myra* weyned? / Are her faire brests made dainty to be hidden? / . . . Doth she cause thee make faults, to make thee beaten?" (*C* 25:7–8, 11). The rendering of this unholy duo, the cruel Myra with her naughty boy, Cupid, mocks Catholic iconography, for Myra is a perverted mother figure, and the little love god is the sinful substitute for her son, Christ.

Greville's use of the mistress Myra and the love-god Cupid is an example of his ability to enrich, complicate, and politicize poetic conventions without resorting to bald topical allegory. In one sonnet, however, Greville explicitly compares Rome and Myra, invoking both his favored "election-affection" theme and the Babylon story. He describes Rome's downfall:

But after thy proud Legions gave thee [Rome] Lawes,
That their bought voices Empire did bestow,
Worthinesse no more was of election cause.

(*C* 29:5–7)

This pattern is repeated in the third stanza:

But after flattring Change did give thee [Myra] lawes,
That her false voices did thy faith bestow,
Worthinesse no more was of affection cause,
Desire did many heads like monsters show.

(*C* 29:13–16)

Rome's denial of election (political preferment) to deserving statesmen parallels and adumbrates Myra's denial of affection to the worthy lover. In linking the decline of Rome and the ascendancy of Myra, Greville loosely adheres to a political interpretation of Revelation 17 as an allegory of the rise of the Roman church following the decline of the empire. The seven-headed beast upon which the scarlet woman rides (Rev. 17:7) is glossed by the Geneva Bible as Rome, a city situated on seven hills: "This is the Romaine empire which being fallen into decay, the whore of Rome usurped autoritie, and proceded from the devil and thether shal returne." This beast is explicitly suggested in line 16 of Greville's sonnet: desire shows "many heads like monsters." Greville (though not his unwary speaker) hereby identifies Myra with the fallen Roman church—to Protestant commentators, the whore of Babylon. The speaker's lust for the inconstant Myra, like Redcrosse's lust for the faithless Duessa, signals the profundity of his error. Here, however, the inconstancy of Myra as Rome is fortunately destabilizing; the speaker exults, "Thus *Rome* and *Myra* acting many parts, / By often changes lost commanding arts" (*C* 29:20–21). Protestants interpreted Revelation 17–18, as they did Genesis 11, as a prophecy of Rome's destruction.[49]

In the inconstant ladies of *Caelica*, Greville figures error as female: Myra alludes to the whore of Babylon, and Caelica is a false heaven. In the final poem of the sequence, the inconstant earthly mistresses become absorbed into one vast female false idol, the wayward church. Addressing the Lord God, no longer Cupid, the speaker repents that we have "Prophan'd thy name, thy worship overthrowne" and "for earthly Idols, have forsaken / Thy heavenly Image" (*C* 109:5, 20–21). Worse yet, "Impiety, o Lord, sits on thy throne" (*C* 109:11). The church, the erstwhile bride of Christ, has fallen into error, and there is no truth in her members:

Mans superstition hath thy truths entomb'd
His Atheisme againe her pomps defaceth,
That sensuall unsatiable vaste wombe,
Of thy seene Church, thy unseene Church disgraceth.

> There lives no truth with them that seem thine own,
> Which makes thee living Lord, a God unknowne.
>
> (*C* 109:13–18)[50]

Greville's distinction between the "seene" church, which disgraces the "unseene" church, echoes Calvin, who distinguishes the visible church (including those who have only the name and outward appearance of Christ) from the invisible church comprising the elect from the beginning of time.[51] The visible church is mother of all believers, and she guides them to the goal of faith. The importance of this metaphoric relation is underscored by Calvin, using the analogy of marriage: "For it is not lawfull that those thynges be severed which God hath conjoyned, that to whom he is a father, the Churche be also their mother."[52] Moreover, the visible church is essential to God's plan of salvation:

> [T]here is no other entrye into life, unlesse she conceive us in her wombe, unlesse she bryng us fourth, unlesse she fede us with her breastes, fynally unlesse she kepe us under her custodye and governaunce, untyll such tyme as beyng unclothed of mortall fleshe we shall be lyke unto Angels.[53]

For Greville, however, the visible church has become a perverted mother of believers. Myra, denying Cupid her breast, is a type of the visible church, fallen from truth. The scarlet woman of Babylon, "the mother of whoredomes" (Rev. 17:5) is also a perverted mother, the antitype of the nurturing true church. Gifford makes explicit the metaphor of the false church as a perverted mother and whore:

> Babylon was a sinke of all abomination . . . a mistress of wickedness, yea a mother and nourse of all evill: all which are most fitlye referred to the Sinagoge of Rome, which althoughe she boaste her selfe to be . . . the mother of all the faithfull, . . . [she is] the mother of all whoredomes and abominations of the earth.[54]

Greville also imagines a female church whose mothering function has gone haywire. With her devouring "sensuall unsatiable vaste wombe," she is not life- and faith-giving but death-dealing. The ironic rhyme of "womb" with "tomb" (*C* 109:13 and 15) reinforces her association with spiritual death, not life.[55] In the poem's final couplet, this sonorous rhyme sounds again as the speaker yearns for the apocalypse: "sweet *Jesus*, fill up time and come, / To yeeld the sinne her everlasting doome." Sin is conceived of a female, but her degenerative ability (that makes the womb a tomb of truth) is canceled by the regenerative power of God's son.[56] It is Jesus who will "fill up" time and "yeeld" sin her doom, canceling the death-delivering power of the "unsatiable vast wombe" (a female black hole), filling it instead with truth and grace.[57]

Greville's representation of profound religious error in terms of the lustful and inconstant lovers of *Caelica* unequivocally condemns the tradition of the amorous sonnet sequence as a trophy of sin. He attempts to reform the love sonnet by investing its language with ideological weightiness and moral wit, introducing a Babylon theme and theological wordplay to ironize the rhyme of "election" with "affection." Invoking Petrarchan and Christian metaphoric traditions, he raises the specter of female evil, first in the false ladies Myra, Cynthia, and Caelica, then in the fallen church they adumbrate. Greville easily surpasses Sidney's *Astrophil and Stella* in moral force, if not in felicity of metaphor.

Caelica, Female Power, and Social Disorder

Greville's exploration of sinful loving in *Caelica* participates in an even larger project, his meditation on the forms of tyranny, sexual and political, which are consequences of the primal Fall.[58] Greville is aware that all human relationships are inescapably hierarchical, based on domination and submission and the manipulation of the emotions of desire and fear. The domestic tyranny of marriage is one theme of Greville's *Letter to an honorable Lady*, in which he offers advice to a lady, perhaps the countess of Cumberland, suffering a wayward husband.[59] He counsels the wife to "suppresse desire, and affections within our selves, by which we shall wither *Hope*, and *Feare (two craftie spies of Power)*" (*Lady* 276). This amounts to passive resistance to her tyrant-husband.[60] Yet, Greville promises the restoration of justice in this near-apocalyptic scenario:

> Therefore *Madame*! untill the smart of sense have so united will and understanding, as all men in like fortunes may have like ends; *till the beasts beginne to know their strengths* [emphasis added]; the unwritten lawes blot out the written; and the temporall cease under the eternall; there is neither in yours, nor in any other subjection, any *true peace* to be gotten by *trust* of *Superiors*; nor *honour* by *strife* against them. (*Lady* 277)

It is impossible not to hear in this passage an echo of Sidney's Ister Bank poem, sung by Philisides in the *Arcadia*. In Sidney's fable, especially the emphasized phrase, the speaker advises the beasts, now tyrannized by man, "in patience bide your hell, / *Or know your strengths, and then you shall do well*" (emphasis added).[61] Greville's echo of Sidney occurs in an apocalyptic context in which the current order is overthrown and the ancient order restored. At that time, he suggests, true peace may be gotten by strife against superiors. Critics continue to question whether Sidney and Greville advocate patient submission to tyranny or rebellion against it, though they generally agree that both ultimately come down on the side of political conservatism.[62] Here and elsewhere, however, Greville manages to raise disturbing and unresolved questions about the value of suffering and obedience.

In the struggle for mastery between husband and wife, the woman's sexuality is the source of her power. Thus the dynamics of the illicit Petrarchan relationship involving a desiring lover and a sexually powerful, denying mistress are reenacted, even in marriage. In the *Letter to an honorable Lady*, the unfaithful husband, now a tyrant, makes his mistress a servant to his desires. She, in turn, uses her sexuality as a tool, "either out of craft, or coldnesse, deny[ing] him the enjoying of her body . . ." (*Lady* 262). The mistress's power inheres in her ability to withhold satisfaction from the man, and the wronged wife's honor consists in her self-denial, her resolute chastity. Such denial, however, only inflames male desire, the denial of which occasions wonder of the wife's

> *well-dignified ashes*, your flesh, while the wheeles of desire are wound up, than when they are run out with injoying. For in this crafty forge are framed wanton modesty, entising shamefac'dnesse, faint reproofes, with what other charmes soever are fit to stirre up the blindnesse of our Selfe-love, or Pitty. (*Lady* 263)

While denial of desire presumably dignifies her flesh, it also makes her subject to inescapable contradictions: she embodies "wanton modesty" and "entising shamefac'dnesse." The description of Stella's rejection of Astrophil provides perhaps the best gloss on this double bind: "While such wise she love denied / As yet love she signified" (*AS* song 8:71–72). In the struggle for mastery, men are invariably subject to their passions, while women, even if they win by denying desire, lose because they nonetheless incite such desire. In Greville's analysis of this dynamic, the distinction between the constant wife and the adulterous mistress is effaced. Both provoke the revolt of man's affection against his reason, awakening sinful desires. Even in this non-Petrarchan, epistolary form, Greville has succeeded in creating a dualistic mistress whose power to evoke and deny desire he reinscribes as sinfulness.

Given Greville's view of the power dynamics within marriage, it is not surprising that he chose to remain unmarried and seek emotional satisfaction in friendships with men. In his analysis, women have the power both to awaken and to deny man's desires, subverting his authority over himself and others. In *Caelica*, the power of Myra, Caelica, and Cynthia alternately to indulge and to deny the lover's desires ensures the continuation both of the sinful desire and of the poetry that celebrates and condemns it. The few fabliaux, which seem so misplaced in *Caelica,* also can be understood in terms of the threat posed by female sexuality. In one, Scoggin's wife cheats on him by sleeping with the Lord (*C* 49); in another, a married woman begets a child with a monk (*C* 23). A wife's ability to cuckold her husband and to jeopardize his patrimony was one form of her power, and a socially disruptive one at that. Inconstant love is not only a violation of the Christian moral code but a practice that undermines the husband's authority and the social order.

While the *Letter to an honorable Lady* and *Caelica* explore domestic and sexual tyranny, Greville is also concerned with the analogous phenomenon of tyranny in the body politic, which springs from the reign of passion in the human body. In his closet drama, *Mustapha*, the chorus remarks how men and states easily succumb to tyranny:

> Mankinde is both the Forme,
> And Matter, wherewith Tyrannies transforme:
> For Power can neither see, worke, or devise,
> Without the Peoples hands, hearts, wit, and eyes:
> So that were Man not by himselfe opprest,
> Kings would not, Tyrants could not make him beast.
>
> (*Certaine Workes,* 117)

Tyranny is enabled from below (and within) and is a symptom of human frailty. For their part, kings exploit the weakness of their subjects and "by false feares and hopes, make people yeild / Their harts for temples unto tyrant's lawes" (*TR* 26).[63] Greville's sonnet speaker decries that "Kings, *Player*-like, act Glories part, / Yet all within them is but Feare and Art" (*C* 101:35–36). Even Queen

Elizabeth exhibits "these flatterings, and threatenings of hope, or fear (which transcendent power is sometimes forced to work by)" (*Life* 202).[64] Moreover, subjects who have resigned their freedom by sinning acquiesce in their enslavement to tyrants. They resemble court flatterers, "Slaves, and yet darlings of Authority" (*C* 78:10) who, "rays'd at Princes cost / Tempt man to throw his libertie away" (*C* 78:21–22). They

> let fall those strengths which make all States great
> By free Truths chang'd to servile flatterie.
> Whence, *while men gaze upon this blazing starre,*
> *Made slaves, not subjects, they to Tyrants are.*
>
> (*C* 78:27–30)

Within the context set by these poems exploring the mechanism of tyranny, occurs Greville's only poem alluding explicitly to Queen Elizabeth.[65] The "blazing starre" of sonnet 78, line 29 (above), is made synonymous and forced to rhyme with the tyrant in line 30. In the next poem, the star becomes a comet, a portent of political upheaval causing men to wonder,

> In restlesse thoughts holding those visions deare,
> Which threaten to rent Government in sunder;
> Yet [they] be but horrors, from vaine hearts sent forth
> To prophecie against Annointed worth.
>
> (*C* 79:3–6)

Despite Greville's condemnation of rebellion, this portentous comet stirs restless thoughts touching the overthrow of God's anointed one. (Similarly, the *Letter to an honorable Lady* alluded to an apocalyptic uprising and the resotration of justice.) Uneasy thoughts are, however, put to rest as the shooting comet is replaced by Queen Elizabeth as the fixed star in this brief sonnet 81 from *Caelica*:

> Under a Throne I saw a Virgin sit,
> The red, and white Rose quarter'd in her face;
> Starre of the North, and for true guards to it,
> Princes, Church, States, all pointing out her Grace.
> The homage done her was not borne of Wit,
> Wisdome admir'd, Zeale tooke Ambitions place
> State in her eyes taught Order how to sit,
> And fixe Confusions unobserving race.
> *Fortune* can here claime nothing truly great,
> But that this Princely Creature is her seat.

Clearly this is no tyrant but a monarch properly graced (*C* 81:4)—a word always carrying religious connotation for Greville. A fixed and guiding star and cynosure of the court, she establishes order in church, state, and society, halting the "unobserving race" towards entropy and destruction. Thus, this Virgin would seem to be the antitype to the poet's changeable mistresses, Caelica, Myra, and Cynthia. The ambiguous praise of her in the couplet, however, casts a backward shadow upon the poem. She is the seat of Fortune, the arbitrary and irrational tyrant who was, as Norbrook reminds us, a negative image of the prince's desired constancy.[66] The Virgin ostensibly controls the change and confusion Fortune sows. But, from Greville's poem, it is not clear who is ultimately in control here; Fortune, identified with the queen, seems to usurp her throne. In the opening line, in fact, the Virgin sits not *upon* the throne but *under* it, in retrospect a less commanding figure. Like Greville's praise of Sidney, his compliment to Elizabeth dissolves under the pressure of its own ambiguous language and imagery. The fixed north star proves an unstable image for the royal virgin.

That Greville manages to turn the subject of his sonnet sequence to a consideration of political tyranny testifies to his humanist concerns with the behavior of courtiers and kings. It also demonstrates the flexibility of Petrarchan idiom, with its ability to signify religious, political, and sexual issues inextricably linked to the virginal Petrarchan mistress occupying the throne. The safe confines of a Petrarchan sonnet sequence allow Greville to explore the theme of inconstancy subversive not only of the Petrarchan ideal but also of the official myth of Elizabeth's unchanging nature, exemplified in the favored motto of her old age, *semper eadem.* As anointed monarch, Elizabeth is, in her body politic, beyond and in control of change, but in her natural body, she is as changeable as any mortal mistress, subject to error and death.[67] This poem may reflect the succession anxiety pervading the last decades of Elizabeth's reign. Possibly Greville reflects on the vagaries of Elizabeth's rule and the shifting fortunes experienced by her courtiers. Greville himself spent many years slowly working his way into her favor, whereupon she died and he was snubbed by Cecil and shortly forced out of his position as treasurer of the navy.[68] Though Greville tended to idealize Elizabeth's reign and pays tribute to her in his *Life of Sidney*, he also alleges and describes "four out of many" instances when the queen's edicts "fell heavy in crossing a young man's ends" (*Life* 168).

Whether or not Greville alludes to Elizabeth in sonnet 81, significantly, he always represents a woman's power as tyrannical and tyranny as allegorically female. In *Caelica* 107, he figures his submission to a powerful female, here the goddess Isis, as galling and humiliating.

> *Isis*, in whom the Poets feigning wit,
> Figures the Goddesse of Authority,
> And makes her on an Asse in triumph sit,
> As if Powers throne were mans humility;
> Inspire this Asse, as well becomming it,
> Even like a Type of wind-blowne vanity:
> With pride to beare Powers gilding scorching heat
> For no hire, but opinion to be great.
>
> (*C* 107:1–8)

The speaker is a poet who, in figuring Isis as a powerful goddess, finds himself in the humiliating role of the ass she rides. The possible pun (in line 7) on "gelding," a castrated horse, appropriately suggests the emasculating nature of this servitude.[69] In the next stanza, the ass connotes a jaded and unsuccessful courtier waiting upon a tyrant,

> Bridled and burdened by the hand of might,
> While he beholds the swarmes of hope and feares,
> Which wait upon ambition infinite,
>
> . . . .
>
> Till wearinesse, the spurre, or want of food,
> Makes gilded curbs of all beasts understood.
>
> (*C* 107:10–16)

Surely Greville remembers this sonnet from *Astrophil and Stella*, in which Astrophil is a "poor beast," a horse ridden by love:

> The raines wherewith my Rider doth me tie,
> Are humbled thoughts, which bit of Reverence move,
> Curb'd in with feare, but with guilt bosse above
> Of Hope, which makes it seeme faire to the eye.
>
> (*AS* 49:5–8)

Both poems even share the image of the gilded curb or bit. In Sidney's poem, the political context is less overt, but the sexual humiliation experienced by the speaker is comparable: "The Wand is Will" and the "horse, he spurres with sharpe desire my hart: / He sits me fast, how ever I do sturre" (*AS* 49:9, 11–12). Peter Herman sees in the image of Sidney as the horse straddled and "managed" by love, homoerotic overtones that reinforce Sidney's powerlessness and consequently, his effeminacy.[70] Partly because *Caelica* 107 lacks the homoerotic element (the rider of the ass is clearly female), it suggests the indignities of service to a female monarch. In this it resembles the ending of *Astrophil and Stella* 107, in which Astrophil asks for his wit to be dismissed from the service of his "Princesse":

> Till it have wrought what thy owne will attends.
> On servants' shame oft Maister's blame doth sit;
> O let not fooles in me thy workes reprove,
> And scorning say, 'See what it is to love.'

Sidney's and Greville's speakers fear being made objects of scorn for their poetry and for their obsequious attendance on the goddess-like female. The mask of the sonnet lover drops to reveal the face of a courtier galled at his forced submission to a powerful queen.

Greville's figurations of female power in *Caelica*, however, signify more than merely his experiences as an Elizabethan courtier.[71] He claims that his association of vice with women is impersonal and general, though surely the issue of Greville's own sexuality is not irrelevant here. He admits to exaggerated representations of female evil in his dramas, explaining that

> my Images [of evil are] beyond the ordinary stature of excesse, wherein again that women are predominant, is not for malice . . . But as Poets figured the vertues to be women . . . so have I described malice, craft, and such like vices in the persons of Shrews, to shew that many of them are of that nature . . . strong in weaknesse; and consequently in these Orbes of Passion, the weaker Sexe. . . . (*Life* 243 [251])

This paradox of women's powerful weakness informs Greville's representations of female power as sexual threat. The sonnet ladies embody the yoking of sexuality and sin. Caelica is a false heaven, and Myra with her Cupid is a perverted madonna; the lady's sexual favor is a demonic parody of divine grace. In *A Treatise of Monarchy*, the decline of the golden age, a favorite Grevillean theme, accords with the rise of a tyrannical power, unambiguously female:

> Whence neither makers now, nor members held
> Men are; but blankes, where pow'r doth write her lust,
> A sprightlesse masse, which for it cannot weld
> It self, at others pleasure languish must;
> Resolve to suffer, and let power doe all;
> Weakenes in men, in children naturall.

From which cras'd wombe of frailtie was brought forth
A giant creature in excesse of might,
To worke in all with every pow'r but worth . . .[72]

Lust is figured as female, recalling Eve's sensual power and signifying, more generally, the rebellion of the lower faculties against reason and will. This force, the primal Other, overcomes men, effacing them as "blankes" and reducing them to effeminate weakness. With its "cras'd wombe" bearing a monster who stamps out religion, honor, nature's laws, and nations, she resembles the "moderne Tyrants" whose power "drownes in this gulfe of vast affections, / Faith, truth, worth, law, all popular protections" (*C* 77:29–30). This tyrant, of course, prefigures the vast female false idol in *Caelica* 109, the "seene Church" whose "sensuall unsatiable vaste womb" engulfs the "unseene Church" of the elect.[73]

This powerful and shocking metaphor of all-encompassing female power yet to be vanquished by divine forces is a fitting conclusion to a sonnet sequence concerned with the debilitating personal, social, and political effects of sinful loving. Anyone who doubts that the "personal" love sonnet is directly engaged in a complex affirmation and critique of political and religious institutions need only read Greville to disperse the illusion that Renaissance lyrics inhabit an independent aesthetic realm. In *Caelica*, all the manifestations of erroneous loving—the inconstant mistresses who fan the flames of man's lust, the false idols he worships and the tyrants to whom he submits, and the disordered personal, social, and political hierarchies resulting from sinful loving—are encompassed by the image of the disgraced church (Christ's spouse) with the vast insatiable womb, female Impiety occupying God's throne.

Redemption from Sinful Loving: Greville as an Aspiring Right Poet

Having shown how Greville swerves from Sidney in his overt consideration of apocalyptic political and religious themes, I wish to realign them, demonstrating how Greville aspires to Sidney's ideal of right poetry, specifically, the use of sonnets to praise immortal goodness and beauty. Greville conceded that true learning, initiated by "gifts of Grace, and Faith" can assist man's regeneration: "Thus are true Learnings in the humble heart / A *spirituall worke*, raising

Gods Image, rased / By our transgression; *a well-framed art*" (*THL* 149, 150). With the homonymic pun "razed-raised," Greville wittily suggests the rebuilding of fallen man in God's image. The placement of "well-framed art" enhances the possible meanings of these lines: the art is godly poetry (a spiritual work of true learning) that restores God's image to defaced man; it is man himself rebuilt by his Maker (hence the rhyme with "humble heart"). In the spiritual poems concluding *Caelica*, the speaker struggles towards personal and poetic redemption, which occurs when the image of Christ, usurped by that of the mistress, is restored to his heart (and to his poetry).

In Greville's religious sonnets, we can see his deliberate effort to surpass and correct his precursor, Sidney. While Sidney allows Petrarchan language to carry spiritual themes, Greville's serious religious concerns condemn and displace Petrarchism altogether. One example is this pair of poems, in which Sidney, then Greville, use the lover's meditation on the darkness of night to figure spiritual blindness. Here is *Astrophil and Stella* 99, which, as I argued in the previous chapter, is a meditation upon the theme of Psalm 130:6.

When far spent night perswades each mortall eye,
   To whom nor art nor nature graunteth light,
   To lay his then marke wanting shafts of sight,
Clos'd with their quivers in sleep's armory;
With windowes ope then most my mind doth lie,
   Viewing the shape of darknesse and delight,
   Takes in that sad hue, which with th'inward night
Of his mazde powers keepes perfit harmony:
   But when birds charme, and that sweete aire, which is
Morne's messenger, with rose enameld skies
Cals each wight to salute the floure of blisse;
In tombe of lids then buried are mine eyes,
   Forst by their Lord, who is asham'd to find
   Such light in sense, with such a darkned mind.

As the mortal eye closes at night, the eye of the mind opens to behold its own darkness, paradoxically palpable and delightfully shaped, like a shadowy Stella.[74] The darkness is inward as well as outward, a mark of Astrophil's "mazde powers" of reason. His senses are impaired as well; he is able to hear, smell, and imagine the sensations of morning but not to see them. He is ashamed and unable to waken, denied the daily resurrection of eyes from sleep and perhaps the final resurrection of his body from the grave.

Greville's speaker also muses on night and sight in *Caelica* 100, but with an almost exclusive focus on the inward darkness:

In Night when colours all to blacke are cast,
Distinction lost, or gone downe with the light;
The eye a watch to inward senses plac'd,
Not seeing, yet still having power of sight.

Gives vaine *Alarums* to the inward sense,
Where feare stirr'd up with witty tyranny,
Confounds all powers, and thorough selfe-offence,
Doth forge and raise impossibility:

Such as in thicke depriving darkenesse,
Proper reflections of the errour be,
And images of selfe-confusednesse,
Which hurt imaginations onely see,
  And from this nothing seene, tels newes of devils,
  Which but expressions be of inward evils.

Of the two poems, Greville's has less to do with love; Sidney's at least has a veiled reference to Cupid's darts. *Caelica* 100 describes the tyranny of sin within the fallen mind as it infects the imagination and provokes terror and confusion. In place of Sidney's pleasantly oxymoric "shape of darknesse and delight," there is a "thicke depriving darkenesse," a "nothing seene." This paradox is suggestive of the deprivation of evil, a psychic vacancy into which self-created demons flow.[75] Greville's sonnet evokes a leaden, rather than a lyrical, despair; at least Sidney's speaker can still *imagine*, even if he is ashamed to behold, the glories of the dawn. Greville's speaker possesses a "hurt imagination" incapable of generating any positive sensory images.

Despite the spiritual resonance of many of Sidney's later sonnets in *Astrophil and Stella*, it is Greville who develops the theological potential of the poetic images in a direction that challenges Petrarchan tradition. Exile from the beloved's heart, at first facetiously called hell, comes to signify the torment of a sinner separated from God. Since tasting of the fruit, the speaker regrets "I have lost my seate" in Paradise and finds "My soule . . . blacke with Shadow is" (*C* 83:86, 87). He further laments, "My saint hath turned away her face, / and made that heaven my hell" (*C* 83:151–52).[76] In a later sonnet, the hell feared is more literal: "Lord, I have sinn'd, and mine iniquity / Deserves this hell, yet Lord deliver me" (*C* 98:5–6). From his "depth of sinne, this hellish grave, / And fatall absence from my Saviours glory," he implores God's mercy—not the lady's (*C* 98:13–15). Yearning for redemption from sinful loving, he prays for God's "sweet mercy [that] opens forth the light, / Of Grace which giveth eyes unto the blind . . ." (*C* 97:5–6). This theological grace displaces the grace that the lover vainly hopes to receive from his mistress; it restores sight to the lover blinded by the false god, Cupid.

Despite his emphatic meditation upon the sinfulness of love, Greville is better able than Sidney to imagine the poet's liberation from the Petrarchan prison house. Here is Astrophil, rejected by Stella, suffering in his prison, a kind of hell:

When sorrow (using mine owne fier's might)
  Melts down his lead into my boyling brest,
  Through that darke fornace to my hart opprest,
There shines a joy from thee my only light;
But soone as thought of thee breeds my delight,
  And my yong soule flutters to thee his nest,
  Most rude dispaire my daily unbidden guest,
Clips streight my wings, streight wraps me in his night.
  And makes me then bow downe my head, and say,
Ah what doth *Phoebus*' gold that wretch availe,
Whom iron doores do keepe from use of day?

(*AS* 108:1–11)

Sidney's language still evokes a primarily courtly context: the furnace is not hell but Astrophil's heart, stoked by his desire; the "iron doores" that keep him from "*Phoebus* gold" (ambiguously daylight or courtly riches) suggest a castle dungeon.[77] Even the fluttering bird is a Neoplatonic image of the soul. In a clearly related sonnet, Greville's language lacks any courtly referent, relying instead upon a religious conception of a tormented soul imprisoned in the body, like a sinner in hell:

Downe in the depth of mine iniquity,
That ugly center of infernall spirits;
Where each sinne feeles her owne deformity,
In these peculiar torments she inherits,
  Depriv'd of humane graces, and divine,
  Even there appeares this *saving God* of mine.

(*C* 99:1–6)

In Greville's theology, God's grace is gratuitous and often sudden: "Immediate grace, true miracle Divine . . . to the harts of sinne, shadowes of death, / The savinge light of truth he doth inspire" (*TR* 60–61). In *Caelica* 99, such grace is manifested, and the speaker begins the process of sanctification, the repairing of the defaced image of God in the soul.[78] Gazing "in this fatall mirrour of transgression" within, he sees the "fruit of his degeneration, / The errours ugly infinite impression" (*C* 99:7–9). The refrain then registers a crucial change from "Depriv'd of humane graces, and divine" to, "Depriv'd of humane graces, *not* divine" (*C* 99:17; emphasis added). Finally, the speaker glimpses within himself an image of the Savior on the cross. This meditative epiphany is the basis for the affirmation of faith that concludes the poem: "Thus hath his death rais'd up this soule of mine" (*C* 99:24). By contrast, Astrophil's soul never takes flight from the dungeon of sonnet 108.

By "raising God's Image, rased / By our transgression" with the "well-framed art" of *Caelica* 99, Greville takes a step towards repairing the fallen imagination and redeeming poetry.[79] His speaker repents of his sinful loving and recovers his spiritual sight, substituting the internal image of the Savior for that of the mistress. In so doing, he radically revises Petrarchan representation and fashions himself as a Sidneian poet who bends the language "to the right use both of matter and manner" (*Defence* 72), praising God's goodness, not mortal love and beauty. Astrophil's poetry, by contrast, rests on the trite, conventional paradox that Stella is the source of his woes and his joys (*AS* 108:14). Greville reapplies the anxieties and alterations of the abject Petrarchan lover to the uneasy Protestant soul, fallen from grace, hoping for and despairing of salvation. Fleshly nature, to which man has subjected himself (as the Petrarchan lover to his mistress), is the root of all pride, which disrupts the divine order and sends persons and states into chaos.

The conversion or election of the individual soul is only the first step of reparation, however. The last two sonnets of *Caelica* depict church and state in desperate need of redemption. Tortured syntax and uneven meter convey the confused rout of warfare: "war and conquest sin / In blood, wrong liberty, all trades of shame" (*C* 108:3–4). In the last poem, "*Syon* lyes waste, and thy *Ierusalem*, / O Lord, is falne to utter desolation" (*C* 109:1–2); impiety and atheism fill the church. The speaker prays, "sweet *Jesus*, fill up time and come, / To yeeld sinne her everlasting doome" (*C* 109:30). The final remedy is beyond man's capability; only God's truth redresses the abuse of power in church and state, allays the tyrant's pride, and reforms the arts: "Showe these [truths] to Arts" and "Those mortall formes, moulded in humane error, / Dissolve themselves by lookinge in this mirror" (*TR* 107). Until this time of apocalypse, man's duty is simply this:

Then man! Rest on this feelinge from above,
Plant thou thy faith on this celestiall way.

. . . .

Finde peace in endlesse, boundlesse, heavenly things;
Place it else where, it desolation bringes.

(*TR* 114)

Here Greville provides a fitting gloss for *Caelica*—and for *Astrophil and Stella*, as Greville must have read it: joys placed in the mortal beauty, Caelica, a bounded, false heaven, bring only desolation to the souls of men and destruction of the social order.

4
Delia, the Countess of Pembroke, and the Literary Career of Samuel Daniel

Greville's avowed intimacy with Sidney spurred his deep and conflicted engagement with his friend's life, works, and philosophical ideals. Without Sidney's prior example, it is hard to imagine his emergence into literary activity. By contrast, Samuel Daniel's appropriation of Sidney's example was more impersonal and occasional, less tormented by an anxiety of influence than motivated by the desire for poetic fame and material gain. While Greville brooded for years over his sonnet sequence, Daniel published *Delia* in 1592, fast upon the heels of *Astrophil and Stella*, and dedicated it to the countess of Pembroke, sister of the renowned Sidney. He presented himself as Sidney's literary heir and an aspiring poet, perfecting the strategies by which poets promoted themselves through Sidney. The earliest elegists had also invoked and emulated Sidney as they sought patronage from his associates. For example, Angel Day presented himself to Walsingham (Sidney's father-in-law) as dedicated and serviceable, in the mold of Sidney, whom he praises for his "love, service, and obedience, to *God*, his *Prince*, and his *Countrie*."[1] John Phillips assumed Sidney's voice in a poem dedicated to the earl of Essex, urging him to emulate Sidney's generosity; Daniel excels at such ventriloquism in *The Complaint of Rosamond*. Thomas Churchyard, in his *A Praise of Poetrie*, proposed a sociopoetic contract: because Sidney enabled his poetry, he will in turn proclaim Sidney's fame as poetic immortality.[2] In *Delia*, Daniel makes a similar promise to Pembroke. Mainly, however, he relies on his admiration for Sidney and a chance association with *Astrophil and Stella* to recommend himself to the countess of Pembroke, beginning a fruitful association with a new patron.

My study of *Delia* is offered as an appreciative account of the subtlety and success with which Daniel exploits Sidney's priority in the service of his own poetic career. Other critics have analyzed Daniel's poetic artistry, and I share their admiration. My focus, however, is on Daniel as a master of strategies of self-promotion and poetic compliment, one who crafts a sonnet persona that significantly refashions Sidney's desiring Astrophil while acknowledging his debt to the prior poet. Unlike Greville, Daniel does not embrace Sidney's ideal of the divine poet or his goal of reforming the lyric; his ambitions tend towards worldly success as an epic poet. Yet even as his literary career advanced and his poetry won him favor, Daniel expressed a strong antipoetic sentiment that shadowed his great achievements in verse. The moralistic poetics and activist ideals of *Musophilus* and *A Defence of Ryme* place him squarely in the company of Sidney and Greville, poets whose humanist aspirations were set back by their simultaneous belief in an imperfectible human nature. In his *Delia* volume, however, Daniel successfully wrests sonnet conventions to signify new relationships and to express and affect the social and political order—specifically, the system of aristocratic patronage.

Daniel and the Countess of Pembroke as Patron

Though he benefited materially from Sidney's posthumous reputation and from the system of patronage his family represented, ironically, Samuel Daniel may never have met Sir Philip Sidney. Almost ten years the junior of Sidney, Daniel followed a similar path of learning, travel, and political apprenticeship, only to become known to posterity as a poet. When Sidney was penning *Astrophil and Stella* and the *Defence of Poetry* at Wilton and seeking ways to regain his position at court, Daniel was a student at Oxford. Like Sidney, he left without taking a degree, but while he was still a student, he translated an Italian work on impresa and devices. *The Worthy Tract of Paulus Jovius* was published in 1585 and dedicated to Sir Edward Dymoke, the queen's champion, a seasoned traveler and lover of Italy. This was Daniel's first attempt to please a patron, and he and Dymoke had a long association.[3] In that same year, 1585, Sidney was appointed governor of Flushing. Meanwhile, Daniel, traveling in France, was bidding for the attention of Sir Francis Walsingham, Sidney's father-in-law, in order to launch his own career as a public servant. In March

1585, from his chambers in Rue St. Jacques in Paris, he wrote to Walsingham of his intent

> to Studie . . . to render my self fit for the service of my Countrie; to whom I am bounde by nature, & of yor Honor, to whom I am vowed by inclination to be always at yor Honors co'maund . . . yf my slender abillitie might be thought worthy the least place about yor Honor. . . .[4]

Clearly, Daniel hoped that Walsingham would see in him a learned young man gaining the experience in foreign affairs that would qualify him for important government service.

Samuel Daniel finally gained notoriety not as a statesman but as a poet when twenty-eight of his poems appeared with the unauthorized edition of *Astrophil and Stella,* which was published by Thomas Newman and printed by John Charlewood with a preface by Thomas Nashe. This 1591 edition was quickly withdrawn, but the damage had been done; both Sidney and Daniel had their toying poems revealed to the public eye. The following year saw the authorized publication of Daniel's sonnet sequence, *Delia,* with *The Complaint of Rosamond.* In the dedication to the countess of Pembroke, he disclaims his earlier poems with the conventional excuse:

> I rather desired to keep in the private passions of my youth, from the multitude, as things utterd to my selfe, and consecrated to silence: yet seeing I was betraide by the indiscretion of a greedie Printer, and had some of my secrets bewraide to the world, uncorrected . . . I am forced to publish that which I never ment.[5]

Most scholars trust Daniel's claim that he was betrayed, that his sonnets were published without his knowledge or approval.[6] Others suspect that he was involved in Newman's surreptitious publication.[7] Germaine Warkentin, following Ringler, believes that Newman used a manuscript belonging to Daniel for his corrections to the second printing. She also notes the haste and success with which Daniel obtained from Newman the copyright to his poems, as *Delia* was registered a few short months after it was printed.[8] His involvement in either edition cannot be proven, but it seems likely for a number of reasons. Putting aside the motive of financial gain, Daniel, an unknown poet, had nothing to lose and everything to gain from an association with Sidney's name and poetry, even in a pirated edition. Furthermore, when Daniel issued his own, authorized version of his poems in 1592, he used the same printer Newman had enlisted for the unauthorized *Astrophil and Stella*, namely John Charlewood.[9] Were he truly "betraide by the indiscretion of a greedie Printer," as he claims, would he have trusted this same unscrupulous printer with his poems in 1592?

Whether Daniel purposely fashioned the opportunity for sudden notoriety or was indeed the victim of literary piracy, the clever way in which he turned the situation to his advantage deserves a closer look. Many significant features of the 1592 volume, including careful revisions and excisions of 1591 sonnets, suggest Daniel's awareness of his desired audience, the countess of Pembroke, and his desire not only to compliment her as Delia but also to convince her that he is worthy to be Sidney's poetic heir.[10] While asserting his poetic aspirations and demonstrating his ability to make Delia live in his rhymes, he affirms the powerful system of patronage that Pembroke represents and on which he depends.[11] The *Delia* volume is Daniel's studied exercise in self-promotion, in which he presents himself as a uniquely gifted devotee of Sidney, using the prior poet's fame to assist his own literary ambitions.[12] In so doing, he demonstrates the social utility of the Petrarchan sonnet and the ability of gracefully wrought poetry to reflect and effect the mutually sustaining relationship of poet and patron.

Both Mary Sidney and her brother Philip were renowned as patrons of learning and poetry, but the nature and extent of their patronage is a matter of dispute. Fulke Greville extolled his friend Philip Sidney as "a generall *Mecaenas* of Learning" (*Life* 39). Invoking the glory of patronage "hereditary to your house" in the dedication of the 1592 *Delia*, Daniel clearly expects the countess to continue her brother's role. John Aubrey later reported that Wilton "was like a College, there were so many learned and ingeniose persons" and the countess was "the greatest Patronesse of witt and learning of any Lady in her time"; he has contributed to the popular view that, because she was the recipient of so many dedications, the countess directed a thriving, experimental literary circle.[13] Mary Ellen Lamb, however, argues that reports of the countess's patronage have been greatly exaggerated, while Margaret Hannay takes the view that the countess actively promoted her brother's literary and political ideals in her own writings and by encouraging selected poets in their work.[14] One of these poets, scholars agree, was Samuel Daniel, though they disagree as to when the association began.[15]

Based on the language of Daniel's dedications to the countess, together with evidence from a reading of *Delia*, it seems fairly certain that, when he first published the sonnets and *The Complaint of Rosa-*

mond, he was seeking admission to her literary circle, such as it was. In 1592, the language of his dedication implies no association with her. He refers to her reputation as "happie and judiciall Patronesse of the Muses," asks for her protection, and looks forward to a beneficial association:

> And if my lines heereafter better laboured, shall purchase grace in the world, they must remaine the monuments of your honourable favour, and recorde the zealous duetie of mee, who am vowed to your honour in all observancy for ever. (sig. A2v)

The language is clearly oriented to the future. Had the countess already shown him favor, we might expect Daniel to express more explicit gratitude here.

Apparently *Delia* succeeded in opening doors for the aspiring poet.[16] In 1594, Daniel prefaced his revised edition of *Delia* with a dedicatory sonnet implying a very different relationship to the countess:

> Great Patroness of these my humble Rymes,
> Which thou from out thy greatnes doost inspire:
> Sith onely thou hast deign'd to rayse them higher,
> Vouchsafe now to accept them as thine owne,
> Begotten by thy hand, and my desire,
> Wherein my Zeale, and thy great might is showne.[17]

Daniel does not ask for her favor; he writes as one enjoying a mutual relationship that sustains his poetry. In the same year, he also published and dedicated to the countess *The Tragedie of Cleopatra*, a play continuing the story line of her own translation of Garnier's neo-Senecan tragedy *Antonie*. In the dedication, he gestures towards his work, which had been inspired by the countess: "Lo heere the worke the which she did impose, / Who only doth predominate my Muse," and he calls her "the starre of wonder, which my labours chose / To guide their way in all the course I use."[18] Evidently, Daniel had been invited to undertake this task, which he performed to satisfy his newly acquired patron.[19] Before, he claims, he was content simply to sing of Delia; now, she has "Call'd up my spirits from out their low repose, / To sing of State, and tragicke notes to frame." He entertains higher poetic ambitions, "Since I perceive the world and thou dost daigne, / To countenance my Song, and cherish me. . . ." The tone of Daniel's dedications bespeaks a confident self-presentation absent from the 1592 volume.

Beyond testifying to his success in gaining Pembroke's attention, the language of Daniel's dedications reveals his strategy for furthering his own literary career. A familiar tactic of poets who dedicated works to the countess was to praise her brother and cite the family's virtue and generosity.[20] Dedicating *The Ruines of Time* to her, Spenser professes his "affection unto that most brave Knight your noble brother deceased" and acknowledges the "straight bandes of duetie" which tied him to Sidney and to his "noble house."[21] Daniel, lacking any close association with the Sidney family, must rely on the "chance" printing of his poems with *Astrophil and Stella* as an occasion to express his admiration of the Sidneys. His strategy in the 1592 dedication of *Delia* is to link his name with Sidney, a similarly wronged poet, but to distinguish Sidney's eternity from his own vulnerable state:

> But this wrong was not onely doone to mee, but to him whose unmatchable lines have indured the like misfortune; Ignorance sparing not to commit sacriledge upon so holy Reliques. Yet *Astrophel*, flying with the wings of his own fame, a higher pitch then the gross-sighted can discerne, hath registred his owne name in the Annals of eternitie, and cannot be disgraced, howsoever disguised. And for myselfe, seeing I am thrust out into the worlde, and that my unholdned Muse, is forced to appeare so rawly in publique; I desire onely to bee graced by the countenance of your protection. . . . (A2r-v)

This technique of self-promoting humility masks his probable complicity in the earlier publication, and his claim of suffering the same wrong as Astrophil is well-designed to gain the countess's sympathy, however angered she might have been at the unauthorized publication of her brother's poetry. Daniel boldly stakes his own success on the popularity of Sidney's poems and the merit of his own, while asserting his dependency on the protection and encouragement of the countess.[22] In a sonnet new to the 1594 volume, he admits that this ploy worked, exulting: "So DELIA, hath mine errour made me knowne"; it is a "strange case, / That errours should be grac'd that merrite shame, / And sinne of frownes bring honor to the face."[23] Conventionally, the "errour" would signify his youthful passion, but it may also allude to his shameful (but successful) appropriation of Sidney, for which he offers a coded apology.

From a number of angles, Daniel's dedication of his sonnets to the countess (and his possible cooperation in Nashe's publication) look like a clever and calculated career move, a bid for recognition as a beginning, lyric poet destined for greater works. The motto on the title page of *Delia* in 1592, *Aetas prima canat Veneres, postrema tumultus*, shows Daniel's awareness of the career path of the aspiring poet who begins with lays of love and progresses to epic and tragic works. (This motto also appears on the title page of the 1609 edition of his epic work, *The Civil Wars*, as if proclaiming how far the poet has advanced in his Virgilian career.) The tragic plaint of Rosamond, appended to the 1592 sonnets, forecasts the future direction of his poetic muse and demonstrates a sympathy for tragic female figures. Indeed, Daniel's progress thereafter was rapid: *Cleopatra* was published in 1594, and in the following year, the first installment of *The Civil Wars* was registered.[24] Daniel must have been working on it while in Mary Sidney's household. He dedicated the work to Lord Mountjoy, a friend of Essex, already looking beyond Wilton's horizons. Others at court recognized and encouraged Daniel's ambition. Spenser, in *Colin Clouts Come Home Againe* (1595), identifies Daniel's aspiring muse who "doth her tender plumes as yet but trie, / In loves soft laies and looser thoughts delight" and urges:

> Then rouze thy feathers quickly *Daniell*,
> And to what course thou please thy selfe advance:
> But most me seemes, thy accent will excell,
> In tragick plaints and passionate mischance.[25]

Granted that the fledgling Daniel enjoyed the patronage of the countess between 1592 and 1595, what form did that favor take? The Sidney family was never particularly wealthy, and the praise accorded to them as patrons, critics agree, was not due to "their power over place or reward but . . . [to] the example and encouragement they gave to poets."[26] The countess was a popular dedicatee in part because she had a wealthy and politically influential husband. She was also deeply committed to her brother's political and religious ideals, a fact Daniel and others certainly considered as they approached her for patronage. Daniel probably held the position of tutor to the Pembroke sons; in addition, he worked with the countess on their Senecan political dramas, and they certainly exchanged poetry. An early draft of "To the Angell Spirit," the countess of Pembroke's elegy on her brother, was found among Daniel's papers;[27] evidently, Astrophil's fellow poet obtained the trust of his sister and provided her with valued poetic guidance.

"Cleer-sighted you": The Countess of Pembroke as the Audience of *Delia*

A poet hoping to attract as discriminating and intelligent a patron as Mary Sidney, countess of Pembroke, however, would do well to demonstrate a skill beyond that of writing pleasing dedications. Unlike some patrons, she could be relied upon to read beyond the dedication, especially when it explicitly invoked her brother's memory. Daniel knew it must be his poetry that would recommend him as a successor to Astrophil. His poetic art entails a complex self-presentational strategy best seen by comparing the "unauthorized" 1591 poems with the 1592 *Delia*. In the pirated edition, Daniel's poetic persona merely mimics features of Sidney's desiring Astrophil, but when Daniel addresses his revised and "authorized" sonnets to the countess of Pembroke, a new decorum is called for. His lover is honest and upright, possessing a "loyall hart and faith unfained" and "chast desire" (*Del* 15:1–2). He accepts his suffering as necessary for writing poetry, eager to demonstrate his literary, rather than erotic, ambition. Daniel's main strategy is to develop the analogy between the situation of the powerful mistress and her submissive lover and that of the female patron and her poet. He writes sonnets to Delia as a subject pays tribute to a prince, never threatening to withdraw his love or to change his allegiance.

In his 1591 sonnets, Daniel crafts a persona who is a rough imitation of the alternately reckless and rueful Astrophil. The poems treat the characteristic Sidneian theme of subversive desire thwarted by a stronger virtue, suggesting that Daniel was familiar with a manuscript copy of *Astrophil and Stella*. In one sonnet, the speaker entertains "rebel thoughts" but is forced into graceful submission by the lady's power: "Yet my soules sovereigne, since I must resigne, / Raigne in my thoughts, my love and life are thine" ("Poems" 8:13–14).[28] This couplet resembles Sidney's 107th sonnet, in which Astrophil resigns his wit to Stella, his "soveraigne part." Like Astrophil, Daniel's speaker attempts a metaphoric assault on his lady but is cast down by "disdaines thunderbolt." He blames his fall on his ambition and the poverty of his poetry; now he languishes in pain and fire "Because th'attempt was far above my Art" ("Poems" 27:7). In its movement from high desire through sudden fall, remorse, and renewed humility, Daniel's first sonnet "sequence" shows him to be a promising disciple of Astrophil. As an apprentice sonneteer, he also employs several conventional Petrarchan conceits: the lady as a cruel tyrant and the shipwrecked lover misled by his pilot, Love, and languishing near death.

Of the original twenty-eight sonnets printed with *Astrophil and Stella*, Daniel omits four from the 1592 *Delia*, a move that shows his awareness of the changed circumstances and purposes of this new publication. He discards the hackneyed sonnet about the shipwrecked lover, in which the lady is compared to a siren ("Poems" 12). In another, the lady's power over her suitor is represented as a deadly witchcraft in which the "slie Inchanter" forms a wax image of "the poore unwitting wretch [s]he meanes to kill" ("Poems" 10:1, 4). Daniel also wisely omits a sonnet charged with sexual tension, one that develops the Sidneian conflict between virtue and desire. It is a bitter complaint against the faithless mistress who "Withholds my right, where I have dearely bought it":

> Dearely I bought that was so highly rated,
> Even with the price of bloud and bodies wasting,
> She would not yeeld that ought might be abated,
> For all she saw my Love was pure and lasting.
> And yet now scornes performance of the passion,
> And with hir presence Justice overruleth,
> Shee tels me flat hir beauty beares no action,
> And so my plee and proces shee excludeth:
>   What wrong shee doth, the world may well perceive it,
>   To accept my faith at first, and then to leave it.
>
> ("Poems" 16:5–14)

The echoes of Sidney here are unmistakable. Lines 5 and 6 recall Sidney's "Thou blind man's marke": "Desire, desire I have too dearely bought, / With price of mangled mind thy worthlesse ware."[29] The legal metaphor in lines 10–12 brings to mind *Astrophil and Stella* 52, in which Love and Virtue sue at the bar for Stella, and the speaker, on Love's side, is willing to settle for Stella's body.[30] Also reminiscent of Sidney is the misunderstanding, whereby the lover believes he has been given rights to the mistress, while the woman insists she has granted no favors.[31] Like Astrophil, the lover hopes for "performance of the passion," while the virtuous mistress expects his love to be "pure and lasting." Daniel's speaker attempts to exonerate himself by blaming the lady, charging her in the last line with inconstancy. Wisely omitting this poem from his 1592 sequence, Daniel acknowledges that such a belligerent posture and the frank admission of sexual desire are inappropriate for a poet hoping to impress a patron. Doubtless the presence of the countess as an expected reader of the 1592 sonnets imposed a decorum on Daniel's representation of Delia; the need for patronage could hardly be served by emphasizing Delia's sorcery, hinting at her inconstancy, or parading the lover's concupiscence.

The fourth sonnet omitted from the 1592 *Delia* at first presents a puzzle. The poem is a supreme compliment to Delia, for it credits her with the ability to make the dying lover live again, like the phoenix:

O Soveraigne light that with thy sacred flame
Consumes my life, revive me after this,
And make me (with the happie bird) the same
That dies to live, by favour of thy blisse.
This deede of thine shall shew a Goddesse power,
In so long death, to grant one living hower.

("Poems" 3:9–14)

The phoenix was a familiar motif for love sonnets. Petrarch, Ronsard, Desportes, and Sidney had all used it; why shouldn't Daniel? For a good reason: the unique bird was already an icon of Sidney, who lived on in his sister. The connection of the phoënix with Sidney had occured as early as 1587 in John Phillip's *Life and Death of Sir Philip Sidney*: "This *Phenix*, sweet *Sidney* was the flower of curtesie."[32] Thomas Nashe, in his preface to the 1591 *Astrophil and Stella*, commands "Poets and Rimers" to burn their "crazed quaterzayns," for Astrophil comes, "Deare *Astrophel*, that in the ashes of thy Love, livest againe like the *Phoenix*." He then praises the countess for keeping green "the Laurel Garlande which thy Brother so bravely advaunst on his Launce" (A3v, A4). Spenser, in a dedicatory sonnet to the 1590 *Faerie Queene*, similarly complimented Pembroke, alluding to her kinship, spiritual as well as physical, with her brother, whose "goodly image liv[es] evermore, / In the divine resemblaunce of your face." Margaret Hannay observes that the phoenix metaphor came to be applied to the countess as the reincarnation of her brother. Nicholas Breton, in *Amoris Lachrimae: for the Death of Sir Philip Sidney* (1586), mourns the tragedy of "kill[ing] a phoenix where there were no moe."[33] Later, in a 1592 publication, he calls the countess a "rare *Phoenix* . . . the sweetest *Phoenix*, whom your wit, pen and art can but well shadow with all your Muses."[34] My point is that Daniel may have realized that expressing his desire to become a phoenix would have been impolitic and highly presumptuous. It was fitting, however, for Daniel to refer to Delia as a phoenix. In fact, Daniel retains in all versions the justly famed sonnet that imagines

Delia's fading beauty and promises to immortalize her:

> When if she grieve to gaze her in her glas,
> Which then presents her winter-withered hew;
> Goe you my verse, goe tell her what she was;
> For what she was she best shall finde in you.
> Your firie heate lets not her glorie passe,
> But Phenix-like shall make her live anew.
>
> (*Del* 30:9–14)

With such praise, addressed to the woman being hailed as her brother's reincarnation, Daniel joins the company of Nashe's poets and rimers creating and sustaining the Astrophil legend.

A reading of *Delia*, together with evidence from dedications and revisions, shows Daniel crafting his work and his own self-presentation with the countess as his ideal reader and desired patron. He may even allude to her privileged status among readers when he addresses "Cleer-sighted you, [who] soone note what is awry, / Whilst blinded ones mine errours never gesse" (*Del* 3:7–8). The opening sonnet of the 1592 sequence has a rich, allusive texture sure to be felt by the countess. Daniel declares Delia's role as protector and source of his poetry, pledging the complete and dutiful submission of his poetry to Delia's honor:

> Unto the boundles Ocean of thy beautie
> Runs this poore river, charg'd with streames of zeale:
> Returning thee the tribute of my dutie,
> Which heere my love, my youth, my playnts reveale.
>
> (*Del* 1:1–4)

Daniel's praise of his mistress is lofty indeed. As mistress of the sea, Delia governs the poet; as the ocean herself, she receives the tribute of the poet, who is like a river. The ocean-river conceit also informs contemporary praise of Queen Elizabeth, for example in Ralegh's *Ocean to Scinthia* and in the sonnet accompanying the Ditchley portrait of the queen.[35] Daniel himself alludes to Ralegh's devotion to the queen in this sonnet, addressed to "My *Cynthia*":

> Th'Ocean never did attende more duely,
> Uppon his Soveraignes course, the nights pale Queene:

Nor paide the impost of his waves more truely,
Then mine to her in truth have ever beene.[36]

(*Del* 40:5–8)

The imagery further exalts Daniel's mistress; as the subject offers tribute to a ruler, the poet reveals his love to Delia, and he expects the protection a prince would grant a subject or steward.[37]

In this opening poem, Daniel also employs a bookkeeping metaphor to express the losses of a youth spent in love and to suggest wittily the poet's own financial need:

Heere I unclaspe the booke of my charg'd soule,
Where I have cast th'accounts of all my care:
Heere have I summ'd my sighes, heere I enroule
Howe they were spent for thee; Looke what they are.
Looke on the deere expences of my youth,
And see how just I reckon with thyne eyes:
Examine well thy beautie with my trueth,
And crosse my cares ere greater summes arise.
Reade it sweet maide, though it be doone but slightly;
Who can shewe all his love, doth love but lightly.

(*Del* 1:5–14)

The lover, casting himself as a bankrupt, asks for grace as remuneration: "crosse my cares ere greater summes arise." Perhaps Daniel also meant for the countess to notice his clever use of a Sidneian conceit; Astrophil similarly referred to his wasted youth and his squandered wealth, calling himself a "banckrout. . . . / Unable quite to pay even Nature's rent, / Which unto it by birthright I do ow" (*AS* 18:3, 5–6). With this sonnet, Daniel discharges a debt to Sidney, demonstrates skillful praise, and strikes the appropriate submissive pose of one seeking patronage.

Interestingly, Pembroke herself uses both the ocean-river conceit and the bookkeeping metaphor in her elegy for her brother, "To the angell spirit":

As little streames with all their all doe flowe
to their great sea, due tribute's gratefull fee:
so press my thoughts my burthened thoughtes in mee,
To pay the debt of Infinits I owe

To thy great worth. . . .[38]

She calls her brother a phoenix and enumerates his virtues, making an "Accompt, this cast upp Summe, / this Reckoning made, this Audit of my woe."[39] It is impossible to say for certain whether Daniel or the countess used these images first, but their occurrence together in both poems is more than coincidental. An early version of the elegy was found among Daniel's papers and initially mistaken for his work. Possibly Daniel saw the poem before he crafted the 1592 *Delia* and purposely echoed it in his opening sonnet, in one stroke both flattering the countess by imitation and paying homage to her brother.[40]

Daniel's use of this image in his opening sonnet sets up an expectation of reciprocity, of mutuality, which is at odds with Petrarchan convention, for a Petrarchan mistress never rewards the poet-lover. Within the larger orbit of the sequence, the origin and return of the poet's "tributary plaints" to Delia, then, runs the familiar cycle of hope and despair. As the poet laments, "The circle of my sorrowes [is] never ending" (*Del* 17:4). He even likens himself to Sisyphus, who was condemned"the never-resting stone of care to roule" (*Del* 9:7), an image of eternal, unfulfilled striving. The circle of the poet's sorrow is inscribed in Delia herself: "My fortunes wheele, [is] the circle of her eyes, / Whose rowling grace deigne once a turne of blis" (*Del* 12:11–12). When Delia merges with the goddess Fortune, Daniel is able to allude wittily to his hopes for patronage. He complains that she "tread[s] me downe with foote of her disgrace: / Whilst I did builde my *fortune* in her eyes" (*Del* 20:10–11), and in the next sonnet she mistakenly "thinkes a looke may *recompence* my care" (*Del* 21:9; emphases added). Like Astrophil murmuring his devotion from behind the iron doors of his prison (*AS* 108), Daniel's speaker ends in a hell of despair, exiled from the lady, though he continues to present to Delia "the impost of a faith unfaining," his "tributary plaints" (*Del* 50:1, 5). The poet's desire for mutual gain will inevitably not be satisfied by a sonnet sequence, for convention demands that it end in grief, alienation, and defeat for the lover. Thus *Delia* highlights the limitations of conventional Petrarchism, while expressing Daniel's anxiety about the success of his bid for patronage.

On the other hand, *Delia* demonstrates Daniel's ability to energize Petrarchism, to rehabilitate sonnet conventions for the purposes of fresh praise and patronage seeking. To see Delia, for example, as an image of the countess as ideal patron drains the implicit erotic content from the sonneteer's plea for reciprocity and highlights the sonneteer's role as a poet, not as an amorist. Even in the poems that sound the carpe diem theme, the poet-lover's aim is not seduction but a gentle reminder of mortality appropriate for his devout reader: "Swift speedy Time, feathred with flying howers, / Dissolves the beautie of the fairest brow" (*Del* 31:11–12). His goal is to preserve, not to destroy, this "pure sweete beautie" (*Del* 30:4) and virtue in his poetry: "Heere see the giftes that God and nature lent thee; / Heere read thy selfe . . ." (*Del* 34:7–8). Daniel realizes that conventional situations and forms provide the necessary means for poetic expression. Hence, he can be a relatively happy Petrarchan lover, describing himself as "content to languish" (*Del* 16:1) and "please[d] to perish in my woe" (*Del* 14:12). He actually prefers Petrarchan misery to its alleviation: "I doubt to finde such pleasure in my gayning, / As now I taste in compas of complayning" (*Del* 40:13–14). In fact, it is the lack of fulfillment in love that makes his poetry possible. In an early sonnet, he describes his mistress using the usual Petrarchan oxymorons. She is both "cruell" and "faire," but

> had she pittie to conjoine with those,
> Then who had heard the plaints I utter now[?]
> O had she not beene faire, and thus unkinde,
> My Muse had slept, and none had knowne my minde.
>
> (*Del* 6:11–14)

Rather than feigning a lover's grief, Daniel simply reveals the mechanism behind conventional poetry, demonstrating how individual expression is wrung from a stylized situation.

Daniel's unique contribution to the English sonnet tradition is his promise to eternize Delia's beauty and her virtue, a theme distinctly un-Petrarchan but well suited to his plea for reciprocity.[41] The eternizing topos was traditionally reserved for the high style of hymns, odes, and epics, not the middle style of the lyric.[42] As a standard feature of the elegy, it was used to commemorate, even sanctify, Sidney. Given *Delia*'s participation in the memorialization of Sidney, Daniel's use of the eternizing topos is an appropriate innovation on sonnet themes, one which elevates and dignifies the lowly love sonnet. By claiming the power to eternize Delia in his poetry, he offers the countess of Pembroke a fame as enduring as that of her brother.

Daniel's demonstration of this immortalizing power begins midway through the sequence with a sonnet in which he likens himself to the high-flying Icarus:

> Now melted with the sunne that hath possest me,
> Downe doe I fall from off my high desiring.

. . . .
Th'Ocean of my teares must drowne me burning,
  And this my death shall christen her anew,
  And give the cruell Faire her tytle dew.

(*Del* 27:7–14)

Situated near the end of the 1591 volume ("Poems" 24), this poem signaled simply the defeat of the poet-lover's erotic ambitions. At the center of the 1592 volume, it introduces the eternizing theme that will raise Daniel's poetry and redefine his ambitions as poetic ones. Daniel transforms the image of Icarus the over-reacher into a symbol of his poetic rebirth and his power to name Delia.

In the second half of the sequence, Daniel exercises his newfound power, asserting that he offers the truest representation of Delia. He warns the lady of the dangers of narcissistic self-absorption and commands her, "leave your glasse, and gaze your selfe on mee" (*Del* 29:9). With this introduction of the second-person address, the speaker's tone becomes both intimate and imperative. He then subjects the beautiful Delia ("the halfe-blowne Rose, / The image of thy blush and Summers honor" [*Del* 31:1–2]) to the depredations of time in his most famous and lyrical group of sonnets. Rejecting mere flattery, he affirms that his own verse not only best represents Delia but also preserves and renews her beauty:

  I once may see when yeeres shall wrecke my wronge,
When golden haires shall chaunge to silver wyer:
And those bright rayes, that kindle all this fyer
Shall faile in force, their working not so stronge.
  Then beautie, now the burthen of my song,
Whose glorious blaze the world dooth so admire;
Must yeelde up all to tyrant Times desire:
Then fade those flowres which deckt her pride so long.
  When if she grieve to gaze her in her glas,
Which then presents her winter-withered hew;
Goe you my verse, goe tell her what she was;
For what she was, she best shall finde in you.
  Your firie heate lets not her glorie passe,
  But Phenix-like shall make her live anew.

(*Del* 30)[43]

The poem compliments Delia, but due to some crucial ambiguity, the poet assertively shares the limelight. In line 6, the "glorious blaze the world dooth so admire" ostensibly refers to Delia's beauty, but it could also describe his verses, which in line 13 are characterized by a "firie heate." Similarly, "Phenix-like" in the final line describes Delia, who will live anew even after she dies. Yet it also characterizes the poet's verses, which (recalling *Del* 27) are reinvigorated by the destruction of the Icarus-poet. Such ambiguity lends a subtle texture to Daniel's poetry, which uses a strategy of self-promotion beyond mere flattery or braggadocio.

Another strategy Daniel employs in *Delia* is to demonstrate with a quiet subtlety his ability to match, even to surpass, the poetic achievements of his precursors Spenser, Sidney, and Petrarch. He offers Delia the well-spoken picture of his own poetry: "Take this picture which I heere present thee, / Limned with a Pencill not all unworthy" (*Del* 34:5–6). The litotes makes his claim simultaneously modest and bold. In the next sonnet, however, he compares himself to Petrarch, assuring Delia,

> Thou canst not dye whilst any zeale abounde
> In feeling harts, that can conceive these lines:
> Though thou a *Laura* hast no *Petrarch* founde,
> In base attire, yet cleerely Beautie shines.
> And I, though borne in a colder clime,
> Doe feele mine inward heate as great, I knowe it:
> He never had more faith, although more rime,
> I love as well, though he could better shew it.
>
> (*Del* 35:1–8)

Characteristically, by the end of the sonnet, Daniel's confidence subsides into modesty:

> And if my penne could more enlarge thy name,
> Then should thou live in an immortall stile.
> But though that *Laura* better limned bee,
> Suffice, thou shalt be lov'd as well as shee.
>
> (*Del* 35:11–14)

This sonnet reveals Daniel's technique of self-promotion through self-effacement; though he distinguishes his poetry first from Sidney's, now from Petrarch's, he in effect implies his resemblance to these famed poets. If the poet can equal or surpass Petrarch's love for Laura, why not his verse too?

Perhaps significantly, this sonnet denying Delia's mortality ("Thou canst not dye whilst any zeale abounde") occurs at the exact seven-tenths mark in all editions of Daniel's sequence.[44] In Petrarch's *Rime sparse*, Laura dies at the same point (*Rime* 267 of 366), after which Petrarch consoles himself by contemplating her memory and longing for his own death. Although Petrarch's poetry established his and Laura's fame, it does not profess to immortalize her. Daniel's allusion to Petrarch's poetry highlights difference as well as likeness. If the countess of Pembroke knew the *Rime sparse* as well as she knew Petrarch's *Trionfi*, she would be impressed at Daniel's skill and subtlety, as well as pleased by his promise to eternize her in verse.

Such confidence in poetry's power proves difficult to sustain, however. In the next poem, Daniel turns again to a contemplation of Delia's death and seems to question the ability of his verses to endure:

How many lives the glory of whose name,
Shall rest in yee [yce], when thine is grav'd in Marble.
  Thou maist in after ages live esteem'd,
Unburied in these lines reserv'd in purenes;
These shall intombe those eyes, that have redeem'd
Mee from the vulgar, thee from all obscurenes.

(*Del* 36:7–12)

Here he imagines Delia's eternal fame as a patron who redeems the poet. Intimations of mortality, however, undermine the poet's confident claims. The pun on "grav'd" in line 8 suggests both Delia's name engraved on a marble tablet and her body interred in a tomb. Lines 10 and 11 present a contradiction that is doubtless intentional, since Daniel preserves it in all editions. He claims that Delia shall live "unburied" in his poetry, but then he immediately promises that his lines shall "intombe those eyes," evoking, despite himself, images of death and burial. By likening his lines to a tomb, Daniel strengthens the association between poetry and death, not eternal life.

The following sonnet further questions the ability of human works to endure. The poet's eyes "Have seene those walles the which ambition reared, / To checke the world, how they intombd have lyen / Within themselves" (*Del* 37:2–4). The walls ambition rears are the works of poetry themselves, ultimately as fragile as any architectural work. The poet urges Delia not to worry, "Though time do spoyle her of the fairest vaile," not because his works will preserve her but because her innate virtue will immortalize her: "That grace, that vertue, all that serv'd t'in woman; / Dooth her unto eternitie assommon" (*Del* 37:10, 13–14). Here, Daniel touches on another of Pembroke's interests, the *ars moriendi* and Senecan Stoicism, which offered women a means to elevate self-sacrifice and equanimity to the status of heroic virtue.[45] The countess also translated Petrarch's *Triumph of Death*, though when this was undertaken we cannot be sure. It seems likely, though, that Daniel was aware of these interests and purposely worked reflections on Petrarch, death, and immortality into the poetry of *Delia*.

Although Daniel is generally modest about proclaiming his poetic skill in the 1592 *Delia*, he does remind Delia of his Homeric potential and her own power to produce his greatest works. In one sonnet, the speaker gestures towards himself as an image of heroic suffering:

> Reade in my face, a volume of despayres,
> The wayling Iliades of my tragicke wo;
> Drawne with my bloud, and printed with my cares,
> Wrought by her hand, that I have honoured so.
>
> (*Del* 39: 1–4)

The Petrarchan exaggeration contains hints of the poet's ambition, which he is careful to distinguish from that of his contemporary, Spenser:

> Let others sing of Knights and Palladines,
> In aged accents, and untimely words:
> Paint shadowes in imaginary lines,
> Which well the reach of their high wits records;
> But I must sing of thee and those faire eyes,
> Autentique shall my verse in time to come,
> When yet th'unborne shall say, loe where she lyes,
> Whose beautie made him speake that els was dombe.
>
> (*Del* 46: 1–8)

Daniel apparently rejects the archaic form and language of the heroic romance as Spenser practices it, for the opening lines recall the first stanza of *The Faerie Queene* and Spenser's intent to "sing of Knights and Ladies gentle deeds" (1.1.1). Yet Daniel goes on to use an "untimely word"—"autentique"—that renders lines 5–6 frustratingly ambiguous. Either the eyes enable the poet's verse to speak with authority or the verse gives an authentic account of the eyes.[46] The *Oxford English Dictionary* cites Daniel's poem as the only example of "autentique" used as a verb, calling it an obsolete by-form of "authenticate." Another reading is possible if the word is considered an adjective, though it relies awkwardly on an incomplete predicate: "Autentique shall [be] my verse in time to come." Here "authentic," that is, authoritative or factual, is opposed to Spenser's "imaginary" allegorical mode. Daniel is signaling a different direction for his muse, which may already be embarked upon his verse epic, *The Civil Wars*. At the same time, by using an archaic word form that generates considerable ambiguity, Daniel pays homage to Spenser's method, as if to say to the countess that he can "do" Spenser as well as he can "do" Petrarch or Sidney.[47]

Daniel's tribute to Spenser (and Petrarch) in *Delia* 46 is profound. By gesturing in the direction of Delia's tomb ("loe where she lyes"), Daniel may also be echoing Ralegh's introductory sonnet to *The Faerie Queene:* "Methought I saw the grave, where *Laura* lay. . . . All suddenly I saw the Faerie Queene / At whose approch the soule of Petrarke wept." Such an echo would be appropriate here, for Daniel repeatedly reminds the countess of his own aspirations and her ability to help him realize them. If Spenser surpassed Petrarch, as Ralegh implies, Daniel indirectly suggests that he, too, may be a worthy poetic rival. In the sestet of this same poem, after rejecting Spenser's epic subject and mode, Daniel declares his own sonnets to be a heroic monument:

These are the Arkes the Tropheis I erect,
That fortifie thy name against old age,
And these thy sacred vertues must protect,
Against the Darke and times consuming rage.

(*Del* 46:9–12)

Once again, Daniel exalts the humble love lyric by proclaiming its eternizing capabilities. In exchange for her protection, requested in the dedication, the poet will protect with these poems (and presumably others to follow) her sacred virtues. (This resembles Churchyard's promise to eternize Sidney, whose example enabled his poetry.) In effect, Daniel invites the countess of Pembroke to be his muse, his Faerie Queene.

Daniel concludes his 1592 sonnets with a poetic gesture towards his two most powerful predecessors, Sidney and Petrarch. "An Ode" recalls song 8 of *Astrophil and Stella*, in which the lovers meet and Stella confesses a kind of love for Astrophil before she departs, "Leaving him so passion rent, / With what she had done and spoken, / That therewith my song is broken" (*AS* song 8:103–4). Daniel's ode, evoking the situation and the meter of Sidney's song, similarly envisions the lady's rejection and the poet's despair. The "cruell Maide"

Doth me, and my true love dispise:
My lives florish is decayde
  That depended on her eyes:
But her will must be obaide,
  And well he'ends for love who dies.

(sig. H2v)

In the final line, Daniel echoes Petrarch's *Rime* 140, a poem familiar because of Wyatt's and Surrey's translations.[48] With this allusion to Petrarchan tradition in a poem that recalls Sidney, Daniel signals his submission to convention (as Sidney did in the final sonnet of *Astrophil and Stella*) while including himself as the latest of the devoted-to-the-death lovers, elevating himself by association with his eminent predecessors.[49]

The Complaint of Rosamond: A Compliment to Pembroke

Given the satisfying coherence and thematic unity of *Delia* alone, it is tempting to overlook the obvious and unexplored question: just what is the complaint of an unchaste woman doing in this volume celebrating the chaste and ideal Delia?[50] My answer is that *The Complaint of Rosamond* completes and unifies the 1592 volume addressed to the countess, further demonstrating Daniel's calculated artistry and control. Like all of Daniel's editorial decisions in the 1592 volume, the inclusion of *Rosamond* was designed to compliment the countess, demonstrate his moral seriousness as a poet, and announce his post-Petrarchan ambitions. The complaint recalls the canzone of Petrarch's own lyric sequence, infused by Daniel with didactic force to show the moral and social disruption resulting from unbridled worldliness. It provides a counterpoint to the sonnets, with their anguished and woebegone male speaker, for it allows the poet to appeal to Delia in a female voice and to demonstrate his sympathy for the plight of women scorned or wronged by men.[51] In *Rosamond,* he can distance himself further from the amorist of the sonnet tradition and condemn adultery while raising pity for the wronged and deceived Rosamond, a sensitive maneuver given his female audience, the countess of Pembroke.

The story of Rosamond Clifford, lover of King Henry II, was widely known in the sixteenth century. The literary antecedents of

Rosamond are also well established and include Thomas Churchyard's tale of Edward IV's mistress, *Shore's Wife*, printed in the 1563 edition of *A Mirror for Magistrates*. Daniel's female-voiced lament thus follows the conventions of *de casibus* tragedy familiar to Tudor readers, even borrowing the rime royal stanza characteristic of the *Mirror*. Rosamond, gifted by nature and fortune, makes her first mistake by leaving the country for the court. There, like a Petrarchan tyrant, she experiences the power of her beauty to subdue men, and she practices the "Sweet silent rethorique of perswading eyes" (*Ros* 121).[52] After attracting the king himself, she finds herself in a double bind: "he is my King and may constraine me, / Whether I yeelde or not I live defamed" (*Ros* 337–38). Rosamond's guilt, though mitigated by her circumstances, is clearly indicated by Daniel's invoking a modified *de casibus* formula. The tragic heroine muses that the "heavenly powers, / . . . worke our fall, yet make the fault still ours" (*Ros* 412–13). Rosamond is a speaking picture of fallen virtue. Ultimately, her tale illustrates the importance of guarding women's chastity against the temptations of the world.

The fallen Rosamond is more than a foil to Delia's perfection, however, and the story's didactic function should not obscure its local intentions: *Rosamond* subtly reiterates Daniel's bid for the countess's patronage. When Rosamond's ghost first appears, she complains that

> *Shores* wife is grac'd, and passes for a Saint;
> Her Legend justifies her foule attaint;
> Her well-told tale did such compassion finde,
> That she is pass'd, and I am left behinde.
>
> (*Ros* 25–28)

Rosamond appears to "sollicit" the poet "To take this taske . . . / . . . and register my wrong" (*Ros* 33–35). Patron-client relationships are established on two levels, as Rosamond enlists the speaker, who, moved with pity, graciously accepts the commission. The reader (the countess) is thus presented with an ideal image of her poet executing the behest of a woman patron, undertaking the difficult assignment of raising pity for an unchaste royal mistress! So that the poet's ultimate goal is clear, Delia's own role is then spelled out as Rosamond addresses the poet:

> *Delia* may happe to deygne to read our story,
> And offer up her sigh among the rest,
> Whose merit would suffice for both our glorie,
> Whereby thou might'st be grac'd, and I be blest,

That indulgence would profit me the best;
  Such powre she hath by whom thy youth is lead,
  To joy the living and to blesse the dead.

(*Ros* 43–49)

This is another version of the "coattail" ploy by which Daniel linked his name and poetry with Astrophil's in the dedication. By having Rosamond use the pronoun "our" in line 43, Daniel assumes Rosamond's distress and links his fortunes with her story. If the story finds favor with Delia, its teller will also be made famous. Rosamond deems the poet's tale a success—for the time being:

And were it not thy favourable lynes,
Reedified the wracke of my decayes:
. . . .
Fewe in this age had knowne my beauties praise.
  But thus renewd, my fame redeemes some time,
  Till other ages shall neglect thy rime.

(*Ros* 715–21)

The poet has fulfilled his commission, and Rosamond submits the matter now to Delia's judgment:

Tell *Delia* now her sigh may doe me good,
And will her note the frailtie of our blood.
  And if I passe unto those happy banks,
  Then she must have her praise, thy pen her thanks.

(*Ros* 732–35)

In brief, *Rosamond* enables Daniel to assert his own power as a poet while complimenting Pembroke as its ultimate source.

Daniel's poem may have pleased the countess, but it provoked a chorus of responses—imitative, admiring, and mocking—from other poets. Much as *Astrophil and Stella* started the sonneteering vogue, *Rosamond* inaugurated a trend for tragic complaints. Churchyard reissued his *Shore's Wife* as *Churchyard's Challenge* in 1593. In the same year appeared Anthony Chute's *Beauty dishonored: written under the name of Shore's wife*. Like Daniel, Thomas Lodge attached his complaint of Elstred to his sonnet sequence, *Phillis*, which appeared in 1593. Shakespeare, too, issued his sonnets with *A Lovers Complaint* in 1609. One admirer praised Daniel as a champion of womankind, "whose sweete refined muse . . . were sufficient amongst men, to gaine pardon of the sinne to *Rosamond*, pittie to distressed

Cleopatra, and everlasting praise to her loving *Delia*."[53]

Apparently, though, some of Daniel's readers thought he was being too forgiving of Rosamond's sin. Drayton's *Matilda* appeared in 1594, as did his sonnet sequence *Idea*. In the voice of the virtuous Queen Matilda, who became a nun rather than give up her chastity, Drayton rebukes writers for immortalizing fallen women.[54] Perhaps sensitive to such criticism, Daniel, in his 1594 edition of *Delia and Rosamond Augmented*, added some strongly worded passages in which the dying Rosamond acknowledges her sin and warns women to "lock up . . . the treasure of your love" and to avoid pride and ambition. He also reiterated the social dangers of women succumbing to unbridled lust, being careful not to blame Rosamond and thus to jeopardize his sympathetic treatment of her. Instead, he has her condemn the "Bed-brokers," women who have

> The blushing fearefull boldned unto sin,
> The wife made subtile, subtile made the mayd,
> The husband scorn'd, dishonored the kin:
> Parents disgrac'd, children infamous been.
> Confus'd our race, and falsi-fied our blood,
> Whilst fathers sonnes, possess wrong Fathers good.[55]

Depicting the progressive breakdown of the family and the social structure, Daniel illustrates the final, fearful consequences of women's unchastity (so vividly explored by Greville in *Caelica*). He thereby affirms one idealizing feature of the Petrarchan configuration: however humiliating the lover's failure to win the lady, her refusal to succumb to his importunate desire ultimately ensures the stability of the social order. Of course, the countess needed no such lesson, and a careful reader could hardly mistake *Delia* for a seduction attempt, but Daniel was apparently very eager to avoid the label of callow sonneteer unaware of the social implications of his sympathetic treatment of Rosamond.[56]

Giles Fletcher's wild burlesque of the female-voiced complaint also highlights the social reference of this newly fashionable genre. *The rising to the crowne of Richard the third*, written in Richard's voice, appeared in 1593 with his sonnet sequence *Licia, or Poems of Love*. The title page of this volume features woodcuts of domineering women, suggestive in this context of the sonnet mistress and the royal concubine. On the left, a woman with an olive branch stands with her foot on the chest of a prone figure, fashionably dressed, gazing into a mirror. To the right, a woman writing in a book stands upon a fallen

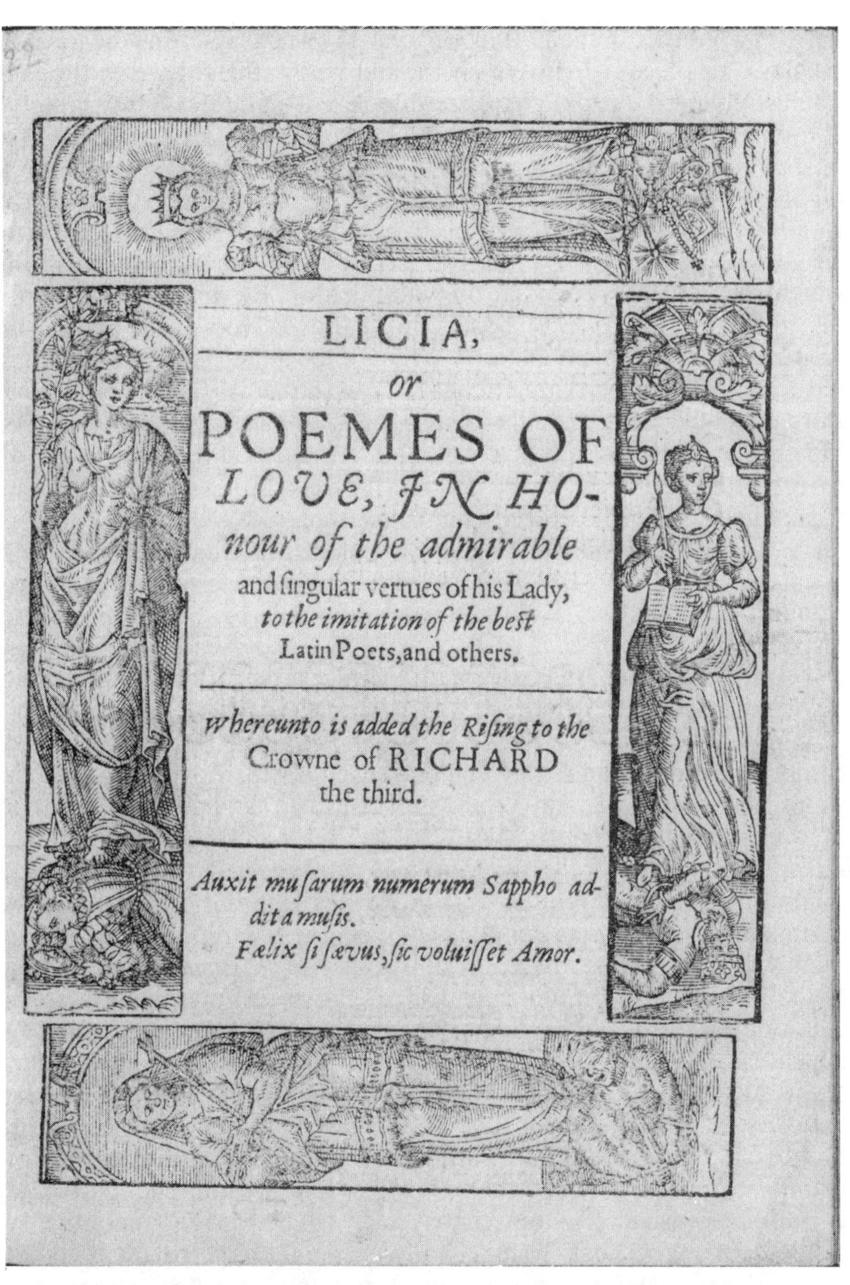

LICIA,

or

POEMES OF

LOVE, IN HO-

nour of the admirable

and ſingular vertues of his Lady,

to the imitation of the beſt

Latin Poets, and others.

Whereunto is added the Riſing to the

Crowne of RICHARD

the third.

Auxit muſarum numerum Sappho ad-

dit a muſis.

Fœlix ſi ſævus, ſic voluiſſet Amor.

Title pages from Giles Fletcher, *Licia, or Poemes of Love* (1593).
Reproduced by permission of The Huntington Library, San Marino, California.

king. Two other female figures, one crowned and one bearing a scepter, are placed sideways above and below the title, like toppled statues, giving the page a haphazard look.[57] The figures are strikingly, if unintentionally, appropriate to Fletcher's iconoclastic volume. His misogynist King Richard speaks like a stand-up comic in a men's nightclub. No wonder Shore's wife fell, he quips; "none can justly wonder, / To see her fall, that useth to lie under."[58] The reference to her sexual posture also alludes to her socially subordinate position, which she violates by her liaison with the king. He mocks the poets of his age who, "Like silly boates in shallow rivers tost" write "of women, and of womens falles, / Who are too light, for to be fortunes balls."[59] Predictably, his Richard raises no pity, for he is a poor storyteller and unrepentantly proud of his ruthless rise to power. As Fletcher's mockery makes clear, Daniel was not the only poet to perceive the gendered power relationships common to the Petrarchan sonnet and the female-voiced complaint. Daniel, however, ably turned these features to his advantage in submitting his poetry to the countess's good will. *Delia* was a subtle, graceful gesture towards the countess of Pembroke, evoking the desired reply, but it was the public response to the *Complaint of Rosamond* that underscored the political and social relevance of Petrarchan themes, particularly that of female dominance in love.

In *Delia* and *The Complaint of Rosamond* alike, Daniel supremely compliments the countess of Pembroke and expresses the dependence of his poetry on her grace. When he praises her as the virtual coauthor of his works, which are "wrought by her hand," he expresses a metaphoric truth, for her presence as an expected reader exerts a shaping force on the sequence. It influences his revisions and his use of imagery; it accounts for his deference to her brother, Sir Philip Sidney, and his choice of a female speaker in *Rosamond.* A reading of the *Delia* volume illuminates Daniel's own self-presentation as an ambitious, skillful, and subtle poet who remains aware of his entire dependence on the favor of a great patron. In *Delia,* he demonstrates his facility with conventional forms and themes while asserting that he is not constrained by them, that his achievement may rank him with Sidney, Spenser, Petrarch, and even Homer. The inclusion of *Rosamond* confirms his moral seriousness and his future ambitions as a tragic historian. Though the system of patronage undoubtedly resulted in much hack writing and servile flattery for the sake of personal gain, *Delia* is a work most certainly enriched, rather than debased, by the demands of the patronage system and the presence of its influential reader, the countess of Pembroke. Enabled by Sidney's growing legend, shaped by the system of clientage, *Delia* in turn seeks, with evident success, to affect the social and literary world in which it is embedded.

Daniel's Philosophy of Poetry, Politics, and the Human Condition

In his 1592 *Delia* volume, Daniel exhibited a faith in the ability of well-wrought poetry to achieve its goals, a faith rewarded in the mutually sustaining relationship with the graceful countess of Pembroke. Daniel continued to mount the ladder of literary achievement, progressing from lyric poetry, tragic complaints, and drama to epic history in verse. From 1595 through 1609, he published installments of *The Civil Wars of England*, in which he pledged to eschew poetic fiction in favor of historical truth, to unfold events "Unintermixt with fictions fantasies. / I versifie the troth, not Poetize."[60] Then the admired and successful poet turned his back on poetry. He never finished his verse epic; instead, he returned to writing prose, "the common tongue of the world,"[61] in *The Collection of the History of England*, which also remained unfinished. In these works, Daniel ponders problems of historical change and relativity and questions his vocation as a poetic historian.[62] More to the point of this study, Daniel's defenses of poetry and learning also express serious doubt about the value of poetry. In *Musophilus* (1599) and *A Defence of Ryme* (1603), Daniel demonstrates that he shares the humanist conviction that learning must result in action and political service, but, like Sidney and Greville, he distrusts the human capacity for active virtue and hence the efficacy of learning and poetry.[63] Daniel's poetic identity, from its auspicious conception in the glow of Sidney's fame, dissipates in self-doubt as he questions the ability of poetry (including fiction and verse) to reform or to outlast the world's moral and social decay.

Musophilus, published in 1599, gestures towards Sidney and Greville both. It is dedicated to the latter, who became Daniel's patron sometime after 1594, obtaining for him a lay holding of a parsonage on the Isle of Wight.[64] Daniel clearly absorbed Greville's influence, and *Musophilus* shows his chameleon-like adaptability to the interests of yet another patron.[65] He now credits Greville with nursing his infant muse (*Mus* 1000–1006), and his poem treats some of Greville's favorite themes: false religion as Babylon ("stately piles we prodigall erect" [*Mus* 298]), the reign of passion, and the decay and confusion of this "rowling world" (*Mus* 677). Even a reference to "*Isis* Asse" recalls *Caelica* 107.[66] The links to Sidney, though indirect, are also apparent. *Musophilus* is, like the *Defence of Poetry*, a project of poetic self-justification, as the dedicatory sonnet to Greville suggests:

Here to revive my selfe my Muse is lead
 . . . t'act her owne part
 Striving to make, her now contemned arte
 As faire t'her selfe as possiblie she can.

Subtitled "a generall defence of learning," the poem, like Sidney's *Defence* and even Gosson's *School of Abuse*, advocates the kind of learning that brings forth virtuous action. The dialogue between Musophilus, lover of the Muses, and Philocosmus, lover of the world, addresses the familiar humanist dilemma embodied by Sidney. The conflict, however, is not as easily resolved as the poem's title would indicate; the debate suggests Daniel's own inner struggle to reconcile the often conflicting values of scholarship and action.[67]

The charges against learning leveled by Philocosmus are familiar and terse: "Men find that action is another thing / Then what they in discoursing papers reade" (*Mus* 486–87). He impugns the masculinity of the man of learning, mocking the false potency of the pen: "This skill wherewith you have so cunning beene, / Unsinewes all your powres, unmans you quite (*Mus* 498–99). Moreover, "Th'unmateriall swellings of your pen / Touch not the spirit that action doth import" (*Mus* 504–5). Musophilus counters that "true knowledge can both speak and do" (*Mus* 836) and affirms that the scholar makes the best statesman, for the "weapons of the mind / Are states best strengths, and kingdoms chiefest grace" (*Mus* 841–42). He asks rhetorically, "Who then holds up the glorie of the state / (Which lettered armes, & armed letters won) / Who shall be fittest to negotiate[?]" (*Mus* 881–83). Within the parenthesis, chiasmus effects a yoking of the scholar and the statesman. The idea and the strategy are both familiar, recalling the poetic efforts to idealize Sidney's achievement and reconcile the contradictions of his life. Daniel, as Musophilus, follows Sidney and Greville in promoting the man of learning as most fit for public governance.

In *The Defence of Ryme*, Daniel also asserts the activist nature of his profession of letters. Like Sidney, he answers one of poetry's detractors, in this case Thomas Campion, who in 1602 published *Observations in the Art of English Poesie*, a treatise attacking rhyme and advocating rules for quantitative, measured verse in English. Daniel rose to the occasion with patriotic aplomb and characteristic self-promotion, making of his *Defence of Ryme* a publication event. It was printed in 1603 with his *Panegyrike Congratulatorie to His Majestie* (King James), a bold poem of admonition, praise, and self-promotion.[68] Of the six additional dedicatory epistles, two were addressed to Sir Thomas Egerton, lord keeper, and Lord Henry Howard, a Privy Council member. The *Defence* itself is a prose epistle addressed to William Herbert, earl of Pembroke. That King James and prominent statesmen were among Daniel's intended readers may account for his use of military analogies, here deployed with a hint of self-mockery resembling Sidney's tone in the *Defence*:

> But yet now, upon the great discovery of these new measures, threatning to overthrow the whole state of Ryme in this kingdom, I must either stand out to defend, or else be forced to forsake my selfe, and give over all. (*DR* 130)

The adversary who impugns poetry wrongs "the honor of the dead . . . the fame of the living" and the "native ornaments" of England (*DR* 153).[69] Such a challenge must be answered, and Daniel rallies poets to repulse the enemy:

> And let no writer in Ryme be any way discouraged in his endevour by this brave allarum, but rather animated to bring up all the best of their powers, and charge with all the strength of nature and industrie upon contempt, that the shew of their reall forces may turne back insolencie into her owne holde. (*DR* 154)

Having an enemy provides poets the opportunity to regain "profit and honor" and to "redeeme backe the good opinion, vanitie and idlenesse have suffered to be wonne from us" (*DR* 154). Thus Daniel presents literary conflicts as matters of national security and personal honor, presenting himself as a bold and forward-looking defender of learning: "It is not the contexture of words, but the effects of Action that gives glory to the times" (*DR* 144).

The question of authority is central to Daniel's *Defence of Ryme*. The volume affirms the king's political authority, establishes Daniel's authority regarding language and poetry, and challenges that of his antagonist, Campion. In support of rhyme, he rejects "the authoritie of Antiquitie" (*DR* 139), proposing as criteria of judgment "Custome that is before all Law, Nature that is above all Arte" (*DR* 131). Despite this seemingly progressive position (adopted in part to counter

Campion's proposal), *A Defence of Ryme* is a fundamentally conservative treatise.[70] Its theme might be paraphrased as "stay the course," and its subject is not only (or not even primarily) poetry but also the practice of statecraft. The twin criteria of custom and nature validate not only the practice of rhyme in English poetry but also the existence and shape of native political institutions (*DR* 145–46). When customs accord with nature, institutions stand fast, but innovation threatens their stability. Taking a politically cautious position, he disavows ambition (associated with innovation), pledging to continue "plodding on the plaine tract I finde beaten by Custome and the Time, contenting me with what I see in use" (*DR* 147). This constitutes a profession of loyalty and submission, for abandoning custom is represented as an explicitly political danger:

> And now in what case were this poore state of words, if in like sorte another tyrant the next yeere should arise and abrogate these lawes and ordaine others cleane contrary according to his humor . . . ? Were it not farre better to holde us fast to our old custome, then to stand thus distracted with uncertaine Lawes, wherein Right shal have as many faces as it pleases Passion to make it. . . . (*DR* 149)

It may come as a surprise to the reader that this *Defence of Ryme* is not simply about the authority of poetic practice; it is a treatise about political authority, condemning tyranny and supporting the customary form of commonwealth. Like the Sidneian right poet, Daniel assumes the mantle of statesman and counselor to the king, responding to concerns raised by James's recent accession. His *Defence* complements the accompanying *Panegyrike*, a poem that praises unity and peace but admonishes the king regarding the dangers of faction and flattery and reminds him of the importance of the social contract. Its final lines carry a strong cautionary tone: "The pedestall whereon thy Greatnesse stands, / Is built of all our hearts, and all our hands."[71] What is customary and common, whether in government or in literary practice, is the source of strength and stability. Together, the *Panegyrike* and the *Defence*, the latter relying on the example of literary practice, warn the king against change and tyranny.[72]

In rejecting the authority of antiquity for that of custom, Daniel exemplifies what Lawrence Manley has identified in the Renaissance as the "increasingly frequent substitution of convention for nature as an adequate test of rectitude and fitness."[73] This growing recognition that social and poetic values and practices are conventional and relative occasions a great deal of anxiety in Daniel and his contemporaries. Francis Bacon warns of the "reign or tyranny of custom" unquestioningly followed and encourages the fostering of good customs.[74] Ben Jonson, like Daniel rejecting the authority of the ancients, wants to retain some standard: "Yet when I name custom, I understand not the vulgar custom . . . [but] the consent of the learned; . . . the consent of the good."[75] For Daniel, the best customs, such as rhyme and constitutional monarchy, are ratified by nature. Potentially, however, custom (characterized by change) may contradict nature (which is unvarying), a conflict Daniel ignores to affirm that "Custome that is before all Law, [and] Nature that is above all Arte" (*DR* 131) both authorize rhyme.

For Daniel, the relation of custom and nature is a complicated system of checks and balances. In distinguishing good from bad custom, nature should play a vital role. Good customs then become established as natural, and custom and nature are in accord. But the system inevitably fails, for human nature, though unchanging, is degraded, thus hardly a fit tool for making such judgments. Human imperfection is manifested in the tyranny of passion, which gives rise to innovation, which the reign (and rein) of customary practice forestalls.[76] Custom is to be followed because change never brings improvement, Daniel proposes in the *Defence*:

> For, let us change never so often, wee can not change man, our imperfections must still runne on with us. . . . [T]herefore let us hold on in the course wee have undertaken, and not still be wandring. Perfection is not the portion of man. (*DR* 147)

Paradoxically, it is custom, not nature, which is here cited as the source of stability. Yet custom is inseparable from—indeed, a product of—imperfect human nature. The cyclical notion of history Daniel espouses in *Philotas* includes a Sidneian affirmation of irremediable human imperfection that binds man to repeat the mistakes of the past:

> These ancient representments of times past
> Tell us that men have, doe, and alwayes runne
> The selfe same line of action, and doe cast
> Their course alike, and nothing can be done,
> Whilst they, their ends, and nature are the same:
> But will be wrought upon the selfe same frame.[77]

The study of history confirmed Daniel's humanist belief in an essential, shared human nature, but his conviction of irremediable human imperfection led him to doubt the value of learning and hence the possibility of progress. In brief, the goodness of established customs is questionable, and the establishment of good customs seemingly impossible.

What, we might ask, is the role of poetry or rhyme in this pathological chain originating in the human psyche and infecting even the institutions of government? Simply, poetry written by unnatural rules is a symptom of the illness, while good poetry can be a force for restraint and stability. Natural rhyme provides "due staies for the minde" (*DR* 134), without which verse "cannot subsist, but runnes wildely on, like a tedious fancie without a close" (*DR* 135). This language of restraint and control is characteristic of Daniel's descriptions of poetic language. At the outset of his *Defence*, he offers this uninspired definition: "All verse is but a frame of wordes confinde within certaine measure" (*DR* 131).

The restraining and ordering function of poetry is also asserted in *Musophilus*, as the threatening tide of ancient errors is brought under control by the power of language:

And do not thou contemne this swelling tide
  And streame of words that now doth rise so hie
  Above the usuall banks, and spreads so wide
  Over the borders of antiquitie:
  Which I confesse comes ever amplifide
  With th'abounding humours that do multiplie
And is with that same hand of happines
  Inlarg'd as vices are out of their bands;
  Yet so, as if let out but to redresse
  And calme, and sway th' affections it commands:
  Which as it stirres, it doth again represse
  And brings in, th'outgone malice that withstands.
Powre above powres, O heavenly *Eloquence*,
  That with the strong reine of commanding words,
  Dost manage, guide, and master th'eminence
  Of mens affections, more then all their swords.

(*Mus* 927–42)[78]

To rein in the flood of abundant humors and freed vices, and to bring his own poetic language back under control, he invokes the divine power of eloquence. Eloquence is not an uplifting or liberating force, however, but a constraining one; Hercules, after all, held his captive audience by chains, not at the end of a kite string. The possibilities for native eloquence Daniel imagines are imperial ones. Who knows, he asks,

whither we may vent
The treasure of our tongue, to what strange shores
This gaine of our best glorie shal be sent,
T'inrich unknowing Nations with our stores?

(*Mus* 957–60)

The "treasure of our tongue" refers to the orator's eloquence here, not to poetry, which is rather the *mother* of eloquence.

That breeds, brings forth, and nourishes this might,
Teaching it in a loose, yet measured course,
With comely motions how to go upright:
And fostring it with bountifull discourse
Adorns it thus in fashions of delight,
What should I say? since it is well approv'd
The speech of heaven . . .

(*Mus* 970–76)

By metaphorizing poetry as a mother who breeds, nourishes, instructs, and dresses the baby eloquence, Daniel, like Sidney, confirms poetry's role as an early teacher and its association with the female world of childhood. Poetry fosters the growth of statesmen who turn language to greater ends: "Or who can tell for what great worke in hand / The greatnes of our stile is now ordain'd? / What powres it shall bring in, what spirits command" (*Mus* 963–65). For Daniel, poetry is instrumental but preliminary to the great work of nation building performed by orators and statesmen.[79]

As in the above passage from *Musophilus*, Daniel acknowledges the platonic beliefs about poetry but almost disavows them: poetry is "well-approv'd / The speech of heaven," but Daniel does not seem to count himself among those who "do with more then humane skils converse" (*Mus* 975-76, 978). His own aims are more modest, even utilitarian. Here he expresses some reservations about the excessive use of rhyme:

> And indeed I have wished there were not that multiplicitie of Rymes as is used by many in Sonets . . . [but] in an eminent spirit whome Nature hath fitted for that mysterie, Ryme is no impediment to his conceit, but rather gives him wings to mount and carries him, not out of his course, but as it were beyond his power to a farre happier flight. (*DR* 137–38)

The shift from first to third person suggests that the experience of flight is not Daniel's and that he considers it something of a mystery. Perhaps Daniel had in mind Sidney's poet, "lifted up with the vigour of his own invention . . . freely ranging only within the zodiac of his own wit" (*Defence* 23–24). But Sidney's Icarus-poet, it must be remembered, descended back to earth, admitting that "our erected wit maketh us know what perfection is, and yet our infected will keepeth us from reaching unto it" (*Defence* 25). Like Sidney, Daniel is more puritanical than platonic. He dwells on the link between poetry and sinfulness, returning to the first-person voice of experience:

> Ryme being farre more laborious then loose measures . . . must needs . . . breed greater and worthier effects in our language. So that if our [poetic] labours have wrought out a manumission from bondage [of sin], and that wee goe at libertie, notwithstanding these ties [of rhyme], wee are no longer the slaves of Ryme, but we make it a most excellent instrument to serve us. (*DR* 138)

(Campion had charged that rhyme was vulgar and easy, hence Daniel's emphasis on its difficulty.)[80] In this appropriately complex and labored passage, Daniel proposes that rhyme, diligently practiced, has a penitential, even salvific effect. The mastery of poetry is akin to a moral and religious victory over sin. The particular efficacy of sonnets is their concise and demanding form, which serves to confine otherwise boundless passion. Daniel continues the religious metaphor:

> For the body of our imagination, being as an unformed *Chaos* without fashion [until] . . . by the divine power of the spirit it be wrought into an Orbe of order and forme, is it not more pleasing to Nature, that desires a certaintie . . . to have these clozes, rather than, not to know where to end . . . especially seeing our passions are often without measure. . . . Besides, is it not most delightfull to see much excellently ordred in a small roome. . . . And these limited proportions, and rests of Stanzas: consisting of 6. 7. or 8. lines are of that happines, both for the disposition of the matter, the apt planting the sentence where it may best stand to hit, the certaine close of delight . . . as neither the Greekes or Latines ever attained unto. For their boundlesse running on, often so confounds the Reader [who becomes lost in uncertainty]. (*DR* 138–39)

This passage, beginning and ending in chaos, centers on the primary satisfaction provided by the sonnet, namely, the "apt planting [of] the sentence" and the attendant delight (presumably at conveying this moral wisdom), all enabled by the sonnet's "proportions" and by its rhyme scheme.

Ultimately, Daniel favors verse that sounds most natural, that is, most like prose. He finds tiresome "those continuall cadences of couplets used in long and continued Poems" (155), preferring rhymed, enjambed lines that employ a kind of *sprezzatura*, hiding their own artistry:

> Besides, me thinkes sometimes, to beguile the eare, with a running out, and passing over the Ryme, as no bound to stay us in the line where the violence of the matter will breake thorow, is rather gracefull then otherwise. Wherein I finde my *Homer-Lucan*, as if he gloried to seeme to have no bounds, albeit hee were confined within his measures, to be in my conceipt most happy. (*DR* 156)

The reader of such verse, unaware of the rhyme, enjoys a vicarious breaking of boundaries, a safe indulgence of passion. Another advantage of unobtrusive rhyme is that one who dislikes poetry or rhyme "may passe it over without taking notice thereof, and please themselves with a well-measured Prose" (*DR* 156). In some cases, Daniel continues, rhyme should be dispensed with altogether: "I thinke a Tragedie would indeede best comporte with a blank Verse, and dispence with Ryme, saving in the *Chorus* or where a sentence shall require a couplet" (*DR* 156). The main purpose of rhyme, apparently, is to highlight a moral lesson, and even then it threatens to become superfluous; the dramatic action, not the marginal verse of a chorus, best conveys the lessons of tragedy. Though custom has ratified the practice of rhyme, custom and nature together favor prose, which Daniel deemed "the common tongue of the world."

Overwhelmed by the weakness and vanity of human nature and the ever-shifting criterion of custom, Daniel concludes his treatise on poetry with an attitude of repentance and submission to the inevitability of change. Like Sidney, who acknowledged himself "sick among the rest" with the "common infection grown among the most part of writers" (*Defence* 72), Daniel confesses the error of his ways as a poet:

> But the greatest hinderer to our proceedings, and the reformation of our errours, is this Selfe-love, whereunto we Versifiers are ever noted to be especially subject; a disease of all other, the most dangerous, and incurable . . . for which there is no cure, but onely by a spirituall remedy . . . this opinion of our sufficiencie makes so great a cracke in our judgement, as it wil hardly ever holde any thing of worth. . . . (*DR* 157)

Sidney similarly observed that "self-love is better than any gilding to make that seem gorgeous wherein ourselves be parties" (*Defence* 17), admitting the impossibility of being objective and banishing self-deceiving ideas of our own merit. Besides pride and self-love, Daniel confesses to the affected and idiosyncratic use of language. Such singularity and novelty assist the rapid shifting of custom, which in Daniel's scheme should ensure continuity. When custom continually changes, it is inevitably at odds with the "Nature that is above all Art," and rules become impossible to establish. Take the case of feminine rhyme, which Daniel used freely in his first verses but systematically purged from his revisions; "ever since I was warned of that deformitie . . . I have alwayes so avoyded it . . . holding feminine Rymes to be fittest for Ditties" (*DR* 156–57). Even this standard dissolves, however, "for indeed there is no right in these things that are continually in a wandring motion, carried with the violence of our uncertaine likings, being but onely the time that gives them their power" (*DR* 157).[81] Daniel is uncomfortable with the fact that, over time, poetic practice pressures conventions. Moreover, time is no ally of poets. Even as Daniel writes, the language is constantly being invaded by foreign words established as "Free-denizens" without a parliament (*DR* 158), a political metaphor appropriate in this watershed year of 1603. In the concluding sentence of his *Defence*, Daniel expresses an anxious despair about the ravages of time on his own works, whose fate is inextricably connected with the fortunes of the larger social and political order they seek to effect:

> But this is but a Character of that perpetuall revolution which wee see to be in all things that never remaine the same, and we must heerein be content to submit our selves to the law of time, which in few yeeres wil make al that, for which we now contend, *Nothing*. (*DR* 158)

Retreating from the relative confidence of *Delia* and *Rosamond*, Daniel in *The Defence of Ryme* submits his work to "the law of time," an apocalyptic force certain to destroy it. Mutability, the final law of nature, will prevail in the end, bringing all to nought. The breathless nihilism of this passage claims everything subject to change and decay, from Delia's fragile beauty to political institutions and social customs, even works of learning and poetry.

5
Spenser's *Complaints*, *Astrophel*, and the Sidney Legend

Spenser and Sidney

The Argument to the October Eclogue of *The Shepheardes Calender* refers to its author's "booke called the English Poete, which booke being lately come to my hands, I mynde also by Gods grace upon further advisement to publish." The book promises a discourse of

> so worthy and commendable an arte: or rather no arte, but a divine gift and heavenly instinct not to bee gotten by laboure and learning, but adorned with both; and poured into the witte by a certain [enthusiasm] and celestiall inspiration.[1]

William Webbe, admirer of Spenser and author of *A Discourse of English Poetrie* (1586), believed the work to be "in ye close cystodye of certaine his freends" and longed to see it published.[2] Unfortunately, *The English Poet*, if it ever existed, is now lost. But it is exciting to suppose that Spenser may have been composing a treatise on poetry at about the same time Sidney was writing or contemplating his own *Defence of Poetry*. More exciting yet is to imagine the discussions at Leicester House during the years Sidney and Spenser could have been in contact there—the period preceding the 1579 publication of *The Shepheardes Calender*, which Spenser dedicated to Sidney, and ending with Spenser's departure for Ireland in 1580.[3] We can glean from Spenser's correspondence with Gabriel Harvey that he considered himself "in some use of familiarity" with Sidney and

Dyer, who, as he reports to Harvey, have "drawen me to their faction."[4] He refers to their experiments in quantitative verse and suggests in a previous letter his own collaboration therein:

> I would hartily wish, you would either send me the Rules and Precepts of Arte, which you observe in Quantities, or else followe mine, that *M. Philip Sidney* gave me, being the very same which *M. Drant* devised, but enlarged with *M. Sidneys* own judgement, and augmented with my Observations, that we might both accorde. . . .[5]

In another letter, Spenser reports the most recent gossip of the literary world:

> Newe Bookes I heare of none, but only of one, that writing a certaine Booke, called *The Schoole of Abuse*, and dedicating it to Maister *Sidney*, was for hys labor scorned: if at leaste it be in the goodnesse of that nature to scorne. Suche follie is it, not to regarde aforehande the inclination and qualitie of him, to whome wee dedicate oure Bookes.[6]

Spenser's judgment that Gosson is a fool for not choosing his dedicatee more carefully is exactly what one would expect of a writer who was also dependent upon the system of patronage but determined to use it with more discretion. His remark about Sidney's good nature, however, bespeaks admiration rather than easy intimacy.

Even in the absence of corroborating biographical evidence, there is no reason to doubt Spenser's claim that Sidney was a formative influence. In his dedication of *The Ruines of Time* to Sidney's sister, the countess of Pembroke, he calls him "the hope of all learned men, and the Patron of my young *Muses*." In a prefatory sonnet to *The Faerie Queene* also addressed to Pembroke, he calls Sidney "that most Heroicke spirit. . . . Who first my Muse did lift out of the flore, / To sing his sweet delights in lowlie laies." In the October eclogue of *The Shepheardes Calendar*, Piers may be a figure of Sidney as a patron, for he urges Cuddie, "Lyft up thy selfe out of the lowly dust: / And sing of bloody Mars, of wars, of guists" (ll. 38–39) and argues that love is a lofty and ennobling subject for poetry (ll. 91–96).[7] He also promises Cuddie a baby kid once his goat gives birth (ll. 119–20), a reward appropriate to pastoral. More than one critic has suggested that Calidore, the knight of courtesy in book 6 of *The Faerie Queene*, may be modeled after Sidney.[8] Until panegyric and pastoral allegory yield their motives, however, we will never know how truly they testify to an association between the two poets.

At the very least, Spenser was confronted with Sidney's inescapable priority as a poet and patron. Beyond that, his poetic tributes to Sidney in *The Teares of the Muses*, *The Ruines of Time*, and the pastoral elegy *Astrophel* participate in the creation and, more importantly, the contestation of Sidney's legendary image. In these works, Sidney is present in his various guises of poet and warrior, lover of learning and scion of a renowned family of patrons. In *The Teares of the Muses* (1591), Spenser advocates Sidneian ideals for right poesy, the "nurse of vertue" (l. 457), and both Erato, muse of love poetry, and Urania, muse of divine poetry, suggest Sidney. In *The Ruines of Time,* Sidney is eternized in the harp of Philisides, a knight borne to heaven on a winged steed, and in a golden ark bearing the ashes of the phoenix. Yet in *Astrophel*, published nine years after Sidney's death, no apotheosis celebrates Sidney's divinity. Instead, Spenser rejects the values celebrated in the myth of Sidney as the soldier-scholar reconciling poetry and heroic action, and he questions the humanist ideal of poetry as an incentive to virtuous action. Disillusioned with the myth of Sidney and its associated humanist agenda, Spenser turns in his later works from public concerns to assert the priority of private experience. This move is evident in the *Amoretti* sonnets, Spenser's critique of Petrarchan loving associated with *Astrophil and Stella.* In his volume, Spenser reforms the traditions of courtly love poetry to articulate Protestant ideals of married love, a radical departure from Sidney's practice that paradoxically confirms the prior poet's ideals for the right use of poetry.

Sidneian Poetics and Spenser's *Complaints*

The Teares of the Muses and *The Ruines of Time*, published in the *Complaints* volume of 1591, reveal Spenser's admiration for Sidney and his shared view of poetry's purpose and limitations. *Teares of the Muses* may even be an earlier work, for its complaints about the woeful state of poetry and patronage echo the commonplace criticisms by Sidney and Gosson, who in 1579–80 groused that military heroism was on the decline, opportunity scarce, and learning scorned.[9] Specifically, Spenser's representation of Erato and Urania, the muses of love poetry and divine poetry, may owe something to Sidney. In his *Defence of Poetry,* Sidney observed with dismay the failure of love poetry to achieve its divine potential, "singing the praises of the immortal beauty: the immortal goodness of that God who giveth us hands to write and wits to conceive." He lamented that love poets, praising mortal beauties, "miss the right use of the material point of poesy" (*Defence* 69–70). Spenser's Erato also laments that love, divine in origin ("pure and spotles . . . sprong / Out of th'Almighties bosome" [*TM* 388–89]), is in decline, abused by lewd lovers and bad poets. She complains that she has been "put from practise of my kindlie skill, / Banisht by those that Love with leawdnes fill" (*TM* 383–84) and that poets merely "rime at riot, and doo rage in love; / Yet little wote what doth thereto behove" (*TM* 395–96), missing the proper end of poetry. Imagining the prelapsarian love poet, Spenser brings Sidney to mind. Erato's initial address to the half-divine love poets, "Ye gentle Spirits breathing from above" (*TM* 362), echoes the beginning of the narrator's description of Sidney in *The Ruines of Time* as a "Most gentle spirite breathed from above, / Out of the bosome of the makers blis" (*RT* 281–82). Whether the repeated line is intentional or not, the implied compliment to Sidney as a heavenly poet, distinct from lewd rhymers, remains.[10]

Urania, muse of religious poetry, expresses Spenser's aspiration towards divine poetry, a desire tethered by a profound sense of limitation. She describes the "noyous pestilence, / That mortall mindes doth inwardly infect / With love of blindness and of ignorance" (*TM* 483–85). Knowledge, however, offers an escape from this mire:

> By knowledge wee do learne our selves to knowe,
> And what to man, and what to God wee owe.
>
> From hence wee mount aloft unto the skie.
>
> . . . .
>
> And there with humble minde and high insight,
> Th'eternall Makers majestie wee viewe.
>
> (*TM* 503–12)

This happiness is available to all who "embrace / The precepts of my heavenlie discipline" (*TM* 517–18). Here, Spenser seems to share Sidney's optimism that knowledge can "lift up the mind from the dungeon of the body to the enjoying his own divine essence" (*Defence* 28). But Sidney, "finding [him]self sick among the rest" of the poets (*Defence* 72), was acutely aware that his erected wit was tethered to an infected will. Astrophil, we recall, is, in the final sonnet, imprisoned in a dungeon, his soul unable to take flight. For Spenser, too, the Neoplatonic progression is interrupted as Urania flees to the heavens: "So loathing earth, I looke up to the sky, / And being driven hence I thether fly. / Thence I behold the miserie of men" (*TM* 527–29) who, lacking wisdom, remain like "brute beasts" (531). By mounting to the heavens, Urania cruelly mocks and frustrates men's aspirations to escape the sinful human condition.[11]

Poetic aspiration and limitation are treated with a mixture of irony and seriousness in *The Ruines of Time*, a work dedicated to the countess of Pembroke. Spenser ventriloquizes a female persona, Verlame, who laments for her fallen city, echoing the lament over the fall of Babylon in Revelation 18, and mourns the deceased Dudleys. Obviously, Verlame's associations with Rome problematize her eulogies of Leicester and Sidney, Protestant men of letters. Carl Rasmussen argues that her defense of poetry's immortalizing power should be seen as morally abhorrent and a mark of her egocentric pride.[12] In my reading, however, Verlame is an image of the poet in a fallen world, vain and self-interested but occasionally inspired to something like right poesy.[13] Her voluble complaint ironically testifies to the absence of poetry celebrating heroic deeds (or moralizing evil ones). Her poetry is skilless, repetitive, and almost comically naive about the business of commemorating a subject. Addressing Leicester's last wife, Anne Russell, Verlame promises:

> Thy Lord shall never die, the whiles this verse
> Shall live, and surely it shall live for ever:
> For ever it shall live, and shall rehearse
> His worthie praise, and vertues dying never,
> Though death his soule doo from his bodie sever.
> And thou thy selfe herein shalt also live;
> Such grace the heavens doo to my verses give.
>
> (*RT* 253–59)

Of the earl of Bedford, she claims, "Ne shall his sister, ne thy father die" (*RT* 260); of Sidney's mother, she promises, "Ne may I let thy husbands sister die" (*RT* 274).[14] Verlame continues along the family tree, repeating her empty promise, finally arriving at Sidney himself.

Verlame's praise of Sidney is keyed to a higher note, expressing a poet's yearning for divine subject matter. She is moved with admiration and wonder for the "Most gentle spirit breathed from above" (*RT* 281). Sidney resembles not only the divine love poet whom Erato addresses in *Teares of the Muses* but also the muse of religious poetry who fled from earth to heaven. Like Urania, he,

> Loathing this sinfull earth and earthlie slime,
> Fled backe too soone unto his native place.

> Too soone for all that did his love embrace,
> Too soone for all this wretched world, whom he
> Robd of all right and true nobilitie.
>
> (*RT* 290–94)

Verlame prays to him, "[D]oo thou my humble spirite raise, / And into me that sacred breath inspire, / . . . Then will I sing" (*RT* 313–16). She becomes, for the moment, an aspiring divine poet, gifted with the sight of Sidney "mongst that blessed throng, / Of heavenlie Poets and Heroes strong" (*RT* 341).[15]

The apotheosis of Sidney as a veritable Christ figure raises some problems, however. The parallel seems natural: like Christ, Sidney died young (just before reaching the significant age of thirty-three); he achieved nothing great, for his nature and kingdom were not of this world. Like Christ, Sidney presents to God

> His bodie, as a spotles sacrifise;
> And chose, that guiltie hands of enemies
> Should powre forth th'offring of his guiltles blood:
> So life exchanging for his countries good.
>
> (*RT* 298–301)

Many of Sidney's elegists freely adapted the convention that the subject's death atones for the sins of his friends and countrymen, making their subject explicitly Christlike.[16] But Verlame's vision of Sidney as Christ borders on idolatry.[17] Perhaps by having a narrator with definite Romish associations apotheosize Sidney, Spenser criticizes excessive poetic grieving for Sidney as a form of idolatry.

Following this visionary moment, Verlame undertakes a defense of poetry's immortalizing power that reflects primarily her own worldly concerns and further distances her from the ideal of right poesy.[18] For Verlame, poetry is a way to buy fame for oneself. Sidney is immortal "through excellent desart,"

> But such as neither of themselves can sing,
> Nor yet are sung of others for reward,
> Die in obscure oblivion. . . .
> . . . .
> Because they living, cared not to cherishe
> No gentle wits, through pride or covetize,
> Which might their names for ever memorize.

> Provide therefore (ye Princes) whilst ye live,
> That of the *Muses* ye may friended bee.
>
> (*RT* 343–66)

That poetry should celebrate heroic deeds in order to inculcate virtue is not part of Verlame's poetics. Not only are her concerns material rather than moral, but her imagination is quite literal; she takes poetry's immortalizing power to mean it can break the sevenfold gates of hell and raise forgotten souls from the "horrid house of sad *Proserpina*" (*RT* 373).[19] Read ironically, as it must be, Verlame's praise resembles Sidney's mockery of poets' claims to immortalize their subjects. In the peroration of his *Defence*, he conjures the reader to believe poets

> when they tell you they will make you immortal by their verses. Thus doing, your name shall flourish in the printers' shops . . . you shall be most fair, most rich, most wise, most all, you shall dwell upon superlatives . . . your soul shall be placed with Dante's Beatrice, or Virgil's Anchises. (*Defence* 75)

But he curses those who scorn poetry "that while you live, you live in love, and never get favour for lacking skill of a sonnet; and when you die, your memory die from the earth for want of an epitaph" (*Defence* 75). Verlame makes a similar pronouncement: "O let the man, of whom the Muse is scorned, / Nor alive, nor dead be of the Muse adorned" (*RT* 454–55). Using personae who elevate the poet's eternizing function as his *raison d'être*, Sidney and Spenser both mock human vanity and the misplaced ambitions of the would-be divine poet. Verlame, for example, remarking the vanity of princes who build stone monuments to their own memory, asks, "For how can mortall immortalitie give?" (*RT* 413), unaware that this is a question one might just as well ask of a poem as a pyramid.

Though Verlame's lament dominates the poem, she disappears two-thirds of the way through, and it is the narrator who witnesses the pageants that apotheosize Sidney. Though he is a foil for Verlame, the naive narrator is not exactly an ideal poet or reader.[20] He finds Verlame's speech incomprehensible, its meaning "above my slender reasons reach" (*RT* 487); her departure and all the visions strike him equally with grief and loss. In that, he might well express Spenser's mute despair at returning to England to find all the great Protestant statesmen dead and Burghley's faction ascendant.[21] But as the poem moves into the series of visions, the words and empty promises of

Verlame's discourse are replaced by vivid (if sometimes inscrutable) "speaking pictures," including the harp, the ark, the knight, and a wooden coffer. These fail to delight the sorrowing narrator; indeed, they only increase his grief. By the end of the poem, however, he has learned to "loath this drosse of sinfull worlds desire" (*RT* 686), a lesson appropriate for an elegy but surely inadequate, given the spectacular allegorical visions the narrator has witnessed. Not an ambitious or especially skillful poet, he pays his "last duties of this broken verse, / Broken with sighes" and adorned with "some few silver dropping teares" (*RT* 678–79, 683) for eloquence. Into the void left by Sidney's death step the proud and persuasive Verlame and the humble, silent narrator-poet. Both momentarily approximate, but never achieve, right poesy, Verlame by her wonder at Sidney's immortal image, the narrator by his moral verse, vivid yet unadorned.

When Verlame rebukes the careless and idle Colin Clout—"Wake shepheards boy, at length awake for shame" (*RT* 231)—she probably represents those who likewise urged Spenser to the task of memorializing his early patrons. In dedicating *The Ruines of Time* to the countess of Pembroke, Spenser aims to pacify those who upbraid him "for that I have not shewed anie thankefull remembrance towards him or any of them; but suffer their names to sleep in silence and forgetfulnesse" (*Yale Edition*, 230). Published shortly after Spenser's return to England, *The Ruines of Time* has been deemed a merely dutiful and hastily assembled tribute to Sidney and Leicester.[22] On the contrary, it is a complex and problematic work, its two inadequate poet-figures expressing Spenser's own unresolved view of Sidney and his uncertainty about the proper way to commemorate him.

Astrophel and Sidney's Heroic Image

By the time Spenser published *Astrophel* in 1595, fully nine years after Sidney's death, his vision of Sidney was less equivocal but darker. Traditionally, the elegy on the shepherd who sings Stella's praises, then ventures forth to perform brave deeds in her service, who is killed in battle and finally transformed into a flower, has been seen as Spenser's tribute to Sidney the poet. Raphael Falco has argued that Spenser led the later elegists in commemorating Sidney as a poet rather than as a patron or soldier.[23] *Astrophel* does mark an important moment in the construction of the Sidney legend, but it is a negative one. The poem celebrates neither the poet nor the military hero; it focuses on the image of the shepherd-turned-warrior and the disturbing intrusion of violence into the pastoral world, as in book 6 of *The Faerie Queene*. Indeed, the poem's deeply ambivalent attitude towards Sidney is hard to overlook. Accordingly, Falco's more recent discussion of *Astrophel* modifies his earlier view; he argues that Spenser acknowledges Sidney's priority but condemns his amateurish poetry, deeming Sidney a failure in order to fashion his own identity as a successful poet.[24] Peter Sacks has argued that, for Spenser, Astrophel's pursuit of violence is a betrayal of language and poetry.[25] I agree with these critics that Spenser holds a deeply ambivalent attitude towards his precursor, but I deny that the elegy marks Spenser's access of confidence in his own art or that it defends poetry. Rather, in *Astrophel*, he questions the values celebrated in the myth of Sidney as the shepherd-knight, criticizes poets for perpetuating that ideal, and expresses despair at the failure of the humanist poetics he and Sidney embraced, namely, the belief that poetry enabled virtuous action.[26]

Sidney was hailed by the elegist John Phillips as the "flower of curtesie"; Spenser's Astrophel is likewise a model of courtesy and grace: "He grew up fast in goodnesse and in grace, / And doubly faire wox both in mynd and face," qualities he augments "With gentle usage and demeanure myld: / That all mens hearts with secret ravishment / He stole away, and weetingly beguyld" (*As* 17–18; 20–22). Nearly identical words describe the *Faerie Queene*'s Calidore, of "manners mylde" and "comely guize" (*FQ* 6.1.2); his "every art and deed, that he did say, / Was like enchantment, that through both the eyes, / And both the eares did steale the hart away" (*FQ* 6.2.3). Such verbal echoes do tempt one to assume that Spenser associated Calidore with Astrophel and hence with Sidney. But while Calidore only visits the pastoral world, neglecting his quest, Astrophel belongs to that world; he is a gentle, merry shepherd who composes "layes of love" (*As* 35) exclusively for Stella:

> To her he vowd the service of his daies,
> On her he spent the riches of his wit:
> For her he made hymnes of immortall praise,
> Of onely her he sung, he thought, he writ.
> Her, and but her of love he worthie deemed,
> For all the rest but litle he esteemed.
>
> (*As* 61–66)

All in all, this is a pretty fair representation of Astrophil's exclusive, obsessive love for Stella; Spenser even includes a Sidneian pun on "rich" (*As* 62) and lightly mocks the idolatry of the lover's "hymns of immortal praise."[27] But just as Sidney esteemed political and military action highly, Astrophel is not content to remain a piping shepherd; his love spurs him to action:

> Ne her with ydle words alone he wowed,
> And verses vaine (yet verses are not vaine)
> But with brave deeds to her sole service vowed,
> And bold atchievements her did entertaine.
> For both in deeds and words he nourtred was,
> Both wise and hardie (too hardie alas).
>
> (*As* 67–72)

Spenser shared with Sidney the belief that poetry could spur virtuous actions, bridging the gap between "ydle words" and truly "brave deeds." As he wrote in the letter to Ralegh prefacing *The Faerie Queene*, he intended his work "to fashion a gentleman or noble person in vertuous and gentle discipline," teaching not by rule but by vivid example. In this passage, however, the narrator's endorsement of activist poetics is less than ringing. Despite the parenthetical correction, "yet verses are not vaine" (*As* 68), the vanity of poetry is suggested and reinforced by the echo.[28] The verses are then syntactically superseded by "brave deeds" and "bold atchievements," seeming to confirm the view that the end of all learning ("words") is virtuous action ("deeds"). But these brave deeds are still only words, vows yet to be acted upon, and the bold achievements are only entertaining tilting games. The thrust of Sidney's eloquent defense is relegated to a weak parenthetical protest, a negative assertion: "yet verses are not vaine." Most critics find that Spenser criticizes Sidney's abandonment of poetic pursuits for military ones.[29] In fact, what the narrator questions is humanist poetics itself, the efficacy and value of poetry as a spur to heroic action. Astrophel's deeds are "too hardie"—foolhardy rather than noble.

Thus, not only Astrophel's poetry but also his heroic activity is called into question by the narrator, as his overeager shepherd leaves the idyllic pastoral world and ventures into the world of history. As soon as Spenser details his skills—"In wrestling nimble, and in renning swift, / In shooting steddie, and in swimming strong: / Well made to strike, to throw, to leape, to lift" (*As* 73–75)—we are in the world of the young courtier-in-training.[30] Astrophel even resembles the naive Redcrosse knight in book 1 of *The Faerie Queene*:

Such skill matcht with such courage as he had,
Did prick him foorth with proud desire of praise:
To seek abroad, of daunger nought y'drad,
His mistresse name, and his owne fame to raise.
What needeth perill to be sought abroad,
Since round about us, it doth make aboad?

(*As* 85–90)

Seeking peril "abroad" on one level simply means "outside Arcadia," but in the chivalric context Spenser also creates, it must surely allude as well to Sidney's appointment in Flushing. The narrator's question ("What needeth perill to be sought abroad"[?]) implies that Astrophel's mission is unwise and surely unnecessary. Given the wider context of this reference, who is the mistress whose name he seeks to raise, along with his own fame? No longer merely the pastoral nymph, Stella, she also signifies Sidney's ultimate mistress, the queen.

As Astrophel moves from the world of innocent pastoral piping to a "forest wide, and waste" (*As* 93), the battlefield of Zutphen, the poem darkens further. In his encounter with the enemy forces, Astrophel resembles one of Spenser's battling knights, not unambiguously good, for he uses "welwoven toyles and subtil traines" to "enwrap" (*As* 97–98) the enemy, and he plunges "greedily" into battle (*As* 104). A bloodthirsty warrior, "His care was all how he them all might kill, / That none might scape" (*As* 109–10). One might think of the merciless Talus, Artegall's deputy (*FQ* 5). Finally, in a fight that rings with the alliterative clashing of swords, he is wounded in the thigh ("So deadly was the dint and deep the wound" [*As* 121]) by an unambiguously bad Spaniard, a "cruell beast of most accursed brood" (*As* 116) who recalls one of Error's offspring (*FQ* 1.1.15–16) or even the Blatant Beast, "begot of foule *Echidna*" (*FQ* 6.6.9). Though the battle becomes a climactic encounter with the forces of evil, Spenser resists any temptation to exalt Sidney as a Christian knight or to deify him. (After all, he loses the battle.) Instead, bitterness is evident in the transformation his poem effects of the "sclender swaine" of "comely shape," "doubly faire . . . both in mynd and face" (*As* 15–18) into the "wretched boy the shape of dreryhead" (*As* 133), bleeding alone on the battlefield of Zutphen, "Unpitied, unplaynd, of foe or frend" (*As* 136). Finally, Astrophel dies: "His wasted life her weary lodge forwent" (*As* 174), "wasted" suggesting not only ravaged or diminished in strength but possibly squandered.[31] In refusing to whitewash the harsh reality of Sidney's death and emphasizing the vast distance between the gentle, happy shepherd piping lays of love and the figure on the battlefield "with crudled blood and filthie gore deformed" (*As* 152), *Astrophel* positively resists association with the idealizing Sidney myth. He questions as well the very foundation of Sidney's poetics, the belief that poetry promotes virtuous action.

Senseless carnage also dogs Calidore, a similarly ambiguous and hapless figure of a shepherd-knight. Chasing the Blatant Beast from the court, he "forced him to flie" right into the shepherds' fields and cots (*FQ* 6.9.3–5). Thus, he is responsible for its rampages and for the violations of courtesy that culminate with the brutal slaying of Meliboe and his wife, the captain, and other innocents. Calidore even contributes to the carnage, slaying and hewing bodies until the carcasses pile up (*FQ* 6.11.46–47, 49). Not only that, but Calidore's presence is positively inimical to poetry; his clumsy intrusion causes Colin's vision of his lady and the graces to vanish (*FQ* 6.10.20). Calidore is sorry that "to thy blisse I made this luckelesse breach, / As now the author of thy bale to be, / Thus to bereave thy loves deare sight from thee" (*FQ* 6.10.29)—an apology he owes to all the inhabitants of Meliboe's world. As he scattered the ordered dance of the graces, so his presence brings chaos and destruction to all the land, a wrong no gracious apology could ever right. Both Astrophel and Calidore behave heedlessly, and their attempts at heroic action end in violence for which they are in part responsible. Calidore may not be an image of Sidney, strictly speaking, but he and Astrophel demonstrate how easily those of exemplary virtue are challenged—and often compromised—by action in the world, however well intentioned.[32]

In *Astrophel*, Spenser seems willfully perverse in undertaking a long-overdue elegy of Sidney and then flaunting so many of its conventions: abandoning the pastoral setting for a gory battlefield, refusing to glorify Sidney's death or to deify him, indeed eschewing consolation altogether, which he leaves to "Clorinda" in the succeeding elegy. Clearly, he was not aiming to flatter or seek the favor of Sidney's widow, Frances Walsingham, now countess of Essex. He even warns in his proem that his "rudely dight" rhymes are "Made not to please the living but the dead" (*As* Pr. 16). Rather, he invokes his fellow poets, whom he addresses in the proem: "Hearken ye gentle shepheards to my song, / And place my dolefull plaint your plaints emong. / To you alone I sing" (*As* Pr. 6–8). The act of contributing a song signals his participation in their communal poetic mourning. However, his imperative tone implies a distinction from them, and his aloneness, an isolation or superiority.[33]

Heading a volume of elegies, five (of seven) of which employ pastoral conventions to praise and commemorate Sidney, *Astrophel* invites a questioning of that very poetic enterprise.[34] Interrupting his gruesome account of Sidney's wounding, he asks his "shepheard peares" "Ah where were ye, when he of you had need, / To stop his wound that wondrously did bleed?" (*As* 127, 131–32). "Piping in Arcadia" is, of course, the answer, but the larger question concerns the relation—and relevance—of that Arcadian world of poetry to the dirty world of history. Spenser treats with some cynicism the response of the poets to the "pitteous spectacle" of Astrophel's death:

And every one did make exceeding mone,
With inward anguish and great griefe opprest:
And every one did weep and waile, and mone,
And meanes deviz'd to shew his sorrow best.
That from that houre since first on grassie greene,
Shepheards kept sheep, was not like mourning seen.

(*As* 205–10)

In the year following Sidney's death alone, the universities of Oxford and Cambridge issued three volumes of academic memorials, several individual elegies appeared, and Thomas Lant published a pictorial account of the funeral procession. Much of this work, dedicated to members of the Protestant faction at court, was surely politically motivated.[35] With his shepherds striving to outdo each other in their grieving, Spenser may allude to this poetic outpouring. He not simply disdains this rivalry but altogether avoids it by postponing his elegy for several years. Moreover, he remains aloof from Stella's grief, declining even to describe it:

The rest of her impatient regret,
And piteous mone the which she for him made:
No toong can tell, nor any forth can set,
But he whose heart like sorrow did invade.

(*As* 169–72)

Seeming to maintain a respectful emotional distance in a poem dedicated, after all, to Sidney's widow, he implies, however, that he cannot tell the "piteous mone" because he does not feel the sorrow, not because his poetry is inadequate. Like Verlame in *The Ruines of Time*, the fellow poets pour forth their plaints; like the narrator who listens to her, the speaker of *Astrophel* is a numb and inarticulate observer of others' woe. He remains outside the process of poetic lamentation, its detached observer and critic.

The speaker of *Astrophel* leaves to "Clorinda," his companion poet, the conventional song of consolation. He does not express personal grief, and his poem eschews the major conventions and rhetorical strategies of the elegy. We can only speculate why. It may be that Spenser considers excessive lamentation, like that expressed by Verlame and the other elegists, inappropriate for a Christian. Perhaps, like Colin Clout peeved at Calidore's intrusion, he would much rather be piping his lady's praises, not writing an elegy for an overrated hero. Perhaps, after seven years, fresh grief for Sidney would seem insincere. Yet in *Prothalamion* (1596), Spenser still expresses grief and loss at the sight of Leicester House:

> Where oft I gayned giftes and goodly grace
> Of that great Lord, which therein wont to dwell,
> Whose want too well, now feeles my freendles case:
> But Ah here fits not well
> Olde woes . . . to tell
>
> (*Pro* 138–42)

Another factor may be his desire to distinguish himself from those poets who have misused poetry to create and enshrine an image of questionable moral value or who have capitalized on Sidney's death for their own ends—those Verlames and grieving, competing shepherd-poets.

Richard Peterson has objected that the interpretation of *Astrophel* as a critique of Sidney ignores Spenser's assimilation of Sidney to the Adonis myth, surely a high compliment and a graceful eternizing gesture.[36] History, he observes, handed Spenser "an allegorist's dream" in the tragic demise of Sidney; "life has cruelly imitated art, and the myth of Adonis has been reenacted with Sidney's blood." Like Adonis, Sidney is gored in the thigh by a cruel beast, bleeds to death, and is discovered and lamented by his beloved. But Spenser is not bound by his Ovidian material; he decorously downplays its eroticism (while including the suggestive thigh wound), and he transforms both lovers (ignoring the fact that Stella still lives).[37] As Stella mourns Astrophel's demise, the gods change them both "Into one flowre that is both red and blew. / It first growes red, and then to blew doth fade, / Like *Astrophel*" bleeding to death (*As* 184–86), "And in the midst thereof a star appeares, / As fairly formd as any star in skyes: / Resembling *Stella* in her freshest yeares" (*As* 187–89). Peterson believes that Spenser, transforming Astrophel to a flower via the Adonis myth, pays Sidney the highest possible compliment, installing him, as it were, at the center of the Garden of Adonis. There, in book 3 of *The Faerie Queene*, Adonis is paradoxically both "subject to mortalitie" and

> . . . eterne in mutabilitie,
> And by succession made perpetuall,
> Transformed oft, and chaunged diverslie:
> For him the Father of all formes they call;
> Therefore needs mote he live, that living gives to all.
>
> (3.6.47)

Adonis lives in "eternall blis," no longer fearing his foe, the wild boar (3.6.48). But there is nothing so transcendent or regenerative in Spenser's pallid and lifeless Astrophel or in the tender flower. Moreover, the laments of the shepherds and the "piteous mone" of Stella do nothing to immortalize him.

It is "Clorinda," Astrophel's sister and the "gentlest shepheardesse" (*As* 212) whose lay Spenser singles out, who succeeds in eternizing her brother in the second poem of the diptych. Though virtually every editor and critic assigns "The Doleful Lay of Clorinda" to Spenser, I follow Margaret Hannay, who persuasively argues that it was written by the countess of Pembroke.[38] Significantly, this poem rejects the Adonis identification so central to Spenser's poem. As Clorinda is aware, the image of the flower underscores Astrophel's mortality, not his eternity; "Untimely cropt . . . And cleane defaced in untimely howre," the "faire flowre" is "gone to ashes" ("Lay" 33–34; 38–39). Moreover, as Sacks has observed, it becomes inadequate to signify Astrophel.[39] Clorinda asks:

> What is become of him whose flowre here left
> Is but *the shadow of his likeness* gone.
> *Scarse like the shadow* of that which he was,
> *Nought like*, but that he like a shade did pas.
>
> ("Lay" 57–60; emphasis added)

Clorinda's questioning causes her to reject, decisively, the resemblance of Astrophel to a flower. (Are we to image Spenser self-deconstructing *Astrophel* by writing these verses?) The speaker moves beyond the unsatisfying pagan myth to assert the eternity of Astrophel's immortal spirit:

> But that immortall spirit, which was deckt
> With all the dowries of celestiall grace:
> . . . .

> Ay me, can so divine a thing be dead?
>
> Ah no: it is not dead, ne can it die,
> But lives for aie, in blisfull Paradise.
>
> ("Lay" 61–68)

Not only is this attitude more appropriate for an elegy, but it also befits the dignity and strong faith of the countess of Pembroke; after all, Astrophel's sister, Clorinda "most resembl[es] both in shape and spright / Her brother deare" (*As* 213–14). If Spenser wrote the poem using a ventriloquized voice, the creation of the Clorinda persona suggests an inability to embrace fully the consolation the poem offers. If the poem is the countess's—and there is no reason to believe it is not—she boldly corrects Spenser's interpretation of her brother and confidently claims a poet's eternizing power. To abandon the assumption of and desire for artistic unity and progression that underlie virtually all discussion of these two poems is to see that the "Doleful Lay" provides a satisfying counterpoint to *Astrophel*, not a completion of it.[40]

Ultimately, Spenser's use of the Adonis myth in *Astrophel* is consistent with his questioning of Sidney's poetic legacy. The poem as a whole, particularly its final image, renders Spenser's judgment on Sidney's persona, the poet-lover of *Astrophil and Stella.* In *Astrophel*, Sidney's image is demoted from the heavenly icons of *The Ruines of Time* to a simple flower with a star in its center, resembling Stella. Sidney lives on, not enshrined in eternizing verse, constellated, or wafted as an immortal spirit, but merged with Stella in a flower. The flower, moreover, is ever subject to decay and death: "when so ever thou it up doest take, / Do pluck it softly for that shepheards sake" (*As* 198). In this lovely acknowledgment of the eternity-in-mortality of lovers (the flower dies but springs anew each year), Astrophel is commemorated as a lover and forever linked with Stella. The flower is as fragile as the lives of the lovers and the leaves of poetry that bear their names. Importantly, there is no apotheosis, only a mere metamorphosis, a testament to Sidney's modest accomplishment which, in Spenser's judgment, earns him no greater immortality; he is not, in the end, a divine poet, just a memorable and mortal love poet.

In sum, Spenser's poetic tributes to his predecessor exemplify the creation and contestation of Sidney's legendary image. His career begins in worshipful admiration as he participates in the eternizing of Sidney as a poet. In *The Teares of the Muses,* Spenser views Sidney as a divine poet who, like Urania, was forced to flee the earth. With *The Ruines of Time*, a belated response to Sidney's death, Spenser's attitude has grown more ambivalent. The absence in that work of a normative poetic voice suggests Spenser's own unresolved view of Sidney and his uncertainty about the proper way to commemorate him. In Astrophel and in Calidore, Spenser openly criticizes the values celebrated in the myth of Sidney as poet and shepherd-knight and questions humanist poetics, the belief that poetry provided an incentive to virtuous action. The narrator of *Astrophel* disdains the comforts of elegy and the company of fellow poets. Neither poetry nor military heroism is celebrated by the poem, which focuses on the destruction, not the apotheosis, of the Sidney figure, Astrophel. The implication is that Spenser deems the rapprochement of poetry and military heroism, promised by Sidney's legendary image, to be an illusion. Both Astrophel and Calidore are failed exemplars through whom Spenser reflects on the difficulty of embodying an ideal of virtue, especially one, such as courtesy, requiring action in an imperfect world.

Spenser's own career and later writings bear out this dismal judgment. Despite his success as a pensioned poet of the queen, Spenser in the 1590s faced a worsening situation in Ireland, and he continued to lament the downfall of his political patron, Lord Grey. In England, most of the activist Protestant statesmen were dead, and Lord Burghley was ascendant, dimming Spenser's hopes of advancement. In his later writings, he negotiates these experiences of loss and threatened failure, often renouncing the burden of public duty. Several critics have noted that in the latter books of *The Faerie Queene*, heroic action is less successful, even brutal, and love is a distraction rather than an inspiration.[41] Calidore abandons his quest in order to woo Pastorella but, as we have seen, brings chaos to her world and destroys the poet's vision. Perhaps necessarily, Spenser leaves off writing *The Faerie Queene* to work on his *Amoretti* sonnets, choosing to court his private mistress and make her his wife; similarly, Colin Clout departs Eliza's court and comes home again to sing the praises of a humble shepherdess. Perhaps Spenser's disillusionment with his epic projects and his foregrounding of private, amorous experience in these later works can be understood as a response to the significance of Sidney's death and its implications for humanist poetics.

6
Amoretti and the Reformation of Love Poetry

Amoretti and Spenser's Humanist Projects

While Spenser was bringing the Sidney myth under close scrutiny in *Astrophel*, he was also writing *Amoretti* and *Epithalamion* for the woman who was to become his wife, Elizabeth Boyle. Both volumes, published in 1595, engage and contest Sidney's exemplarity. While in *Astrophel* Spenser calls into question the values associated with the legend of Sidney as a military hero, in *Amoretti* he criticizes the values of Petrarchan loving associated with the sonnet tradition Sidney had popularized in *Astrophil and Stella*.[1] Rejecting the model of the tyrannous lady and her subordinate, desiring lover, Spenser refashions his poet-lover and lady after the ideal husband and wife depicted by contemporary writers on marriage. These lovers aspire to higher, godly ideals: "Let us love, deare love, lyke as we ought, / love is the lesson which the Lord us taught" (*Am* 68:13–14). Elizabethan conventional wisdom about marriage, specifically its emphasis on mutuality within a divinely ordained hierarchy, shapes Spenser's *Amoretti* volume, radically revising Petrarchan conventions of loving and writing.[2]

Spenser's *Amoretti* participate in his ongoing project of "fashioning a gentleman or noble person in virtuous and gentle discipline," a humanist aim of *The Faerie Queene* whereby poetry provides models for action in the world. While his epic poem aims to fashion myriad virtuous gentlemen and women, however, the *Amoretti* sonnets fashion two lovers, Spenser and his lady-bride. The poet's models are not legendary heroes like Arthur or the Italian lovers Petrarch and Laura but a Protestant everyman and everywoman, the gently authoritative husband and his humble, chaste wife. Their marriage is informed not by an ethic of domination and force but by the value of peaceful mutuality: the lady lifts the poet-lover from his selfish desire and self-absorption, while he in turn educates her to renounce her improper pride. The love poet celebrates not sterile, illicit Petrarchan eroticism but the power of virtuous, licit love (and the poetry that celebrates it) to renew future generations. As he promises his lady:

> my verse your vertues rare shall eternize,
> and in the hevens wryte your glorious name,
> Where whenas death shall all the world subdew,
> our love shall live, and later life renew.
>
> (*Am* 75:11–14)

While the poet of *Astrophel* despaired at the failures of humanist poetics, the poet-lover of *Amoretti* reconceives his mission, emphasizing private virtues that nourish married love and transform the individual, his poetry, and the social world.

Spenser thus fulfills Sidney's ideal of right poesy, even as he rejects his example as a love poet. The speaker of *Amoretti* is a Sidneian right poet who uses sonnets for their proper end: not merely applying fiery speeches to persuade a lady of his love but praising (in Sidney's words) "the immortal goodness of God who gives us hands to write and wits to conceive." He praises and fashions the lady's divine virtue and provides models for godly, Christian loving. For Spenser, the right relationship of husband and wife is an analogy for the well-ordered state; their virtuous love renews the Christian commonwealth, both physically and spiritually. This redirection of erotic love obviates the possibility, imagined by Greville in *Caelica*, of apocalyptic destruction brought about by disordered lust. Spenser also surpasses Daniel's purposeful application of the sonnet conventions to effect an ideal patron-client relationship, affirming instead the broader possibilities of social transformation, even personal redemption, in the right use of poetry.

The aspiring right poet must still, however, struggle to negotiate the contrary, worldly pressures of private desire and public obligation. This is a recurring theme in Spenser's late poetry. *Astrophel* and book 6 of *The Faerie Queene* both feature a shepherd-knight weighing his obligation to pursue his public quest against his desire to remain in the pastoral world and woo his beloved. The outbreak of senseless and uncontrollable violence in both works condemns the efforts of both heroes to fulfill their missions of service. Moreover, in these works the roles of shepherd-poet and questing knight are dramatically at odds. Astrophel cannot reconcile these roles; he abandons poetry, and his heroism is rendered pathetic by his ignoble end. In *The Faerie Queene*, the scene on Mount Acidale points up the utter disparity between the poet Colin and the knight Calidore, whose clumsy intrusion causes Colin's vision to vanish irrevocably, to the poet's enormous irritation and despair. In *Colin Clouts Come Home Againe*, written in 1591 but published in 1595 with *Astrophel*, Colin leaves court and returns to his fellow shepherds, abandoning his efforts to reform courtly loving. In these works, Spenser openly doubts the possibility of reconciling Mars and the Muses, the hope of humanist poetics and the promise of Sidney's legendary image.[3]

Possibly the sense that heroic action is doomed to failure occasions the growing inwardness of Spenser's late poetry. In *The Faerie Queene*, even as he explores courtesy, a social virtue, Spenser stresses its source within: "But vertues seat is deepe within the mynd, / And not in outward shows, but inward thoughts defynd" (*FQ* 6. pr. 5). This is the only book in which an avatar of Elizabeth / Gloriana is not celebrated; rather, Colin Clout elevates his mistress, Rosalind, as the fourth grace (*FQ* 6.10.15). Aware of the conflict his devotion to Rosalind occasions, Colin / Spenser begs Gloriana's indulgence (*FQ* 6.10.28), freeing himself to celebrate his private desire. Ironically, as Michael O'Connell observes, Spenser begins *The Faerie Queene* "by insisting upon the public dimension of the essentially private virtue of holiness, and he ends . . . with a vision of the inwardness of the social virtue of courtesy."[4] O'Connell also links Spenser's growing interiority to his loss of faith in the humanist goals for poetry. Or, as David Lee Miller puts it, Spenser "has come to see his art not as the shaping of culture but as its refuge"; poetry is something private and contemplative rather than a form of action.[5]

Though private and public obligations compete in Spenser's mind, in the *Amoretti* volume personal concerns take priority, and the poet sings not to Queen Elizabeth or to fellow elegists (as in *Astrophel*) but to Elizabeth Boyle, who alone inspires and redeems his poetry: "Leaves, lines, and rymes, seeke her to please alone, / whom if ye please, I care for other none" (*Am* 1:13–14). His beloved, however, bears the same name as his queen, and indeed his poetic lovemaking is interrupted by expressions of guilt at neglecting his greater obligations as a poet of the queen.[6] Like Astrophil's friend who rebuked his pursuit of Stella, Spenser's friend, Lodowick Bryskett, has apparently criticized him. The poet defends his work, first admitting,

Great wrong I doe, I can it not deny,
to that most sacred Empresse my dear dred,
not finishing her Queene of faery,
that mote enlarge her living prayses dead.

(*Am* 33:1–4)

His excuse is that since his wit is "tost with troublous fit / of a proud love, that doth my spirite spoyle," he has no wit or energy to complete his *magnum opus*. The reverse is possible, however: that the "taedious toyle" (*Am* 33:10) of writing *The Faerie Queene* interferes with his own courtship and the *Amoretti* sonnets, his immediate and greater concerns. In sonnet 80, Spenser considers his pursuit of love a refreshing and well-deserved vacation after his wearying race through Faery land. Reluctant to assail the next installment, he begs leave "to sport my muse and sing my loves sweet praise: / the contemplation of whose heavenly hew, / my spirit to an higher pitch will rayse" (*Am* 80:10–12). After claiming his beloved (not the queen) as his muse, he acknowledges in a cursory (and unconvincing) way the queen's priority: "But let her prayses yet be low and meane, / fit for the handmayd of the Faery Queene" (*Am* 80:13–14). Here Spenser is conscious of the indiscretion of publicly elevating his own mistress above the queen. No such hesitation appears, however, in the sonnet in which he praises his three Elizabeths: mother, queen, and, above all, his mistress;[7]

The third my love, my lives last ornament,
by whom my spirit out of dust was raysed:
to speake her prayse and glory excellent,
of all alive most worthy to be praysed.

(*Am* 74:9–12)

In *Amoretti*, the conflict between public obligations and private desire is resolved in favor of the latter, and Spenser's decision to foreground private desire, his love for his lady, enables the transformation of his life and his poetry.

Spenser's Revision of Petrarchism

There can be little doubt that Spenser deemed Petrarchism, as an ethic of love and a poetic convention, inimical to proper loving and right poetry. In *The Faerie Queene*, Spenser often draws attention to the abuses wrought by lovers and poets in the Petrarchan tradition. Perpetrators include Mirabella, the classic beautiful-but-cruel mistress who can save or destroy men with a mere twinkle of her eye (*FQ* 6.7.31), and the cannibals who subject the naked Serena to their lust in a parody of the blason poem (*FQ* 6.8.41–43). The sonneteer who would compel his lady's love is figured in the enchanter, Busyrane, who "cruelly pen[s]" Amoret (*FQ* 3.11.11), writing his magic charms with her heart's blood (*FQ* 3.12.31). In virtuous but victimized characters like Amoret, Serena, and the ever-chased / chaste Florimell (not to mention her plastic counterpart, the false Florimell), Spenser acknowledges that Petrarchan courtship (and forms of representation) dehumanize women and men alike. Over and against the tableaux of lustful cruelty and compulsion stands Spenser's embodiment of chaste married love, Britomart, whose quest is devoted to finding her destined husband, Artegall, and submitting to him in marriage. She also frees Amoret from the abusive Busyrane and releases Artegall from the tyranny of Radigund.[8] Her first words, an allusion to Chaucer's *Franklin's Tale*, condemn mastery in love:

> Ne may love be compeld by maisterie:
> For soone as maisterie comes, sweet love anone
> Taketh his nimble wings, and soone away is gone.
>
> (*FQ* 3.1.25)

In *The Faerie Queene*, Spenser makes it clear that male and female lovers alike can exercise—and overcome—the mastery that destroys virtuous love. Moreover, they can effect social change. After freeing Artegall, her husband-to-be, Britomart restores justice and rebuilds the commonwealth under his authority (*FQ* 5.7.42–43).

That Britomart restores women to subjection, dealing "true Justice," promises only to prolong the debate on mastery. This issue becomes an urgent and personal one for a poet contemplating his own marriage in poetry addressed to, or intended for, his own wife. Spenser's response in *Amoretti* is to reject the Petrarchan terms of the debate and to advocate instead a Christian ethic of love as mutual submission within a divinely ordained hierarchy. The convention that love remain unfulfilled yields to the lover's expectation that it will be reciprocated, that he and the lady will "knit the knot that ever shall remaine" (*Am* 6:14). In preparation for marriage, the lady of the *Amoretti*, like Britomart, is encouraged to overcome her pride and her desire for mastery and to submit to her husband's love. In turn, the poet-lover abandons both abject submission and forceful desiring and prepares to assume the role of husband, the benevolent ruler and teacher. *Epithalamion* then confirms the transformation of the proud Petrarchan mistress into a humble wife, as the courtship is completed and the Christian marriage consummated.

The confident persona of *Amoretti* immediately signals the new, un-Petrarchan direction of his poems by sounding the Christian theme of redemption and forecasting the lovers' fulfillment. In the opening sonnet, he imagines his leaves of poetry being held by his lady's hands, a loving gesture that releases him from enthrallment:

> Happy ye leaves when as those lilly hands,
> which hold my life in their dead doing might
> shall handle you and hold in loves soft bands,
> lyke captives trembling at the victors sight.
>
> (*Am* 1:1–4)

Unlike Astrophil, whose poetry is never able to please or move Stella, Spenser's speaker exhibits the confident expectation that his love and his poetry will find acceptance. The power of the lady to destroy the poet is eased by the softness of love's bands and the lady's trembling hands, which cause the poet's leaves to shake. Importantly, these lines also prefigure the Easter sonnet, with its promise of redemption offered by the "Most glorious Lord of lyfe" who "didst bring away / captivity thence captive us to win" (*Am* 68:1, 4). Significantly, *Amoretti* 68 echoes Psalm 68 (and other biblical passages) that celebrate the paradox of liberating captivity.[9] Like Christ, the lady is the "victor," or liberator; indeed, her "lilly hands" suggest an icon of the Resurrection, an angel holding a lily. Christ's example teaches perfect love—one characteristic of which is reciprocity, or mutuality. Thus the poet instructs his beloved in turn: "So let us love, deare love, lyke as we ought, / love is the lesson which the Lord us taught" (*Am* 68:13–14). Another characteristic of Christlike love is willing submission. This occurs in the prior sonnet as the deer, a symbol for the lady, allows herself to be captured. Explains the hunter, recalling the ambiguous and mutual trembling of sonnet 1: "I in hand her yet halfe trembling tooke, / and with her owne goodwill hir fyrmely tyde" (*Am* 67:11–12).[10] This betrothal anticipates their binding in marriage, a captivity that frees the lovers from the conventional erotic chase. By contrast, the bondage in which Petrarchan lovers found themselves absolutely precluded the possibility of love's fulfillment in any form, let alone in marriage.[11]

Depicting the gentle, unforced capture of the deer in *Amoretti* 67,

Spenser rewrites in a stroke Petrarch's dreamy *Rime* 190 ("Una candida cerva") and Wyatt's bitter "Whoso list to hunt." As he revises the notion of captivity, Spenser rewrites other Petrarchan conceits in order to praise his lady and to raise her above the bevy of literary cruel mistresses. One obvious example of such revision is his treatment of the related motifs of his lady's eyes and love's inception. Traditionally, the lady's glance unleashes Cupid's arrows, which wound the poet's heart.[12] Spenser at first invokes this convention, addressing his mistress's fair eyes: "both lyfe and death forth from you dart / into the object of your mighty view" (*Am* 7:3–4). He then begs her not to destroy him but to "kindle living fire within my brest" (*Am* 7:12). In the next sonnet, this living fire has a heavenly origin. The lady's eyes, "More then most faire, full of the living fire, / Kindled above unto the maker neere" (*Am* 8:1–2), are elevated to membership in a divine trinity, mediating the heavenly fire to the poet-lover. Cupid is disabled by their angelic power:

> Thrugh your bright beams doth not the blinded guest
> shoot out his darts to base affections wound:
> but Angels come to lead fraile mindes to rest
> in chast desires on heavenly beauty bound.
>
> (*Am* 8:5–8)[13]

The lady is even likened to the creator, bringing order out of chaos, forming the poet and his speech:

> You frame my thoughts and fashion me within,
> you stop my toung, and teach my hart to speake,
> you calme the storme that passion did begin,
> strong thrugh your cause, but by your vertue weak.
> Dark is the world, where your light shined never;
> well is he borne, that may behold you ever.
>
> (*Am* 8:9–14)

Beholding the mistress is like being in the sight of God. This point is also made in the next sonnet as the poet rejects all comparisons between her eyes and things of the earth, concluding, "Then to the Maker selfe they likest be, / whose light doth lighten all that here we see" (*Am* 9:13–14). This final line could modify either "the Maker selfe" or the mistress's eyes. The ambiguity contributes to Spenser's analogy between his mistress and his God, both of whom sustain his life with their light.

Neither irreverent nor fanciful, this comparison of his lady to Christ serves a number of purposes. First, it distinguishes his lady and his love from profane Petrarchism. Second, it assists Spenser's didactic purpose. William Johnson has argued ably that the *Amoretti* is a semi-autobiographical account of the education of Spenser as a poet and lover, a process crucially assisted by the redemptive lady-Christ.[14] Importantly, likening the lady to Christ also instructs *her*. The poet compares his lady's love to divine grace in order to persuade her to love him: "Then sith to heaven ye lykened are the best, / be lyke in mercy as in all the rest" (*Am* 55:13–14). Similarly, sonnet 53 concludes, "But mercy doth with beautie best agree, / as in theyr maker ye them best may see" (ll. 13–14). These are the pleas not of a manipulative suitor but of a confident poet instructing his lady to "love . . . lyke as we ought," to heed Christ's example and exhibit mercy, love, and submission to the will of heaven. His language teaches her not to fashion herself after the literary model of the disdainful lady, for her image is divine and her behavior ought to imitate Christ's.

Spenser also draws on Neoplatonism to revise Petrarchan poetic practice. Neoplatonic idealism proves useful for establishing the lady's divine resemblance, as when the poet makes her eyes bearers of heavenly light. Taken to its philosophical extreme, however, a fully spiritualized Neoplatonic love is incompatible with consummated marital love.[15] Accordingly, Spenser does not allow his beloved to become an idealized abstraction, available only for worship and contemplation. While the early sonnets are more likely to elevate and idealize the lady, several later sonnets repudiate Neoplatonic love in favor of an earthly and physical expression of love. When the poet's spirit, attempting to "mount up to the purest sky," sees the lady "resembling heaven's glory in her light: / drawne with sweet pleasures bayt, it back doth fly, / and unto heaven forgets her former flight" (*Am* 72:2, 6–8). The poet opts for "none other happinesse, / but here on earth to have such hevens blisse" (*Am* 72:13–14). In sonnets 76 and 77, too, the poet's idealizing impulses are countered by the strong pull of the flesh; he likens his lady's breast to a table richly spread with fruits of paradise, "Exceeding sweet, yet voyd of sinfull vice," and his thoughts to the "guests, which would thereon have fedd" (*Am* 77:9, 14). This lover climbs no ladder of love; he does not progress from enjoyment of his mistress to communion with God. As Ellrodt sums it up, for Spenser, "love is of heavenly nature, but its consummation is earthly."[16]

Spenser's syncretism of Neoplatonism and Christianity elevates his subject, assists his rewriting of Petrarchan poetry, and promotes the spiritual element in married love.[17] Clearly, Spenser sought to reform the conventions and contexts of the love sonnet, rising to the challenge of being a godly poet who sings "the praises of the immortal beauty: the immortal goodness of that God who giveth us hands to write and wits to conceive." Sidney's phrasing implicitly opposes mortal beauty (Stella) to immortal beauty and goodness (God), and his own sonnets ultimately censure that earthly love "which reachest but to dust" (*Certaine Sonnets* 32:1). Unlike Sidney, however, Spenser conflates his "immortal beauty" (Elizabeth Boyle) and the "immortal goodness" of God, undoing the opposition between earthly love and heavenly love that grounds Petrarch's sonnets and still prevails in Sidney's sequence. Spenser's sonnets instead affirm the highest form of earthly love, marriage. He situates the courtship in the framework of the Christian liturgical year, a structuring device Petrarch also used, but to a different purpose.[18] In Petrarch's *Rime sparse*, the anniversary poems recapitulate time and again the poet's first sighting of Laura. Thus they underscore the stasis of their relationship Spenser's calendrical and liturgical references, on the other hand, establish progress in the relationship as well as movement towards spiritual redemption. Spenser's lovers imitate Christ's immortal love not in order to transcend carnality (Petrarch's goal) but in order to bring their own earthly love to fruition in marriage.

Amoretti and Christian Marriage

Gently but firmly repudiating Petrarchan models and Neoplatonic ideals alike, Spenser's *Amoretti* are firmly situated in the Renaissance discourse on marriage, an important but hitherto neglected context. Spenser is clearly steeped in his culture's conventional wisdom regarding marriage and shares its anxieties over women's pride and man's sometimes tenuous authority. The roles he envisions for the lover and his lady accord with ideal behavior expected of Christian husbands and wives and expressed time and again by sixteenth- and seventeenth-century writers on marriage.[19]

For Spenser, spiritualized Neoplatonic love has its place as the foundation of married love. He is among the many writers who stress that love based on spiritual rather than material gifts is the only firm basis for marriage. Henry Smith, in *A Preparative to Marriage*, advises that "the goods of the world are good, and the goods of the bodie are good, but the goods of the mind are better" (30). Edmund Tilney advises that women's "vertues . . . ought to be accounted [their] chiefest dowrie" (108). Early in the sequence, Spenser establishes that his beloved is virtuous, a fit partner for marriage. In a sonnet that blazons his lady's beauty in terms of "the goods of the world"—treasures of the Indies, rubies, ivory, and gold—the poet renounces them in favor of the intangible and invisible "goods of the mind." Though his "love doth in her selfe containe / all this worlds riches that may farre be found" (15:5–6), her virtue caps all her beauties: "that which fairest is, but few behold, / her mind adornd with vertues manifold" (*Am* 15:5–6, 13–14).[20] Likewise, he affirms that though she is beautiful, "the trew fayre, that is the gentle wit, / and vertuous mind, is much more praysd of me" (*Am* 79:3–4). He admits that her physical beauties are subject to "frayle corruption," but her true beauty is eternal; it

> doth argue you
> to be divine and borne of heavenly seed:
> deriv'd from that fayre Spirit, from whom al true
> and perfect beauty did at first proceed.
> He onely fayre, and what he fayre hath made,
> all other fayre lyke flowres untymely fade.
>
> (*Am* 79:9–14)

That his love is grounded on spiritual rather than material virtue makes him an ideal Christian husband-to-be. Juan Luis Vives, in *The Office and Duetie of a Husband* (1553), distinguishes husbands "that love the beautye, or the ryches of their wives, [who] are blynde and subjecte to that earthly love" from those "true husbandes, [who] love the soule and vertue" of their wives and are "inspired wyth the strengthe and spirite of that celestiall love" (M8r). Spenser and his contemporaries drew on Neoplatonic ideals to shore up the spiritual side of the economic, contractual matter of marriage.

Given the expectation that the courtship will end in marriage, the central task facing the poet is to fashion his proud lady into a humble companion of a wife. He does this by presenting a negative image of the mistress, renouncing it, and re-presenting the ideal image, one that depends upon, even as it denounces, the negative image. This process of "differential repetition" is one which David Lee Miller finds intrinsic to Spenser's poetics.[21] It is useful for understanding *Amoretti*, in which Elizabeth Boyle emerges into representation only through the presence—and the rejection—of the archetypal Petrarchan mistress whose qualities pervert the ideal of a Christian wife. This view helps to account for Spenser's reversion to exaggerated Petrarchan attitudes. In one sonnet, for example, the lady is a woman of heavenly virtue, and in the next sonnet she is a "Tyrannesse [who] doth joy to see / the huge massacres which her eyes do make" (*Am* 10:5–6) or a savage beast who "taketh glory in her cruelnesse" (*Am* 20:12). Louis Martz, rightly noting Spenser's sense of humor, sees elements of parody or even comedy in the exaggerated sonnets, as the lovers knowingly and mockingly strike the conventional poses for each other.[22] Perhaps through humor, Spenser hopes to get his lady to see that the laws of the "Unrighteous Lord of love" and the behavior of a lady who "lordeth in licentious blisse" (*Am* 10:1, 3) seriously transgress God's law (as Spenser's puns on "lord" suggest). By presenting the negative example, he invites her to renounce it and refashion herself in its counterimage.

The presentation of a negative image through which an ideal form is summoned into being is not solely a feature of Spenser's poetics. It is evident as a persuasive and instructive tactic in two prominent wedding sermons of the period, the Elizabethan sermon "Of the State of Matrimony" in the Elizabethan *Book of Homilies* (1562) (hereafter cited as *Homily*) and William Whately's *A Bride-Bush* (1617), works alike enough in their attitudes and advice to be considered compendia of conventional wisdom regarding marriage. In the following passage from the *Homily*, the specter of a domineering wife is raised, horror is invoked, the example is rejected, and a vignette of ideal wifely behavior is substituted:

> Now as concerning the Wives duty. What shall become her? Shall she abuse the gentleness and humanity of her husband? and, at her pleasure, turn all things upside down? No surely. For that is far repugnant against GODS Commandment, for thus doth St. *Peter* preach to them, ye Wives, be ye in subjection to obey your own husbands. To obey, is another thing than to controle or command, which yet they may do, to their Children, and to their Family: But as for their Husbands, them must they obey, and cease from commanding, and perform subjection. For this surely doth nourish concord very much, when the Wife is ready at hand at her husbands commandment, when she will apply her self to his will, when she endeavoureth her self to seek his contentation, and to do him pleasure, when she will eschew all things that might offend him. (*Homily* 311)[23]

Writers on marriage agree without question that pride is most unfitting for a Christian wife, who was enjoined to be humble, chaste, and silent, an obedient subordinate to her husband.

The submission of wives is justified by the common analogy between marriage and the commonwealth, here expansively set forth by Daniel Rogers, author of *Matrimoniall Honour*:

> Marriage is the Preservative of Chastity, the Seminary of the Commonwealth, seed-plot of the Church . . . supporter of lawes, states, orders, offices, gifts and services . . . the ambition of virginity, the foundation of Countries, Cities, Universities, succession of Families, Crownes, and Kingdomes; yea . . . the very furniture of heaven . . . depending thereupon.[24]

This encomium on matrimony includes its interconnected personal, political, and spiritual dimensions. Understandably, preaching the widespread consequences of wifely disobedience would provide a strong incentive for families to adhere to traditional, stabilizing roles. Extending the commonwealth comparison, writers on marriage typically liken the husband to a king who must be obeyed and the wife to a "Deputie subordinate" who, if not governed reasonably, will "breake out into open act of rebellion" (Whately 16, 23). Because women's pride upsets the divine and natural orders, it is denounced in the strongest language; William Gouge, in his handbook *Of Domesticall Duties* (1622), writes that for a wife "to imagine that she her selfe is not inferiour to her husband, ariseth from monstrous self-conceit, and intolerable arrogancy, as if she her selfe were above her owne sex, and more then a woman" (273). He deems pride the most "pestilent vice for an inferiour. . . . [I]t is the cause of all rebellion, disobedience, & disloyalty" (331). In short, women's pride is the vice most disruptive to a Christian marriage, which in turn is the foundation of all social and political order.

With his representation of the dominatrix Radigund in *The Faerie Queene*, Spenser confirms the view that women's pride imperils the proper order that ought to exist between men and women in the private realm of marriage and in the public realm of governance.[25] As the negative image of Britomart, Radigund exemplifies what Gouge describes as the "ambitious and proud humour in women, who must needs rule" (286–87). She occasions Spenser's condemnation of women's rule: "vertuous women wisely understand, / That they were borne to base humilitie, / Unlesse the heavens them lift to lawfull soveraintie" (*FQ* 5.5.25). Women such as Radigund "thwart Gods ordinance, pervert the order of nature, deface the image of Christ, [and] overthrow the ground of all dutie" (Gouge 287). One recalls Greville's fearful imagination of "female Impiety" occupying God's throne (*C* 109), the ultimate consequence of women's sinful dominance in love. Disorder on all levels—personal, natural, political, and spiritual—results from women's ambitions to rule.

Pride, of course, is the most notable characteristic of the Petrarchan mistress, and the *Amoretti* poet's concern with his lady's pride is almost obsessive. Over half of the poems before sonnet 62 treat the lady's pride or cruelty.[26] Importantly, however, Spenser's sonnets focus on the personal dimensions of the lady's pride, not its political ramifications. Pride is associated with a descent in the scale of being, a perversion of nature's order like that which Gouge decries. For Spenser, pride and cruelty destroy the lady's divine likeness, the "fayre Idea of [her] celestiall hew" (*Am* 45:7). He complains that her "pryde depraves each other better part, / and all those pretious ornaments deface" (*Am* 31:3–4). He then likens the lady to a cruel or proud beast about to kill her prey, the poet. Elsewhere the lady is a deceptive enchantress whose pride, represented as rampant, animal sexuality, threatens the poet's very life:

> So she with flattring smyles weake harts doth guyde
> unto her love and tempte to theyr decay,
> whome being caught she kills with cruell pryde,
> and feeds at pleasure on the wretched pray:
>
> . . . .
>
> O mighty charm which makes men love theyr bane,
> and thinck they dy with pleasure, live with payne.
>
> (*Am* 47:5–14)

The sexual overtones of pride and dying in this sonnet cannot be overlooked. A woman who uses her sexuality to master and devour her lover, Spenser warns, upsets the divine order and debases her own humanity.[27] This exaggerated Petrarchan lady who deceives and destroys her prey is, to borrow Miller's terms again, the "negative moment" that summons the poems' ideal into existence. Extreme inversions of virtue are represented in order to be renounced, that the woman who embodies ideal virtue may spring into clear relief.

The negative image of the proud enchantress is countered by Spenser's representation of his lady as a woman with an abundance of proper pride:

> Such pride is praise, such portliness is honor,
> that boldned innocence beares in hir eies:
> and her faire countenance like a goodly banner,
> spreds in defiaunce of all enemies.

Was never in this world ought worthy tride
  without some spark of such self-pleasing pride.

(*Am* 5:9–14)

This virtuous pride is informed by a consciousness of what befits one's position; it prevents one from behaving unworthily. This pride is a mark of the lady's well-tempered nature, in which "Myld humblesse [is] mixt with awfull majesty," but it still threatens to compromise her humility:

  for looking on the earth whence she was borne,
  her minde remembreth her mortalitie:
  what so is fayrest shall to earth returne.
But that same lofty countenance seemes to scorne
  base thing, and thinke how she to heaven may clime:
  treading downe earth as lothsome and forlorne,
  that hinders heavenly thoughts with drossy slime.
Yet lowly still vouchsafe to looke on me,
  such lowlinesse shall make you lofty be.

(*Am* 13:6–14)[28]

The poet, in his role as teacher, warns his lady that by scorning earth as "lothsome" and "drossy slime," she risks tipping the virtuous balance on the side of false pride. He reminds her that, ultimately, she attains her exalted position by humbling herself to her lover-husband.

The scales of pride tip back and forth again in sonnet 58, which condemns her self-assurance as vanity, and in sonnet 59, which praises it as a sign of steadfastness. There, the mistress is a paragon of controlled, chaste sexuality, a "steddy ship," firm "in the stay of her own stedfast might" (*Am* 59:5, 11).[29] Such pride and self-control make her eminently suitable for marriage, but the emergence of false pride remains an ever-present possibility, as "that cloude of pryde, which oft doth dark / her goodly light with smiles she drives away" (*Am* 81:7–8). In the *Amoretti*, renunciation of false pride is not a once-and-for-all event but a process requiring continual vigilance and self-control. Not until the *Epithalamion* does the lady display the proper synthesis of pride and humility that befits a virtuous wife.[30]

In his attempt to discourage false pride and inculcate wifely virtue in his beloved, the speaker of the *Amoretti* assumes a tone of gentle authority, in effect rehearsing his own role of husband. Conduct writers agree that one duty of the husband is gently and lovingly to reform his wife's faults (Tilney 114–15). Henry Smith, in *A Preparative to Marriage*, reminds the husband that, in taking a wife, he takes on a vineyard that he must nurture before it will bear fruit: "So hee must not looke to finde a wife without a faulte, but thinke that she is committed to him to reclaime her from her faults" (69). The poet assumes this role when he praises his lady's virtuous pride while gently warning her not to succumb to the temptation to master her beloved. A tone of gentle authority characterizes many of the sonnets, especially the imperative and epigrammatic concluding couplet:

Then you faire flowre, in whom fresh youth doth raine,
  prepare your selfe new love to entertaine.

(*Am* 4:13–14)

Faire be no lenger proud of that shall perish,
  but that which shal you make immortall, cherish.

(*Am* 27:13–14)

Then fly no more fayre love from Phebus chace,
  but in your brest his leafe and love embrace.

(*Am* 28:13–14)[31]

This poet-lover, addressing gentle admonitions to his beloved, is a striking departure from the conventional sonneteer who alternately indulges his despair and seeks to satisfy his desire. As these examples show, Spenser's gently didactic tone changes the thrust of the couplet, helping to modify the sonnet form. Sidney had perfected the oxymoron expressive of the poet-lover's insoluble dilemma and his perpetual frustration. Astrophil wails that Stella "So sweets my paines that my paines me rejoyce" (*AS* 57:14); he begs "Deare, love me not, that you may love me more" (*AS* 62:14). Spenser, by contrast, often builds up to such a Sidneian conclusion but neatly evades its seemingly inescapable contradiction. For example, the poet invokes the metaphor of courtship as a siege of the lady's castle, but in the final couplet he simply gives over the battle:

Bring therefore all the forces that ye may,
  and lay incessant battery to her heart;
  playnts, prayers, vowes, ruth, sorrow, and dismay,
  those engins can the proudest love convert.
And if those fayle fall downe and dy before her,
  so dying live, and living do adore her.

(*Am* 14:9–14)

Now, Spenser is certainly able to sustain the idea of love as an assault, but he rejects it in favor of an image of submissive love, reinforced by the "feminine" end-rhyme of lines 13–14. His references to converting the proud mistress and to the paradox of dying in order to live point to the promise of redemption offered by the Easter sonnet and give Petrarchan paradoxes a Christian flavor. As Spenser softens the couplet and defuses the tensions of the conventional siege motif, he subverts the expectations raised by his use of Petrarchan conceits and the sonnet form.

Sonnet 14, in which the lover gives up the siege, prefigures sonnet 67, in which the hunter gives up the chase; their "message" is that the renunciation of force enables the act of submission. Indeed, writers on marriage consistently reject the use of force to compel a wife's obedience. They offer alternative strategies for a husband: setting a good example for the wife to follow, yielding to her in trivial matters, using indirection, and even dissembling to win her will. Men who use force, according to Vives, are responsible for turning love into hate in their wives; he further advises,"Love is gotten by love; by honestie & fidelitie, not by violence" (C7v). Likewise, the Elizabethan marriage homily counsels that "frowardness and sharpness is not amended with frowardness, but with softness and gentleness" (*Homily* 316). Rather, the duty of a husband, says Vives, is to set an example "the which to informe and fashion the womans life" (Q4r). Such a process occurs in this sonnet, a response to something like a domestic quarrel:

> Shall I then silent be or shall I speake?
> And if I speake, her wrath renew I shall:
> and if I silent be, my hart will breake,
> or choked be with overflowing gall.
> What tyranny is this both my hart to thrall,
> and eke my toung with proud restraint to tie?
>
> (*Am* 43:1–6)

The poet-lover tempers his initial anger, which would break out in harsh words. Instead of condemning or attacking the mistress, he recommends silence and submission through his own example and even manages a compliment to her "deep wit":

> Yet I my hart with silence secretly
> will teach to speak, and my just cause to plead:
> and eke mine eies with meeke humility,
> love learned letters to her eyes to read.

> Which her deep wit, that true harts thought can spel,
> wil soone conceive, and learne to construe well.
>
> (*Am* 43:9–14)

Such a strategy befits a good husband, who maintains authority

> by being an ensample in love, gravitie, pietie, honesty, &c. The fruits of these and other like graces shewed forth by husbands before their wives and family, cannot but worke a reverend and dutifull respect in their wives . . . for by this means they shall more cleerely discerne the image of God shine forth in their faces. (Gouge 354)

A good husband, says Whately, asserts authority not by "big looks, & great words, & cruel behavior . . . but by a milder & more artificiall course" (19). In correcting a wife's fault, he continues, a husband should never speak in anger, always be gentle, and mingle praise and reproof, thus enticing obedience. He should "neither shew himselfe rigorous in every thing, but bee content to gratifie his wife in some things, that she may less unwillingly, yea with more cheerefulnesse bee subject in other things" (27). In this advice, Whately echoes his predecessors; Tilney also recommends that a husband sometimes dissemble, consent to his wife in "trifling matters," and "deale with his wife, rather by subtiltie, than by crueltie" (121–22). This advice the speaker of *Amoretti* 43 follows to the letter: he swallows his anger and speaks no harsh words; rather, he teaches virtuous humility by his own example and compliments the lady's virtuous wisdom.

The alternatives of force and subtlety to fashion the lady are also treated in another pair of sonnets. In one, the poet is a blacksmith who beats "with his heavy sledge" on "th'andvyle of her stubberne wit" (*Am* 32:3, 8), which only hardens her resistance: "she frieseth in her wilfull pryde: / and harder growes the harder she is smit" (*Am* 32:10–11). Later in the sequence, he approaches the problem from a new perspective, considering that her hardness may signal steadfastness and opting for a more subtle means of persuasion:

> Ne ought so hard, but he that would attend,
> mote soften it and to his will allure:
> so doe I hope her stubborne hart to bend,
> and that it then more stedfast will endure.
>
> (*Am* 51:9–12)

The word "attend" implies both attention and waiting, suggesting a paradoxical attitude of patient persistence. The speaker has concluded that the eventual concord of hearts will be achieved not by force but by indirection, by allurement, a hope realized as the "gentle deare" finally submits in sonnet 67.

In advocating allurement and dissembling, conduct writers extend to husbands those strategies cultivated by courtiers, lovers, and allegorical poets alike.[32] Whately advises husbands, "Obedience would be inticed and allured, and as it were by committing it to it[s] own disposing. . . . So carry thy selfe to thy wife, that she may perceive herselfe to have entred, not into servile thraldome, but loving subjection" (28).[33] The speaker of *Amoretti* 67 almost uncannily enacts this advice. The huntsman forsakes the chase and reclines in a shady place, whereupon the "gentle deare" returns in search of water and submits to him voluntarily:

There she beholding me with mylder looke,
sought not to fly, but fearelesse still did bide:
till I in hand her yet halfe trembling tooke,
and with her owne goodwill hir fyrmely tyde.
Strange thing me seemd to see a beast so wyld,
so goodly wonne with her owne will beguyld.

(*Am* 67:9–14)

In this sonnet, mutual "beguiling" occurs; the hounds are "beguiled of their pray" (l. 4) by the escaping deer, who gains the freedom to set the terms of her own surrender. Then the woman-deer is ambiguously "with her owne will beguyld," suggesting both that she has been deceived of "her owne goodwill" and that she has exercised it. Another apt gloss on his poem is Vives's comment that husbands who love spiritually will use gentle persuasion, not force, "for pure and holye love dothe not vyolentlye compel them . . . but prudentelye doth both guyde, and conduct the gently perswaded to the place they would go unto" (M8r-v).[34] The hunter unwittingly guides his deer (dear) to the place she would go, the brook. There she, unsurprised and fearless, submits to being tied willingly, but only after he abandons the chase. The husband-lover, importantly, does not compromise his authority by granting the lady her will. David Lee Miller perceptively notes the replacement of the tremors of line 11 with masculine firmness in line 12 and the "quiet reassertion of masculine authority in the active voice, as the speaker muses on what he has 'wonne.'"[35]

In *Amoretti* 65, Spenser addresses a mistress who has apparently shown a reluctance to marry and seeks to assuage her doubts about forfeiting her freedom. Here is Spenser's most thorough affirmation of companionate marriage based on mutual love and submission:

> The doubt which ye misdeeme, fayre love, is vaine,
> That fondly feare to loose your liberty;
> when loosing one, two liberties ye gayne,
> and make him bond that bondage erst dyd fly.
> Sweet be the bands, the which true love doth tye,
> without constraynt or dread of any ill:
> the gentle birde feeles no captivity
> within her cage, but singes and feeds her fill.
> There pride dare not approch, nor discord spill
> the league twixt them, that loyal love hath bound:
> but simple truth and mutuall good will
> seekes with sweet peace to salve each others wound.
> There fayth doth fearlesse dwell in brasen towre,
> and spotlesse pleasure builds her sacred bowre.

He characterizes marriage as a liberating captivity but recognizes that without loving harmony—the bird singing in its cage—it can become a prison. As Vives counsels, "[T]her shalbe in wedlocke a certayne swete and pleasaunt conversation, without the whiche it is no maryage but a prysone, a hatred & a perpetual torment of the mynde" (N7r). In an eclogue from the third book of Sidney's *Arcadia*, Histor imagines such a marriage. When the wife is proud and shrewish,

> The house is made a very lothsome cage,
> Wherein the bird doth never sing but cry;
> With such a will that nothing can asswage.[36]

In short, conventional wisdom agrees that spouses must also be friends. Marriage is considered the highest form of friendship, as the title of Tilney's discourse on marriage, *The Flower of Friendship*, suggests. Vives also describes matrimony as the perfection of friendship; marriage is "the supreme and most excellent part of all amitie" that "farre differeth from tiranny." There can be no marriage, he says, where the husband and wife "agree not in wyll and minde" (K8r). The association of marriage and friendship is natural to Spenser, too, for the meeting, courtship, and engagement of Artegall and Britomart occur in book 4, the legend of friendship.

Though sonnet 65 seeks to assuage the lady's fears of marriage, it also betrays some of the speaker's own fears as well, as the metaphors for marriage oscillate between negative and positive meanings.

Marriage is first characterized as "bondage" from which the poet himself has admittedly fled; then these bonds become sweet bands. The "brasen towre" of line 13 connotes not only strong faith but is also reminiscent of the kind of tower in which maidens or offenders are immured. Finally, marriage is affirmed to be a "sacred bowre," a place of sinless pleasure, an enclosed and fruitful garden—an image that replaces the unsettling metaphor of the caged bird. The tower and the bower both prefigure the description of the bride in *Epithalamion*, whose

> Snowie necke [is] lyke to a marble towre,
> And all her body like a pallace fayre,
> Ascending uppe with many a stately stayre,
> To honors seat and chastities sweet bowre.
>
> (*Epi* 177–80)

Though a Spenserian bower can also be a place of sensual and sexual excess, these bowers and towers are firmly associated with a lady chaste in body and mind.

Sonnet 65 also affirms the responsibility of spouses with "mutuall good will" to seek "with sweet peace to salve each others wound." One thinks of the wounds of Cupid's arrow and the gash in Amoret's heart (*FQ* 3.12.20–21), the remains of Petrarchan loving. More generally, the wounds are the legacy of sinfulness in general, the daily hurts that men and women inflict and suffer. Writers on marriage agree that husband and wife share the duty to provide solace, to reform each other's vices, and to foster each other's virtues. Smith advises spouses in *A Preparative to Marriage*:

> To begin this concord well, it is necessarie to learne one anothers nature, and one anothers afflictions, and one anothers infirmities. . . . [T]herefore they must learne of Paule, to fashion themselves one to the other, if they would win one another. (59)

On the occasion of the New Year, Spenser invites his mistress to

> chaunge eeke our mynds and former lives amend,
> the old yeares sinnes forepast let us eschew,
> and fly the faults with which we did offend.
>
> (*Am* 62:6–8)

This is a poet-lover who takes seriously the admonishment to be the "Leader and Author of Love" (*Homily* 310), to initiate reconciliation and foster concord. Elsewhere, he instructs the lady:

Leave lady in your glasse of christall clene,
Your goodly selfe for evermore to vew:
and in my selfe, my inward selfe I meane,
most lively lyke behold your semblant trew.

(*Am* 45:1–4)

With the mirror motif alluding to a long instructive tradition, he urges her to repair her "goodly ymage": "if your selfe in me ye playne will see, / remove the cause by which your fayre beames darkned be" (*Am* 45:13–14). In Tilney's dialogue, the wife is advised to look to her husband, "whose face must be hir daylie looking glass . . . wherto she must alwayes frame her own countenance" (138).[37] The Christian wife ought to look to her husband as the image of Christ; there she will see her own divine nature mirrored. While conduct writers do not in turn urge the husband to behold his wife as a glass, Spenser does grant his lady the power to illuminate and teach him with her goodness:

You frame my thoughts and fashion me within,
you stop my toung, and teach my hart to speake,
you calme the storme that passion did begin,
strong thrugh your cause, but by your vertue weak.
Dark is the world, where your light shined never;
well is he borne, that may behold you ever.

(*Am* 8:9–14)

The point is that in the *Amoretti*, mutual fashioning occurs; the poet is drawn to goodness by his mistress's virtue, and he in turn seeks to amend her faults by frequent moral exhortations and by his own example of patience and love. By making such reciprocity central to his sonnet cycle and by grounding his poetry in the ethics of Christian marriage, Spenser fundamentally reworks the amorous Petrarchan sonnet he inherited from Sidney and his contemporaries.

Epithalamion and the Fulfillment of Desire

Spenser's blushing bride, emerging on her wedding day, exemplifies in all respects the virtuous Christian wife. She is clad in virgin white, and though she resembles Phoebe, an angel, or a "mayden Queene," she is the soul of humility:

Her modest eyes abashed to behold
So many gazers, as on her do stare,
Upon the lowly ground affixed are.
Ne dare lift up her countenance too bold,
But blush to heare her prayses sung so loud,
So farre from being proud.

(*Epi* 159–64)

Henry Smith would approve of the sight, murmuring that "a modest countenance, and womanly shamefastnesse, do commend a chaste wife" (37). As in the *Amoretti*, Spenser makes clear that the bride's physical beauty is surpassed by the beauty of her soul:

But if ye saw that which no eyes can see,
The inward beauty of her lively spright,
Garnisht with heavenly guifts of high degree,
Much more then would ye wonder at that sight,
And stand astonisht lyke to those which red
Medusaes mazeful hed.

(*Epi* 185–90)

Among these gifts are virtues that befit a wife, namely "sweet love and constant chastity, / Unspotted fayth and comely womanhood, / Regard of honour and mild modesty" (*Epi* 191–93). This "regard of honour" could suggest several things: that she regards her own honor, or the honor bestowed on her by marriage and its requisite mildness and modesty, or her husband's honor, which implies her own modest subordination.[38] Moreover, "mild modesty" is a virtue that lends honor to a wife. Mildness and modesty, says Gouge, are marks of a wife's reverence for her husband (277–78). Yet a measure of self-regard is appropriate for the wife, who ranks just below her husband in the hierarchy of the family. Humility involves an acknowledgment of this proper place; it is "that grace that keepes one from thinking highly of himself *above that which is meet*" (Gouge 331; emphasis added); it will also make a wife "thinke better of her husband then of her selfe, and . . . make her more willing to yeeld all subjection unto him" (ibid.). "Regard of honour" and "mild modesty" are thus not contradictory but essentially complementary. By praising his bride's virtues of chastity, modesty, and honor, Spenser continues to promote his culture's ideal of a godly wife.[39]

But even here, on the day of the wedding and at the portal to the temple, the specter of the demonic wife puts in a final, brief appearance. In a troublesome comparison, the power of the bride's virtue to astonish the viewer is likened to that of "Medusaes mazefull head," which could turn men into stone. On one level, the speaker is simply awed by his lady's beauty and virtue. Medusa could suggest chastity, say the editors of the Yale edition, citing Milton's *Comus*; the lady's "rigid looks of Chaste austerity . . . dash't brute violence / With sudden adoration and blank awe."[40] More relevant, however, may be Medusa's less benign association with lawless female sexuality, which Nancy Vickers notes. In Gerard Leigh's *Accedence of Armorie* (1591), Medusa is transformed into a monster with snaky locks as a punishment for practicing

> her filthy lust, with that same godde Neptune, wherof as she openly fled the discipline of womanly shamefastness, she was by the godes decree for hir so foule a fault, bereft of all dame Bewties shape. . . . transformed into loathsome annoiance . . . horrible to mankind, a mirror for Venus minions.[41]

The fearsome Gorgon's face, a reverse of the chaste Lucrece's face, is an appropriate image for a nervous bridegroom to conjure, if only momentarily, on his wedding day. Medusa was also, as Vickers points out, a victim of violence; in Ovid's account, she was raped by Neptune. Thus the nightmare image suggests not only the possibility of female transgression but also that of male violence (present in the *Comus* allusion to Medusa). Both dangers the lovers of *Amoretti* have renounced but not entirely banished.[42] Finally, Medusa was associated with artful female eloquence that strikes men dumb, providing yet another occasion of anxiety for the poet-lover fearful of losing his lyric voice.[43] (Satisfied lovers seldom write sonnets.)

Spenser's final words on pride and humility present an apparent conundrum, an oxymoron that resolves itself into an affirmation of the bride's honorable virtue. Entering the bridal bower, the speaker exclaims, "Behold how goodly my faire love does ly / In proud humility" (*Epi* 305–6). "Proud humility" is not really the contradiction it seems, for Spenser and writers on marriage agree that it is possible to be simultaneously humble and proud, though not "above that which is meet." (*Amoretti* 13, discussed above, describes such a coexistence of humility and pride, "mild humblesse" and "awfull majesty," and promises that "such lowlinesse shall make you lofty be.") The emphasis of the phrase rests on "humility," which is modified and qualified by a pride as "goodly" as the fair bride herself. Good pride, for a wife, involves the consciousness that humility befits her, indeed, that it exalts her. Good pride also describes the virtuous sexuality of the wife humbled before her husband, her lord. Reclining in "proud humility," the bride exhibits (and awakens) a sexual desire that now occurs in its proper context of marriage. Heather Dubrow observes that the bride is strikingly (even disturbingly) passive, like "Maia, when as Jove her tooke, / In Tempe, lying on the flowry gras, / Twixt sleepe and wake, after she weary was . . ." (*Epi* 307–9); she is drained of all threatening sexual aggressiveness.[44] Her sexuality is now contained and controlled by the loving bonds of marriage and by the husband's (and the poet's) authority. The phrase "proud humility" also suggests that her qualities of modesty, humility, temperance, and chaste desire for her husband are virtues of which the bride can justly be proud. Finally, this oxymoron expresses the conflict of Petrarchism with Christian loving and a redefinition of their conventional languages. The phrase echoes the lady's vain pride and the lover's humiliation while rewriting and reconciling them as a Christian paradox.

Still, however, the phrase "proud humility" resonates with Petrarchan conflicts, and the poet-lover's success raises a nagging possibility: perhaps he has not after all renounced the Petrarchan ethic, only effected a turnabout by loving a woman he can dominate by marrying.[45] Has he merely substituted for a Petrarchan hierarchy a patriarchal one, incarnating with his art the ideal of a shamefast and silent wife and parading himself as a masterful poet and husband? Admittedly, the poet's public celebration of mastery over his chaste and submissive bride, who blushes inordinately but speaks not a word, is problematic.[46] But the intimate, mutual relationship represented in the *Amoretti* qualifies our view of the spouses presented to public view on the marriage day. Of crucial significance is the fact that the poet-lover is also conformed to the ideology of Christian marriage. While Elizabeth Boyle is transformed into a godly wife, Spenser recreates himself as the ideal husband; his affection for his wife, his reverence for her heavenly virtues, and his gentle authority in correcting her faults help to establish the peace and concord deemed necessary for marriage. Both poet-lover and lady learn to embrace a higher law, Christ's law of love. The *Amoretti*, then, can be considered Spenser's legend of humility; its protagonists are the mistress who must learn that her pride imperils the proper order that should exist between husband and wife and the poet-lover who wins her only after repudiating force.

The *Amoretti* sonnets thus enact Spenser's self-fashioning as a Protestant—versus a Petrarchan—poet and lover. The conventions, metaphors, and paradoxes of Petrarchan poetry and loving are redeemed and overwritten by the ideals of sixteenth-century marriage, with its own unique paradox: that mutual love and responsibility can and ought to exist within the hierarchical relationship of marriage. By pairing his sonnets with the *Epithalamion,* Spenser further corrects and surpasses contemporary poetic practice. Daniel, Lodge, and other sonneteers concluded their sequences with female complaints, "testaments to sexual weakness . . . and to the fragility and instability of human affections."[47] Sidney himself got no farther than a kind of retraction of love in *Certaine Sonnets* 31 ("Thou blind men's marke") and 32 ("Leave me ô Love"). Spenser, on the other hand, completes his *Amoretti* with a wedding hymn celebrating passion that is mutual and legitimate, sanctioned and stabilized by marriage. This constitutes a return to and a reaffirmation of the humanist goals for poetry.

The Reaffirmation of Humanist Poetics

When he turned from celebrating Elizabeth Tudor in *The Faerie Queene* to celebrate Elizabeth Boyle in *Amoretti* and *Epithalamion*, Spenser also seemed to realize that, paradoxically, his temporary retreat from his role as laureate poet was necessary for a renewed commitment to the great work of humanist poetics, fashioning virtuous members of the queen's commonwealth and God's kingdom. When Spenser acknowledges his error in abandoning his epic poem, he may be expressing a genuine crisis of his poetry and his spirit, not simply the distraction of his love:

How then should I without another wit:
  thinck ever to endure so taedious toyle,
  sins that this one is tost with troublous fit
  of a proud love, that doth my spirite spoyle.

(*Am* 33:9–12)

The transformation of his "proud love" into a humble wife occasions the poetic and personal reformation that leads to a reaffirmation, not a rejection, of the world. Spenser climbs no ladder of love, achieving his lady only to renounce her, desiring to embrace (like Sidney and Petrarch) a heavenly love instead. Rather, he realizes that until he attains this earthly love, he cannot become a divine poet. Were he assured of attaining the "happie port [of his mistress's love] for ever," he promises in "An Hymne in Honour of Love,"

Then would I sing of thine immortall praise
An heavenly Hymne, such as the Angels sing,
And thy triumphant name then would I raise
Bove all the gods, thee onely honoring,
My guide, my God, my victor, and my king;
Till then, dread Lord, vouchsafe to take of me
This simple song, thus fram'd in praise of thee.[48]

Though the hymn praises human love and pleasure lorded over by Cupid, not Christ, it is no illicit Astrophiliac passion but one "devoyd of guilty shame" ("Hymne" 290); it is no temporary gratification but a permanent one such as the *Amoretti* and *Epithalamion* celebrate. Breaking with convention, *Amoretti* redeems mortal love and argues that it is a precursor and herald of divine love.[49]

Though Sidney wrote that love poetry might be employed with "heavenly fruit, both private and public, in singing the praises of the immortal beauty," in *Astrophil and Stella* he enacted the human inability to realize these ambitions. In despair and resignation, Astrophil remained estranged both from Stella and from the experience of divine grace. Nor do marriage and passion ever reconcile in Sidney's works. The epithalamic eclogues concluding book 3 of the *Arcadia* celebrate the marriage of the rustics Thyrsis and Kala, not the principles Pyrocles and Philoclea, who have just been described making illicit love. Spenser would approve Dicus's depiction of the "honest Bridegroome and the bashfull Bride" who are "[l]ike to the Elme and Vyne" in their "mutuall embracements," virtue "the knot of this their open vowe."[50] But Sidney moves no higher; he only sanctions, he does not sanctify, desire. In another eclogue, Geron sings that "holy marriage, [is] sweete and surest meane / Our foolish lustes in honest rules to stay."[51] For Sidney, marriage is important as a form of social and sexual control; its praise here implicitly censures the illicit and even subversive passion of Pyrocles and the princess Philoclea.[52] For Spenser, by contrast, marriage redeems sensuality—one thinks of the lover's delight in his lady's "Fayre bosom," "her paps like early fruit in May," and those "twoo golden apples" he longs to taste (*Am* 76:1, 9; 77:6).

Though human love and beauty adumbrate the divine and lead virtuous lovers thereto, Spenser affirms that loving well entails not renouncing the world but living well in it. In the proem to book 4 of *The Faerie Queene*, the narrator praises the "kindly flame" of love that

> of honor and all vertue is
> The roote, and brings forth glorious flowres of fame,
> That crowne true lovers with immortal blis,
> The meed of them that love, *and do not live amisse.*
>
> (*FQ* 4 pr. 2; emphasis added)

Promoting virtuous loving is the aim of the reformed Petrarchan poet, promoting well-living the end of the confirmed humanist poet. Both aims meet in Spenser's praise of matrimonial love in *Amoretti* and *Epithalamion.* Marriage is, after all, primarily a social contract, and hence the couple's obligation to its own posterity is stressed in the Renaissance epithalamion. Spenser prays

> That we may raise a large posterity,
> Which from the earth, which they may long possesse,
> With lasting happiness,
> Up to your haughty pallaces may mount
> And for the guerdon of their glorious merit
> May heavenly tabernacles there inherit,
> of blessed Saints for to increase the count.
>
> (*Epi* 417–23)

What better way to fashion virtuous subjects and eventual saints than to beget and raise them oneself? Sidney's defender of marriage, Geron, reminds his opponent in the debate of his obligation to marry and produce children:

> Nature above all things requireth this,
> That we our kind doo labour to maintaine;
> Which drawne-out line doth hold all humane blisse.[53]

If Histor "murders" his posterity by refusing to marry, "Thy common-wealth may rightly grieved be, / Which must by this immortall be preserved."[54] In Rogers's eulogy, marriage is, remember, the "preservative of chastity, the Seminary of the Commonwealth . . . succession of Families, Crownes, and Kingdomes" on which "the very furniture of heaven" depends. Unlike Petrarchan lovers such as Astrophil and Stella, whose passion is illicit and ultimately sterile, spouses in a Christian marriage represent and reproduce the proper order—social, political, and divine. Procreation, beyond poetic making, may be the best way to imitate the heavenly Maker.

Spenser's celebration of his private love in *Amoretti* and *Epithalamion* is thus no shirking of his laureate responsibility but a reconception of it. The humanist poet's ambition to be an arbiter of culture and morality, expressed in Sidney's *Defence*, is redrawn on a more modest scale and addressed within the lowly but hardly insignificant love sonnet. What is at stake in Spenser's courtship of his lady is the very ground of his identity as a humanist and Protestant, a poet and public servant. As a poet and as a sinner, he depends for his life and salvation upon the grace of the lady, which prefigures and mediates God's grace and love. For Spenser, as for Sidney and his followers, the reformation of the practices of love poetry is an enterprise with serious moral and political implications, enabling the transformation of individuals and social institutions alike.

Postscript
Reformations of Petrarchism in Seventeenth-Century Poetry: Herbert, Wroth, and Carew

I have argued here that the Elizabethan love sonnet was deeply engaged with the question of poetry's value and ultimate purpose, an issue highlighted and problematized by Sidney's own writings and by his heroic image. Importantly, Sidney's occupation of the persona of Astrophil, an equivocally exemplary poet, lover, and courtier, enabled successive poets to envision new possibilities for the sonnet—beyond Petrarchan imitation, flattery, or seduction—as a means of engagement with culturally central issues of humanist activism, scholarship, and even the soul's salvation. My approach has challenged both the traditional view that conventional forms of expression and prior models impede (rather than complexly enable) the sonneteer's voice and the new historicist assumption that, where courtly sonnets are concerned, the personal is actually political. Rather, a conflict between the indulgence of "private" passions (expressed in conventional rather than individual terms) and the performance of one's public obligations as a humanist poet animates the lyric poetry of Sidney, Spenser, and their successors, even into the next century. Like the tensions inherent in Sidney's exemplary image, the question of the role of private desire in public discourse is never fully resolved. Looking ahead to the seventeenth century, I have selected three very different figures—a devotional poet and a female sonneteer, both with ties to Sidney, and a cavalier love poet—in order to glance at the fortunes of Sidneian poetics and Petrarchism in the post-Elizabethan years. In their poetry, George Herbert, Lady Mary Wroth, and Thomas Carew disengage themselves (to varying degrees) from humanist concerns to embrace the personal and private, a move associated (as in Spenser's poetry) with the critique or revision of Elizabethan Petrarchism as a literary convention and as a sociopolitical configuration.

When the subject is Elizabethan poetry, privacy is often a fiction and publicity a self-promoting ruse. While Sidney had circulated his love sonnets among a coterie audience, other poets rushed to publish their supposedly private amours. Daniel protested in the dedication of his 1592 *Delia*, "I rather desired to keep in the private passions of my youth, from the multitude as things utterd to my selfe, and consecrated to silence: yet seeing I was betraide. . . . I am forced to publish that which I never ment" (A2^{r}). Publication rendered paradoxical the poetry's claims to privacy, and the sonnet became an arena in which the poet laid bare his passion, his repentance, and his poetic ambitions. But this self-disclosing sonneteer is no forerunner of the romantic lyric poet, recollecting his powerful feelings in tranquillity. To the contrary, Elizabethan sonnets rely on conventions in part to obscure and problematize their relation to the personal. For example, Astrophil alludes to Philip Sidney but also eludes the identification; the name means star-lover (and Stella is his star). The sequence depends on a measure of deniability. Under the contrived privacy of courtship, veiled by conventional conceits and forms of representation, a sonneteer could meditate upon various experiences of subordination, including that of a subject to a powerful, denying queen, a client to a patron, a sinner to his God. The "private" emotions of Petrarchan lovers became public currency, circulated by poets who aspired to higher forms of poetry and positions of prominence and service. It is Spenser who most urgently questions the goals of humanist poetics in his critical portrayal of Sidney and reverses the priority of public ambition and private desire in his sonnet sequence. He is the only sonneteer not to disguise his beloved behind an abstract name and to refuse to play the courtly game of Petrarchan domination. In the *Amoretti* volume, he publicizes his choice to pursue private desire rather than royal favor.

Whether they published or only circulated their "private" amours, Sidney, Greville, Spenser, and Daniel all ultimately questioned whether their poetry deserved any place of honor in the wider culture. When it came to "that lyrical kind of songs and sonnets," the answer seemed to be "no"; without serious reformation and redirection, the love sonnet was undeserving of praise, a misuse of wit at best and a grave sin at worst. Ultimately, it would seem, the values of the Elizabethan court, which enforced a Petrarchan configuration upon the poetry and practice of courtship, were profoundly at odds with the reformist tendencies of the era's most committed poet-courtiers. This tension is most visible in Spenser's *Amoretti* volume. One cannot serve both the little love god, Cupid, and the Lord God. More to Greville's point, to serve the tyrannizing mistress in whatever incarnation she assumes—Myra, Caelica, Isis/Elizabeth—is a form of idolatry that defaces the image of one's divine Master. The moral imperative to use poetry rightly impels Sidney, Greville, and Spenser to reform the love sonnet and to promote proper attitudes of submission and service. Astrophil struggles, without much success, to control his aggressive desire and submit to Stella; Spenser's poet-lover, with more success, submits to the divinity his beloved adumbrates.

The Elizabethan courtly sonnet was a site of reformation, in several senses of the word. Poets of the reformed religion, including Sidney, Spenser, and Greville, sought to bring their poetry into accord with Protestant and humanist values. They mused upon the inevitability of human frailty and its implications for politics and society. They sometimes chafed at their submission to authority, pondering rebellion against or reformation of the sociopolitical order. These men were all poetic reformers, too, and despite the reputation of the sonnet sequence for being derivative, imitative, and repetitious, they wrought some profound changes in its practice. They refashioned the Petrarchan sonnet into a form capable of articulating forms of desire and negotiating forms of authority—amorous, political, and poetic. Of course, they also re-formed Sidney's image and legacy. It was Sidney who first enabled the sonnet to speak with several voices simultaneously, expressing desire for and estrangement from Stella, the queen, and God alike, confusing and conflating personal and political goals. Greville then exploited the potential for multiple ironies by developing the analogies between lust, political tyranny, and religious idolatry. Spenser renounced Petrarchism altogether, reforming its values with those of Protestant Christianity, replacing its clichés with his culture's wisdom about marriage. Daniel's reformations, sociopoetic rather than religious, made the sonnet sequence an effective tool for currying the favor of a patron and demonstrating his admiring imitation of Sidney as well as his own lyrical skill.

The traditional wisdom of literary history has it that Petrarchism and the courtly sonnet sequence became obsolete with the passing of Elizabeth and faded from practice, enabling the tradition of religious poetry to reemerge with the metaphysical and meditative sonnets of Donne and Herbert.[1] This evolutionary version of the sonnet story has some shortcomings, however. It generally underestimates the variety and richness of what was occurring in the Elizabethan sonnet, beyond veiled praise and blame of Queen Elizabeth. It privileges early seventeenth-century devotional poetry as serious and heartfelt, while dismissing Elizabethan lyrics as insincere and derivative.[2] It also exaggerates the divide between amorous and religious poetry, evident in criticism of Donne.[3] The Elizabethan love sonnet was already a site of intense concern with religious issues of sin, salvation, and the proper use of one's God-given wits. Even during the height of the sonnet vogue, poets heeded Sidney's call to reform the love sonnet. Barnabe Barnes, for one, followed his courtly sequence *Parthenophil to Parthenophe* (1593) with *A Divine Centurie of Spirituall Sonnets* (1595), in the opening sonnet of which he renounces his "lewde laies of Lighter loves" and takes the Holy Spirit for his muse. Well into the seventeenth century, however, the attraction of lewd love lays persisted, amorous Petrarchan language dying hard with Herbert, reviving easily with Carew.

* * *

When Herbert asks "My God. . . . Doth Poetry / Wear *Venus* Livery? only serve her turn? / Why are not *Sonnets* made of thee?"[4] he is addressing an old question, one posed by Sidney in his *Defence* and never far from the conscience of an Elizabethan sonneteer. Herbert is not the first poet, though he may be the most famed, to reform Petrarchism by redirecting its language of love to a divine object. The originary exemplar of the divine poet is, of course, the psalmist David, and Lewalski has shown how thoroughly Herbert assimilates the Davidic voice into his own poems.[5] Herbert's more immediate precursor, however, is Sidney, whose voice in *Astrophil and Stella* he echoes in poems of *The Temple*.[6] Herbert is a shining example of a successor who admired and imitated Sidney but, recognizing the deeper issues of his poetics, sought to correct and overgo his example.

Herbert clearly ascribes to some features of Sidney's poetics. In "Love (I)" and "Love (II)," Herbert, like Sidney in the *Defence,* laments the misuse of poetry to praise mortal rather than divine love. "Immortal Love, author of this great frame," is parceled out

> While mortall love doth all the title gain!
> Which siding with invention, they together
> Bear all the sway, possessing heart and brain,
> (Thy workmanship) and give thee share in neither.[7]

Herbert here makes explicit Sidney's suggestion that poetic makers with their witty inventions usurp the role of the "heavenly Maker" (*Defence* 24) and fail to honor Him. Concluding "Love (I)," Herbert's speaker asks, "Who sings thy praise? onely a skarf or glove / Doth warm our hands, and make them write of love" (ll. 13–14). This image of the unwilling poet overmastered by the force of his (mortal) love recalls Astrophil, forswearing the title of poet but confessing helplessly to Stella that "all my words thy beauty doth endite, / And *love doth hold my hand, and makes me write*" (*AS* 90:13–14; emphasis added). "Love (II)," a stichomythic response to "Love I," picks up on its last line, invoking "Immortal Heat, O let thy greater flame / Attract the lesser to it" (ll. 1–2); when this flame warms the poet's cold hand, he writes hymns rather than sonnets, his "usurping lust" (l. 12) consumed by true desires. Purging as well as warming, this heat reforms the wit and redirects it to praise of God, the Maker: "All knees shall bow to thee; all wits shall rise, / And praise him who did make and mend our eies" (ll. 13–14). Significantly, "Love (I)" and its response, "Love (II)," are sonnets, the form associated with profane love; in this pair of poems, Herbert corrects himself, enacting the reformation of the love poet and his sonnets.

Most critics assume that Herbert's sonnets straightforwardly declare their independence from Elizabethan practice and that he excels in what Louis Martz calls "the art of sacred parody," exposing and remedying the errors of popular love poetry.[8] One example of Herbert correcting Sidney, however, will suffice to show how complex is his engagement with the prior poet. In one of Sidney's most justly famed sonnets, Stella is a book who teaches Astrophil virtue—but without much success:

Who will in fairest booke of Nature know,
  How Vertue may best lodg'd in beautie be,
  Let him but learne of *Love* to reade in thee,
Stella, those faire lines, which true goodnesse show.

(*AS* 71:1–4)

For all Stella's perfection, however, she fails to move Astrophil to goodness; in the sonnet's final line, his "Desire still cries, 'give me some food.'" Stella is an authoritative text but one that fails to satisfy Astrophil's less bookish needs. Herbert's pair of sonnets on the Holy Scriptures directly responds to Sidney. Unlike the "book of Nature," scripture is a book that fully satisfies and heals:

Oh Book! infinite sweetnesse! let my heart
    Suck ev'ry letter, and a hony gaine,
    Precious for any grief in any part;
To cleare the breast, to mollifie all pain.

Thou art all health, health thriving till it make
    A full eternitie . . .

("H. Scriptures [I]" 1–6)

Herbert's text thus "corrects" Sidney's, and it aims to teach as well—"Ladies, look here; this is the thankfull glasse, / That mends the lookers eyes" (ll. 8–9). "H. Scriptures (II)" is more explicit in its criticism of Stella and Astrophil, concluding with this aphoristic, didactic couplet: "Starres are poore books, & oftentimes do misse: / This book of starres lights to eternall blisse" (ll. 13–14). Though the message could not be more clear, Herbert's break from Sidney is not complete. In "H. Scriptures (I)," the poet, sounding like Astrophil, addresses his book as a beloved mistress he would kiss. Herbert preserves, even intensifies, the metaphor of feeding that subverts Sidney's sonnet; the activity of sucking honey suggests nourishment more erotic than spiritual.[9] Besides healing the heart, the Scriptures provide the sensual satisfaction that Stella denies. Herbert's impulse to reform the love sonnet capitulates to his shared weakness with Sidney: the human desire for sensual gratification and the related delight in the rich language of love poetry. This is the poet, after all, who laments, "Lovely enchanting language, sugar-cane, / Hony of roses, whither wilt thou flie?" ("The Forerunners" 19–20), embracing with difficulty the simpler language of religious devotion.

For Herbert, as for Spenser, poetic reformation and individual salvation are inseparable from each other, and they take precedence over humanist goals, the transformation of church and society. It is sometimes easy to forget, however, that Herbert's "private" devotional poetry is also socially embedded in religious institutions (witness the title and structure of *The Temple*) and in residual courtly practices. John Wall argues that the speaker of "The Church" is a member of a community of love, oriented towards God and working for the establishment of the Christian commonwealth on earth.[10] Michael Schoenfeldt has shown how, in *The Temple,* Herbert both assimilates and supplants the courtly tradition. Under Herbert's pen, the tropes of courtesy become weapons for the weak, means of complying with and rebelling against authority, divine or earthly; "the ingratiating power of humility offers the surest way to rise."[11]

Among the Elizabethan sonneteers, Daniel used the posture of humility to advance himself with his patroness, and Spenser's lover gently enticed the submission of his beloved deer/dear. Herbert further complicates this courtly strategy to articulate profound mysteries of salvation. One example is a sonnet that, like Spenser's *Amoretti* 68, enacts the paradox of redemptive humility. Its speaker is an aggrieved tenant desiring new terms on his lease; seeking his "rich Lord" among those of high estate, he unwittingly locates him among "theeves and murderers: there I him espied, / Who straight, *Your suit is granted*, said, & died" ("Redemption" 13–14). The lord reveals himself as simultaneously the most humble and most powerful, the God-man, who trumps the speaker's (false) humility with his radical humility, his powerfully redemptive dying. By granting his suit even before it is spoken, the lord silences the speaker's bold words and redeems the poet and his unspoken language of pleading. In this poem, Herbert's God confounds the *raison d'être* of the amorous sonnet sequence, the perpetual, unsatisfied suing for grace.

* * *

Related to the reformist impulse of the Elizabethan sonneteer is an emerging iconoclasm, as poets challenge the courtly status quo and undermine its Petrarchan images and values. Redeeming the errors of sinful loving and poetry, Greville and Spenser dethrone or deface Petrarchan icons, restoring holy images (Greville) or crafting men and women in the divine image (Spenser). In the sonnet sequence of Lady Mary Wroth, *Pamphilia to Amphilanthus*, there are no Petrarchan icons, no blasons of beauty; indeed, the beloved is never described. The female speaker, bemoaning her lover's inconstancy, brings a different set of values to the sonnet sequence. The effort to achieve self-control and self-possession replaces the desire to dominate and control the beloved. She writes not to convince her lover to pity her or to remain faithful but to console herself and to prove her own worth/wroth. In a tradition defined and dominated by male writers, particularly her uncle, Sir Philip Sidney, Wroth truly breaks the Elizabethan sonnet mold as she struggles to affirm her identity as a poet and a virtuous lover.

Lady Mary Wroth never met her famous uncle, for she was born probably just after his death. She had a number of literary authorities within her immediate family; her father, Robert Sidney, was also a poet, albeit a minor one, and her aunt, the countess of Pembroke, was known for her translations of the Psalms, among other literary activities. It was her uncle Philip's example, however, that Mary Wroth followed, publishing one installment of a lengthy romance, *The Countess of Montgomery's Urania* (1621). This work gestures towards its predecessor, Sidney's *New Arcadia*, which opened with shepherds mourning the departure of the goddess Urania from the earth. Wroth also appended to her romance a sonnet sequence, *Pamphilia to Amphilanthus*. Such evidence of admiring imitation has led one critic to the conclusion that Wroth writes in (or is written by) the language of her father figures, that she does not succeed in expressing herself as a desiring subject or in modifying the Petrarchan tradition.[12] Others find that Wroth writes against tradition, that her female speaker disrupts the expectation that women be passive and silent and achieves a measure of subjectivity.[13] My brief discussion of Wroth's sonnets will consider how the values promoted by a woman writer encroaching upon the male preserve of Petrarchan sonneteering challenge and modify its conventions of aggressive praise and persuasion.[14] Her virtues of chastity and constancy enable her to write love poetry without compromising her reputation, yet those virtues also render the purpose of sonneteering (namely, seduction) irrelevant. Wroth thus attempts to reform courtly loving and to authorize herself not by invoking prior poets and following received conventions but by asserting the authority of her own virtue of chaste constancy.

The value of privacy and the impulse towards publicity compete in Wroth's life and works.[15] She had been at the center of the Jacobean court, a friend of Queen Anne, but her adulterous affair with her own cousin (by whom she bore two children), her husband's death, and her ensuing bankruptcy resulted in her isolation. Partly out of financial necessity, and perhaps to end her exile from court, she took the risks attending publication of her work.[16] Because contemporary intrigues and scandals were but thinly disguised in *Urania*, she offended many readers. One of these was Baron Edward Denny, who attacked her virtue with the obscene charge that "common oysters such as thine gape wide / And take in pearles or worse at every tide" and advised her to "leave idle bookes alone / For wise and worthyer women have writte none." He urged her to follow the example of her "virtuous and learned aunt," the countess of Pembroke, and to "redeem the time with writing as large a volume of heavenly lays and holy love as you have of lascivious tales and amorous toys."[17] This incident underscores the precarious position of a woman writer in a culture that tended to identify a woman's silence with chastity and to punish her for publishing in male modes—romance and love sonnets—rather than in pious genres approved for women.

Wroth's gendered experience of writing and loving leads her to revise significantly the poetic conventions she inherits. An example is this poem from *Pamphilia to Amphilanthus*, in which the destructive conquest that Petrarchan poets ascribed to the lady's eyes is redefined as the power to pierce falsehoods. The traditional values of feminine modesty and secrecy are modified to authorize a female gaze that is shameless and morally triumphant:

Take heed mine eyes, how you your lookes doe cast
  Least they beetray my harts most secrett thought;
  Bee true unto your selves for nothings bought
  More deere then doubt which brings a lovers fast.
Catch you all waching eyes, ere they bee past,
  Or take yours fixt where your best love hath sought
  The pride of your desires; let them bee taught
  Theyr faults for shame, they could noe truer last;
Then looke, and looke with joye for conquest wunn
  Of those that search'd your hurt in double kinde;
  Soe you kept safe, lett them themselves looke blinde
  Watch, gaze, and marke till they to madnes runn,
While you, mine eyes injoye full sight of love
Contented that such hapinesses move.[18]

The cautious looks that conceal Pamphilia's thoughts are emboldened in the second stanza, becoming the gaze that catches all watching eyes and refuses to blink. The unflinching gaze of the woman rebukes those (presumably men) who look away and thereby admit their inability to match her steady gaze, her constancy. Hers is not the male gaze that anatomizes and possesses the beloved; indeed, Pamphilia never even describes Amphilanthus. This is a looking that unmasks untruth in others while revealing nothing, secure in its virtue, triumphant because it preserves the lady's secret thoughts. In an environment where self-exposure and publicity threaten a woman's reputation, Pamphilia's eyes are warders of her privacy and integrity, making her invulnerable to prying eyes.[19] The power of her eyes signifies virtue, not the destructive potential of the Petrarchan mistress.

Wroth's female poet-lover finds Petrarchan courtship as unsatisfying as her male counterparts had, though for a fundamentally different reason: not female intransigence but male infidelity. Indeed, she articulates the Petrarchan bind from the lady's perspective; the likeliest explanation for her desertion is that Amphilanthus sought out a more yielding mistress. The abandoned Pamphilia, in turn, seeks out a more enduring kind of love. The corona of fourteen sonnets within the larger sequence is Wroth's attempted reformation of courtly loving. Lost in a "strang labourinth," Pamphilia is threatened by love, danger, suspicion, and shame, those allegorical attributes of courtly loving. She resolves "to leave all, and take the thread of love" (P 77:1, 14), which leads to a kind of inward, feminized paradise. There, "chaste thoughts guide us" and the "Light of true love, brings fruite which none repent" (P 78:5, 7). Constant love is the "Image of fayth, and wombe for joyes increase" (l. 12). In this paradise of abundance, the female poet-lover's confidence burgeons and her self-knowledge grows:

It [true love] doth inrich the witts, and make you see
That in your self, which you knew nott before,
Forcing you to admire such guifts showld bee
Hid from your knowledg, yett in you the store;

(P 82:9–12)

The image of the internal paradise of egalitarian love, however, is succeeded by that of the hierarchical court of love, and here Wroth's attempt to reform the courtly love tradition begins to falter. Wroth's court is presided over not by Cupid but by a noble lord of love, who is at once a benevolent monarch, virtuous husband, and Christlike teacher:

Hee may owr profitt [prophet] and our Tuter prove
In whom alone wee doe this power finde,
To joine two harts as in one frame to move;
Two bodies, butt one soule to rule the minde;

(P 82:1–4)[20]

But the sequence does not resolve itself like Spenser's *Amoretti*, praising marriage. In the penultimate sonnet, the speaker seemingly submits to this lord:

To thee then lord commander of all harts,
Ruller of owr affections kinde, and just
Great King of Love, my soule from fained smarts
Or thought of change I offer to your trust

This crowne, my self, and all that I have more
Except my hart which you beestow'd beefore.

(P 89:9–14)

In the last line (which is the first line of the next sonnet), however, she revokes part of the gift:

Except my hart which you beestow'd before,
And for a signe of conquest gave away
As worthles to bee kept in your choyse store
Yett one more spotles with you doth nott stay.

(P 90:1–4)

As if reminded of her ill usc by Amphilanthus, Pamphilia now bitterly castigates this lord of love as an ungrateful monarch, even a tyrant. The sequence ends where it began, in the same court of danger and suspicion, and with the same question: "In this strange labourinth how shall I turne?" Clearly Pamphilia disdains submission within this courtly, Petrarchan hierarchy that signals its affinity to the institutions of Christian commonwealth and patriarchal marriage, but there is no answer to her question, no escape from the labyrinth.[21]

Before the attempted reform short-circuits, however, Wroth's speaker affirms that among the benefits of her truth in love is an access of confidence in her identity as a poet and as a lover. She imagines love enabling her poetry:

Love will a painter make you, such, as you
Shall able bee to *drawe your only deere*
More lively, parfett, lasting, and more true
Then rarest woorkman, and *to you more neere*,

(P 83:9–12; emphasis added)

This sounds much like the sonneteer's practice of idealized representation, but Wroth neither depicts nor idealizes the unfaithful Amphilanthus. Rather, I am reminded more of Spenser's gentle speaker in *Amoretti*, enticing his deer/dear. I see in the rich ambiguity of the emphasized phrases a suggestion of tenderness in the speaker's desire to draw or attract the beloved and to fashion or portray him as a true lover, thus making him resemble the speaker (the workman) and drawing him into intimacy with her. These connotations are present in the word "neere."[22] The speaker's self-confidence persists, even when she contemplates the loveless Amphilanthus:

And cursed hee whos spiritt not admires
The worth of love, wher endles blessednes
Raines, and commands, maintaind by heavnly fires

> Made of vertu, join'de by truth, blowne by desires
> Strengthned by worth. . . .
>
> (P 84:2–6)

Not once, but twice, Wroth puns on her own name, associating it (and her female speaker) with virtuous, heavenly love. Finally, convinced of her virtue, Wroth's Pamphilia lays her muse to rest in the final sonnet:

> My muse now hapy, lay thy self to rest,
> Sleepe in the quiett of a faithfull love,
> Write you noe more, butt lett thes phant'sies move
> Some other harts. . . .
>
> (P 103:1–4)

Perhaps imitating her uncle, Sir Philip Sidney, who also renounced earthly for heavenly love,[23] Pamphilia vows to address her thoughts to higher joys, "And thus leave off, what's past showes you can love, / Now lett your constancy your honor prove" (P 103:13–14). For Wroth, her identity as a chaste and confident lover authorizes her to write poetry; in turn, the poetry proves her truth in love, confirming her virtue. As a poet, Wroth aims less to engage her poetic predecessors, not at all to persuade a reluctant lover; rather, she fashions herself as a model of virtue. Confirmed chaste, she has no use for the love sonnet's traditional ploys of seduction and praise. Having proved herself a true lover, Wroth can relinquish her public identity of poet, drawing her identity from the private virtue of constancy.

In one respect, Wroth is true to the spirit of Petrarch; her Pamphilia, though scorned and disdained, is an ever-faithful lover. This fidelity, however, has more to do with Wroth's affirmation of the virtue of constancy and her recognition of the cultural expectation of female chastity than her allegiance to a poetic tradition. Similarly, Wroth's departures from Petrarchism issue from an impulse to critique the moral rather than the political arrangements of society. She also recognizes that its conventions are inappropriate to the situation of a female lover concerned with matters of personal honor and integrity. In that sense, her poetry is less germane to the larger humanist concerns that impelled Sidney and his followers and that inform even George Herbert's devotional poetry.

* * *

Fidelity in love and female chastity, as Petrarchan ideals or as Christian virtues, are hardly values one would associate with poets of the Caroline court, whose designation "Cavalier" has become synonymous with libertine attitudes towards women and love and a thorough repudiation of Elizabethan idealism. Caroline poets have traditionally been criticized as a group of effete courtiers and time-servers disengaged from the moral and political issues of their day. This view has been recently challenged by Kevin Sharpe, who argues that Thomas Carew, for one, was firmly in the tradition of Renaissance humanism and that he "reemployed, adapted, and even subverted" the conventions of Petrarchan love poetry to examine contemporary social and political relationships.[24]

Thomas Carew, a poet and Caroline courtier par excellence, offers an opportunity to study the fate of humanist poetry and the fortunes of Petrarchism at the Stuart court. Anthony Low has remarked the "general stripping away of dead Petrarchan conventions which no longer suit the new age"[25] and linked Carew's new, libertine lover to the rise of a market economy. To the contrary, Carew's poetry is deeply indebted to Petrarch,[26] and his libertine lover has precursors in the Elizabethan tradition.[27] Caroline Petrarchism differs somewhat from the Elizabethan version, however; while Sidney and his fellows invoked Petrarch to legitimize their poetic ambitions and to negotiate their submission to royal authority, the Caroline poet adopts a Petrarchan stance to assert sexual and poetic prowess, perhaps even to repudiate the platonic cult fostered at court by Henrietta Maria. In my brief discussion of Carew, I will consider how his libertine speaker exposes the strategies of the Petrarchan poet-lover and effects a turnabout of Petrarchan power relations; the cavalier poet deconstructs, rather than reforms, the conventions. Moreover, his allegiance to pleasure and power, together with a demystification and devaluation of poetry, prevent his submission to the higher humanist goals embraced by his Elizabethan predecessors.

Carew's speaker exposes what surely everyone, including the lady addressed, recognized as the function of love poetry, namely, seduction. The speaker advises a young maid: "Netts, of passions finest thred, / Snaring Poems, will be spred, / All, to catch thy maiden-head."[28] Carew openly practices the art of seduction while mocking those ploys Elizabethan sonneteers used to convince the lady to relent:

Then give me leave to love, and love me too,
Not with designe
To rayse, as Loves curst Rebells doe,
When puling Poets whine,
Fame to their beautie, from their blubbr'd eyne.[29]

Instead of promising his lady fame, he proposes a different kind of pact if she succumbs:

Rich Natures store, (which is the Poets Treasure)
I'le spend, to dresse
Your beauties, if your mine of Pleasure
In equall thankfulnesse
You but unlocke, so we each other blesse.[30]

With words like "store," "treasure," "spend," "dresse," and "mine," Carew manages to suggest a material dimension to the exchange, sounding less like a poet promising to eternize his beloved than a courtier decking his mistress with finery. His use of "blesse" also mocks any pretense of spiritual transcendence in love.[31] Here Carew promotes a reciprocity very different in spirit from the mutuality advocated by Daniel, Spenser, and Wroth. In another seductive poem, Carew's speaker promises mutual pleasure in the sexual encounter. He points out that women are also framed for pleasure and urges "'twere a madnesse not to grant / That which affords (if you consent) / To you the giver, more content / Then me the beggar."[32] As Braden points out, in libertine poetry "the reciprocity of sexual pleasure is . . . among the seducer's most compelling arguments."[33] This tactic mocks the Elizabethan poet's attempts to seduce his lady by promising her a mere sonnet in return.

A darker side to this egalitarian ethic emerges in "A Rapture," Carew's most famed poem, an explicit and erotic fantasy that invites women to share the speaker's libertine morality. The speaker urges Celia to give in to his sexual advances, using an appeal to female liberty that turns out, however, to be quite suspect. He urges her to bypass the "Gyant, Honour, that keepes cowards out, / . . . and the servile rout / Of baser subjects. . . ." Honor is no more than "a weake modell wrought / By greedy men, that seeke to enclose the common, / And within private armes empale free women." Celia is invited to depose this usurper who unjustly "fetter[ed] your soft sex with Chastitie, / Which Nature made unapt for abstinence."[34] One wonders what Wroth would have made of this attempt to demonize and subvert a principle so germane to her virtuous identity. In "A Rapture,"

Carew imagines, as Wroth did in her corona, a prelapsarian paradise, though hardly a chaste one, for there even Petrarch lies with his Laura. Carew's Eden is also characterized more by Adamic mastery over nature than the tender mutuality of Wroth's feminized Eden. His lover proclaims that, like a bee, he "will rifle all the sweets . . . and swell / My bagge with honey, drawne forth by the power / Of fervent kisses . . . I'le seize the Rose-buds . . . the smooth, calme Ocean, invade / With such a tempest. . . ." In "A Rapture" and other poems, mutuality is belied by the aggression of the male lover. Carew champions the ethic of mastery in love repudiated by Spenser in *Amoretti*, and he disdains marital chastity as well: "the hated name / Of husband, wife, lust, modest, chaste, or shame, / Are vaine and empty words. . . . All things are lawfull there."[35]

Not only as a lover but also as a poet, Carew celebrates his mastery over Celia:

> That killing power is none of thine,
> I gave it to thy voyce, and eyes:
> Thy sweets, thy graces, all are mine;
> Thou art my starre, shin'st in my skies;
> . . . .
> Tempt me with such affrights no more,
> Lest what I made, I uncreate;[36]

Sidney likewise threatens his lady with his power as a poet in song 5 of *Astrophil and Stella*, but there Astrophil's petulance contrasts to the cold and confident tone of Carew's speaker, who sounds like a jealous, possessive god. He then rejects Celia, the Petrarchan mistress who is revealed as nothing more than an empty icon:

> I have searcht thy soule within,
> And find nought, but pride, and scorne;
> I have learn'd thy arts, and now
> Can disdaine as much as thou.[37]

The Petrarchan tables have been turned, and the male poet, not the mistress, is in control. Petrarchism is demystified but also repoliticized, as human sexual relationships both resemble and replicate the political order, where the poet-lover is the monarch and the mistress the submissive member of the body politic.[38]

Though Carew exposes the mechanisms of Petrarchan poetry and mocks the humility of the poet-lover, he never reforms the conventions or embraces a higher purpose than poetic lovemaking. True, he can be ironic, refusing the "dull wayes, by which base pens, for hire" elegize beauty: "One shall enspheare thine eyes, another shall / Impearle thy teeth; a third, thy white and small / Hand, shall besnow." Mocking these trite, monotonous tactics, he offers nothing new. Instead, he dismisses poetry altogether: "Thou art the Theame of Truth, not Poetrie."[39] But no higher truth emerges; Sharpe's attempts notwithstanding, Carew resists repatriation into a humanist tradition that linked poetry to action in the public sphere. Reluctantly responding to an invitation to elegize the king of Sweden, Carew objects that the subject of the king is outside poetry, whose purview is matters of love and revelry, not heroic deeds:

> Alas! how may
> My Lyrique feet, that of the smooth soft way
> Of Love, and Beautie, onely know the tread,
> In dancing paces celebrate the dead
> Victorious king . . .
> . . . .
>
> His actions were too mighty to be rais'd
> Higher by Verse, let him in prose be prays'd . . .

Carew uses the occasion to promote an insular, antipolitical stance:

> But let us that in myrtle bowers sit
> Under secure shades, use the benefit
> Of peace and plenty, which the blessed hand
> Of our good King gives this obdurate Land,
> Let us of Revels sing. . . .
> . . . .
> Tourneys, Masques, Theaters, better become
> Our *Halcyon* dayes; what though the German Drum
> Bellow for freedome and revenge, the noyse
> Concernes not us, nor should divert our joyes.[40]

One can hardly imagine a view more distant from Sidney's ideal of the poet as statesman and his belief that poetry provided models for the practice of virtue.[41]

Carew's poetry, if it seems remote from Sidney's humanism, represents an access of meaning for a revised Petrarchism that releases, rather than represses, desires for erotic pleasure and power. Herbert and Wroth, on the other hand, are recognizably indebted to Sidney's example as a poet and humanist, and their Petrarchism sublimates, rather than celebrates, erotic desire. Yet they, together with Carew, begin to grant priority to private experience: Herbert expresses the soul's love for God, not a mistress; Wroth affirms personal virtue over her public identity as a poet; and Carew celebrates (perhaps with some irony) sexual license, pleasure, and power. Whether religious or amorous, chaste or cavalier, however, this love poetry reveals its Elizabethan roots. Herbert, Wroth, and even Carew still concern themselves with the value of poetry and its role in fostering virtuous engagement in the world, if only to retreat into a realm of private virtue or desire. They all consider the relevance of the Petrarchan ethic of domination and submission to social and personal relationships, especially those associated with court. They also participate, inevitably, in the ongoing revision and reformation of prior conventions and models in the construction of their poetic authority.

Notes

Introduction: The Exemplary Sir Philip Sidney

1. B. W., "A commemoration of the generall mone, the honorable and solemne funerall made for . . . Sir Phillip Sidney," appended to "Sir Phillip Sidney, his honorable life, his valiant death, and true vertues" by George Whetstone, in *Elegies for Sir Philip Sidney (1587)*, ed. A. J. Colaianne and W. L. Godshalk (New York: Scholars' Facsimiles and Reprints, 1980), C3v. B. W. is Bernard Whetstone, brother of George Whetstone, Sidney's elegist.

2. Ibid.

3. Thomas Lant, *Sequitur celebritas & pompa funeris*, in *Elegies for Sir Philip Sidney* (1587). Transcriptions are taken from Sander Bos et al., "Sidney's Funeral Portrayed," in *Sir Philip Sidney: 1586 and the Creation of a Legend*, ed. Jan van Dorsten et al. (Leiden: E. J. Brill, 1986), 58.

4. B. W., "A commemoration."

5. Thomas Churchyard, "The Worthie Sir Phillip Sidney Knight his Epitaph," in Samuel Butler, ed., *Sidneiana* (London: Shakespeare Press, 1837), 35–36.

6. A. J. Colaianne and W. L. Godshalk, Introduction to *Elegies for Sir Philip Sidney* (1587), ix. Facsimiles of *Academiae Cantabrigiensis Lacrymae*, *Exequiae illustrissimiequitis D. Philippi Sidnaie* and *Peplus illustrissimi viri D. Philippe Sidnaei* are reprinted in this volume.

7. Theodore L. Steinberg provides a translation of these "standard epitaphic verses" (4) in "Weeping for Sidney," *Sidney Newsletter and Journal* 11.2 (1991): 3–15, and Anne Prescott notes some common conceits in her letter to the editor in *Sidney Newsletter and Journal* 12.1 (1992): 29–31.

8. Raphael Falco, "Instant Artifacts: Vernacular Elegies for Philip Sidney," *Studies in Philology* 89 (1992), 3. See also G. W. Pigman III, *Grief and English Renaissance Elegy* (Cambridge: Cambridge University Press, 1985), 53.

9. For a Marxist analysis of the participation of the general populace in Sidney's death, see Ronald Strickland, "Pageantry and Poetry as Discourse: The Production of Subjectivity in Sir Philip Sidney's Funeral," *ELH* 57 (1990): 19–36. J. F. R. Day counters Strickland's subversive reading with a proudly traditional one, situating the

event within aristocratic funeral practices and claiming a conscious motive of glorifying Sidney ("Death be very proud: Sidney, Subversion, and Elizabethan Heraldic Funerals," in *Tudor Political Culture*, ed. Dale Hoak [Cambridge: Cambridge University Press, 1995], 179–203).

10. See Theodore Zouch, *Memoirs of the Life and Writings of Sir Philip Sidney* (York, 1808), 284; B. W., "A commemoration," ("The Flushingers made sute his breathles corps to have, / And offered a sumptuous Tombe the same for to engrave" [C3v]); Fulke Greville, *The Life of the Renowned Sir Philip Sidney* (1652; rpt., Delmar, N.Y.: Scholars' Facsimiles and Reprints, 1984), 165. Holland's offer may be part of the myth, for as Bos et al. point out, there is no documentary evidence to support the claim (49–50).

11. Quoted in Bos et al., 58; see Katherine Duncan-Jones, *Sir Philip Sidney: Courtier Poet* (New Haven: Yale University Press, 1991), 300.

12. See Alan Hager, "The Exemplary Mirage: Fabrication of Sir Philip Sidney's Biographical Image and the Sidney Reader," *ELH* 48 (1981), 8. For a contrary view, see John Buxton, "The Mourning for Sidney," *Renaissance Studies* 3 (1989), 50.

13. On Elizabeth's policy in the Low Countries as part and parcel of a complex strategy involving the French and aimed at curbing Spanish power, see Wallace T. MacCaffrey, *Queen Elizabeth and the Making of Policy, 1572–1588* (Princeton: Princeton University Press, 1981), chaps. 7–14.

14. *Lant's Roll* closely resembles Goltzius's *Haec pompa funebris* (1584), a frieze of William's funeral. See Walter L. Strauss, *Hendrick Goltzius: The Complete Engravings and Woodcuts* (New York: Abaris Books, 1977), vol. 1, plates 192–203. It may have been Leicester who, familiar with Goltzius's work, conceived of a like frieze for his nephew; upon his arrival to join Sidney in the Netherlands, he stayed at the house in Delft in which William had been assassinated. R. E. Giesey, in *The Royal Funeral Ceremony in Renaissance France* (Geneva: E. Droz, 1960), prints a similar frieze-like rendering of the funeral of Henry IV in 1610 (plate 10). See the brief discussion of continental models in Bos et al., 42.

15. Bos et al., 51; Hager, "The Exemplary Mirage," 9. On the political process at work in public festivities, and the interpenetration of public and private therein, see Richard C. Trexler, *Public Life in Renaissance Florence* (New York: Academic Press, 1980), esp. chap. 8, "The Ritual of Celebration."

16. Bos et al., 39.

17. Dominic Baker-Smith, in "'Great Expectation': Sidney's Death and the Poets," in *Sir Philip Sidney: 1586 and the Creation of a Legend*, ed. Jan van Dorsten et al. (Leiden: E. J. Brill, 1986), argues that these volumes are "part of a wider campaign to exploit Sidney's death in favor of an interventionist policy in the Netherlands" (90).

18. On Waldegrave's Puritan publishing record, see Patrick Collinson, *The Elizabethan Puritan Movement* (Berkeley and Los Angeles: University of California Press, 1967), 273–74.

19. See A. L. Bennett, "The Principal Rhetorical Conventions in the Renaissance Personal Elegy," *Studies in Philology* 51 (1954): 107–26, for an overview of these conventions.

20. John Phillips, "The Life and Death of Sir Phillip Sidney," in *Elegies for Sir Philip Sidney (1587).*

21. Sir Philip Sidney and Arthur Golding, trans., *A Woorke Concerning the Trewnesse of the Christian Religion,* by Philippe de Mornay (1587; rpt., Delmar, N.Y.: Scholars' Facsimiles & Reprints, 1970), Epistle Dedicatory.

22. George Gifford, *The Manner of Sir Philip Sidney's Death*, in *Miscellaneous Prose of Sir Philip Sidney*, ed. Katherine Duncan-Jones & Jan van Dorsten (Oxford: Clarendon, 1973), 166–72. See also Greville's *The Life of the Renowned Sir Philip Sidney*, chap. 13; Thomas Moffet, *Nobilis*, ed. Virgil B. Heltzel and Hoyt L. Hudson (San Marino: Huntington Library, 1940), 91–92.

23. Falco argues that the 1595 *Astrophel* collection begins Sidney's canonization as a poet. This point was noted by Colaianne and Godschalk as well as by William A. Ringler in "Sir Philip Sidney: The Myth and the Man," in *Sir Philip Sidney: 1586*, 12–13.

24. Margaret Hannay, "'This Moses and This Miriam': The Countess of Pembroke's Role in the Legend of Sir Philip Sidney," in *Sir Philip Sidney's Achievements*, ed. M. J. B. Allen et al. (New York: AMS Press, 1990), 217–26.

25. Arthur Golding, Epistle, Sir Philip Sidney and Arthur Golding, trans., *A Woorke Concerning the Trewnesse of the Christian Religion.*

26. Katherine Duncan-Jones concurs, noting that Golding was closely associated with Oxford, Sidney's enemy (*Sir Philip Sidney: Courtier Poet*, 251–52). See also Victor Skretkowicz, "Building Sidney's Reputation: Texts and Editors of the *Arcadia*," in *Sir Philip Sidney: 1586,* 113.

27. John Phillips, "The Life and Death of Sir Phillip Sidney."

28. On the importance of Sidney's precedent as a published poet, see Arthur Marotti, *Manuscript, Print, and the English Renaissance Lyric* (Ithaca: Cornell University Press, 1995), 228–38. He briefly discusses how Davison uses the Sidney legend to authorize his *Poetical Rhapsody* (London, 1602) (235–36).

29. Ringler compares STC citations for Spenser (130), Shakespeare (72), and Sidney (207) through 1625, omitting some 200 allusions to Sidney that do not deal with his writings or his role as man of letters ("Sir Philip Sidney," 14 n. 34). See also Jackson Boswell and H. R. Woudhuysen, "Some Unfamiliar Sidney Allusions," in *Sir Philip Sidney: 1586* , 221–37.

30. Dudley Digges, *Foure paradoxes, or politique discourses. All newly published* (1604) (STC 6872), 74. Cited in Boswell & Woudhuysen, 224.

31. George Wither, *Abuses stript, and whipt* (1613) (STC 25894), sig. R2. Cited in Boswell & Woudhuysen, 224.

32. John Aubrey, *Aubrey's Brief Lives*, ed. Oliver Lawson Dick (Ann Arbor: University of Michigan Press, 1957), 279.

33. Ibid., 280.

34. John Nichols, *Progresses and Public Processions of Queen Elizabeth* (London, 1823; rpt. New York: Burt Franklin, 1964), 2: 483. It was just under 8 in. wide.

35. Jacques LeGoff, *History and Memory*, trans. Steven Rendall and Elizabeth Claman (New York: Columbia University Press, 1992), 95.

36. Pierre Nora, "Between Memory and History: *Les Lieux de Mémoire*," trans. Marc Roudebush, *Representations* 26 (1988), 8.

37. Exact definitions of *mentalité* are always tentative, but its theoretical and methodological opposition to traditional historical inquiry seems clear. See Jacques LeGoff, "Mentalities: a history of ambiguities," trans. David Denby, in *Constructing the Past: Essays in Historical Methodology*, ed. LeGoff and Pierre Nora (Cambridge: Cambridge University Press, 1974; rpt., 1985), 166–80; Michel Vovelle, *Ideologies and Mentalities*, trans. Eamon O'Flaherty (Cambridge: Polity Press, 1990), esp. 2–9.

38. In turn, most studies of authority, imitation, and originality in Renaissance literature assume the primacy of classical models of writing and action. For examples, see Thomas M. Greene, *The Light in Troy: Imitation and Discovery in Renaissance Poetry* (New Haven: Yale University Press, 1982), G. W. Pigman III, "Versions of Imitation in the Renaissance," *Renaissance Quarterly* 33 (1980): 1–32; Nancy S. Struever, *The Language of History in the Renaissance: Rhetoric and Historical Consciousness in Florentine Literature* (Princeton: Princeton University Press, 1970). On vernacular models for Renaissance poets, see John N. King, *English Reformation Literature: The Tudor Origins of the Protestant Tradition* (Princeton: Princeton University Press, 1982); Barbara K. Lewalski, *Protestant Poetics and the Seventeenth Century Religious Lyric* (Princeton: Princeton University Press, 1979).

39. Lodowick Bryskett, "The Mourning Muse of Thestylis," in *Spenser: Poetical Works*, ed. J. C. Smith and E. deSelincourt (New York: Oxford University Press, 1912), ll. 186–89; Walter Ralegh, "An Epitaph upon the right Honourable sir *Phillip Sidney* knight: Lord governor of Flushing," in *Spenser: Poetical Works*, l. 58.

40. Anne Bradstreet, "An Elegy Upon that Honorable and Renowned Knight Sir Philip Sidney . . .," in *The Works of Anne Bradstreet*, ed. Jeannine Hensley (Cambridge: Belknap Press, 1967), ll. 55, 63, 94–95.

41. Sir Philip Sidney, *A Defence of Poetry*, ed. J. A. Van Dorsten (Oxford University Press, 1966), 40. Further citations to the *Defence* refer to this edition and will be included in the text.

42. See Greville, *The Life of the Renowned Sir Philip Sidney*, 145 (149).

43. David Loades, *The Tudor Court* (London: B. T. Batsford, 1987), 1–2.

44. See Stephen Greenblatt, *Sir Walter Ralegh: The Renaissance Man and His Roles* (New Haven: Yale University Press, 1973), 16.

45. My claim is related to Timothy Hampton's thesis in his excellent work, *Writing from History: The Rhetoric of Exemplarity in Renaissance Literature* (Ithaca: Cornell University Press, 1990), namely, that in the Renaissance "the representation of exemplarity underwent a series of transformations which undermined the authority of ancient exemplars as models of action" and generated "new modes of representing virtue, of understanding the relationship between politics and literature, and of depicting the self" (vii). Hampton, however, does not discuss native, contemporary, or

conflicted models as I do. John D. Lyons also finds a crisis in the authority of example "as the figure that tied past to future through the present" in early modern France and Italy (*Exemplum: The Rhetoric of Example in Early Modern France and Italy* [Princeton: Princeton University Press, 1989], 237). Robert C. Jones has a complementary discussion of the exemplarity of Shakespeare's medieval kings in the Renaissance in *These Valiant Dead: Renewing the Past in Shakespeare's Histories* (Iowa City: University of Iowa Press, 1991), xii. See also the useful article by Mary E. Hazard, "Renaissance Aesthetic Values: 'Example' For Example," *Art Quarterly* 2 (1979): 1–36.

46. On Sidney as an originary figure for an Elizabethan poetic genealogy, see Raphael Falco, *Conceived Presences: Literary Genealogy in Renaissance England* (Amherst: University of Massachusetts Press, 1994). I am grateful to Professor Falco for sharing with me the proofs of his book before its publication.

47. Gabriel Harvey, *Pierce's Supererogation* (London, 1593), 52. Additional examples of Harvey's "Englishing" of models include his note of "an Inglishe Petrarch [Sidney?] . . . a singular Gentleman, and a sweete Poet" (46) and his praise for John Astley, author of a treatise on horsemanship, as "our Inglish Xenophon" (53). Harvey also praises Sidney for writing "in the veine of Salust, Livy, Cornelius Tacitus . . . and the most sententious Historians" (53).

48. Lyons cites seven characteristics of Renaissance example, three of which are relevant here: artificiality (an example is invented), undecidability (it is openended, always insufficient as complete proof), and excess ("any fiction adduced to support a generalization will have characteristics that exceed what can be covered by the generalization") (33, 34). The feature of equivocality I identify is not among those he discusses.

49. Anthony Stafford, *The Guide of Honor* (London, 1634), "To the Noble Reader." Subsequent quotations in this section are from this epistle. Alan Hager would argue here that because chambermaids read the *Arcadia*, Sidney has fulfilled his exoteric (vs. esoteric) aim of reaching a popular audience. See *Dazzling Images: The Masks of Sir Philip Sidney* (Newark: University of Delaware Press, 1991), 20, 34–36.

50. Hampton, 5.

51. Although we think of Petrarch primarily as the lover of Laura, he was a classical scholar, author of a Latin verse epic as well as of vernacular poetry, and an outspoken critic of abuses in the Roman church; he was patronized by the influential Cardinal Giovanni Colonna and became poet laureate in 1341. I cannot claim, however, that Renaissance English poets were aware of the fulness of his exemplarity. With Robert Coogan, I am inclined to believe they saw him as primarily a love poet. See "Petrarch's *Trionfi* and the English Renaissance," *Studies in Philology* 67 (1970): 306–27, esp. 307, 321.

52. The *Trionfi* were translated by Henry Parker, Lord Morley (who published them between 1553 and 1556), and, in part, by the countess of Pembroke. See Aldo S. Bernardo, *Petrarch, Laura, and the Triumphs* (Albany: State University of New York Press, 1974); D. G. Rees, "Petrarch's 'Trionfo Della Morte' in English," *Italian Stud-*

ies 7 (1952): 82–96; Gary Waller, ed., *The Triumph of Death and Other Unpublished and Uncollected Poems by Mary Sidney, Countess of Pembroke (1561–1621)* (Salzburg: Institut für Englische Sprache und Literatur, 1977), esp. 12–17.

53. Hyder Edward Rollins, ed., *The Phoenix Nest* (London, 1593; rpt., Cambridge: Harvard University Press, 1931), xi.

54. The literature on these traditions is copious. Two representative volumes, one old, one new, are Lisle Cecil John, *The Elizabethan Sonnet Sequences: Studies in Conventional Conceits* (New York: Columbia University Press, 1938), and Michael R. G. Spiller, *The Development of the Sonnet: An Introduction* (London: Routledge, 1992).

55. See Jonathan Dollimore, *Radical Tragedy: Religion, Ideology, and Power in the Drama of Shakespeare and his Contemporaries* (Chicago: University of Chicago Press, 1984), 9–11, whose definition, drawn from Marx and Althusser, I have paraphrased. Louis Althusser, in "Ideology and Ideological State Apparatuses," in *Lenin and Philosophy and Other Essays*, trans. Ben Brewster (London: New Left Books, 1971), is known for a critique of ideology as mere false consciousness and his focus on the material system of social practice and how subjects become constituted ideologically. Pierre Macherey, following Althusser, focuses on the ideological effects of a work in the society in which it is read; see Etienne Balibar and Pierre Macherey, "On Literature as an Ideological Form," in *Untying the Text: A Post-Structuralist Reader*, ed. Robert Young (London: Routledge and Kegan Paul, 1981), 79–99.

56. For a discussion of political Petrarchism and the creation of Elizabeth's identity, see Leonard Forster, *The Icy Fire: Five Studies in European Petrarchism* (Cambridge: Cambridge University Press, 1969), chap. 4; Roy Strong, *Portraits of Queen Elizabeth I* (Oxford: Clarendon Press, 1963); Greenblatt, *Sir Walter Ralegh*, chap. 3; Catherine Bates, *The Rhetoric of Courtship in Elizabethan Language and Literature* (Cambridge: Cambridge University Press, 1992). See Mary Thomas Crane, "'Video et Taceo': Elizabeth I and the Rhetoric of Counsel," *Studies in English Literature 1500-1900* 28 (1988): 1–15, for a slightly different emphasis on Elizabeth's self-fashioning.

57. *The Poems of Queen Elizabeth*, ed. Leicester Bradner (Providence: Brown University Press, 1964). In a personal discussion, Jeredith Merrin, drawing on Ivor Winters, notes in this poem characteristics of the "plain style" and makes the intriguing suggestion that Elizabeth wished to sound "native," especially given the context.

58. Marie Axton, in *The Queen's Two Bodies: Drama and the Elizabethan Succession* (London: Royal Historical Society, 1977), chap. 2, traces the development of this doctrine and its revival in the succession debate during Elizabeth's reign.

59. Sir John Harington, *Nugae Antiquae*, ed. Henry Harington (London, 1804), 1:167.

60. *The Complete Works of George Gascoigne*, 2 vols., ed. John W. Cunliffe (Cambridge: Cambridge University Press, 1907–10), 2:510.

61. Sir Walter Ralegh, "A Vision Upon this Conceipt of the Faery Queene," commendatory verses to *The Faerie Queene*, in *The Works of Edmund Spenser: A Variorum Edition*, ed. Edwin Greenlaw et al. (Baltimore: Johns Hopkins University Press,

1945), ll 1, 6–10. Further references to *The Faerie Queene* refer to this edition and are cited parenthetically in the text.

62. Harvey, 46–47.

63. "Yet of all those that newly wrate / In prose or verse of state / Let Sydney weare . . . / The garland lawreate" (Thomas Churchyard, *A Praise of Poetrie* [London, 1595] published with *A Consort of Heavenly Harmonie*). See Barnabe Barnes, "Parthenophil and Parthenophe," (1593), canzon 2, in *Elizabethan Sonnets*, ed. Sidney Lee (New York: Cooper Square Publishers, 1964), 1:274.

64. *Astrophil and Stella* 90:7–8. Hereinafter referred to as *AS*. All references to Sidney's poetry, unless otherwise indicated, are from *The Poems of Sir Philip Sidney*, ed. William A. Ringler (Oxford: Clarendon Press, 1962) and are hereafter abbreviated and cited in the text.

65. Admittedly, Sidney was not the first to nativize Petrarch in a sonnet sequence; Thomas Watson's *Hecatompathia, or Passionate Centurie of Love* was published in 1582 but never caught on like *Astrophil and Stella*, perhaps in part because its author lacked Sidney's postmortem charisma. See William M. Murphy, "Thomas Watson's *Hecatompathia* (1582) and the Elizabethan Sonnet Sequence," *Journal of English and Germanic Philology* 56 (1957): 418–28.

66. John Guillory, *Poetic Authority: Spenser, Milton, and Literary History* (New York: Columbia University Press, 1983), x. Others who discuss the struggle between autonomy and submission to authorities include Jacqueline Miller, *Poetic License: Authority and Authorship in Medieval and Renaissance Contexts* (New York: Oxford University Press, 1986), 29; David Quint, *Origin and Originality in Renaissance Literature: Versions of the Source* (New Haven: Yale University Press, 1983), x. Both Miller and Guillory acknowledge Hannah Arendt's discussion of the source of authority in antiquity in "What is Authority?" in *Between Past and Future: Eight Exercises in Political Thought* (New York: Penguin Books, 1977), 91–141, esp. 98, 121.

67. In Harold Bloom's words, poetic influence "always proceeds by a misreading of the prior poet, an act of creative correction that is actually and necessarily a misinterpretation. The history of fruitful poetic influence . . . is a history of anxiety and self-saving caricature, of distortion, of perverse, wilful revisionism" (*The Anxiety of Influence: A Theory of Poetry* [New York: Oxford University Press, 1973], 30).

Bloom's emphasis on a writer's protean skill to shape himself informs John Freccero's influential account of Petrarch's self-fashioning in "The Fig Tree and the Laurel: Petrarch's Poetics," *Diacritics* 5 (1975): 34–40. Also indebted to Bloom is Jonathan Crewe's *Trials of Authorship: Anterior Forms and Poetic Reconstruction from Wyatt to Shakespeare* (Berkeley and Los Angeles: University of California Press, 1990).

68. The critical literature on the reception of Petrarch in Tudor poetry is vast. See, for a sampling, George Watson, *The English Petrarchans: A Critical Bibliography of the "Canzoniere"* (London: Warburg Institute, 1967); Patricia Thomson, *Sir Thomas Wyatt and His Background* (London: Routledge and Kegan Paul, 1964); Hallett Smith, "The Art of Sir Thomas Wyatt," *Huntington Library Quarterly* 9 (1946): 323–55; Lisa Klein, "The Petrarchism of Sir Thomas Wyatt Reconsidered," in *The Work of Dissimilitude: Essays from the Sixth Citadel Conference on Medieval and Renaissance*

Literature, ed. David G. Allen and Robert H. White (Newark: University of Delaware Press, 1992), 131–47; Michael Holahan, "Wyatt, the Heart's Forest, and the Ancient Savings," *English Literary Renaissance* 23 (1993): 46–80. On Sidney and Petrarch, see Gary F. Waller, "The Rewriting of Petrarch: Sidney and the Languages of Sixteenth-Century Poetry," and Marion Campbell, "Unending Desire: Sidney's Reinvention of Petrarchan Form in *Astrophil and Stella*," both in *Sir Philip Sidney and the Interpretation of Renaissance Culture*, ed. Gary F. Waller and Michael D. Moore (London: Croom Helm, 1984), 69–83, 84–94.

69. These refer to strategies identified by Bloom. Jon A. Quitslund uses Bloom's scheme to discuss "Sidney's Presence in Lyric Verse of the Later English Renaissance," in *Sidney and the Interpretation of Renaissance Culture*, 110–23.

70. *The Works of Michael Drayton*, ed. T. William Hebel (Oxford: Shakespeare Head Press, 1931), 1:96.

71. On the political implications of Sidney's subversion of Petrarchism, see Paul Allen Miller, "Sidney, Petrarch, and Ovid: Imitation as Subversion," *ELH* 58 (1991): 499–522, esp. 513–14. For some earlier views on conventional forms as outlets for sexual impulses, see Forster on the epithalamium and G. M. Matthews's proto-Marxist "Sex and the Sonnet," *Essays in Criticism* 2 (1952): 119–37. An important and influential feminist reading of Petrarch's sexual-textual poetics is Nancy J. Vickers, "Diana Described: Scattered Women and Scattered Rhyme," *Critical Inquiry* 8 (1981): 265–79.

72. Miles Coverdale, *Remains of Myles Coverdale*, ed. G. Pearson (Parker Society, 1846), 537. Cited in Hallet Smith, "English Metrical Psalms in the Sixteenth Century and Their Literary Significance," *Huntington Library Quarterly* 9 (1946), 258.

73. Giles Fletcher, *Licia*, in *Elizabethan Sonnets*, 2:27.

74. See the discussions in Gary Waller, *English Poetry of the Sixteenth Century* (London: Longman, 1986), 98; Alan Sinfield, *Literature in Protestant England, 1560–1660* (London: Croom Helm, 1983); Lewalski, *Protestant Poetics*.

75. Sir Thomas Wyatt, *The Complete Poems*, ed. R. A. Rebholz (New Haven: Yale University Press, 1978), no. 17. Other faithful translations are Thomas Watson, *Hecatompathia,* sonnet 40; and William Alexander, *Aurora* (London, 1604), sonnet 68, though nearly every sonneteer uses the oppositions.

76. For corresponding theological views in Bullinger's *Second Helvetic Confession* (1566) and Calvin's *Institutes*, see Andrew Weiner, *Sir Philip Sidney and the Poetics of Protestantism: A Study of Contexts* (Minneapolis: University of Minnesota Press, 1978), 8–12.

77. This presents a minor disagreement with Stephen Greenblatt, *Renaissance Self-Fashioning from More to Shakespeare* (Chicago: University of Chicago Press, 1980), 9, and chap. 3. Recent studies focusing on Protestant theology and Renaissance poets include Lewalski, *Protestant Poetics;* Andrew Weiner, *Sir Philip Sidney and the Poetics of Protestantism, A Study of Contexts* (Minneapolis: University of Minnesota Press, 1978); and John N. King, *Spenser's Poetry and the Reformation Tradition* (Princeton: Princeton University Press, 1990).

78. A recent study that focuses on Petrarch's legacy as a spiritual poet is Thomas P. Roche, Jr., *Petrarch and the English Sonnet Sequences* (New York: AMS, 1989).

79. Fulke Greville, *Caelica*, in *Certaine Learned and Elegant Workes* (1633) (Delmar, N.Y.: Scholars' Facsimiles and Reprints, 1990), sonnet 109. Further references to Greville's sonnets from this edition are cited in the text and abbreviated as above.

80. Edmund Spenser, *Amoretti*, in *The Yale Edition of the Shorter Poems of Edmund Spenser*, ed. William Oram et al. (New Haven: Yale University Press, 1989), sonnet 68: 13–14. All references to *Amoretti* and to Spenser's shorter poems are taken from this edition and will hereafter appear in an abbreviated form in the text.

81. See the summary of trends in sonnet criticism by Janet H. MacArthur, *Critical Contexts of Sidney's* Astrophil and Stella *and Spenser's* Amoretti, in *English Literary Studies* 46 (University of Victoria Press, 1989), esp. chaps. 1–2.

82.. C. S. Lewis, *English Literature in the Sixteenth Century* (Oxford: Clarendon Press, 1954), 327. For the persistence of biographical issues in Sidney criticism, see Katherine Duncan-Jones, "Sidney, Stella, and Lady Rich," in *Sir Philip Sidney: 1586,* 170–92; Clark Hulse, "Stella's Wit: Penelope Rich as Reader of Sidney's Sonnets," in *Rewriting the Renaissance: The Discourses of Sexual Difference in Early Modern England*, ed. Margaret Ferguson et al. (Chicago: University of Chicago Press, 1986), 272–86. Hulse links the creation of poetry to "the creation of actual human relationships and . . . the shaping of the political arrangements of their society" (285), assimilating biographical and "new historical" approaches.

83. The following works are characteristic, influential works on the sonnet: J. W. Lever, *The Elizabethan Love Sonnet* (London: Methuen, 1956); John; Janet Scott, *Les Sonnets Élisabethains* (Paris, 1929); Hallet Smith, *Elizabethan Poetry: A Study in Conventions, Meaning and Expression* (Cambridge: Harvard University Press, 1952), chap. 3. Much recent criticism of Renaissance sonnets tends not to treat their cultural function or conventional elements but stresses poetic subjectivity. See Joel Fineman, *Shakespeare's Perjured Eye: The Invention of Poetic Subjectivity in the Sonnets* (Berkeley and Los Angeles: University of California Press, 1986); Sandra Berman's introduction to *The Sonnet Over Time: A Study in the Sonnets of Petrarch, Shakespeare, and Baudelaire* (Chapel Hill: University of North Carolina Press, 1988); Anne Ferry, *The Inward Language: Sonnets of Wyatt, Sidney, Shakespeare, Donne* (Chicago: University of Chicago Press, 1983). Jane Hedley, in *Power in Verse: Metaphor and Metonymy in the English Renaissance Lyric* (University Park: Pennsylvania State University Press, 1988) sees Elizabethan sonneteers as self-focused rather than context-oriented. The literature on *Astrophil and Stella*, discussed in more detail in the next chapter, epitomizes changing and persistent critical concerns. See, for example, Theodore Spencer, "The Poetry of Sir Philip Sidney," *ELH* 12 (1945): 251–78; Richard B. Young, "English Petrarke: A Study of Sidney's *Astrophil and Stella*," in *Three Studies in the Renaissance: Sidney, Jonson, Milton* (New Haven: Yale University Press, 1958), 1–88; Robert Montgomery, *Symmetry and Sense: The Poetry of Sir Philip Sidney* (Austin: University of Texas Press, 1961); David Kalstone, *Sidney's Poetry: Contexts and Interpretations* (Cambridge: Harvard University

Press, 1965). Roland Greene's *Post-Petrarchism: Origin and Innovations of the Western Lyric Sequences* (Princeton: Princeton University Press, 1991) is evidence that some critical issues (narrative and dramatic elements in sonnets, the character of the speaker) will never die. See especially his chap. 2.

84. Louis Montrose's chiastic formulation is the "historicity of texts" and the "textuality of history"; see "Renaissance Literary Studies and the Subject of History," *English Literary Renaissance* 16 (1986): 8, and his more recent "Professing the Renaissance: The Poetics and Politics of Culture," in *The New Historicism*, ed. H. Aram Veeser (New York: Routledge, 1989), 15–36; Montrose and Stephen Greenblatt are the primary architects of American "new historicism," a term coined by Greenblatt in his introduction to *The Power of Forms in the English Renaissance* (Norman, OK: Pilgrim Books, 1982), 5–6 and roughly synonymous with "poetics of culture," an often preferred term, introduced also by Greenblatt in *Renaissance Self-Fashioning*, 5. Other recent attempts to set forth the assumptions and methodology of this critical practice include Jean E. Howard's "The New Historicism in Renaissance Studies," *English Literary Renaissance* 16 (1986), 13–43; Lee Patterson, *Negotiating the Past: The Historical Understanding of Medieval Literature* (Madison: University of Wisconsin Press, 1987), 41–74. Critics of new historicism include Edward Pechter, "New Historicism and its Discontents: Politicizing Renaissance Drama," *PMLA* 102 (1987): 292–303, a work that frequently misrepresents or exaggerates its target; from a feminist standpoint, Lynda E. Boose, "The Family in Shakespeare Studies," *Renaissance Quarterly* 40 (1987): 707–61; with a crotchety tone, G. W. Pigman III, "Self, Subversion, and the New Historicism," *Huntington Library Quarterly* 52 (1989): 501–8; with a considered and generous tone, A. Leigh DeNeef, "Of Dialogues and Historicisms," *South Atlantic Quarterly* 86 (1987): 497–517. (Both Pigman and DeNeef want to preserve a modicum of transhistorical essentialism.) The movement has merited a full-length study by the skeptical Brooke Thomas, *The New Historicism and Other Old-Fashioned Topics* (Princeton: Princeton University Press, 1991).

85. Pierre Nora, cited in LeGoff, *History and Memory*, 95.

86. LeGoff, *History and Memory*, 97.

87. Ibid., 95.

88. For a cogent defense of the new historicist methodology (including use of the exemplary anecdote), see the introduction to Howard Dobin, *Merlin's Disciples: Prophecy, Poetry and Power in Renaissance England* (Stanford: Stanford University Press, 1990); see G. W. Pigman III, "Limping Examples: Exemplarity, the New Historicism, and Psychoanalysis," in *Creative Imitation: New Essays on Renaissance Literature in Honor of Thomas M. Greene*, ed. David Quint et al. (Binghamton, N.Y.: Medieval and Renaissance Texts and Studies, 1992), 281–95, for a paradoxical defense of using examples. For a contrary view criticizing unself-conscious reliance on historical narration, see Leeds Barroll, "A New History for Shakespeare and His Time," *Shakespeare Quarterly* 39 (1988): 441–64.

89. In their introductory remarks, these authors of recent works avowedly bring formalist grounding to their new historical endeavors: Michael C. Schoenfeldt, *Prayer and Power: George Herbert and Renaissance Courtship* (Chicago: University of

Chicago Press, 1991), and Heather Dubrow, *A Happier Eden: The Politics of Marriage in the Stuart Epithalamion* (Ithaca: Cornell University Press, 1990).

99. Stephen Greenblatt, *Shakespearean Negotiations: The Circulation of Social Energy in Renaissance England* (Berkeley and Los Angeles: University of California Press, 1988), 6–7.

91. Michel Foucault, *The History of Sexuality*, trans. Robert Hurley (New York: Vintage Books, 1980), 1:92–93. See also his *Power/Knowledge: Selected Interviews and Other Writings 1972–1977*, ed. Colin Gordon, trans. Colin Gordon et al. (New York: Pantheon, 1988), 98.

92. Even Richard C. Helgerson comes close to prioritizing systems when he claims in *Self-Crowned Laureates: Spenser, Jonson, Milton, and the Literary System* (Berkeley and Los Angeles: University of California Press, 1983) that literary acts "have authors, though authors who are themselves authorized by the systems that make those acts possible" (20).

93. Among anthropologists, the new emphasis is on *praxis*, the study of all forms of human action in the world, specifically how systems are produced and reproduced by human action and intention. For example, see Pierre Bourdieu, *Outline of a Theory of Practice* (1972), trans. Richard Nice (Cambridge: Cambridge University Press, 1978); Anthony Giddens, *Central Problems in Social Theory: Action, Structure and Contradiction in Social Analysis* (Cambridge: Cambridge University Press, 1979); for a good summary and assessment of this approach, see Sherry B. Ortner, "Theory and Anthropology since the Sixties," *Comparative Studies in Society and History* 26 (1984): 126–66, esp. 144–60.

94. For example, Deborah Shuger's study of Renaissance "habits of thought" stresses "the mediating role of the psyche in all cultural production: that ideology is . . . the creation of people feeling, thinking, interpreting, persuading, and struggling for meaning" (*Habits of Thought in the English Renaissance: Religion, Politics, and the Dominant Culture* [Berkeley and Los Angeles: University of California Press, 1990], 255). Among literary scholars working to reconstruct an understanding of intentionality in the Renaissance are Luke Wilson, "*Hamlet*: Equity, Intention, Performance," *Studies in the Literary Imagination* 24 (1991), 91–113; and "*Hamlet*, Hales v. Petit, and the Hysteresis of Action," *ELH* 60 (1993): 17–55; Reed Way Dasenbrock, *Imitating the Italians: Wyatt, Spenser, Synge, Pound, Joyce* (Baltimore: Johns Hopkins University Press, 1991), 9–13. In the words of Lee Patterson,

> a text is also a function of specific human intentions, in the sense both of self-consciously maintained purposes and of impulses that may be incapable of articulation but nonetheless issue from a historical intentionality, and it is a large part of our task to understand how these intentions went into its making (73).

Even Foucault allows for human agency in the strengthening, transformation, or breakdown of power. Individuals "are not only its [power's] inert or consenting target; they are always also the elements of its articulation" (*Power/Knowledge*, 98).

95. See, for example, Montrose, "Renaissance Literary Studies," 10; Anthony Appiah, "Tolerable Falsehoods: Agency and the Interests of Theory," in *Conse-*

quences of Theory, ed. Jonathan Arac and Barbara Johnson (Baltimore: Johns Hopkins University Press, 1991), 74.

96. Ortner, 157; Giddens, 49–95. Or, in Foucault's words, "People know what they do; they frequently know why they do what they do; but what they don't know is what what they do does" (Ortner, 157 n. 18.).

97. LeGoff, *History and Memory*, xi.

98. Most practitioners of cultural poetics have focused on the ambitious public works of aspiring laureates such as Spenser's *The Faerie Queene*, not their seemingly private passions, the sonnets. For examples of new historicist approaches to sonnet sequences, see Ann Rosalind Jones and Peter Stallybrass, "The Politics of *Astrophil and Stella*," *Studies in English Literature* 24 (1984): 53–68; Arthur Marotti, "'Love is Not Love': Elizabethan Sonnet Sequences and the Social Order," *ELH* 49 (1982): 396–428; Hulse, "Stella's Wit"; Paul Allen Miller.

99. See, however, the following sampling of works arguing that conventional poetic forms negotiate various forms of authority: Louis Adrian Montrose, "'Eliza, Queene of shepheardes,' and the Pastoral of Power," *English Literary Renaissance* 10 (1980): 153–82, "Of Gentlemen and Shepherds: The Politics of Elizabethan Pastoral Form," *ELH* 59 (1983): 415–59, and "'The perfecte paterne of a Poete': The Poetics of Courtship in *The Shepheardes Calender*," *Texas Studies in Literature and Language* 21 (1979): 34–67; Helgerson, *Self-Crowned Laureates*; David Norbrook, *Poetry and Politics in the English Renaissance* (London: Routledge and Kegan Paul, 1984). See also Lauro Martines, *Society and History in English Renaissance Verse* (Oxford: Basil Blackwell, 1985); John Barrell, *Poetry, language, and politics* (Manchester: Manchester University Press, 1988).

100. See Helgerson's *Self-Crowned Laureates*, an indispensable work for the study of the careers of Elizabethan poets. I find his laureate/amateur divide somewhat too distinctly drawn, however.

1: "Mars and the Muses meete": The Divided Aims of Sidney's *Defence of Poetry*

1. George Whetstone, "Sir Phillip Sidney, his honorable life," sig. C3r.

2. Ibid., sigs. B2v, B1v.

3. Sidney and Golding, trans., *A Woorke*, Epistle Dedicatory.

4. Greville, *The Life of the Renowned Sir Philip Sidney*, 40, 171–72.

5. George Peele, *Polyhymnia*, in *The Life and Minor Works of George Peele*, ed. David H. Horne (New Haven: Yale University Press, 1952), 236.

6. Ralegh, "An Epitaph," l. 58. On Sidney as a courtly hero and master of conflicting voices, see Hager, *Dazzling Images*, 33.

7. Whetstone, sig B2v.

8. Sir Arthur Gorges,*Vannetyes and Toyes*, in *The Poems of Sir Arthur Gorges*, ed. Helen Estabrook Sandison (Oxford: Clarendon Press, 1953), 118.

9. Falco, *Conceived Presences*, 89.

10. Baldassare Castiglione, *The Book of the Courtier*, trans. Sir Thomas Hoby (1561, 1588; rpt., London: J. M. Dent, 1928), 70. Further citations are given parenthetically in the text.

11. George Pettie, "The Preface to the Readers," in *The Civile Conversation of M. Steeven Guazzo* (1581; rpt., London: Constable, 1925), 8. Further citations occur in the text.

12. This is the main theme of Neil Rudenstine's *Sidney's Poetic Development* (Cambridge: Harvard University Press, 1967), in which the balance tips easily on the side of retirement and scholarship.

13. Dorothy Connell, *Sir Philip Sidney: The Maker's Mind* (Oxford: Clarendon Press, 1977), 4–5; witness the title of Roger Howell's biography, *Sir Philip Sidney: The Shepherd Knight* (London: Hutchinson, 1968). Richard C. Helgerson, in *The Elizabethan Prodigals* (Berkeley and Los Angeles: University of California Press, 1976) emphasizes the *concordia discors* of his life and art (chap. 7). Duncan-Jones also rejects the idea of conflicting allegiances; in taking up his post in the Netherlands, Sidney "was not abandoning the life of the mind" but he "viewed active military service as an occasion for new and intensified study, not for action divorced from contemplation" (*Sir Philip Sidney,* 275, 276).

14. A. C. Hamilton, *Sir Philip Sidney: A Study of His Life and Works* (Cambridge: Cambridge University Press, 1977) posits a double identity, describing a Sidney who "lived two separate lives: a known life as a Renaissance courtier seeking political office, and a private life as a poet" (9).

15. Lever finds that "the exploration of Sidney's own personality is the subject of most of his serious sonnets" (71); Kalstone measures Sidney's achievement in "fashion[ing] the Petrarchan sonnet into a form responsive to the antagonisms he felt so deeply," conflicts "between love and heroic obligation, between desire and virtuous affection" (180, 179). For Steven May, Sidney's verse "grew out of his experiences as a courtier yet subordinated that experience to the art it inspired" (*The Elizabethan Courtier Poets: The Poems and Their Contexts* [Columbia: University of Missouri Press, 1991], 97–98, 102). Focus on aesthetic and personal concerns also characterized Richard B. Young's influential study "English Petrarke."

16. Duncan-Jones, *Sir Philip Sidney*, 222. See also Hamilton, *Sir Philip Sidney,* 108.

17. Kenneth Myrick, *Sir Philip Sidney as a Literary Craftsman* (1935; rpt., Lincoln: University of Nebraska Press, 1965), chaps. 2 and 8.

18. See, for example, Rudenstine, 51. The work's status as a sublime literary artifact has not been shaken even by charges that it is derivative, inconsistent, lacking in unity, even politicized. See O. B. Hardison, "The Two Voices of Sidney's *Apology for Poetry,*" *English Literary Renaissance* 2 (1972): 83–99. For contrary, defensive views, see Martin Raitiere, "The Unity of Sidney's *Apology for Poetry,*" *Studies*

in English Literature 1500–1900 21 (1981): 37–57; John C. Ulreich Jr., "'The Poets Only Deliver': Sidney's Conception of *Mimesis*," *Studies in the Literary Imagination* 15 (1982): 67–84. Critics interested in Sidney's borrowings that make him the proverbial Renaissance bee include John P. McIntyre, "Sidney's Golden World," *College Literature* 14 (1962): 356–65; Geoffrey Shepherd, Introduction to *An Apology for Poetry*, by Sir Philip Sidney (London, 1965); D. H. Craig, "A Hybrid Growth: Sidney's Theory of Poetry in *An Apology for Poetry*," *English Literary Renaissance* 10 (1980): 183–201; S. K. Heninger, *Touches of Sweet Harmony: Pythagorean Cosmology and Renaissance Poetics* (San Marino: Huntington Library, 1974), 288; Anthony Miller, "Sidney's *Apology for Poetry* and Plutarch's *Moralia*," *English Literary Renaissance* 17 (1987): 259–76; John Hunt, "Allusive Coherence in Sidney's *Apology for Poetry*," *Studies in English Literature 1500–1900* 27 (1987): 1–16.

19. For example, for Richard McCoy, Sidney exhibits irreconcilable conflicts between his various roles (*The Rites of Knighthood: The Literature and Politics of Elizabethan Chivalry* [Berkeley and Los Angeles: University of California Press, 1989]). In an earlier work (*Sir Philip Sidney: Rebellion in Arcadia* [Sussex: Harvester Press, 1979]), McCoy traced problems with development and closure in Sidney's works to his inability to resolve his conflicts with political authority.

20. This analogy informs George Puttenham's *Arte of English Poesie* (ed. Gladys Doidge Willcock and Alice Walker [1589; Cambridge University Press, 1936]) and was first explored by G. K. Hunter, *John Lyly: The Humanist as Courtier* (Cambridge: Harvard University Press, 1962), and Daniel Javitch, *Poetry and Courtliness in Renaissance England* (Princeton: Princeton University Press, 1978). The high valuation of Puttenham is questioned by Roger Kuin in "Sir Philip Sidney: The Courtier and the Text" *English Literary Renaissance* 19 (1989): 249–71. Influential new historicist readings of *Astrophil and Stella* include Jones and Stallybrass; Marotti's "'Love is Not Love,'" which explores the "sociopolitical encoding of love poetry," which mediates the courtier's desires and the constraints of established order (397, 399); and Maureen Quilligan, "Sidney and His Queen," in *The Historical Renaissance: New Essays on Tudor and Stuart Literature and Culture*, ed. Heather Dubrow and Richard Strier (Chicago: University of Chicago Press, 1988), 171–96. Sidney's most recent biographer, Duncan-Jones, mostly disdains these efforts, as when she disagrees with Marotti: "There is no doubt that . . . Sidney was exploring sexual rather than political frustration" (*Sir Philip Sidney*, 239).

21. Alan Sinfield, "The Cultural Politics of the *Defense of Poetry*," in *Sidney and the Interpretation of Reniassance Culture*, 124.

22. Margaret Ferguson, *Trials of Desire: Renaissance Defenses of Poetry* (New Haven: Yale University Press, 1983), chap. 4. Countering Montrose and Sinfield, Robert Matz finds Sidney defending courtly pleasures against Protestant criticisms; like Ferguson, he sees Sidney as negotiating personal anxieties; see his "Sidney's *Defence of Poesie*: The Politics of Pleasure," *English Literary Renaissance* 25 (1995): 131–47.

23. Sinfield, "Cultural Politics," 136; Quilligan, "Sidney and His Queen," 191; see also Marotti, for whom Sidney retreats into an ideal poetic world ("Love is Not Love," 406)—and McCoy for the view that in Sidney's sonnets "conflict is internal-

ized and reduced to purely romantic terms, and less is finally at stake . . . and wit maintains its extraordinary composure and control" (*Sir Philip Sidney*, 109).

24. Many critics take up this humanist-Protestant tension. Åke Bergvall argues in *The "Enabling of Judgement": Sir Philip Sidney and the Education of the Reader* (Stockholm: Almqvist, 1989) for the importance of right reason in maximizing human potential, and he demonstrates in "Reason in Luther, Calvin, and Sidney," *Sixteenth Century Journal* 23 (1992): 115–27, that humanism and Protestantism were not at odds in their views on human reason. See also Andrew Weiner, "Sidney, Protestantism, and Literary Critics: Reflections on Some Recent Criticism of *The Defence of Poetry*," in *Sir Philip Sidney's Achievements*, 117–26. M. J. Doherty examines continuities between Sidney's Protestant poetics and ancient and medieval theological traditions, claiming for feminized "mistress knowledge" redemptive capabilities in *The Mistress-Knowledge: Sir Philip Sidney's* Defence of Poesie *and Literary Architectonics in the English Renaissance* (Nashville: Vanderbilt University Press, 1991). Frank B. Evans, in "The Concept of the Fall in Sidney's *Apologie*," *Renaissance Papers* (1969): 9–14, argues that Sidney's crediting fallen man with erected wit was a theological position unusual for his time, while Calvin and Luther were reviving the harsher Augustinian view that man's fall involved a total corruption of his nature. (The less-harsh Aquinian position, I might note, allows Sidney the euphonious "erected wit–infected will" dichotomy, even if his faith in wit's potential does not match that of Aquinas.) Though she acknowledges the humanist vs. Protestant tension, Margo Todd shows the Puritans' debt to activist, Erasmian humanism in *Christian Humanism and the Puritan Social Order* (Cambridge: Cambridge University Press, 1987), 17, 178–79.

25. On the contagion of original sin, see Jean Calvin, *Institutes of the Christian Religion*, 2 vols., ed. John T. McNeill, trans. Ford Lewis Battles (Philadelphia: Westminster Press, 1960), bk. 2, chap. 1, secs. 5–9 (Original sin is a "hereditary depravity and corruption of our nature. . . . this perversity . . . continually bears new fruits—the works of the flesh. . . . [1:251]); on the will's unfreedom except by God's grace, see bk. 2, chap. 2, sec. 8, and chap. 3, sec. 5 (The will "bereft of freedom is of necessity either drawn or led into evil" [1:295]) and Romans 7:13–25 ("I can will what is right, but I cannot do it. For I do not do the good I want, but the evil I do not want is what I do"). On the Calvinist base of Sidney's Protestantism, see Weiner, *Poetics of Protestantism*, chap. 1.

26. See Margaret Ferguson, 159–60. For Luther and Calvin, David was also a type of the reformed Protestant, prince, and a champion of the Gospel. See Lewalski, *Protestant Poetics*, 133–38; Weiner, *Poetics of Protestantism*, 12–14. Anne Lake Prescott shows how David was a figure of the slandered courtier, especially for Protestants ("Evil Tongues at the Court of Saul: The Renaissance David as a Slandered Courtier," *Journal of Medieval and Renaissance Studies* 21 [1991]: 163–86). On the pattern of the literary career in which the poet is a repentant prodigal, see Helgerson, *The Elizabethan Prodigals*.

27. Anne Lake Prescott, "King David as a 'Right Poet': Sidney and the Psalmist," *English Literary Renaissance* 19 (1989), 134. Roche (*Petrarch*, 215–16) provides as a gloss on Sidney's definition and examples of divine poesy Ephesians 5:1–21

("Speaking unto your selves in psalmes, and hymnes, and spiritual songs, singing and making melodie to the Lord in your hearts . . ."). But see Bergvall for the claim that "right poetry remains a human skill without aspirations to divinity" ("Reason," 125)

28. Thomas Becon, *Davids Harpe ful of most delectable harmony* (1542), sig. A7.

29. *Remains of Miles Coverdale*, cited in Smith, "English Metrical Psalms," 258.

30. See Hager, *Dazzling Images*, 109, on the "egoistic bias" of Sidney's persona in this passage.

31. Compare the poet Fitzgeffrey: "I write not voluntarily, but fatally; neither did I seeke occasion, but occasion sought me. . . ." (J. W. Saunders, "The Stigma of Print: A Note on the Social Bases of Tudor Poetry," *Essays in Criticism* 1 [1951], 149).

32. Weiner, *Poetics of Protestantism*, 35. See also Sinfield, "Cultural Poetics," 136.

33. William Craft, *Labyrinth of Desire: Invention and Culture in the Work of Sir Philip Sidney* (Newark: University of Delaware Press, 1994), chap. 1. Craft's larger claim is that invention, or "counterfeiting a fictional image . . . reconfigures the culture that prompted it" (x).

34. See William Rossky, "Imagination in the English Renaissance: Psychology and Poetic," *Studies in the Renaissance* 5 (1958): 49–73, for an excellent overview of the psychology of the imagination. Rossky finds that poetic feigning is deemed a good use of imagination because it is controlled and moral, though he does not acknowledge the doubts poets (especially Protestant ones) entertained about poetic feigning. See also Weiner, *Poetics of Protestantism*, 39–40.

35. For a good account of the Platonic conception of imitation, see Richard McKeon, "Literary Criticism and the Concept of Imitation in Antiquity," in *Critics and Criticism*, ed. R. S. Crane (Chicago: University of Chicago Press, 1952), 152, 158–59.

36. Victoria Kahn, *Rhetoric, Prudence, and Skepticism in the Renaissance* (Ithaca: Cornell University Press, 1985), 20. While Sidney's *Defence* is a judicial rather than a deliberative oration proper, it can be seen as a debate between different conceptions of poetry, a dialogue of various authorities.

37. See Arthur F. Kinney, *Humanist Poetics: Thought, Rhetoric, and Fiction in Sixteenth-Century England* (Amherst: University of Massachusetts Press, 1986), 16; Ronald Levao, *Renaissance Minds and Their Fictions* (Berkeley and Los Angeles: University of California Press, 1985), 139, 155.

38. My discussion of Sidney's strategy in the exordium and peroration is indebted to Catherine Barnes, "The Hidden Persuader: The Complex Speaking Voice of Sidney's *Defence of Poetry,*" *PMLA* 86 (1971): 422–27. For Barnes, the persona wins support by "appealing to the listener's self-interest" and arousing "an emotional identification between listener and speaker" (422, 425).

39. See Hager, *Dazzling Images*, 111–14, for a similar reading of the Pugliano anecdote.

40. Thomas Churchyard, "A Praise of Poetrie" (London, 1595), 32, 35. Further citations are included in the text.

41. See *OED*, s.v. "note" (verb 1) 1; (verb 2) I.1, 3, II.6.a, 6.b,6.d; (substantive 2) III.13.d, 14; IV.19 for current and possibly relevant meanings.

42. Churchyard had been a page to Henry Howard, earl of Surrey; he contributed to Tottel's *Miscellany* (1554) and authored the popular *Shore's Wife* (1563), a military treatise, and numerous broadsheets and small volumes. He was also a soldier in the Low Countries. Spenser, in *Colin Clout,* called him "old *Palemon* . . . that sung so long untill quite hoarse he grew" (*The Oxford Companion to English Literature*, 5th ed., ed. Margaret Drabble [New York: Oxford University Press, 1985], 198).

43. Rosalie Colie includes the *Defence* in the tradition of the rhetorical paradox, a formal defence of an unexpected, unworthy, or indefensible subject. See her *Paradoxical Epidemica: The Renaissance Tradition of Paradox* (Princeton: Princeton University Press, 1966), 3. See also Connell, 5–8. Alan Hager's Sidney is a jester wearing a variety of masks, writing the *Defence* as a mock encomium in the tradition of Agrippa and Erasmus (*Dazzling Images*, chap. 6); also see A. C. Hamilton, "Sidney and Agrippa," *Review of English Studies* 7 (1965): 151–57, for a discussion of Agrippa's influence on Sidney; and Margaret Ferguson, chap. 4.

44. Persius, *Satire I*, trans. G. G. Ramsay, in *Juvenal and Persius* (Cambridge: Harvard University Press, 1979), 328–29.

45. Ovid, *Metamorphoses*, 11:164–216. See *Shakespeare's Ovid: Being Arthur Golding's Translation of The Metamporphoses*, ed. W. H. D. Rouse (1567; rpt. London, 1904). Midas has "a head more fat than wyse, and doltish wit . . ." (166).

46. For another example from Sidney's works, see book 4 of The Countess of Pembroke's *Arcadia*, ed. Maurice Evans (Harmondsworth, Middlesex: Penguin Books, 1977), when Dametas, digging for a buried treasure but finding only some poems, "his hope of wealth turned to poor verses," imagined "Midas' fancy when, after the great pride he conceived to be made judge between Gods, he was rewarded with the ornament of an ass's ears" (715). The structure of the sentence reinforces the parallel (hope : poor verses :: pride : ass's ears). Further references to the *Arcadia* are to this edition and are cited parenthetically in the text.

47. Ovid, *Metamorphoses*, bk. 8.

48. Contrast the anxious self-image of Midas with the empowering one of Menenius Agrippa, a figure for the poet as judge and victor (*Defence,* 41–42), which Margaret Ferguson discusses in *Trials* (140–42).

49. Kahn, 189.

50. See the introduction to *William Temple's* Analysis *of Sir Philip Sidney's* Apology for Poetry, ed. and trans. John Webster (Binghamton: Medieval and Renaissance Texts and Studies, 1984), 99–117. According to Webster, Temple's aim is to argue for poetry's logical character and to emphasize its *common* enterprise with philosophy and history.

51. Anthony Esler, *The Aspiring Mind of the Elizabethan Younger Generation* (Durham: Duke University Press, 1966). Esler characterizes Sidney's cohort as aspir-

ing, reined in by the cautious older generation, and channeling their idealism into a cult of military honor, ultimately to be frustrated by the system. In their spiritual alienation and rejection of humanist principles of the older generation, they resemble radicals of Esler's own generation.

52. See Edward Berry, "The Poet as Warrior in Sidney's *Defence of Poetry*," *Studies in English Literature 1500–1900* 29 (1989): 21–34. Sidney's primary goal is public service; thus, in the *Defence* he seeks to "redefine poetry in such a way as to make it serve this very goal" (24).

53. See Hayden White, *Metahistory: The Historical Imagination in Nineteenth-Century Europe* (Baltimore: Johns Hopkins University Press, 1973), 37–38.

54. In chapter 3 of *Squitter-Wits and Muse Haters: Sidney, Spenser, Milton and Renaissance Antipoetic Sentiment* (Detroit: Wayne State University Press, 1996), Peter C. Herman argues that Sidney is deeply imbued with anxiety about poetry and its defensibility, hence the *Defence* shuttles between the authoritative positions of humanist poetics and Protestant antipoetics. (He also argues that this suspicion of poetry is figured in *Astrophil and Stella* as a threat to masculinity.) I am indebted to Professor Herman for sharing with me his work-in-progress.

55. Reprinted in James M. Osborn, *Young Philip Sidney 1572–1577* (New Haven: Yale University Press, 1972), 537–40.

56. A. C. Hamilton points out that none of the 165 known letters to Sidney and the 117 by him discuss even indirectly his own writing (*Sir Philip Sidney*, 8). Despite the slight exaggeration, his point is well taken. Herman reads Sidney's letters as evidence of his ambivalence towards poetry and as an effort to fashion a public self. See "'Do as I Say, Not as I Do': The *Apology for Poetry* and Sir Phillip Sidney's Letters to Edward Denney and Robert Sidney," *Sidney Newsletter* 10 (1989): 13–24.

57. Berry, 22.

58. For the letter of advice to his brother, see *The Prose Works of Sir Philip Sidney*, ed. Albert Feuillerat (Cambridge: Cambridge University Press, 1962), 3:132–33. In *The Book named the Governor,* ed. S. E. Lehmberg (London: J. M. Dent, 1962), Elyot recommends that, beginning at the age of seven, a child read Aesop's fables, the dialogs of Lucian, comedies of Aristophanes, Homer, Virgil's *Aeneid* and *Georgics*, and Ovid's *Metamorphoses*. A "child's courage [will be] enflamed by the frequent reading of noble poets" (bk. 1, chap. 10, p. 33). See also Myrick, 9.

59. For maternal metaphors, see *AS* 1 and 50. For examples of Sidney's infantile persona, see *Certain Sonnets* 6 ("Sleepe Babie mine, Desire; nurse Beautie singeth"), in *The Poems of Sir Philip Sidney*; *AS* 15 ("If. . . . You seeke to nurse at fullest breasts of Fame, / *Stella* behold"); *AS* 71 ("Desire still cries, 'give me some food'"). Cristina Malcolmson, in the unpublished essay "Politics and Psychoanalysis: Sidney's Imagery of the Child," proposes a psychoanalytic reading of this network of imagery. I am grateful to her for sharing with me a copy of this essay.

60. Duncan-Jones facetiously states, "In the winter of 1579–80 Sidney and his sister Mary were both pregnant," he with the *Arcadia* (*Sir Philip Sidney*, 168).

61. On the association of fosterage with patronage in Sidney's allegory, *The Fortress of Perfect Beauty*, see McCoy, *Rites*, 61. For a discussion of Elizabeth's fos-

ter/forester children of desire, see my next chapter.

62. In "Sidney's Truant Pen" (*Modern Language Quarterly* 46 [1982]: 128–42]), Joseph Loewenstein reads *AS* as a reflection of larger cultural frustrations of courtiers like Sidney "doomed to arrest and immaturity" (141), presumably out of a stifling dependence on the mother-queen.

63. *The Correspondence of Philip Sidney and Hubert Languet*, ed. William Aspenwall Bradley (Boston: Merrymount Press, 1912), 159. As early as 1574, Sidney wrote to Languet of the diminishing opportunities for service: "[T]he Turk can make no great movement this year for want of seamen; and the same is commonly reported of our Queen. . . . all our English sailors have for some time past found employment in the Prince of Orange's ships (ibid., 74). Incidentally, Rudenstine uses the Sidney-Languet correspondence to a contrary end, to confirm Sidney's strong disposition towards retirement, love, and poetry; the *Defence* "banishes all the conflicting feelings . . . and the doubts which the letters to Languet . . . reveal" (52).

64. On Sidney's ill health, often attributed to his studious nature, see Duncan-Jones, *Sir Philip Sidney*, 29, 56, 73.

65. Moffet, 87, fols. 20–21. Moffet's motives of representation must take into account his audience: Sidney's young nephew, William Herbert, the dedicatee. The work was completed in 1593.

66. Elyot, bk. 1, chap. 6, p. 19.

67. Plutarch, *Moralia*, trans. Harold North Fowler (Cambridge: Harvard University Press, 1949), 223, 225.

68. Richard Willes, *De re poetica* (London, 1573), cited by Richard Todd, "Humanist Prosodic Theory, Dutch Synods, and the Poetics of the Sidney-Pembroke Psalter," *Huntington Library Quarterly* 52 (1989), 279.

69. For a discussion of Pallas as an appropriate figure for the realization of Sidney's "Scipionic ideal" and as a figure for the queen, see Dominic Baker-Smith, 98. Puttenham, in his dedication to Elizabeth, cites Pallas as a figure of government worth imitating (5).

70. Katherine Duncan-Jones, in her Introduction to *Miscellaneous Prose of Sir Philip Sidney* (Oxford: Clarendon Press, 1973), doubts the connection, for which no direct evidence exists, but sees no reason to deny it (62). Arthur Kinney thoroughly traces critical views of the relation between the two works in a lengthy note in *Markets of Bawdrie: The Dramatic Criticism of Stephen Gosson* (Salzburg: Institut für Englische Sprache und Literatur, 1974), 44–46. See also Matz, 135–41.

71. I have used a facsimile edition of Stephen Gosson's *Schoole of Abuse* (London, 1579) based on the Cambridge copy but have cited the signature numbers from Kinney's transcription since the facsimile is only intermittently paginated. Hereafter the work will be cited by signature numbers in the text.

72. There are resemblances between the two critics beyond those I have discussed. Gosson is, overall, more critical of the abuses of players than of poets. For a further discussion of the agreement between Gosson and Sidney, see Arthur F. Kinney, "Parody and its Implications in Sidney's *Defence of Poesie*," *Studies in English Literature 1500–1900* 12 (1972): 1–19.

73. See Christopher Martin, "Sidney's *Defence*: The Art of Slander and the Slander of Art," *Sidney Newsletter* 9 (1988): 3–10.

74. See MacCaffrey, esp. chap. 12.

75. On this point, see Duncan-Jones, *Sir Philip Sidney*, 280–81. For the general account of Sidney's activities, I have relied primarily on Malcolm Wallace, *The Life of Sir Philip Sidney* (Cambridge: Cambridge University Press, 1915), chaps. 14–15, secondarily on Duncan-Jones.

76. *Correspondence*, 161.

77. Ibid., 163.

78. Ibid., 173.

79. Ibid., 185.

80. Other examples of his pugnacity include his letter to Edmund Molyneux, a family retainer, threatening "that if ever I know yow do so muche as reede any lettre I wryte to my Father, without his commandement, or my consent, I will thruste my Dagger into yow" (Sidney, *Prose Works*, 3:124) and his *Defence of the Earl of Leicester*, in which he challenges its author to a duel (*Miscellaneous Prose*, 140–41). See Duncan-Jones's account of Sidney's 1577 quarrel with the earl of Ormond, a dispute also motivated by family loyalty (*Sir Philip Sidney*, 135–37).

81. *Correspondence*, 224.

82. Percy Bysshe Shelley, *Shelley's Poetry and Prose*, ed. Donald H. Reiman and Sharon B. Powers (New York: W. W. Norton, 1977), 508.

83. Sidney indirectly claims for the poet a position Puttenham makes explicit. Poets were

> the first lawmakes to the people, and the first politicians, devising all expedient meanes for th'establishment of commonwealth, to hold and containe the people in order and duety by force and vertue of good and wholesome lawes. . . . (*Arte,* 7)

I agree with Kinney's fine statement that the *Defence* is "a political document as well as a poetics . . . designed to enable the poet." Sidney

> enfranchises himself by giving the "right poet" a central political role and access to rulers; on the other hand, the poet gains this authority on the grounds and by the means of a morality that forwards the claims of the Puritan faction at court. ("Rhetoric at the Court of Elizabeth I," in *Sir Philip Sidney's Achievement,* 44)

84. This letter is reprinted in Sidney, *Prose Works*, 3:166–67, and subsequent citations here refer to this source. Duncan-Jones discusses this letter as evidence of Sidney's depression and anxiety in *Sir Philip Sidney*, 287–90. The queen's opposition and lack of financial support are common themes in Sidney's letters of this period. See the following letters, all reprinted in *Prose Works*: 71 (to Leicester, 19 February 1586); 107 (to the Council, 14 August 1586); and 109 (to Walsingham, 14 August 1586).

2: *Astrophil and Stella* and the Failure of the Right Poet

1. 3 May 1577; Sidney, *Prose Works*, 3:109–14.

2. Cited by Wallace, 182.

3. Greville, *The Life of the Renowned Sir Philip Sidney*, 49.

4. Roger Howell agrees that Sidney took license in negotiating with Protestant princes, and he proposes that Elizabeth knew of Sidney's activities and attempted to recall him (40). Howell claims the marriage negotiation was a personal matter separate from the political matter of the alliance (45–46). Osborn, in *Young Philip Sidney* (448–50), claims that Walsingham may have proposed Sidney for the mission, but he agrees that the ulterior purpose of exploring a Protestant union is not mentioned in or sanctioned by the queen's instructions.

5. *Correspondence*, 121.

6. 14 June 1577; Ibid.

7. 15 July 1577; Ibid., 124.

8. Ibid., 132.

9. Wallace, 187; Duncan-Jones, *Sir Philip Sidney*, 134. Roger Kuin, in "The Middleburg Weekend: More Light on the Proposed Marriage Between Philip Sidney and Marie of Nassau," *Sidney Newsletter and Journal* 12 (1993): 3–13, adds new evidence to confirm that the courtship proceeded against the background of the proposed Protestant League, both of which were impossible ventures.

10. Cited by Wallace, 187. Osborn believes that the queen knew of the proposal, while Duncan-Jones finds no mention of it in the public documents. It is hard to believe Elizabeth could remain ignorant of the proposal.

11. 1 March 1578; *Correspondence*, 160.

12. Cited by Osborn, 496.

13. Osborn, 496.

14. See Duncan-Jones, *Sir Philip Sidney*, 46–52, for an account of the Cecil-Sidney engagement and 164–67 for the quarrel with Oxford.

15. Ibid., 148–49.

16. See MacCaffrey, 243–66. In 1574, the Frenchman attained the title held by his elder brother, duke of Anjou, but according to convention and to avoid confusion, I will call him Alençon throughout.

17. Duncan-Jones, *Sir Philip Sidney*, 90.

18. Sidney, *The Lady of May,* in *Miscellaneous Prose*, 29.

19. See Louis Adrian Montrose, "Celebration and Insinuation: Sir Philip Sidney and the Motives of Elizabethan Courtship," *Renaissance Drama* 8 (1977): 3–35. Kalstone suggests that the queen failed to notice Sidney's unorthodox use of pastoral and chose the shepherd as the usual hero of pastoral (46). See also the influential article by Stephen Orgel, "Sidney's Experiment in Pastoral: *The Lady of May*" *Journal of the*

Warburg and Courtauld Institutes 26 (1963): 198–203, in which he argues that Sidney reassesses underlying assumptions of pastoral (198).

20. Those who believe Elizabeth made the "right" choice include May, 171, and Duncan-Jones, Introduction to *The Lady of May* in *Miscellaneous Prose*, 14–15, and *Sir Philip Sidney*, 148–51. Duncan-Jones also argues that Espilus, or "felt-presser," alludes to Leicester, who was licensed to export felt, and that Elizabeth's choice of Espilus expresses a preference for her hosts. For Bates, however, Sidney insists on the impossibility of choice between the two suitors, fashioning a text that accommodates either judgment (61–69).

21. *Lady of May*, 12. Quilligan perceptively remarks of Sidney's strategy here: "Humility and a profound sense of social inferiority allows [sic] Sidney not merely to triumph over, but to obliterate, Elizabeth's challenge to his authority" ("Sidney and His Queen," 177). Wendy Wall, in *The Imprint of Gender: Authorship and Publication in the English Renaissance* (Ithaca: Cornell University Press, 1993), argues that Sidney uses this opportunity to suppress the queen's/May Lady's language of desire (140–50).

22. Sidney, *Prose Works*, 3:51. Further references to Sidney's *Letter to Queen Elizabeth* will be cited parenthetically in the text.

23 *Amoretti* 24:13–14. *The Yale Edition of the Shorter Poems of Edmund Spenser*, ed. William A. Oram et al. (New Haven: Yale University Press, 1989). Further citations from *Amoretti* refer to this edition and are abbreviated in the text.

24. Jean Wilson, *Entertainments for Elizabeth I* (Woodbridge, England: D. S. Brewer, 1980), 83. Further citations from this work will be given parenthetically, including page number, in the text.

25. See Montrose, "Celebration and Insinuation," 29; Bates, 74.

26. William Camden, *Remaines Concerning Britaine, Fift Impression* (London, 1636), 357.

27. The following is a brief sample of works on the relations between language, desire, selfhood, and narrative: A Lacanian approach informs Jonathan Goldberg's *Endlesse Worke: Spenser and the Structures of Discourse* (Baltimore: Johns Hopkins University Press, 1981), esp. 73–121; Michel Foucault, in "The Order of Discourse," in *Untying the Text: A Post-Structuralist Reader,* ed. Robert Young (London: Routledge and Kegan Paul, 1981), shows how "discursive rules are linked to the exercise of power" (48) and states that discourse both manifests desire and is the object of desire (52–53). Drawing on Augustine's awareness that language both engenders and originates in desire (*Confessions*, 1:7–8), Guiseppe Mazzotta discusses Petrarchan self-construction in "The *Canzoniere* and the Language of Self," *Studies in Philology* 75 (1978): 271–96, esp. 290–91. For a deconstructive reading of desire in *Astrophil and Stella*, see Campbell, "Unending Desire." Obviously, the paradoxical relations are not unique to Sidney, but they are seldom better articulated than in his texts.

28. By contrast, most critics emphasize the ironic distance between Sidney and Astrophil; see, for example, Richard Lanham, "*Astrophil and Stella*: Pure and Impure Persuasion," *English Literary Renaissance* 2 (1972): 100–115; Alan Sinfield, "Astrophil's Self-Deception," *Essays in Criticism* 28 (1978): 1–17, and "Sidney and

Astrophil," *Studies in English Literature 1500–1900* 20 (1980): 25–41; Robert Montgomery, "The Poetics of Astrophil," in *Sir Philip Sidney's Achievement,* 145–56.

29. Quilligan nicely captures the double thrust of these lines: "He desires not only Stella but also the riches, fame, and achievement he would happily throw away for her" ("Sidney and His Queen," 191).

30. 24 September 1580; *Correspondence*, 202–4.

31. Jones & Stallybrass similarly conclude that sonnets 23 and 27 concern both private love and public ambition; Astrophil is "obsessed by erotic ambition. . . . Thus the structure of desire turns out to resemble the structure of ambition" (57).

32. See Forster for a classic discussion of epithalamic conventions as an authorized "safety valve" for poets' sexual passion.

33. For a related discussion of Lady Rich's significance, see Quilligan, "Sidney and His Queen," 185–86.

34. See Margaret Ferguson, 140–43.

35. Stella resembles Musidorus chastising his friend Pyrocles for his "relenting . . . [and] slackening of the main career you had so notably begun . . . whereas you were wont . . . to give yourself vehemently to the knowledge of those things which might better your mind. . . . you now leave all these things undone; you let your mind fall asleep" (*Arcadia*, 110).

36. See Ringler's commentary on *AS* 46 in Sidney, *Poems*, 475.

37. Helgerson also reads Stella's failure to move the poet as akin to the failure of a "poem that dared incite passion in the interest of well-doing" (*Elizabethan Prodigals*, 146). See Kalstone's analysis of this poem as a "devastating comment on the whole Petrarchan vision" (119).

38. Castiglione, 315.

39. This network of imagery cries out for psychoanalytic interpretation. I here acknowledge an unpublished essay by Cristina Malcolmson that applies object-relations theory to an analysis of Sidney's sonnets. She discusses weaning as a ritual of disillusionment reenacted in the Petrarchan lover's dependency upon a woman, alternately maternal and erotic.

40. Osborn, 503.

41. *1 Henry IV*, 5.2.16–18, in *The Riverside Shakespeare* (Boston: Houghton Mifflin, 1974).

42. See also the sonnets following the stolen kiss, esp. 74, 77, 79–83, which dramatize Astrophil's poetic decline as his desire for Stella intensifies.

43. The *OED* lists several relevant meanings of "feign" and "fain" current in Sidney's day. "Feign" can variously signify "to fashion fictitiously or deceptively" (II); to "represent in fiction" (3); to "imagine, believe erroneously" (4.b); "to disguise, dissemble, conceal" (6). "Fain" means simply "glad" (1); "necessitated, obliged" (2.b); or "disposed, inclined or willing" (3). See William Empson's discussion of this pun in Shakespeare in *Some Versions of Pastoral* (London: Chatto and Windus, 1935), 136–38.

44. Puttenham, 186.

45. For the idea of Sidney's role-playing I am indebted to Alan Hager, who reads *Astrophil and Stella* as a "consciously crafted tragicomedy" (64) where Astrophil is the busy, loving courtier of Roman comedy (*Dazzling Images*, chap. 4).

46. See Jacqueline Miller, "'Love doth hold my hand': Writing and Wooing in the Sonnets of Sidney and Spenser," *ELH* 46 (1979), 541–58; see also her *Poetic License*, chap. 4. Nona Fienberg, in "The Emergence of Stella in *Astrophil and Stella*," *Studies in English Literature 1500–1900* 25 (1985), 5–19, traces the emergence of a Stella who generates her own language and is not simply a projection of the speaker's desires. Maria Teresa Micaela Prendergast finds Stella usurping the role of Orphic poet in "The Unauthorized Orpheus of *Astrophil and Stella*," *Studies in English Literature 1500–1900* 35 (1995): 19–34. In "Stella's Wit," Hulse links the struggle for control over poetry to the love game enacted between Sidney and Penelope Rich.

47. Cicero, *De Oratore,* trans. H. Rackham. (Cambridge: Harvard University Press, 1942), 2.169.

48. See Jacqueline Miller's related analysis of the orator sonnet in terms of a dynamic reading and misreading in "'What May Words Say': The Limits of Language in *Astrophil and Stella*," in *Sidney and the Interpretation of Renaissance Culture,* 95–109. Gary Waller also focuses on the role of the audience in "Acts of Reading: The Production of Meaning in *Astrophil and Stella*," *Studies in the Literary Imagination* 15 (1982), 25–35.

49. *Wilson's Arte of Rhetorique*, ed. G. H. Mair (1553; Oxford: Clarendon Press, 1909), sig. A2v.

50. This work is in the Folger Shakespeare Library. The emblem is reproduced on the frontispiece to Erasmus, *Collected Works of Erasmus*, ed. Craig R. Thompson (Toronto: University of Toronto Press, 1978), together with a brief commentary on which I have drawn.

51. Puttenham, 142.

52. On the importance of the Hercules legend, see Theodor E. Mommsen, "Petrarch and the Story of the Choice of Hercules," *Journal of the Warburg and Courtauld Institutes* 16 (1953): 178–92; Hallet Smith, *Elizabethan Poetry*, 292–302. In another legend Smith cites, Hercules rescues England from a tyrant; thus he also becomes for Elizabethans a figure of resistance to political oppression, even a Protestant champion.

53. Cicero, *De Officiis*, trans. Walter Miller (Cambridge: Harvard University Press, 1956), 3.5.25. The tale is told in Xenophon's *Memorabilia*, 2.1.21–34.

54. Petrarch, *The Life of Solitude*, trans. Jacob Zeitlin (Champaign: University of Illinois Press, 1924), 286–87.

55. Greville, *The Life of the Renowned Sir Philip Sidney*, 40–41.

56. Based on this sonnet, Duncan-Jones argues that *Astrophil and Stella* was written as a kind of courtly game at the behest of Penelope Rich ("Sidney, Stella and Lady Rich," 170–92).

57. Edmund Spenser, *Teares of the Muses*, l. 577, in *Complaints* (1591), in *Yale Edition*, 290; Puttenham, 4.

58. A few critics explore Astrophil's spiritual state via the sonnets. See Thomas P. Roche, who attempts to prove that Sidney uses "Astrophil's journey from hope to despair" to analyze "human desire in Christian terms" (*Petrarch*, 196), and, briefly, Margreta De Grazia, "Lost Potential in Grammar and Nature: Sidney's *Astrophil and Stella*," *Studies in English Literature 1500–1900* 21 (1981), 33–35.

59. The seven penitential psalms are 6, 32, 38, 51, 102, 130, and 143. See Wyatt's "Paraphrase of the Penitential Psalms" in *The Complete Poems*. Other sixteenth-century versions include William Hunnis, *Seven Sobs of a Sorrowful Soule for Sinne* (London, 1583), Spenser's now lost translation, and, of course, the Sidney-Pembroke version of the complete Psalter. On the importance of the Psalms in sixteenth-century poetic and devotional practice, see Lily Campbell, *Divine Poetry and Drama in Sixteenth Century England* (Cambridge: Cambridge University Press, 1959); Smith, "English Metrical Psalms"; Rivkah Zim, *English Metrical Psalms: Poetry as Praise and Prayer, 1535–1601* (Cambridge: Cambridge University Press, 1987).

60. On the importance of the persona of Psalmist to seventeenth-century religious poets, see Lewalski, *Protestant Poetics*, 237–50.

61. This sonnet provides a subtly ironic echo of the speaker's identification with the moon's "languisht grace" in *AS* 31, which connoted merely romantic failure, not the existential despair of a sinner.

62. Biblical references are to the Geneva Bible (1560; rpt., Madison: University of Wisconsin Press, 1969) and are cited in the text.

63. See, for example, *AS* 29, 36, 40, 47, and 61.

64. Prescott also believes that Sidney has Psalm 51 in mind ("King David," 147–50).

65. Sidney, *Certaine Sonnets* 32:1–2, 14, in *Poems*.

66. Psalm 10:2; *The Psalms of Sir Philip Sidney and the Countess of Pembroke*, ed. J. C. A. Rathmell (New York: Anchor Books, 1963), 21. The connection to Astrophil is made in Roche, *Petrarch*, 216–17.

67. Here my interpretation differs from that of Hager, who does a "humorous" reading of the late sonnets in terms of Astrophil's love melancholy and argues that there *is* a resurrection in the artful expression of passion (*Dazzling Images*, 79–80).

3: *Trophaeum Peccati*: Fulke Greville's Monuments to Sidney

1. Quoted by Warren W. Wooden, Introduction to *The Life of Sidney*, by Fulke Greville, iii. I have used the earlier-cited facsimile edition, *The Life of the Renowned Sir Philip Sidney* (London, 1652). Though Greville titled the work *Dedication to Sir*

Philip Sidney, I refer to it as the *Life of Sidney* (or *Life*, for short), according to custom, and include citations within the text.

2. See R. A. Rebholz, *The Life of Fulke Greville, Lord Brooke* (Oxford: Clarendon Press, 1971), 318; Joan Rees, "Fulke Greville's Epitaph on Sidney," *Review of English Studies* 19 (1968): 47–51.

3. The unnamed epitaph was printed with Spenser's *Astrophel* in 1595 and has been attributed to Greville. See *Spenser: Poetical Works*, 559–60, ll. 32, 36, 39–40.

4. Quoted by Rebholz, 74.

5. Ibid., 317. See Joan Rees, "Fulke Greville's Epitaph," for more details. Rees speculates that *Caelica* 82, an unfinished epitaph, may have been Greville's attempt to recast Sidney's epitaph (49).

6. See Skretkowicz, 111–24, esp. 113–16. Possibly Greville also hoped to gain advantages from his privileged association with Sidney; writing to Walsingham in 1586, hoping to forestall the "mercenary printing" of the old *Arcadia*, he admits: "Gayn ther wilbe no doubt to be disposed by you, let it helpe the poorest of his servants, I desyre only care to be had of his honor . . ." (Joan Rees, "Fulke Greville's Epitaph," 47).

7. For the view that Greville's representation of the heroic Sidney is the product of his disillusionment with King James and his idealizing nostalgia regarding Elizabeth, see Rebholz, chap. 12, passim; Norbrook, 158–59. Joan Rees, in "Fulke Greville's Epitaph," claims that Greville sought to keep Sidney's memory "alive as a force potentially active in the moral and political life of the present" (49).

8. Regarding the dating of Greville's *Life*, I follow John Gouws, ed. *The Prose Works of Fulke Greville, Lord Brooke* (Oxford: Clarendon, 1986), xxii-xxiii. A generally accepted, more precise date is 1610–11.

9. Judith H. Anderson, *Biographical Truth: The Representation of Historical Persons in Tudor-Stuart Writing* (New Haven: Yale University Press, 1984). Greville's role as an involved, interpretive biographer most closely resembles Walton's practice as Anderson describes it. See esp. the introduction and chap. 5.

10. Crewe, 117.

11. Christopher Martin, "Between Duty and Selfness: Greville's *Life of Sidney*," *Mid-Hudson Language Studies* 9 (1986), 19. Richard Lanham charges Greville with using Sidney's name to gild his own theories ("Sidney: The Ornament of His Age," *Southern Review* 2 [1967], 324). Others defend Greville's reliability as a biographer; among them are Myrick, 12; John Gouws, "Fact and Anecdote in Fulke Greville's Account of Sidney's Last Days," in *Sir Philip Sidney: 1586*; Mark Caldwell, "Sources and Analogues of the *Life of Sidney*," *Studies in Philology* 74 (1977): 279–300.

12. Greenblatt, *Renaissance Self-Fashioning*, 3.

13. F. J. Levy, in "Fulke Greville: The Courtier as Philosophic Poet," *Modern Language Quarterly* 33 (1972): 433–48, sees Greville's writings as a commentary on the shared experiences, careers, and crises of his contemporaries (447).

14. Puttenham includes him in the "crew of Courtly makers" among Elizabeth's men (61).

15. See John 8:31–32 ("If ye continue in my worde, ye are verely my disciples, And shal knowe the trueth, & the trueth shal make you fre").

16. One of Greville's aims in portraying an indulgent Elizabeth is to show James an example of princely grace to a possibly out-of-line suitor. The main thrust of his defence of Sidney as courtier is to establish how astute, even prophetic, were his political judgments (*Life*, 162–65). By allying himself to Sidney's politics, he hopes to persuade James that he, too, is an indispensable counselor.

17. This is essentially Duncan-Jones's conclusion; she describes Sidney as "hot tempered, arrogant" (*Sir Philip Sidney,* xii), impetuous and rebellious in general.

18. Martin, in "Between Duty and Selfness," also notes Greville's questioning of Sidney's judgment (26–27). For Duncan-Jones, the voyage marks a crisis for Sidney, who is desperate for action; Drake sees him as a "poet and dreamer, as well as a political embarrassment" (*Sir Philip Sidney*, 272–74).

19. See Skretkowicz, 113–16.

20. There is a pagination error in the original text. The brackets indicate the actual page.

21. See Morris W. Croll, *The Works of Fulke Greville* (Philadelphia, 1903), 23–35; Ivor Winters, *Forms of Discovery: Critical and Historical Essays on the Forms of the Short Poem in English* (Chicago: Alan Swallow, 1967), 51; Thom Gunn, Introduction, *Selected Poems of Fulke Greville* (Chicago: University of Chicago Press, 1968), 35–36; Douglas Peterson, *The English Lyric from Wyatt to Donne: A History of the Plain and Eloquent Styles* (Princeton: Princeton University Press, 1967), 264–66. For a critique of the "plain-style" critics, see Roche, *Petrarch*, 295–96.

22. Moffet, who may have been present at the battle, claims that Sidney was wounded while hastening to free Willoughby, implying his carelessness (102, fol. 31). Sir John Smythe, author of *Certain discourses . . . concerning the forms and effects of diverse sorts of weapons* (London: 1590), suggests that Sidney may have been following the continental fashion of abandoning heavy armor. Gouws, in "Fact and Anecdote," and Ringler, in "Sir Philip Sidney: The Myth and the Man," consider additional motivations, the latter claiming that Sidney went to battle without his cuisses "for the calculated and practical purpose of more efficient fighting" (8). Duncan-Jones rather implausibly diagnoses Sidney with accident proneness brought about by stress due to the recent death of his mother (*Sir Philip Sidney*, 292).

23. For a more optimistic view of Greville's (and Sidney's) ideals for writing enabling virtuous action, see Levy, "Fulke Greville," and Joan Rees, *Fulke Greville, Lord Brooke 1554-1629: A Critical Biography* (Berkeley and Los Angeles: University of California Press, 1971), 199–206.

24. Fulke Greville, *Treatise of Religion*, stanza 39, *The Remains: Being Poems of Monarchy and Religion* (1670), ed. G. A. Wilkes (Oxford: Oxford University Press, 1965). This text will hereafter be abbreviated as *TR* and cited by stanza number in the text.

25. Fulke Greville, *A Treatie of Humane Learning*, st. 3. In *Certaine Learned and Elegant Workes* (London, 1633). (Delmar, New York: Scholars' Facsimiles and

Reprints, 1990). Further references to this work, the *Letter to an Honorable Lady*, and *Caelica* are to this edition and will be abbreviated in the text as *THL* or *Lady* or *C* and cited by stanza, page, or sonnet and line number.

26. Richard Waswo discusses the Calvinist tenor of Greville's thought but contrasts his distrust of delight to Sidney's faith in poetry in *The Fatal Mirror: Themes and Techniques in the Poetry of Fulke Greville* (Charlottesville: University Press of Virginia, 1972), chap. 1. Because of the way I read the *Defence*, I find Greville agreeing with and intensifying Sidney's views of poetry.

27. For a definition of pride as sexual desire, see *OED*, s.v. "pride," 11.

28. See also *Caelica* 65 on the sorry state of learning; books "of vaine humanity / . . . dazell truth, by representing it, / And so entayle clouds to posterity" (ll. 44–46).

29. For a different reading, arguing that poetry has the power to restore the prelapsarian balance in man and nature, see David Roberts, "Fulke Greville's Aesthetic Reconsidered," *Studies in Philology* 74 (1977): 388–405, esp. 394–99.

30. For a brief discussion of Greville's treatment of the Babel story as it guides Greville's attitude towards the proper use of language, see June Dwyer, "Fulke Greville's Aesthetic: Another Perspective," *Studies in Philology* 78 (1981), 261. Dwyer is another critic influenced by the "plain style" tradition.

31. George Gifford, *Praelections upon the Sacred and holy Revelation of S. John* (London, 1573), 112.

32. Martin Luther, *Lectures on Genesis*, trans. George V. Schick. *Luther's Works*, vol. 2, ed. Jaroslav Pelikan (St. Louis: Concordia, 1960), 220, 224.

33. See Colie for a discussion of the *Treatie* as a paradoxical epistemology raising its own imponderables: "If the arts and sciences, those tools of truth, are based on error, how can a man . . . reach any final, ultimate truth?" (411).

34. See Duncan-Jones, *Sir Philip Sidney*, 240–41; Rebholz, 54; Joan Rees does not consider the question. Duncan-Jones cautiously identifies Greville as homosexual and wonders about the circumstances of his death: stabbed by a disgruntled servant, Ralph Hayward, he desired to let Hayward escape, possibly because he wished not to expose details of their relationship in court; the servant shortly thereafter committed suicide (240; Rebholz, 314–16).

35. Sidney, "Two pastoralls, made by Sir Philip Sidney," in *Poems,* 260; originally published in Francis Davison's *A Poetical Rapsody* (1602).

36. Sidney, "Dispraise of a Courtly Life," in *Poems*, 263. Sidney and Edward Dyer, a courtier, mediocre poet, and friend eleven years older than Sidney, collaborated (or competed) in writing verse in classical measures (Duncan-Jones, *Sir Philip Sidney*, 101–6).

37. Wendy Wall, 39–40.

38. On the probable chronology of *Caelica*, see Joan Rees, *Fulke Greville*, chap. 5, 221 n. 2; Rebholz, 325–28, 338–40. Rebholz breaks down the composition as follows: 1–76, 83 (1577–87); 77–81 (1587–1603); 82, 84–105 (1604–14); 106 (1614–21); 107–9 (1622–28). He assumes the order is chronological and that the

poems reflect Greville's experience, particularly a conversion, and the evolution of his thought; he finds such evidence internally.

39. This comparative study was the metier of Greville's early critics. See Croll, 8–11; J. M. Purcell, "Sidney's *Astrophel and Stella* and Greville's *Caelica*," *PMLA* 50 (1935): 413–22; Douglas Peterson, 265–66.

40. Roland Greene, 108.

41. Roche links this purpose to the sequence's "two-part structure in which the poet-lover is seen to shift his allegiance from the one love to the other" (*Petrarch*, 295), yet a few pages later he rejects this structural distinction, finding the poetry more complicated somehow but suggesting by way of clarification only that the final twenty-five poems serve as a retraction (316) of profane love. I find Roche's treatment of *Caelica* not erroneous but simply incomplete. Consideration of the structure of *Caelica* is implicit in most discussions, explicit in Gary L. Litt, "'Images of Life': A Study of Narrative and Structure in Fulke Greville's *Caelica*," *Studies in Philology* 69 (1972): 217–30. Recently, Elaine Y. L. Ho has argued that *Caelica* is a Calvinist narrative of the self and a critique of "ideologically alien" Petrarchan discourse ("Fulke Greville's *Caelica* and the Calvinist Self," *Studies in English Literature 1500–1900* 32 [1992]: 35–57).

42. Augustine, *De Civitate Dei*, 13.24. On the association of lust and sexuality and shame see 14.16–18; also *De Peccarorum Meritis et Remissione,* 2.2 and 22. See the summary in Elaine Pagels, *Adam, Eve, and the Serpent* (New York: Random House, 1988), 110–12.

43. Dwyer also comments on this poem's use of the Babel story. The speaker is punished for lusting after the lady by being unable to communicate with her (268).

44. Peterson, 256.

45. Scholars disagree whether Greville counted himself among the elect. Waswo summarizes the controversy (131); Joan Rees believes he distinguished two types of election: that available to all believers and that reserved for God's chosen band; Greville counted himself among the former (*Fulke Greville*, 114–15). For Gary Waller, Greville departs from Calvin; his elect souls are not those predestined by God's will but "those who live by faith and in obedience to their princes" ("Fulke Greville's Struggle with Calvinism," *Studia Neophilologica* 44 (1972): 309). Rebholz believes Greville followed du Plessis-Mornay's more generous doctrine of predestination rather than Calvin's, allowing more worth to human virtue and effort (24–25).

46. On these traditions, see John, 39–77.

47. See, in particular, *Caelica* 26, 27, and 36. Waswo compares Greville's and Sidney's use of the Cupid convention in specific poems, but he claims only Greville uses the convention ironically, and he does not discuss the idolatrous implications of Cupid as a god (54–58).

48. See *Caelica* 12, 15, 22, 25, 27–28, 31–34, and 36.

49. See John Bale, *The Image of Both Churches After the Most Wonderfull and Heavenly Revelacion of Sainct John the Evangelist* (1548; Amsterdam, 1973), commentary on Revelation 18; Jan van der Noot, *Theatre for Worldlings* (1569), translated by Spenser (in *Spenser: Poetical Works*). Sonnet 12 and its commentary consti-

tute a commentary on Revelation 17–18. For more anti-Roman invective, see Greville's *TR* 16–33, 93–96.

50. Waswo perceptively notes the "literally shocking metrical variations" of lines 12–16 and the contrasting "regular meter of the heavy, slow-moving monosyllables" of line 17 but focuses on the personal grief behind the public utterance (151).

51. Jean Calvin, *The Institution of Christian Religion* (London, 1561), 4.1.7. Greville also treats this distinction in *TR* 62–67.

52. Calvin, *Institution,* 4.1.1.

53. Ibid., 4.1.4.

54. Gifford, *Praelections*, 113.

55. Compare Spenser's representation of theological Error (*The Faerie Queene,* 1.1.15–26) as a perverted mother figure, itself one source of Milton's allegorical image of Sin and her hellhounds (*Paradise Lost*, 2:655–58). For a positive occurrence of the womb/tomb rhyme, see the Friar's speech in *Romeo and Juliet*:

> The earth that's natures mother is her tomb;
> What is her burying grave, that is her womb;
> And from her womb children of divers kind
> We sucking on her natural bosom find.
>
> (2.3.9–12)

56. For another use of this image, in reference to the idolatrous Israelites in captivity, see *TR* 88: "In this times wombe, this uttermost defection / Of fleshlie *Israel*, came the Virgins seed."

57. Most critics find Greville's seeming condemnation of all institutional religion extreme. Waswo observes that neither Calvin nor William Perkins, his English disciple, "would have permitted the logical extension of the effects of sin so far into the visible Church" (150). Douglas Peterson finds that Greville's Protestantism allows no church intermediary (279); for Shuger, Greville is, like Milton, "a church unto himself" (217).

58. See Augustine, *De Civitate Dei*, 19.15.

59. Gouws examines the circumstantial evidence for this identification and notes that the letter is a deliberative oration (xxvii-xxix).

60. Norbrook, 168.

61. Sidney, *Arcadia*, 708; also in *Poems*, 102–3.

62. See, for example, Martin Raitiere, *"Faire Bitts": Sir Philip Sidney and Renaissance Political Theory* (Pittsburgh: Duquesne University Press, 1984); Norbrook, who observes that in Greville, "radical sentiments keep emerging . . . and have to be repressed" (159). Levy links Greville with the antityrannical school of thought centered around the interpretation of Tacitus and possibly including Essex ("Fulke Greville," 445–46). See also Norbrook, 172–74, and Rebholz, 293–302.

63. See also *Lady* 276.

64. Greville's critique of the mystification and abuse of power is a theme of *Mustapha* (Shuger, 210, 214–15) and *Caelica* (Norbrook, 158).

65. Geoffrey Bullough (ed., *Poems and Dramas of Fulke Greville* [New York: Oxford University Press, 1945], 1:42) mentions sonnets 17, 46 (45 in the 1633 edition), and 55 (54) as poems possibly touching Greville's relationship to Elizabeth, to which number Marotti adds *Caelica* 7 for its possible reference to Elizabeth's motto *semper eadem* ("Love is not Love," 427 n. 71). Norbrook finds explicit reference to Elizabeth in sonnets 55 (54) and 81 but finds a political metaphor implicit in *Caelica*, which shades into a condemnation of the cult of Elizabeth (158–59).

66. Norbrook, 152–54.

67. See Ernst H. Kantorowicz, *The King's Two Bodies: A Study in Medieval Political Theology* (Princeton: Princeton University Press, 1957); Axton.

68. See Rebholz, chaps. 9–10.

69. A similar pun may be operating in Sidney's *Defence* when the persona, resisting Pugliano's arguments about the superiority of horses, admits he has learned "that self-love is better than any *gilding* to make that seem gorgeous wherein ourselves be parties" (17; emphasis added).

70. Professor Herman has shared with me his perceptive chapter on *Astrophil and Stella* from his forthcoming book.

71. The weakness of Norbrook's reading of *Caelica* is his assumption that the poetry is an allegory of Greville's experience of political submission to Elizabeth, a view that narrows the sonnets' potential range of meanings.

72. *A Treatise of Monarchy*, stanzas 55–56, in *Remains: Poems of Monarchy and Religion*.

73. Cf. Lear's attempt to repress the "mother" overtaking him, the hysteria caused by the wandering womb, the female element; also the emphasis on female cruelty and monstrosity (*King Lear* 2.4. 56–57; 4.2; 4.6).

74. Contrast *AS* 39, where Astrophil begs for sleep, when "thou shalt in me, / Livelier then elsewhere, *Stella's* image see" (13–14).

75. See Waswo's discussion of the psychological insight of this poem (132–34). He compares it to Herbert's "Sinne (II)." See also Dennis Danielson, "Sidney Greville, and the Metaphysics of 'Naughtiness,'" *English Studies in Canada* 10 (1984): 267–70, for a discussion of the poem in terms of Augustinian theology of evil as privation.

76. Cf. *AS* 100:8 ("the hell where my soul fries"), in which the complaint is that of the sorrowing poet-lover, not of a repentant sinner.

77. In *Arcadia*, Dorus complains of his distance from Pamela in similar language: "So far from the mark of my desires that I rather think it such a light as comes through a small hole to a dungeon, that the miserable caitiff may the better remember the light of which he is deprived" (221).

78. See Lewalski, *Protestant Poetics*, 18. Critics agree that this is Greville's greatest poem; see Waswo, 127–30; Gunn, 37–39; Winters calls it a "Calvinistic version of the dark night of the soul" (50).

79. To a different end, Quitslund contrasts *AS* 99 with *Caelica* 100 to show Greville's religious treatment of what is for Sidney love melancholy (114–15).

4: *Delia*, the Countess of Pembroke, and the Literary Career of Samuel Daniel

1. Angel Day, "Upon the life and death of the most worthy . . . Sir Phillip Sidney," in *Elegies for Sir Philip Sidney* (1587).

2. See the introduction and chapter 1 for a discussion of the elegists and Churchyard, respectively.

3. Joan Rees, *Samuel Daniel: A Critical and Biographical Study* (Liverpool: Liverpool University Press, 1964), 305; on the Daniel-Dymoke relationship, see Mark Eccles, "Samuel Daniel in France and Italy," *Studies in Philology* 34 (1937): 160–67, who places Daniel in Dymoke's household in March 1591/92, at the time of publication of *Delia*.

4. Quoted in Eccles, 153.

5. Samuel Daniel, *Delia With the Complaint of Rosamond* (1592; rpt., Menston, England: Scolar Press, 1969), sig. A2r. All references to the 1592 *Delia* and sonnets will be cited parenthetically in the text.

6. According to Eccles, Daniel was in Italy with Sir Edward Dymoke at the time of Newman's publication (167).

7. See Christopher R. Wilson, "*Astrophil and Stella*: A Tangled Editorial Web," *The Library*, 6th ser., 1 (1979): 338.

8. Germaine Warkentin, "Patrons and Profiteers: Thomas Newman and the 'Violent Enlargement' of *Astrophil and Stella*," *The Book Collector* 34 (1985): 483–84.

9. Warkentin notes this fact as merely "ironic," not a key to Daniel's role (487). See the bibliographical studies by J. A. Lavin, "The First Two Printers of Sidney's *Astrophil and Stella*," *The Library*, 5th ser., 26 (1971): 251; and MacD. P. Jackson, "The Printer of the First Quarto of *Astrophil and Stella*," *Studies in Bibliography* 31 (1978): 201–3.

10. For me, the identity of Delia is not a critical issue, but then I do not assume that sonnets record real emotion experienced in an actual courtship. Most of the controversy surrounds a sonnet in the 1592 *Delia* addressed to "M. P." and sonnet 48, which refers to Delia's home being near the Avon. Those who reject the identification of Mary Sidney as Delia believe that Daniel wrote the sonnets before he came to Wilton and assume that Delia *must* refer to some actual woman. See Alexander B. Grosart, *The Complete Works in Verse and Prose of Samuel Daniel* (London, 1885; rpt. New York: Russell and Russell, 1963), 1:xviii; Joan Rees, *Samuel Daniel*, 13–17; Cecil Seronsy, *Samuel Daniel* (New York: Twayne Publishers, 1967), 25–26, and Margaret Hannay, *Philip's Phoenix: Mary Sidney, Countess of Pembroke* (New York: Oxford University Press, 1990), 116–17, for a summary of the controversy. See John

Pitcher, "Samuel Daniel, the Hertfords, and A Question of Love" (*Review of English Studies* 35 [1985]: 450–54), for an account of how Daniel flatters a subsequent patron by likening her to Delia.

11. See the related discussions of the social functions of Sidney's and Daniel's sonnets by Hulse in "Stella's Wit," and "Samuel Daniel: The Poet as Literary Historian," *Studies in English Literature 1500–1900* 19 (1979): 59. Wendy Wall also situates sonnets within the institution of patronage and codes of manuscript exchange it promoted (55).

12. Most critics of *Delia* have treated its poetic merits or its relation to lyric poetry of Sidney, Shakespeare, or the French sonneteers, neglecting its social function and context. Edwin H. Miller, in "Samuel Daniel's Revisions in 'Delia,'" *Journal of English and Germanic Philology* 53 (1954): 58–68, confirms his inferiority; more appreciative of Daniel's craft is C. F. Williamson's "The Design of Daniel's *Delia,*" *Review of English Studies* 19 (1968): 251–60. On Daniel and the French poets, see Anne Lake Prescott, *French Poets and the English Renaissance: Studies in Fame and Transformation* (New Haven: Yale University Press, 1978), passim; D. G. Rees, "Italian and Italianate Poetry," in *Elizabethan Poetry*, ed. John Russell Brown and Bernard Harris (New York: St. Martin's Press, 1960), 53–69. See also Joseph Kau, "*Delia*'s Gentle Lover and the Eternizing Conceit in Elizabethan Sonnets," *Anglia* 92 (1974): 334–48; Lars-Haken Svensson, *Silent Art: Rhetorical and Thematic Patterns in Samuel Daniel's* Delia (Lund: CWK Gleerup, 1980), 35–49; Erik S. Ryding, *In Harmony Framed: Musical Humanism, Thomas Campion, and the Two Daniels* (Kirksville, Mo.: Sixteenth Century Essays & Studies, 1993), 155–73; Lowry Nelson, "The Matter of Rime: Sonnets of Sidney, Daniel, and Shakespeare," in *Poetic Traditions of the English Renaissance*, ed. Maynard Mack and George de Forest Lord (New Haven: Yale University Press, 1982), 123–42. Hulse briefly discusses Daniel's awareness of the social utility of literature in "Samuel Daniel," 55–69.

13. Aubrey, 138. See also Frances B. Young, *Mary Sidney, Countess of Pembroke* (London: David Nutt, 1912), chap. 5; Gary Waller, following John Buxton, agrees that her patronage was extensive (*Mary Sidney, Countess of Pembroke: A Critical Study of her Writings and Literary Milieu.* Elizabethan and Renaissance Studies 87 [Salzburg, 1979]).

14. Mary Ellen Lamb, "The Countess of Pembroke's Patronage," *English Literary Renaissance* 12 (1982): 162–79, and "The Myth of the Countess of Pembroke: The Dramatic Circle," *Yearbook of English Studies* 11 (1981): 194–202; Hannay, *Philip's Phoenix,* esp. chap. 5. On the motives and forms of patronage in this period, see Patricia Thomson, "The Literature of Patronage, 1580-1630," *Essays in Criticism* 2 (1952): 267–84; Jan van Dorsten, "Literary Patronage in Elizabethan England: The Early Phase," in *Patronage in the Renaissance*, ed. Guy Fitch Lytle and Stephen Orgel (Princeton: Princeton University Press, 1981), esp. 191–98.

15. Grosart, based on Daniel's claim in the dedication of *A Defence of Ryme* (1603) that the countess first encouraged his writing at Wilton, his "best Schoole," and its "worthy Lord, [was] the fosterer of mee and my *Muse*," places Daniel in the household in the mid 1580s (Daniel, *Complete Works*, 1:xv-xvii). For a different

chronology, see Margaret Farrand, "Samuel Daniel and his 'Worthy Lord,'" *Modern Language Notes* 45 (1930), 23–24. Eccles's research, placing Daniel in Paris during this period, makes their conjectures less likely and supports Lamb's suggestion that he dedicated the 1592 *Delia* to the countess in order to gain a position at Wilton ("Pembroke's Patronage," 177–78).

16. Saunders's observation points up a crucial difference between Sidney and Daniel: "Paradoxically, whereas the Courtier who printed his poems might endanger his career, the social climber found that a printed book of poetry would often admit him to . . . the Court" (157).

17. Daniel, *Poems and A Defence of Ryme,* ed. Arthur Colby Sprague (1930; rpt. Chicago: University of Chicago Press, 1965), 170–71.

18. This and the following quotations from the dedication are taken from Daniel's *Complete Works*, 3:23–24.

19. Lamb, "Pembroke's Patronage," 167.

20. For further examples of allusions to Sidney in works dedicated to family members, see Boswell & Woudhuysen, 225–27.

21. Spenser, *Yale Edition*, 230.

22. Beth Wynne Fisken argues that the countess adopts a similar strategy of self-abnegating dependence on her brother while asserting her own ambitions ("'To the Angell Spirit . . .' : Mary Sidney's Entry into the World of Words," in *The Renaissance Englishwoman in Print: Counterbalancing the Canon*, ed. Anne M. Haselkorn and Betty Travitsky [Amherst: University of Massachusetts Press, 1990], 263–75).

23. Samuel Daniel, *Delia and Rosamond augmented* (London, 1594), 51:5, 10–12.

24. Joan Rees, *Samuel Daniel*," 61–62; Hannay, *Philip's Phoenix,* 118–19.

25. Spenser, *Yale Edition*, pp. 541–42, ll. 416, 420–27.

26. See Waller, *Mary Sidney*, 274.

27. Hannay, *Philip's Phoenix,* 66.

28. Sonnet 8, "Poems and Sonets," in Philip Sidney, *Astrophil and Stella* (1591; rpt., Menston, England: Scholar Press 1970). References to Daniel's 1591 "pirated" sonnets will hereafter occur in parentheses in the text in an abbreviated form that will distinguish them from the 1592 *Delia.*

29. Sidney, *Certain Sonnets* 31:1–2, in *Poems*, 161.

30. "Well, *Love*, since this demurre our sute doth stay, / Let *Vertue* have that *Stella's* selfe; yet thus, / That *Vertue* but that body graunt to us" (*AS* 52:12–14).

31. See *AS* 66–69, 83, songs 2, 4, and 8.

32. This occurrence was noted by Rollins, x.

33. *Amoris Lachrimae*, in *The Works in Verse and Prose of Nicholas Breton*, ed. Alexander Grosart (1879; rpt., New York: AMS Press, 1966), 1:4, l. 156.

34. Cited in Hannay, *Philip's Phoenix*, 82.

35. Svensson, 35–49. On the relation between Ralegh's poetry and his efforts to gain the queen's patronage, see Leonard Tennenhouse, "Sir Walter Ralegh and the Literature of Clientage," in *Patronage in the Renaissance*, 235–58.

36. In 1594, Daniel changes "Cynthia" to "Delia," which further specifies the addressee and clarifies the analogy of patroness as queen.

37. See McCoy on the ocean-river conceit used in *The Civil Wars* in the context of Daniel's criticism of tyranny, "all-drowning Sov'raintie" (*Rites*, 116–18).

38. In *The Psalms of Sir Philip Sidney and the Countess of Pembroke*, xxxvi, ll. 32–36.

39. Ibid., ll. 43–44.

40. This supposition accords with Hannay's reconstruction of the poem's probable chronology (*Philip's Phoenix,* 66–69). The version mistakenly attributed to Daniel and printed in *The Whole Workes of Samuel Daniel* (1623) also includes the stanzas I have cited. See also Ringler's comment in Sidney, *Poems,* 509. Svensson concludes from the verbal parallels that the countess's poem was written first and that Daniel's poem improves on its images (likely) and hence Daniel was at Wilton before 1590 (debatable) (41–45).

41. Surprisingly, only twice in the *Rime sparse* does Petrarch suggest that his rhymes may immortalize (actually, sanctify) Laura. In *Rime* 297, Petrarch tentatively suggests, "[P]erhaps it will happen that I shall consecrate her lovely noble name with this weary pen." In *Rime* 327, Petrarch imagines Laura already among the elect spirits, concluding that "if my rhymes have any power, among noble intellects your name will be consecrated to eternal memory" (*Petrarch's Lyric Poems: The "Rime sparse" and Other Lyrics*, ed. and trans. Robert M. Durling [Cambridge: Harvard University Press, 1976]). As many commentators have pointed out, the theme of eternizing the mistress comes into the Elizabethan sonnet via Ronsard.

42. Kau, 335–36.

43. This sonnet, says Prescott, is closely patterned after Desportes's *Cleonice* lxii (*French Poets*, 146–47). She and Sidney Lee (*Elizabethan Sonnets* [New York: Cooper Square Publishers, 1964], lv-lix) agree that, of the French poets, Daniel is most indebted to Desportes, though Prescott admits that his "seize the day" and rose sonnets resemble Ronsard's.

44. Even as Daniel tinkers in subsequent editions, adding poems, this poem retains its symbolic position: 35 (of 50) in 1592; 40 (of 57) in 1594, 1595, and 1598; 43 (of 60) thereafter.

45. Mary Ellen Lamb, "The Countess of Pembroke and the Art of Dying," in *Women in the Middle Ages and the Renaissance*, ed. Mary Beth Rose (Syracuse: Syracuse University Press, 1986), 207–26.

46. Williamson, 259.

47. A useful gloss on Daniel's "autentique" is Dante's etymology of "authority," from the Greek word "'Autentim' which in Latin means 'worthy of faith and obedience.' And thus 'Autore' (Author), derived from this, is taken for any person worhy to be believed and obeyed. . . ." (*Il Convito: The Banquet of Dante Alighieri*, cited in Jacqueline Miller, *Poetic License*, 32).

48. Petrarch: "che bel fin fachi ben amando more" (For he makes a good end who dies loving well [Durling trans.]); Wyatt: "Good is the life ending faithfully" ("The

long love, "Poems," 77); Surrey: "Sweet is the death that taketh end by love" ("Love that doth raine," Henry Howard, Earl of Surrey, *Poems*, ed. Emrys Jones [Oxford: Clarendon Press, 1964], 3).

49. See Roche's discussion of this ode in *Petrarch*, 368 ff.

50. Few, if any, commentators on *Rosamond* address the question of the unity of the 1592 volume as a whole. Joan Rees, *Samuel Daniel*, 34–42, and Seronsy, *Samuel Daniel* (34–37), account for it via *The Mirror for Magistrates*, Daniel's source. Gotz Schmitz divorces the poem from *Delia* to link it with the complaint tradition in *The Fall of Women in Early English Narrative Verse* (Cambridge: Cambridge University Press, 1990), 127–33. Roche's attempt to consider the poems together is unconvincing, even alien. He calls the whole work "an ironic sequence . . . in which the poet-lover is found wanting in his love and in the false immortality proffered to the lady"; he calls *Rosamond* a "fitting conclusion to his sophistical desires to gain his Delia" (*Petrarch*, 378, 379). Harsh condemnations of Rosamond's immorality are issued on Daniel's behalf by Ira Clark in "Samuel Daniel's 'Complaint of Rosamond,'" *Renaissance Quarterly* 23 (1970): 152–62, and Ronald Primeau, "Daniel and the *Mirror* Tradition: Dramatic Irony in *The Complaint of Rosamond*," *Studies in English Literature 1500–1900* 15 (1975): 21–36.

51. Wendy Wall focuses on this impersonation, arguing that the complaint trend Daniel initiated became a site of male rivalry and self-authorization; the female respondent is a double for the writer, used "to introduce his own authority through masquerade" (260). Wall's discussion of *Rosamond* (esp. 250–60; 266–68) is the most incisive I have read, and though our emphases are different, our interpretations occasionally intersect. Elizabeth D. Harvey only briefly mentions the complaint in her *Ventriloquized Voices: Feminist Theory and English Renaissance Texts* (London: Routledge, 1992), but her view that such ventriloquism is a means to control female sexuality and silence women's voices (12, 141) seems extremely narrow when applied to Daniel's poem in its contexts.

52. Quotations from *The Complaint of Rosamond, Musophilus*, and *A Defence of Ryme* are taken from Samuel Daniel, *Poems and A Defence of Ryme*, and are cited parenthetically within the text by page or line number, using the abbreviations *Ros*, *Mus*, and *DR*, respectively.

53. Seronsy, *Samuel Daniel*, 58, citing William Covel, *Polimanteia* (1595), sigs. R2v-R3r. On *Rosamond*'s popularity and imitators, see Hallet Smith, *Elizabethan Poetry*, 104–11.

54. See *Matilda. The Faire and Chaste Daughter of the Lord Robert Fitzwater*, in *The Works of Michael Drayton*, 1:209–46.

55. A lengthy passage, from which these and the above lines were taken, was added in 1594 after line 602. See Daniel, *Poems and A Defence of Ryme*, 197–201, ll. 71, 128–33.

56. For a related discussion of female dominance as a sign of political and religious corruption, see Hulse, "Samuel Daniel," 60–61, and *Metamorphic Verse: The Elizabethan Minor Epic* (Princeton: Princeton University Press, 1981), 60–62.

Heather Dubrow assigns Daniel's poem to a subgenre of complaint concerned with the nature of sexual and political power in "A Mirror for Complaints: Shakespeare's *Lucrece* and Generic Tradition," in *Renaissance Genres: Essays on Theory, History, and Interpretation*, ed. Barbara K. Lewalski (Cambridge: Harvard University Press, 1986), 401–3.

57. The woodcuts, as John King pointed out to me, originated from John Day's 1578 *A Booke of Christian Prayers*, where they represent virtues: Knowledge and Love of God, Patience, and Humility. From there, as Samuel Chew observes, they appear (under new names) in various publications, and when they appear on *Licia*, he contends, they are but "nameless and meaningless decoration" ("The Iconography of *A Booke of Christian Prayers* [1578] Illustrated," *Huntington Library Quarterly* 8 [1945]: 293–305).

58. [Giles Fletcher], *Licia, or Poems of Love* and *The Rising to the Crowne of Richard the Third* (London, 1593), sig L2r.

59. Ibid., sig L2v.

60. Daniel, *Complete Works* 2:12, stanza 6.

61. Samuel Daniel, *The Civil Wars*, ed. Laurence Michel (New Haven: Yale University Press, 1958), Epistle Dedicatory, 69.

62. Daniel's vocation as a historian is beyond the scope of this study, though much excellent critical work on the subject exists. On the changing practices in Renaissance historiography generally, see Phyllis Rackin, *Stages of History: Shakespeare's English Chronicles* (Ithaca: Cornell University Press, 1990), chap. 1; F. J. Levy, *Tudor Historical Thought* (San Marino: The Huntington Library, 1967); Arthur B. Ferguson, *Clio Unbound: Perception of the social and cultural past in Renaissance England* (Durham: Duke University Press, 1979). For particular applications to Daniel, see Arthur B. Ferguson, "The Historical Thought of Samuel Daniel: A Study in Renaissance Ambivalence," *Journal of the History of Ideas* 32 (1971): 185–202; D. R. Woolf, "Community, Law and State: Samuel Daniel's Historical Thought Revisited," *Journal of the History of Ideas* 49 (1988): 61–83. On the conflict of history and poetry for Daniel, see Joan Rees, "Past and Present in the Sixteenth Century," *Trivium* (1985), 110–11; Jean Brink, "Framing Philosophy: Sidney and Daniel,"in *Perspective as a Problem in the Art, History and Literature of Early Modern England*, ed. Mark Lussier and S. K. Heninger (Lewiston, Ky.: Edwin Mellen Press, 1992), 86–91. On Daniel's place within the emergent practice of politic history, see F. J. Levy, "Hayward, Daniel, and the Beginnings of Politic History in England," *Huntington Library Quarterly* 53 (1987), 26. On providential and cyclical views of history in Daniel, see R. B. Gill, "Moral History and Daniel's *The Civil Wars*," *Journal of English and Germanic Philology* 76 (1977): 334–45; Cecil Seronsy, "The Doctrine of Cyclical Recurrence and Some Related Ideas in the Works of Samuel Daniel," *Studies in Philology* 54 (1957): 387–407.

63. In 1930, a nameless reviewer observed that Daniel's attitude is in fact inimical to poetry and that both he and Greville were "really opposed to poetry, to its metaphor, its hyperbole, its rhetoric. . . . [N]ominally defending rhyme, [they] were introducing a philosophy which made poetry futile" ("Samuel Daniel and Fulke

Greville," *Times Literary Supplement*, 5 June 1930, p. 475). This view, not elaborated then or since, here receives consideration and modification.

64. See Joan Rees, *Samuel Daniel*, 62–65, for circumstances of Greville's aid to Daniel. For a discussion of literary and philosophical backgrounds to *Musophilus*, see Raymond Himelick's introduction to *Samuel Daniels' Musophilus: Containing a General Defense of All Learning* (West Lafayette: Purdue University Press, 1965).

65. Himelick cites Bullough for the notion that Greville's skeptical Calvinism was the catalyst for the humanist defence in *Musophilus*, finding Daniel as moralistic as Greville but not overtly Christian; Montaigne was a strong influence on Daniel, too (Introduction to *Musophilus,* 38–39).

66. For a discussion of literary links between Greville and Daniel, particularly versifying practices, see Croll, 15–49 passim. Croll and other critics generally agree that Daniel is more optimistic than Greville about the state of learning. Another important strain in Daniel's work is Senecan Stoicism, bolstered by the reading of Montaigne at this time. See Raymond Himelick, "Samuel Daniel, Montaigne and Seneca," *Notes and Queries* 3 (1956): 61–64.

67. Himelick calls the dialogue "a kind of spiritual autobiography" suggesting "some of the ambivalences inherent in the age but not always so consciously rationalized" (Introduction to *Musophilus*, 15, 31). For further evidence of the conflict in Daniel and its attendant despair, see John Pitcher, "Samuel Daniel's Letter to Sir Thomas Egerton," *Huntington Library Quarterly* 47 (1984): 55-61.

68. Samuel Daniel, *A Panegyrike with a Defence of Ryme* [1603] (Menston: Scolar Press, 1970). See Seronsy, *Samuel Daniel,* 111–12.

69. Daniel's native pride and patriotism are also noted by Howard C. Cole in *A Quest of Inquirie: Some Contexts of Tudor Literature* (New York: Bobbs-Merrill, 1973), 155–57.

70. Those who view the work as progressive include J. W. H. Atkins, *English Literary Criticism: The Renascence* (New York: Barnes and Noble, 1947), 195–207; Derek Attridge, *Well-Weighed Syllables: Elizabethan Verse in Classical Metres* (London: Cambridge University Press, 1974), 233. Also see the discussion of Daniel and Campion in Ryding, 83–92.

71. Daniel, *Panegyrike*, sig. B4r.

72. McCoy's analysis of *The Civil Wars* in terms of Daniel's ambivalence toward royal authority confirms my observations here (*Rites*, 116; chap. 5 passim). Laurence Michel, in the introduction to Daniel's *The Tragedy of Philotas* (New Haven: Yale University Press, 1949), finds Daniel sympathetic to Essex's case and the play an indictment of tyranny (62–63).

73. Lawrence Manley, *Convention 1500–1740* (Cambridge: Harvard University Press, 1980), 11.

74. Francis Bacon, "Of Custom and Education," in *The Essayes or Counsels, Civill and Morall* (1625), in *Francis Bacon: A Selection of His Works*, ed. Sidney Warhaft (New York: Odyssey Press, 1965), 148–49.

75. Ben Jonson, *Timber: or Discoveries*, in *The Complete Poems*, ed. George Parfitt (New Haven: Yale University Press, 1975), 432.

76. For the view that Custom and Nature are different and unreconciled poles in Daniel's thought, see Arthur B. Ferguson, *Clio Unbound*, 65–66 and "Historical Thought," 185–202.

77. Epistle, *Philotas*, 26–31, in *Complete Works*, 3:100. This passage also enables Daniel to deny his play's particularity; any resemblance between his character and the earl of Essex is a coincidence of human nature.

78. Similar praise of the power of eloquence occurs in Thomas Wilson's *Arte of Rhetorique*, echoing Cicero's *De Oratore*: "Such force hath the tongue, and such is the power of eloquence and reason, that most men are forced even to yelde in that, whiche most standeth against their will" (sig. A3v). The passage is cited in Kinney, *Humanist Poetics*, 7.

79. See Richard C. Helgerson's "Barbarous Tongues: The Ideology of Poetic Form in Renaissance England" (in *The Historical Renaissance*, 288–89) for the point that Daniel's *Defence* contributes to English poets' nationalist project of establishing "the kingdom of their own language" by inventing traditions such as the sonnet and rhyme.

80. See G. B. Harrison, introduction to Samuel Daniel, *A defence of ryme . . .* (1603) and Thomas Campion, *Observations in the Art of English poesie* (1602). (London: John Lane, 1925), vi.

81. Disagreements between poets on rhyming practices only reinforce Daniel's observations here. Ben Jonson, his rival, tells William Drummond that he has written a treatise of poetry against both Campion and Daniel wherein "he proves couplets to be the bravest sort of verses, especially when they are broken, like hexameters; and that cross-rhymes and stanzas . . . were all forced" (*Conversations with William Drummond*, in *Ben Jonson: The Complete Poems*, 461).

5: Spenser's *Complaints*, *Astrophel*, and the Sidney Legend

1. Spenser, *Yale Edition*, 170. Quotations from *The Shepheardes Calender*, *The Ruines of Time*, *The Teares of the Muses*, *Astrophel*, *Amoretti*, *Epithalamion*, and *Prothalamion*, "The Doleful Lay of Clorinda," refer to this edition and are cited in the text, using abbreviated titles where necessary for clarification.

2. William Webbe, *A Discourse of English Poetrie*, ed. Edward Arber (Westminster: A. Constable and Co., 1895), 23. Webbe graduated from Cambridge in 1572–73, while Spenser was attending, though they were not members of the same

college. He professed to admire Harvey and Spenser but may have known of the reputed *English Poet* only through E. K.'s reference in *The Shepheardes Calendar.*

3. Those who reconstruct a possible early relationship between Sidney and Spenser (including Spenser's biographer, Alexander C. Judson), rely on Wallace, who suggests that they may have met at Cambridge but is certain that "by the latter part of 1579 Spenser had come to London and was living at Leicester House, that he was on terms of familiarity with Sidney and Dyer, and that they together discussed literary questions" (228). The Spenser-Harvey correspondence of 1580 (*Three Proper, and wittie, familiar Letters* and *Two Other very commendable Letters,* in *Spenser: Poetical Works*) is also taken as evidence. Duncan-Jones suggests Harvey could have brought Spenser to Sidney's notice around 1577 (when Spenser was Henry Sidney's courier or secretary in Ireland), though she doubts the letters' intimation that Spenser was in close association with Sidney and Dyer (*Sir Philip Sidney*, 119, 191–92). Sidney's editor, Ringler, believes they were not closely acquainted and never had truly substantive discussions of poetic craft (*Poems,* xxxi-xxxv). He suggests that Sidney may have helped Spenser to his position as secretary to Lord Grey as a reward for Spenser's dedication of *The Shepheardes Calender* to him in 1579 (xxxiii). Duncan-Jones believes Sidney surely rewarded Spenser for this dedication (229), and she frequently refers to the latter as Sidney's "protege," finding a grain of truth in John Aubrey's apocryphal account of their meeting. Jan van Dorsten also deems the evidence points to Sidney as "patron and leader of a group of intellectuals" that included Spenser ("Literary Patronage," 201–6, 204).

4. *Two Other very commendable Letters,* 635.

5. *Three Proper and wittie, familiar Letters*, 612. Wallace does not rely on the Spenser-Harvey correspondence as evidence of any warm personal friendship between Sidney and Spenser (230). Duncan-Jones also doubts its credibility; she deems the correspondence a self-aggrandizing attempt by a marginal member of Sidney's group. The experimentation in meters to which he alludes formed only a small part of Sidney's literary interests in 1580 (*Sir Philip Sidney*, 191–92).

6. *Two Other very commendable Letters,* 635.

7. Piers also slyly promotes the Leicester family by referring to their crest: "Or if thee please in bigger notes to sing, / Advaunce the worthy whome shee loveth best, / That first the white beare to the stake did bring" (ll. 46–48), supporting Wallace's view that Spenser's friendship with Sidney at Cambridge helped him to secure Leicester as his early patron.

8. Sidney as a prototype for Calidore was first suggested by John Upton in his edition of *The Faerie Queene* (London, 1758), 657–58. For a summary of earlier critical views, *Works of Edmund Spenser*, 6:371–76. Few have recently addressed this relationship; an exception is Judith Dundas's "'The Heaven's Ornament': Spenser's Tribute to Sidney," *Etudes Anglaises* 42 (1989), 131–34.

9. W. L. Renwick, in his edition of Spenser's *Complaints* (London, 1928) assigns it a date of 1579–80, noting the general resemblance to Sidney's *Defence* and doubting the validity of its criticisms in 1590, when Spenser was a successful poet. Jean Brink, in "Who Fashioned Edmund Spenser?: The Textual History of *Complaints*,"

Studies in Philology 88 (1991): 153–68, reopens matters of dating and unity; she cautions against the assumption that Spenser organized and oversaw the publication of his *Complaints* in 1591, pointing out that its satires on Burleigh and the court might compromise Spenser's not-yet-authorized pension.

10. Renwick notes the coincidence of lines (204).

11. At the outset of book 1 of Sidney's revised *Arcadia*, Urania similarly mounts to the heaven, having moved Strephon and Claius to a higher love. Spenser may have drawn on the *Arcadia*, first published in 1590, for his own *Complaints*, published in 1591, but most likely both Spenser and Sidney drew from Du Bartas's *L'Uranie ou Muse Celeste* (1574). Protestant poetics is also the subject of Carl J. Rasmussen's "'Quietnesse of Minde': *A Theatre for Worldlings* as a Protestant Poetics," *Spenser Studies* 1 (1980): 3–27.

12. Carl J. Rasmussen, "'How Weak Be the Passions of Woefulness': Spenser's *Ruines of Time*," *Spenser Studies* 2 (1981): 159–81. See also Deborah Cartmell, "'Beside the shore of silver streaming *Thamesis*': Spenser's *Ruines of Time*," *Spenser Studies* 6 (1985): 77–82, for the view that Verlame is a type of Babylon, the Roman church, and the narrator's refusal to sing "implies a Protestant criticism of Verlame's values" (79).

13. See A. Leigh DeNeef, "'The Ruins of Time': Spenser's Apology for Poetry," *Studies in Philology* 76 (1979), 262–71. He briefly observes that Verlame may be unreliable but that at times she "clearly speaks with authorial sanction" (271 n. 14).

14. Lawrence Manley, ignoring the problem of Verlame's reliability, finds this elegiac praise of the Dudleys a "civic act, a creation of exemplary images whose suasive powers can reorder society" ("Spenser and the City: The Minor Poems" *Modern Language Quarterly* 43 [1982], 215).

15. Rasmussen arrives at this conclusion from a different perspective, showing Verlame's awareness that "Sidney need not be eternized: he is eternal" ("How Weak Be the Passions," 168).

16. Churchyard, for example, calls him the "Lords elekt" and a "chosen Lam;" in Bryskett's "The Mourning Muse of Thestylis," Sidney conforms himself to the example of Christ, and his death, like Christ's crucifixion, is attended by disorder in nature. See my introduction to this book. For the conventional nature of this praise, see Bennett, 119–20.

17. See Kenneth Gross, *Spenserian Poetics: Idolatry, Iconoclasm, and Magic* (Ithaca: Cornell University Press, 1985), 28–31.

18. Until recently, most readers have read Verlame's praise of poetry as a straightforward statement of Spenser's own beliefs and his confidence in poetry's power. See Renwick, 198. Alfred W. Satterthwaite, in *Spenser, Ronsard, and Du Bellay: A Renaissance Comparison* (Princeton: Princeton University Press, 1960), sees no conflict, in Spenser or in his poem, between pagan views of poetry and the Christian belief that only the soul is immortal (101).

19. As Rasmussen comments, "Poetry is for Verlame the most efficient possible House of Pride" ("How Weak Be the Passions," 171).

20. Here I disagree both with Cartmell, who sees the narrator as a divinely inspired, proper Protestant poet who refuses to use Verlame's secular language, and Rasmussen, who finds that the final visions provide the true *consolatio* that directs the narrator to heavenly things and liberates him from weak passions.

21. See Spenser's own *Vewe of the Present State of Ireland*, believed to be written in the mid-1590s. For criticism of Burghley, see *RT* 214–17, 447–53. Not only Henry Sidney and his son Philip were dead, but also Philip's uncles Robert and Ambrose Dudley (earls of Leicester and Warwick), Francis Walsingham, and the earl of Bedford.

22. See Renwick, 189–90.

23. Falco, "Instant Artifacts," 19. Michael O'Connell made a similar observation in "*Astrophel*: Spenser's Double Elegy," *Studies in English Literature* 11 (1971), 29–30. Dennis Kay observes that with *Astrophel*, the English elegy turns from simple praise to engage the artistic tradition and issues of culture and politics. See *Melodious Tears: The English Funeral Elegy from Spenser to Milton* (Oxford: Clarendon Press, 1990), 78.

24. Falco, *Conceived Presences*, chap. 2.

25. Peter Sacks, "*Astrophel*," a selection from *The English Elegy: Studies in the Genre from Spenser to Yeats*, reprinted in *Edmund Spenser: Modern Critical Views*, ed. Harold Bloom (New York: Chelsea, 1986), 241–43.

26. See Theodore Steinberg's related discussion of the poem in "Spenser, Sidney, and The Myth of Astrophel," *Spenser Studies* 11 (1994): 187–201; he argues that *Astrophel* "simultaneously glorifies and criticizes its subject" (187) and that Spenser refuses to accept the Sidney myth (194). Steinberg's article appeared at the same time as my own "Spenser's *Astrophel* and the Sidney Legend," *Sidney Newsletter and Journal* 12 (1993): 42–55, an earlier version of the present chapter.

27. Biographical questions sometimes emerge from this poem: Walter G. Friedrich, concerned about propriety, argued that the Stella of *Astrophel* is meant to refer to Sidney's widow ("The Stella of Astrophel," *ELH* 3 [1936]: 114–39). Modern critics are less troubled by these issues; O'Connell even suggests that Stella may be the queen or even Sidney's sister, on both of whom he spends the riches of his wit ("*Astrophel*," 30–32). See also Thomas P. Roche Jr., "Autobiographical Elements in Sidney's *Astrophil and Stella*," *Spenser Studies* 5 (1984): 209–29, who deems the assessment of Penelope Rich by later writers to have been "essentially literary" rather than biographical (223).

28. Sacks finds that Spenser's reversals instill a sense of "vertiginous instability" in language, as in life, and prefigure the catastrophe to come (242). Steinberg finds that the narrator is disagreeing with Astrophel, who deems words merely idle ("Spenser, Sidney," 189).

29. Falco, "Instant Artifacts," 15, and *Conceived Presences*, 111; Sacks; Steinberg, "Spenser, Sidney," 192.

30. Castiglione details such desirable physical accomplishments as swimming, running, throwing, playing tennis, and horsemanship. Roger Ascham, in *The*

Scholemaster (1570), advocates riding, shooting, tilting, running, wrestling, and swimming as appropriate pastimes for a gentleman, and recommends Castiglione's work (in *Prose of the English Renaissance,* ed. John William Hebel et al. [New York: Appleton Century Crofts, 1952], 108–10).

31. Leonard Tourney finds Spenser suggesting in Astrophel's fatal heroism "a darker psychology than mere recklessness, a malaise bordering in its self-destructiveness on the pathological" ("Spenser's *Astrophel*: Myth and the Critique of Values," *Essays in Literature* 3 [1976], 148). Ultimately, however, he finds that the poem affirms the possibility of pure and heroic human love in a fallen world (150).

32. Astrophel recalls Sidney's own image of wasted promise, Amphialus, whose consuming desire for Pamela and Philoclea feeds his rebellion, which eventually dissipates in empty chivalric show and tragic deaths (*Arcadia*, 501–75). Josephine Roberts says of Amphialus, "He believes in the model of the self-centered warrior and does not recognize that the heroic life may consist of higher values" (*Architectonic Knowledge in the* New Arcadia*: Sidney's Use of the Heroic Journey, Salzburg Studies in English Literature* 69 [Salzburg, 1978], 246). In Amphialus, Sidney criticizes the cult of martial courage by which men embrace destruction in the name of courtly love. Calidore also alludes to a higher ideal than chivalry while commending Tristram's "high desire / To love of armes," which

> I may not certes without blame denie;
> But rather wish, that some more noble hire,
> (Though none more noble then is chevalrie,)
> I had, you to reward with greater dignitie. (*FQ* 6.2.34)

For an alternate reading of Amphialus that emphasizes his moral weakness, see Joan Rees, *Sir Philip Sidney and* Arcadia (London: Associated University Press, 1991), chap. 1. Rees's reading would not support an Amphilaus-Astrophel connection. Spenser surely has Sidney's *Arcadia* in mind when Calidore saves Pastorella from the tiger, a scene that closely parallels the rescue by Pyrocles-Zelmane of Philoclea from the lion (*Arcadia*, 176–82). The nature and extent of Spenser's engagement with Sidney's romance is beyond the scope of this chapter.

33. Falco believes Spenser's delay can be accounted for by two factors: a decline in support from Sidney's family and Spenser's "establishment of a shared literary descent" that both acknowledges and necessarily repudiates Sidney (*Conceived Presences*, 98).

34. It is not necessary to claim Spenser's shaping hand behind the 1595 *Astrophel* volume. Indeed, Hyder Rollins notes that the printer of *Colin clouts come home againe* used *The Phoenix Nest* as a copy to set the text of the last three elegies (Introduction to *The Phoenix Nest*). Remember Brink's argument, from textual and bibliographic evidence, for the unlikelihood of Spenser's involvement in the 1591 *Complaints*.

35. See my discussion in the Introduction.

36. Richard S. Peterson, "'Who Ever Made Such Layes of Love as He?'" unpublished response to my "Spenser's *Astrophel* and the Sidney Legend," presented at the 28th International Congress on Medieval Studies, Kalamazoo, Michigan, May 1993. I am grateful for Professor Peterson's comments urging me to address Spenser's use of the Adonis myth more fully.

37. Spenser is simply not bound by biographical facts or by his sources, which include Ronsard's "Adonis," an adaptation of Bion's "Lament for Adonis" (Prescott, *French Poets*, 109–10). He is perhaps consciously decorous, however, since the poem's dedicatee was Frances Walsingham, Sidney's widow, now wife of the earl of Essex. See, by contrast, the Ovidian eroticism present in Spenser's depiction of the legend in the tapestries in Malecasta's castle (*FQ* 3.1.34–38) and in versions such as Thomas Lodge's *Scillaes Metamorphosis* and Shakespeare's *Venus and Adonis*.

38. Arguments against her authorship hinge on the weak assumption that she could not skillfully imitate Spenser's style. Hannay draws on strong textual and contextual evidence, including Spenser's own attribution of the "Lay" to Sidney's sister (*Astrophel* 211–216), a reference in *RT* 316–20, and epistolary evidence. See Hannay, *Philip's Phoenix*, 63–68, for a fuller account and summary of the critical controversy.

39. See Sacks, 246.

40. O'Connell's essay is the prime example of a critical effort to forge a unified whole from two disparate halves that he asserts are "carefully bound together by the symbolic flower" ("*Astrophel*," 35).

41. See Helgerson, *Self-Crowned Laureates*, 89–90; Judith Anderson, *The Growth of a Personal Voice: Piers Plowman and The Faerie Queene* (New Haven: Yale University Press, 1976), 173; David L. Miller, "Abandoning the Quest," *ELH* 46 (1979): 173–92.

6: *Amoretti* and the Reformation of Love Poetry

1. I do not wish to claim that Spenser responded directly to Sidney's sequence. Unlike the sonnets of Greville and Daniel, there are very few verbal or thematic links to specific poems of Sidney. (An exception might be the images of leaves and the bird in the first and last *Amoretti*, gentle echoes of the leaves and the bird/soul of Sidney's first and last sonnets.) However, Spenser undoubtedly knew his French Petrarchists Ronsard, DuBellay, and Desportes well, as Anne Lake Prescott has shown in *French Poets*. Thomas P. Roche Jr. finds the fact that *Astrophel* has 216 lines, exactly double the number of sonnets in *Astrophel and Stella*, evidence that Sidney is trying to overgo Sidney (review of *The Yale Edition of the Shorter Poems of Edmund Spenser*, *Spenser Newsletter* 22.2 [1991]: 10).

2. I made this argument in "'Let us love, dear love, lyke as we ought': Protestant Marriage and the Revision of Petrarchan Loving in Spenser's *Amoretti*," *Spenser Studies* 10 (1992): 109–37, which forms the core of the present chapter. A few of my

points are anticipated by John N. Wall, whose discussion of the "Homiletics of Marriage" in *Transformations of the Word: Spenser, Herbert, Vaughan* (Athens: University of Georgia Press, 1988), centers on the *Epithalamion* and emphasizes Spenser's promotion of Christian community. For other perspectives on Spenser's engagement with and revision of Petrarchan convention see Joseph Loewenstein, "Echo's Ring: Orpheus and Spenser's Career," *English Literary Renaissance* 16 (1986), 294–95; A. Leigh DeNeef, *Spenser and the Motives of Metaphor* (Durham: Duke University Press, 1982), 73; Reed Way Dasenbrock, "The Petrarchan Context of Spenser's *Amoretti*," *PMLA* 100 (1985): 38–50, and *Imitating the Italians*, chap. 2.

3. See Helgerson's discussion of the Mount Acidale episode in *Self-Crowned Laureates*, 89–96; Richard Neuse, "Book VI as Conclusion to *The Faerie Queene*," *ELH* 35 (1968): 350.

4. Michael O'Connell, *Mirror and Veil: The Historical Dimension of Spenser's* Faerie Queene (Chapel Hill: University of North Carolina Press, 1977), 193.

5. Miller, "Abandoning," 190, 173–74. For the opposite view, that retirement energizes and inspires Spenser's laureate projects, see Helgerson, *Self-Crowned Laureates*, 97.

6. As Bates observes, Spenser's *Amoretti* volume is "shot through with allusions to the court and to Queen Elizabeth, inviting an obvious parallel between the wooing of his beloved and his difficult 'courtship' of the sovereign" (138).

7. See Donald Cheney's complementary discussion of sonnets 74 and 80 in "Spenser's Fortieth Birthday and Related Fictions" *Spenser Studies* 4 (1983): 3–31. See also Joanne Craig's discussion of Spenser's dual roles of public and private poet in "The Queen, Her Handmaid, and Spenser's Career," *English Studies in Canada* 12 (1986): 256.

8. See the analysis of Britomart's role by Thomas P. Roche Jr. in *The Kindly Flame: A Study of the Third and Fourth Books of Spenser's* Faerie Queene (Princeton: Princeton University Press, 1964) and A. Kent Hieatt, *Chaucer, Spenser, Milton: Mythopoeic Continuities and Transformations* (Montreal: McGill-Queens University Press, 1975).

9. Roche notes the relevant scriptural glosses as Ephesians 4:8 and Psalm 68:18 ("You have gone up on high and led captivity captive"). The Song of Deborah (Judges 5:12) rejoices, "Up Deborah, up, arise, & sing a song: arise Barak & lead thy captivite captive" (Review of *The Yale Edition*, 10).

10. See Ann Lake Prescott's discussion of the deer's Christlike connotations and liturgical and biblical associations in "The Thirsty Deer and the Lord of Life: Some Contexts for *Amoretti* 67–70," *Spenser Studies* 7 (1986): 47 ff. DeNeef finds that the Song of Songs, with its central metaphor of the *hortus conclusus*, affords Spenser's lover the means of transforming his previously literal understanding of captivity (*Spenser*, 70).

11. See King, *Spenser's Poetry*, chap. 4. *Amoretti* and *Epithalamion* feature "a distillation of Spenser's position concerning love and marriage and a *modification* of imported literary models in line with Protestant ideology" (182; emphasis added). Though his focus differs, his reading of *Amoretti* complements and supports my own.

12. See, for example, Petrarch's *Rime sparse* 39 ("I so fear the assault of those lovely eyes where Love and my death dwell"); 61 ("Blessed be the day . . . where I was struck by the two lovely eyes that have bound me; and blessed be . . . the bow and the arrows that pierced me, and the wounds that reach my heart!"); and 75 ("The lovely eyes that struck me in such a way that they themselves could heal the wound"). (Translations are Robert Durling's.)

13. The resemblance of this sonnet to *Caelica* 3 must be noted; Greville's poem begins: "More than most faire, full of that heavenly fire, / Kindled above to shew the Makers glory." This poem may point to an association between Spenser and Greville (and hence Sidney) dating from 1579–80 (Rebholz, 326), though it is hard to say which poem is prior. Rebholz gives a probable date of 1579 to Greville's poem, in which case Spenser is echoing—and correcting—Greville, whose lady wrongly displaces Christ. She is the "pride of spirits" and "prison of mans pure affection" (*C* 3:7, 10), not, as for Spenser, an image of God's own grace and beauty.

14. William C. Johnson, *Spenser's* Amoretti: *Analogies of Love* (London: Associated University Presses, 1990), 18–22. Most critics are reluctant to see Spenser in the role of teacher, as if direct didacticism compromises Spenser's artistry. Instead, they insist on separating Spenser from his poet-lover persona and tracing the spiritual growth of the latter. See, for example, Johnson's "Amor and Spenser's *Amoretti*," *English Studies* 54 (1973): 217–26; Peter M. Cummings, "Spenser's *Amoretti* as an Allegory of Love," *Texas Studies in Literature and Language* 12 (1970): 163–79; DeNeef, *Spenser*, 69.

15. According to Robert Ellrodt, Louis LeRoy, whose commentary on the *Symposium* Spenser may have known secondhand, is the only other Renaissance Platonist to agree with Spenser that the perfection of human love is generation. Most Renaissance Platonists (Castiglione, for example) separated the consideration of marriage from the platonic philosophy of love and even contrasted the two. See Ellrodt, *Neoplatonism in the Poetry of Spenser* (Geneva: E. Droz, 1960), 105, 146.

16. Ellrodt, 146. William Nelson also establishes that, for Spenser, earthly love and heavenly love are comparable and not incompatible in *The Poetry of Edmund Spenser* (New York: Columbia University Press, 1963), 97–101.

17. On the relationship of Spenser's Christianity and his Platonism, see Ellrodt, 129–30; William Nelson, 114. Most recently, Elizabeth Bieman treats the subject in *Plato Baptized: Towards the Interpretation of Spenser's Mimetic Fictions* (Toronto: University of Toronto Press, 1988).

18. On the calendrical structure of Petrarch's *Canzoniere* see Roche, *Petrarch*, 32–69. One entire vein of *Amoretti* criticism deals with its calendrical contexts. See, for example, Alexander Dunlop, "The Unity of Spenser's Amoretti," in *Silent Poetry: Essays in Numerological Analysis*, ed. Alastair Fowler (New York: Barnes and Noble, 1970), 153–69; G. K. Hunter, "'Unity' and Numbers in Spenser's *Amoretti*," *Yearbook of English Studies* 5 (1975): 39–45; A. Kent Hieatt, "A Numerical Key for Spenser's *Amoretti* and Guyon in the House of Mammon," *Yearbook of English Studies* 3 (1973): 14–27; Johnson, *Spenser's* Amoretti, chap. 1. More recently, Prescott's "The Thirsty Deer" expands the liturgical contexts of the sequence.

19. I have drawn on the following works: Juan Luis Vives, *The Office and Duetie of a Husband* (London, 1553), and William Gouge, *Of Domesticall Duties* (London, 1622), both conduct manuals; *An Homily of the State of Matrimony*, in *Certain Sermons* (London, 1562), Henry Smith, *A Preparative to Marriage* (London, 1591), and William Whately, *A Bride-Bush, or a Wedding Sermon* (London, 1617), all sermons; and Edmund Tilney, *The Flower of Friendship: A Renaissance Dialogue Contesting Marriage* (1568), ed. Valerie Wayne (Ithaca: Cornell University Press, 1992), a courtly work akin to Castiglione's *Book of the Courtier*. Citations from these works appear parenthetically in the text.

Literary critics and social historians disagree concerning the status of marriage in late Elizabethan times. Some point to the new Puritan ideal of marriage emphasizing love and domestic relations and find that it elevated a wife's position. Among them are William Haller, "Hail Wedded Love," *ELH* 13 (1946): 79–97; William and Malleville Haller, "The Puritan Art of Love," *Huntington Library Quarterly* 5 (1942): 235–72; C. S. Lewis, *The Allegory of Love* (New York: Oxford University Press, 1958), and Juliet Dusinberre, *Shakespeare and the Nature of Woman* (London: MacMillan, 1975); Mark Rose, *Heroic Love: Studies in Sidney and Spenser* (Cambridge: Harvard University Press, 1968). Lawrence Stone, on the other hand, while acknowledging the new emphasis on domesticity, sees the period 1580–1640 as one of increasing patriarchal control over the wife and family (see *The Family, Sex and Marriage in England 1500–1800* [New York: Harper & Row 1977], chap. 5). Margaret J. M. Ezell rejects Stone's idea of restrictive patriarchy as a bugbear in *The Patriarch's Wife: Literary Evidence and the History of the Family* (Chapel Hill: University of North Carolina Press, 1987). Kathleen M. Davies, in "Continuity and Change in Literary Advice on Marriage," in *Marriage and Society: Studies in the Social History of Marriage*, ed. R. B. Outhwaite (London: Europa, 1981), 58–80, agrees with Stone but finds that attitudes expressed towards domestic relations changed very little from the mid-sixteenth to the mid-seventeenth century, despite changes in theological views about the status of marriage. Because my own reading of the above primary texts bears out Davies's conclusions, I refer to their advice and prescriptions regarding men's and women's roles in marriage as the "conventional wisdom" of Spenser's culture. Like Davies, Keith Wrightson emphasizes the continuity between pre- and post-Reformation tradition regarding marriage, in *English Society 1580–1680* (New Brunswick: Rutgers University Press, 1982), 91. See also Margo Todd, who stresses the humanist origins of many supposedly puritan ideas about marriage (chap. 4). Most recently, Heather Dubrow has refueled the debate; noting the contradictions within and between conduct books on marriage, she denies there was a single, coherent "Protestant discourse of marriage" in Tudor and Stuart England (*Happier Eden*, 4, 12–14).

20. Prescott believes this poem to be a paraphrase and refashioning of Desportes' *Diane* I, xxxii (*French Poets*, 150–51).

21. See David Lee Miller, "Spenser's Poetics: The Poem's Two Bodies," *PLMA* 101 (1986): 171, 175. In *The Poem's Two Bodies: The Poetics of the 1590* Faerie Queene (Princeton: Princeton University Press, 1988), Miller writes of Una:

> Like the truth of the heavenly hymns, [which depends on the presence of the earthly hymns and on their renunciation], Una emerges into representation only through a differential repetition that sets her apart from herself and so makes her dependent on what she is not—dividing Truth to assert its self-resemblance in a phrase that echoes, as it opposes, Duessa's counterepiphany. (81–82)

This passage also occurs verbatim in the earlier *PMLA* article.

22. Louis Martz, "The Amoretti: 'Most Goodly Temperature,'" in *Form and Convention in the Poetry of Edmund Spenser*, ed. William Nelson (New York: Columbia University Press, 1961), 146–68. O. B. Hardison explains these clashing motifs of the *donna angelicata* and the "cruel fair" as the legacy of the Italian tradition in his "*Amoretti* and the Dolce Stil Nuovo," *English Literary Renaissance* 2 (1972), esp. 211, 216.

23. The same rhetorical strategy is employed by Whately in a somewhat less concise passage of *A Bride-Bush*, 36–37.

24. Daniel Rogers, *Matrimoniall Honour* (London, 1642), 7.

25. See bk. 5, cantos 4, 5, and 7, especially 5.5.25 and 5.7.42–43.

26. Before sonnet 62, twenty poems refer to pride: 2, 5, 6, 13, 14, 19, 21, 27, 28, 31–33, 38, 43, 47, 49, 56, 58, 59, and 61. *Amoretti* 62 is the New Year's sonnet; shortly thereafter is the "engagement" sonnet (67), after which references to pride are scarce. In addition to the above twenty sonnets, several refer to the mistress as cruel, a tyrant, or a beast: 10, 11, 20, 25, 36, 41, 45, 53, and 57. Five poems describe her as "hard" or "stubborn": 18, 29, 30, 51, and 54. Spenser's preoccupation with his lady's pride and its manifestations, cruelty and hard-heartedness, is without precedent or match in his contemporaries.

27. See also *Amoretti* 20, 31, 38, 47, 53, and 56. As Gail Cohee has pointed out to me, the prideful women in Lucifera's dungeon include Semiramis and Cleopatra, known for unnatural and insatiable lust (*FQ* 1.5.50). For the definition of pride as sexual desire or excitement, see *OED*, s.v. "pride," II. 11; "proud," 8. Sexual pride is apparent in Shakespeare's Dark Lady, who "Tempteth my better angel from my side, / And would corrupt my saint to be a devil, / Wooing his purity with her foul pride" (144:6–8) (*Shakespeare's Sonnets*, ed. Stephen Booth [New Haven: Yale University Press, 1977]). In conduct books, the association of pride with sexuality is implicit in the endorsement of "shamefastness" as a primary virtue for women. Vives inextricably links the two: "Chastitie is kept with shamefastnes, nor the one can not be without the other" (R3v). (Its opposite, shamelessness, still connotes sexual looseness.)

28. Compare the description of Urania in *TM* 523–28: "I feede on sweet contentment of my thought, / And please my selfe with mine owne selfe-delight. . . . So loathing earth, I looke up to the sky. . . ."

29. King discusses these two poems in terms of Protestant doctrine concerning grace and justification by faith. In sonnet 58, her spiritual autonomy suggests original sin, while in sonnet 59, she displays "assurance," a term Protestants used to define election (*Spenser's Poetry*, 166).

30. See the discussions of pride by William Nelson, 89–90; Martz, "*Amoretti*," 162–64. Carol Kaske, in "Spenser's *Amoretti* and *Epithalamion* of 1595: Structure,

Genre, and Numerology," *English Literary Renaissance* 8 (1978): 271–95 finds that sonnets 58, 59, and 61 fail to resolve the issue of pride or the "conflicts of sexual desire with virtue and virginal pride with wifely submission" (285), but she sees the debate settled with sonnet 67 (281).

31. See also sonnet 13, discussed above, and sonnets 38, 41, 45, 49, 50, 53, 55, 57, 58, 68, 79, and 82.

32. Puttenham discusses allegory as an art of dissembling essential to courtiers and princes, as well as to poets (155–56).

33. Tilney expresses the same idea: the married man "little by little must gently procure that he maye also steale away hir private will, and appetite, so that of two bodies there may be made one onely hart . . ." (112).

34. In this advice to husbands, I am reminded of Peter Ramus's "prudential method," characterized by indirection and used to persuade an inattentive or unfriendly audience. See John Webster, "'The Methode of a Poete': An Inquiry Into Tudor Conceptions of Poetic Sequence," *English Literary Renaissance* 11 (1981): 22–43.

35. David Lee Miller, *Poem's Two Bodies*, 219–20. Incidentally, the courtship of Artegall and Britomart, like that of the *Amoretti* lovers, begins in a contest for mastery and ends with the establishment of loving concord. In *The Faerie Queene* 4.6.12, Artegall greedily assails Britomart, like a hound cornering a hind. Her own "hart"-heart leaps with "sudden joy, and secret feare" (4.6.29) as she recognizes her mate. Glauce reconciles the battling lovers, and Artegall proceeds to woo Britomart properly, "with meeke service and much suit" until she consents to marry him (4.6.40–41).

36. Poems from *The Countess of Pembroke's Arcadia* 67:49–51, in Sidney, *Poems*, 105.

37. In Erasmus's colloquy "Marriage," first published in England in 1557, the same idea is expressed in virtually identical wording to Tilney's. See *The Colloquies of Erasmus*, trans. Craig R. Thompson (Chicago: University of Chicago Press, 1965), 119. Another example of the mirror conceit used in an advice book for married Christians is Robert Snawsell's *A Looking Glasse for Married Folkes. Wherein they may plainly see their deformities; and also how to behave themselves one to another, and both of them towards God* . . . (London: 1610).

38. Britomart exhibits such "regard of honour" at Artegall's departure. Though she grieves, she "wisely moderated her owne smart, / Seeing his honor, which she tendred chiefe, / Consisted much in that adventures priefe" (*FQ* 5.7.44). Like a proper wife, she puts her husband's honor before her own desires and represses her own complaints; here she embodies humility, sincerity, cheerfulness, and constancy, the four virtues which "season a wives subjection" (Gouge, 331).

39. John Milton shares this ideal; his description of Eve exhibits a similar tension between "regard of honour" and "mild modesty": "Innocence and Virgin Modesty, / Her virtue and the conscience of her worth" (*Paradise Lost*, 8: 501–2, in *Complete Poems and Major Prose*, ed. Merrit Y. Hughes [Indianapolis: Odyssey Press, 1957]).

40. *Comus* 450–52, in Milton, *Complete Poems*.

41. Quoted by Nancy Vickers, "'The blazon of sweet beauty's best': Shakespeare's Lucrece," in *Shakespeare and the Question of Theory*, ed. Patricia Parker and Geoffrey Hartman (New York: Methuen, 1985), 109.

42. Similar themes emerge in Britomart's allegorical dream in the temple of Isis, where she tames the threatening crocodile/Artegall who is "swolne with pride of his owne peerelesse powre" (*FQ* 5.7.15).

43. For these associations of Medusa and contemporary citations, see Vickers, 109–12.

44. Dubrow, *Happier Eden,* 37–38. In Kaske's differing interpretation, the oxymoron "proud humility" expresses "mutuality of desire, the bride humble in her surrender to her husband, but the groom also now a servant to her awakened desire" (282). Dubrow and other critics of *Epithalamion* find Spenser expressing, containing, controlling, or resolving tensions and anxieties about marriage, variously personal and cultural. See Dubrow's introduction for a good summary.

45. For this observation, I am indebted to Ann Prescott. Bates also sees Spenser's husbandly subordination of a woman called Elizabeth as a wishful power play (140).

46. Carol Thomas Neely, in a paper delivered at the Ohio Shakespeare Conference in March 1989, discussed the discontinuity between the roles of maid and wife in Renaissance drama; she referred to the letters of Leonard Wheatcroft, which trace a mid-seventeenth-century courtship after the manner of sonneteers; at the wedding, however, the woman disappears as a speaker ("Representing Women: Disjunctions, Divisions, Disappearances").

47. Bates, 139.

48. Spenser, "An Hymne in Honor of Love," st. 44, in *Fowre Hymnes, Yale Edition.*

49. DeNeef calls *Fowre Hymnes* Spenser's "affirmation and demonstration of a Sidneyan poetic" enabling man, by God's grace, to transcend the fallen human state (*Spenser*, 88). Enid Welsford, by contrast, argues that Spenser "emphasizes the contrast between the two loves and only hints at a possible reconciliation" (*Fowre Hymns, Epithalamion: A Study of Edmund Spenser's Doctrine of Love* [New York: Barnes and Noble, 1967], 63). Ellrodt believes Spenser is sincere, if exaggerated, in his rejection of earthly love (147).

50. Poems from *Arcadia* 63:13, 15, 16, 47, in Sidney, *Poems*, 91–92.

51. Poems from *Arcadia* 67:2–3, in Sidney, *Poems*, 103.

52. See Dubrow, *Happier Eden*, 31–32.

53. Poems from *Arcadia* 67:70–72, in Sidney, *Poems*, 105.

54. Ibid., ll. 76–77.

Postscript: Reformations of Petrarchism in Seventeenth-Century Poetry

1. See Lever, 273–75; Spiller, 176–77. William L. Stull ascribes to this scenario, while also situating religious sonneteering in a tradition stretching back to Tudor times in "'Why Are Not *Sonnets* Made of Thee?' A New Context for the 'Holy Sonnets' of Donne, Herbert, and Milton," *Modern Philology* 80 (1982): 129–35.

2. This judgment is so common it scarce needs attribution, but see, for one example, C. S. Lewis, "Donne and Love Poetry in the Seventeenth Century," in *Seventeenth-Century Studies Presented to Sir Herbert Grierson* (Oxford: Clarendon Press, 1938), 64–66.

3. The critical habit of reading "Jack Donne's" love poems against "Dr. Donne's divine poems" originated with Izaak Walton and was canonized by Helen Gardner in her dating of the poems to distinct periods of Donne's life. See her introductions to John Donne, *The Divine Poems*, (Oxford: Clarendon Press, 1978), and John Donne, *The Elegies and the Songs and Sonnets* (Oxford: Clarendon Press, 1956). Recently, Dennis Flynn questions Gardner's theories of the poems' composition in "'Awry and Squint': The Dating of Donne's Holy Sonnets," *John Donne Journal* 7 (1988): 35–46.

4. From *The Works of George Herbert*, ed. F. E. Hutchinson (New York: Oxford University Press, 1941), 206. This sonnet and another were first printed in Walton's *Lives* (1670).

5. Lewalski, *Protestant Poetics*, 246–47, 298–304.

6. See Louis L. Martz, *The Poetry of Meditation* (New Haven: Yale University Press, 1954; rpt. 1962), 263–78; Joseph H. Summers, "Sir Calidore and the Country Parson," in *Like Season'd Timber: New Essays on George Herbert*, ed. Edmund Miller and Robert DiYanni (New York: Peter Lang, 1987), 207–18; John N. Wall, who argues that *Astrophil and Stella* is a "site where Herbert performs his eucharistic work as priest/poet, breaking . . . received conventions" and exploiting them "to articulate and further the divine-human relationship" (224–37; 227).

7. Quotation from Herbert's *The Temple* are taken from *The English Poems of George Herbert*, ed. C. A. Patrides (London: J. M. Dent, 1974) and are cited parenthetically in the text.

8. See, for example, Chauncey Wood, "Sin and the Sonnet: Sidney, St. Augustine, and Herbert's 'The Sinner,'" *George Herbert Journal* 15 (1992): 19–32; Martz, *Poetry*, 271. For Anthony Low, Herbert's move from secular to sacred is uncomplicated; see *The Reinvention of Love: Poetry, politics and culture from Sidney to Milton* (Cambridge: Cambridge University Press, 1993), 93–102.

9. On the erotic dimensions of Herbertian spirituality, see Schoenfeldt, chap. 6.

10. John Wall, 235–37.

11. Schoenfeldt, 6.

12. Janet H. MacArthur, "'A Sydney, Though Un-Named': Lady Mary Wroth and her Poetic Progenitors," *English Studies in Canada* 15 (1989): 12–20.

13. See Naomi J. Miller, "Rewriting Lyric Fictions: The Role of the Lady in Lady Mary Wroth's *Pamphilia to Amphilanthus*," and Nona Fienberg, "Mary Wroth and the Invention of Female Poetic Subjectivity," both in *Reading Mary Wroth: Representing Alternatives in Early Modern England*, ed. Naomi Miller and Gary Waller (Knoxville: University of Tennessee Press, 1991), 295–310, 175–90; Barbara K. Lewalski, *Writing Women in Jacobean England* (Cambridge: Harvard University Press, 1993), 251–63. On the "discursively empowering" relationship with her cousin, William Herbert, see Maureen Quilligan, "Lady Mary Wroth: Female Authority and the Family Romance," in *Unfolded Tales: Essays on Renaissance Romance*, ed. George M. Logan and Gordon Teskey (Ithaca: Cornell University Press, 1989), 257–80, esp. 271 ff.

14. For a contrary view that downplays the role of gender, see Heather Dubrow, *Echoes of Desire: English Petrarchism and its Counterdiscourses* (Ithaca: Cornell University Press, 1995), 134–61. Dubrow finds that both Petrarchism and its counterdiscourses express Wroth's ambivalence towards writing and "the problematics of female subjectivity as well as male" (161).

15. See Jeff Masten's "'Shall I turne blabb?': Circulation, Gender, and Subjectivity in Mary Wroth's Sonnets, in *Reading Mary Wroth*, 67–87, for the contention that the poems "encode a withdrawal from circulation" (69) that signals Wroth's refusal to circulate herself or her words.

16. See Ann Rosalind Jones, who also addresses the public-private tension, arguing that Wroth, from her position of exclusion, writes *Pamphilia to Amphilanthus* in an attempt to end that isolation ("Designing Women: The Self as Spectacle in Mary Wroth and Veronica Franco," in *Reading Mary Wroth*, 135–53).

17. For an account of Wroth's life and the controversy over her work, see Josephine Roberts's excellent introduction to *The Poems of Lady Mary Wroth* (Baton Rouge: Louisiana State University Press, 1983). Denny's poem is quoted on pp. 32–33, the message on p. 34. Though Wroth boldly returned Denny's invective, the second installment of her romance was never published.

18. *Poems of Lady Mary Wroth*, P36. Further quotations from *Pamphilia to Amphilanthus* are cited parenthetically in the text, using Roberts's notation and numbering.

19. Of this poem, Gary Waller says that it attempts, though without complete success, to appropriate the gaze and its pleasure, that it enacts a "fantasy of female agency" (*The Sidney Family Romance: Mary Wroth, William Herbert, and the Early Modern Construction of Gender* [Detroit: Wayne State University Press, 1993], 213). Waller does not find that Wroth achieves a measure of subjectivity: "Only dimly graspable subject positions are being tentatively and partly unconsciously explored, interacting with more powerful discourses of restriction" (219).

20. See also P 79–81 and P 85–86.

21. Elaine V. Beilin, by contrast, sees Pamphilia successfully moving from blind love for Amphilanthus to a fervent, divine love (*Redeeming Eve: Women Writers of*

the English Renaissance [Princeton: Princeton University Press, 1987], 238–42). Jones finds the conceit of love's labyrinth a figure for the "entrapping anxiety of courtiers in quest of favor" ("Designing Women," 150); Dubrow stresses Wroth's ambivalence in the corona as she notes the "propensity of . . . counterdiscourses for reenacting what they aim to reject" (*Echoes*, 152).

22. See *OED*, s.v. "near," adv. I.1, 14; the phrase "near and dear," suggesting kinship (I.13), is also current, admitting the possibility of Wroth's reference to her own cousin; see also examples of adjectival usage I.1, 2.

23. "Leave me o Love, which reachest but to dust. . . . Eternall Love maintaine thy life in me" (*Certaine Sonnets* 32:1, 14; *Poems*, 161–62).

24. Kevin Sharpe, "Cavalier Critic? The Ethics and Politics of Thomas Carew's Poetry," *Politics of Discourse: The Literature and History of Seventeenth-Century England*, ed. Kevin Sharpe and Steven N. Zwicker (Berkeley and Los Angeles: University of California Press, 1987), 119, 125.

25. Low, *Reinvention*, 151. But then, for Low, Petrarchism is no more than "sighs and tears, begging and dutiful subservience . . . [the] ideal of unconditionally faithful love" (151). Gordon Braden comments that libertine poetry is characterized not by "the rejection of Petrarchism, but the bringing of the Petrarchan ego into the sexual arena where it must confront psychic otherness" ("Beyond Frustration: Petrarchan Laurels in the Seventeenth Century," *Studies in English Literature* 26 [1986]: 14).

26. See, for example, "Song. Murdring Beauty," "A prayer to the Wind," "To her in absence. A ship," "Song. Eternitie of love protested," and "Upon some alterations, etc.," a few of the opening poems of his *Poems* (1640). Quotations from Carew's poetry are taken from *The Poems of Thomas Carew*, ed Rhodes Dunlap (Oxford Clarendon Press, 1949). Because of some lengthy titles, citations will occur in notes.

27. Astrophil flirts with other ladies in Stella's absence (*AS* 106); Greville's speaker has several mistresses; in *Idea* (1599), Drayton's speaker professes himself a libertine ("To the Reader of these Sonnets").

28. "Good counsel to a young Maid," ll. 10–12, in *Poems of Carew*, 12.

29. "To a Lady that desired I would love her," ll. 11–15, in *Poems of Carew*, 81–82.

30. Ibid., ll. 31–35.

31. Recall the first sonnet of *Astrophil and Stella*, where Sidney employs "grace" with similar irony, praying that "Knowledge might pitie winne, and pitie grace obtaine."

32. "To A. L. Perswasions to Love," ll. 22–25, in *Poems of Carew*, 4. Sharpe does point out that in this poem, as in others, Carew promotes marriage as the best reconciler of love and passion (123); the speaker urges A. L. to choose "one that may / Love for an age, not for a day" (ll. 57–58).

33. Braden, 13.

34. "A Rapture," ll. 3–5, 18–20, 149–53, in *Poems of Carew*, 49–53. On the complexity of Honor as a perverter of good, discredited by the final lines of the

poem, see M. L. Donnelly, "The Rack of Fancy and the Trade of Love: Conventions of *Precieux* and *Libertin* in Amatory Lyrics by Suckling and Carew," in *Renaissance Discourses*, 123–26.

35. Ibid., ll. 107–11.

36. "Ingratefull beauty threatned," ll. 7–10, 13–14, in *Poems of Carew*, 17–18..

37. "Disdaine returned," ll. 15–18, in *Poems of Carew*, 18.

38. See Achsah Guibbory, "Sexual Politics/Political Sex: Seventeenth-Century Love Poetry," in *Renaissance Discourses*, 206–22, esp. 206–12. See also Carew's celebration of "Boldnesse in Love" and the king's potency in "A New-yeares gift. To the King."

39. "Obsequies to the Lady Anne Hay," ll. 39, 51–53, 46, in *Poems of Carew*, 68. Anne Hay was Carew's distant cousin.

40. "In answer of an Elegiacall Letter upon the death of the King of Sweden," ll. 5–9, 15–16, 45–49, and 95–98, in *Poems of Carew*, 74–77, . Reid Barbour, whose readings provide a good foil for those of Sharpe, calls this poem Carew's conservative manifesto, which reverses poetic hierarchies and calls on English poets to dwell on careless pleasure, not European politics. See "'Wee, of th'adult'rate mixture not complaine': Thomas Carew and Poetic Hybridity," *John Donne Journal* 7 (1988), 103.

41. On the other hand, for a defense of theatrical fiction as providing better examples of virtue than truth itself, see "To Will. Davenant my Friend," in *Poems of Carew*, 98.

Bibliography

Primary Works

Alciata. *Emblemata*. Antwerp, 1574.

Alexander, William. *Aurora*. London, 1604.

Ascham, Roger. *The Scholemaster*. London, 1570. Excerpted in *Prose of the English Renaissance*. Edited by John William Hebel, et al. New York: Appleton Century Crofts, 1952.

Aubrey, John. *Aubrey's Brief Lives*. Edited by Oliver Lawson Dick. Ann Arbor: University of Michigan Press, 1957.

[B. W.] "A commemoration of the generall mone, the honorable and solemne funerall made for . . . Sir Phillip Sidney." Appended to "Sir Phillip Sidney, his honorable life, his valiant death, and true vertues," by George Whetstone. In *Elegies for Sir Philip Sidney (1587)*. Edited by A. J. Colaianne and W. L. Godshalk. Delmar, N.Y.: Scholars' Facsimiles and Reprints, 1980.

Bacon, Francis. *The Essayes or Counsels, Civill and Morall*. 1625. In *Francis Bacon: A Selection of His Works*. Edited by Sidney Warhaft. New York: Odyssey Press, 1965.

Bale, John. *The Image of Both Churches After the Most Wonderfull and Heavenly Revelacion of Sainct John the Evangelist*. 1548. Reprint, Amsterdam, 1973.

Barnes, Barnabe. *A Divine Centurie of Spirituall Sonnets*. London, 1593.

———. *Parthenophil and Parthenophe*. In *Elizabethan Sonnets*, edited by Sidney Lee, vol. 1. New York: Cooper Square Publishers, 1964.

Becon, Thomas. *Davids Harpe ful of most delectable harmony*. 1542.

The Bible. Geneva, 1560. Reprint, Madison: University of Wisconsin Press, 1969.

Bradstreet, Anne. *The Works of Anne Bradstreet*. Edited by Jeannine Hensley. Cambridge: Belknap Press, 1967.

Breton, Nicholas. *The Works in Prose of Nicholas Breton*. Edited by Alexander Grosart. 1879. Reprint, New York: AMS Press, 1966.

Bryskett, Lodowick. "The Mourning Muse of Thestylis." In *Spenser: Poetical Works*. Edited by J. C. Smith and E. deSelincourt. New York: Oxford University Press, 1912.

Calvin, Jean. *Calvin: Institutes of Christian Religion.* 2 vols. Edited by John T. McNeill. Translated by Ford Lewis Battles. Philadelphia: Westminster Press, 1960.

———. *The Institution of Christian Religion.* London, 1561.

Camden, William. *Remaines Concerning Britaine, Fift Impression.* London, 1636.

Campion, Thomas. *Observations in the Art of English Poesie* (1602). With Samuel Daniel, *A defence of ryme* (1603). Edited by G. B. Harrison. London: John Lane, 1925.

Carew, Thomas. *The Poems of Thomas Carew.* Edited by Rhodes Dunlap. Oxford: Clarendon Press, 1949.

Castiglione, Baldassare. *Book of the Courtier.* Translated by Sir Thomas Hoby. 1588. Reprint, London: J. M. Dent, 1928.

Churchyard, Thomas. *A Praise of Poetrie* and *A Consort of Heavenly Harmonie.* London, 1595.

Churchyard, Thomas. "The Worthie Sir Phillip Sidney Knight his Epitaph." In *Sidneiana.* Edited by Samuel Butler. London: Shakespeare Press, 1837.

Cicero. *De Officiis.* Translated by Walter Miller. Cambridge: Harvard University Press, 1956.

———. *De Oratore.* Translated by H. Rackham. 2 vols. Cambridge: Harvard University Press, 1942.

The Correspondence of Philip Sidney and Hubert Languet. Edited by William Aspenwall Bradley. Boston: Merrymount Press, 1912.

Coverdale, Miles. *Remains of Myles Coverdale.* Edited by G. Pearson. Parker Society, 1846.

Daniel, Samuel. *The Civil Wars.* Edited by Laurence Michel. New Haven: Yale University Press, 1958.

———. *The Complete Works in Verse and Prose of Samuel Daniel.* 5 vols. Edited by Alexander B. Grosart. 1885. Reprint, New York: Russell and Russell, 1963.

———. *Delia With the Complaint of Rosamond.* 1592. Reprint, Menston, England: Scolar Press, 1969.

———. *Introduction to a breviary of the History of England.* London, 1693.

———. *A Panegyrike with a Defence of Ryme.* 1603. Reprint, Menston, England: Scolar Press, 1970.

———. *Poems and A Defence of Ryme.* Edited by Arthur Colby Sprague. 1930. Reprint, Chicago: University of Chicago Press, 1965.

Davison, Francis. *A Poetical Rapsody.* London, 1602.

Day, Angel. "Upon the life and death of the most worthy . . . Sir Philip Sidney." In *Elegies for Sir Philip Sidney (1587).* Edited by A. J. Colaianne and W. L. Godshalk. Delmar, N.Y.: Scholars' Facsimiles and Reprints, 1980.

Digges, Dudley. *Foure paradoxes, or politique discourses. All newly published.* 1604.

Drayton, Michael. *The Works of Michael Drayton.* Edited by J. William Hebel. 5 vols. Oxford: Shakespeare Head Press, 1931–41.

Elizabeth I. *The Poems of Queen Elizabeth.* Edited by Leicester Bradner. Providence: Brown University Press, 1964.

Elyot, Sir Thomas. *The Book named the Governor.* Edited by S. E. Lehmberg. London: J. M. Dent, 1962.

Erasmus. *Collected Works of Erasmus*. Edited by Craig R. Thompson. Toronto: University of Toronto Press, 1978.

———. *The Colloquies of Erasmus*. Translated by Craig R. Thompson. Chicago: University of Chicago Press, 1965.

Fletcher, Giles. *Licia, or Poems of Love* and *The Rising to the Crowne of Richard the Third*. London, 1593.

Gascoigne, George. *The Complete Works of George Gascoigne*. 2 vols. Edited by John W. Cunliffe. Cambridge: Cambridge University Press, 1907–10.

Gifford, George. (Gyffard, George.) *The Manner of Sir Philip Sidney's Death*. In *Miscellaneous Prose of Sir Philip Sidney*. Edited by Katherine Duncan-Jones and Jan van Dorsten, 166–72. Oxford: Clarendon Press, 1973.

———, *Praelections upon the Sacred and holy Revelation of S. John*. London, 1573.

Gorges, Sir Arthur. *The Poems of Sir Arthur Gorges*. Edited by Helen Estabrook Sandison. Oxford: Clarendon Press, 1953.

Gosson, Stephen. *Schoole of Abuse*. London, 1579.

Gouge, William. *Of Domesticall Duties*. London, 1622.

Greville, Fulke. *Certaine Learned and Elegant Workes*. London, 1633. Reprint, Delmar, N.Y.: Scholars' Facsimiles and Reprints, 1990.

———. *The Life of the Renowned Sir Philip Sidney*. London, 1652. Reprint, Delmar, N.Y.: Scholars' Facsimiles and Reprints, 1984.

———. *The Prose Works of Fulke Greville, Lord Brooke*. Edited by John Gouws. Oxford: Clarendon Press, 1986.

———. *The Remains: Being Poems of Monarchy and Religion*. Edited by G. A. Wilkes. New York: Oxford University Press, 1965.

———. *The Works in Verse and Prose Complete*. 4 vols. Edited by Alexander B. Grosart. 1870.

Harington, Sir John. *Nugae Antiquae*. Vol. 1. Edited by Henry Harington. 2 vols. London, 1804.

Harvey, Gabriel. *Pierce's Supererogation*. London, 1593.

Herbert, George. *The English Poems of George Herbert*. Edited by C. A. Patrides. London: J. M. Dent, 1974.

———. *The Works of George Herbert*. Edited by F. E. Hutchinson. New York: Oxford University Press, 1941.

An Homily of the State of Matrimony. In *Certain Sermons*. London, 1562.

Howard, Henry, earl of Surrey. *Poems*. Edited by Emrys Jones. Oxford: Clarendon Press, 1964.

Hunnis, William. *Seven Sobs of a Sorrowful Soule for Sinne*. London, 1583.

Jonson, Ben. *Conversations with William Drummond*. In *Ben Jonson: The Complete Poems*. Edited by George Parfitt. New Haven: Yale University Press, 1975.

———. *Timber: Or Discoveries*. In *Ben Jonson: The Complete Poems*. Edited by George Parfitt. New Haven: Yale University Press, 1975.

Lant, Thomas. *Sequitur celebritas & pompa funebris*. In *Elegies for Sir Philip Sidney (1587)*. Edited by A. J. Colaianne and W. L. Godschalk. Delmar, N.Y.: Scholars' Facsimiles and Reprints, 1980.

Luther, Martin. *Lectures on Genesis*. Translated by George V. Schick. Vol. 2 of *Luther's Works*. Edited by Jaroslav Pelikan. St. Louis: Concordia, 1960.

Milton, John. *Complete Poems and Major Prose*. Edited by Merrit Y. Hughes. Indianapolis: Odyssey Press, 1957.

Moffet, Thomas. *Nobilis* and *Lessus Lugubris*. Edited by Virgil B. Heltzel and Hoyt L. Hudson. San Marino: Huntington Library, 1940.

Peele, George. *The Life and Minor Works of George Peele*. Edited by David H. Horne. New Haven: Yale University Press, 1952.

Persius. *Satire I*. Translated by G. G. Ramsay. In *Juvenal and Persius*. Cambridge: Harvard University Press, 1979.

Petrarch. *The Life of Solitude*. Translated by Jacob Zeitlin. Champaign: University of Illinois Press, 1924.

———. *Petrarch's Lyric Poems: The "Rime sparse" and Other Lyrics*. Edited and translated by Robert M. Durling. Cambridge: Harvard University Press, 1976.

Pettie, George. *The Civile Conversation of M. Steeven Guazzo*. 1581. Reprint, London: Constable, 1925.

Phillips, John. "The Life and Death of Sir Phillip Sidney." In *Elegies for Sir Philip Sidney (1587)*. Edited by A. J. Colaianne and W. L. Godshalk. Delmar, N.Y.: Scholars' Facsimiles and Reprints, 1980.

Plutarch. *Moralia*. Translated by Harold North Fowler. Cambridge: Harvard University Press, 1949.

The Psalms of Sir Philip Sidney and the Countess of Pembroke. Edited by J. C. A. Rathmell. New York: Anchor Books, 1963.

Puttenham, George. *Arte of English Poesie*. 1589. Reprint, edited by Gladys Doidge Willcock and Alice Walker. Cambridge: Cambridge University Press, 1936.

Ralegh, Sir Walter. "An Epitaph upon the right Honourable sir Sir Phillip Sidney knight, Lord of Flushing." In *Spenser: Poetical Works*. Edited by J. C. Smith and E. de Selincourt. New York: Oxford University Press, 1912.

Rogers, Daniel. *Matrimoniall Honour*. London, 1642.

Rouse, W. H. D., ed. *Shakespeare's Ovid: Being Arthur Golding's Translation of the Metamorphoses*. London, 1904.

Shakespeare, William. *The Riverside Shakespeare*. Boston: Houghton Mifflin, 1974.

———. *Shakespeare's Sonnets*. Edited by Stephen Booth. New Haven: Yale University Press, 1977.

Shelley, Percy Bysshe. *Shelley's Poetry and Prose*. Edited by Donald H. Reiman and Sharon B. Powers. New York: W. W. Norton, 1977.

Sidney, Sir Philip. *Astrophil and Stella*. 1591. Reprint, Menston, England: Scholar Press, 1970.

———. *The Countess of Pembroke's Arcadia*. Edited by Maurice Evans. Harmondsworth, Middlesex: Penguin Books, 1977.

———. *A Defence of Poetry*. Edited by J. A. Van Dorsten. Oxford: Oxford University Press, 1966.

———. *Miscellaneous Prose of Sir Philip Sidney*. Edited by Katherine Duncan-Jones and J. A. von Dorsten. Oxford: Clarendon Press, 1973.

———. *The Poems of Sir Philip Sidney*. Edited by William A. Ringler. Oxford: Clarendon Press, 1962.

———. *The Prose Works of Sir Philip Sidney*. 4 vols. Edited by Albert Feuillerat. Cambridge: Cambridge University Press, 1962.

———, and Arthur Golding, trans. *A Woorke Concerning the Trewnesse of the Christian Religion*, by Philippe de Mornay. 1587. Delmar, N.Y.: Scholars' Facsimiles and Reprints, 1970.

Smith, Henry. *A Preparative to Marriage*. London, 1591.

Smythe, Sir John. *Certain discourses . . . concerning the forms and effects of diverse sorts of weapons*. London, 1590.

Snawsell, Robert. *A Looking Glasse for Married Folkes*. London, 1610.

Spenser, Edmund. *Spenser: Poetical Works*. Edited by J. C. Smith and Ernest deSelincourt. New York: Oxford University Press, 1912.

———. *The Works of Edmund Spenser: A Variorum Edition*. Edited by Edwin Greenlaw, et al. 11 vols. Baltimore: Johns Hopkins University Press, 1966.

———. *The Yale Edition of the Shorter Poems of Edmund Spenser*. Edited by William A. Oram, et al. New Haven: Yale University Press, 1989.

Stafford, Anthony. *The Guide of Honor*. London, 1634.

Temple, William. *William Temple's Analysis of Sir Philip Sidney's* Apology for Poetry. Edited and translated by John Webster. Binghamton, N.Y.: Medieval and Renaissance Texts and Studies, 1984.

Three Proper, and wittie, familiar Letters. Two Other very commendable Letters. 1580. In *Spenser: Poetical Works*. Edited by J. C. Smith and E. De Selincourt. New York: Oxford University Press, 1912.

Tilney, Edmund. *The Flower of Friendship: A Renaissance Dialogue Contesting Marriage*. 1568. Edited by Valerie Wayne. Ithaca: Cornell University Press, 1992.

Vives, Juan Luis. *The Office and Duetie of a Husband*. London, 1553.

Watson, Thomas. *Hecatompathia, or Passionate Centurie of Love*. London, 1582.

Webbe, William. *A Discourse of English Poetrie*. 1586. Reprint, edited by Edward Arber, Westminster: A Constable and Co., 1895.

Whately, William. *A Bride-Bush, or a Wedding Sermon*. London, 1617.

Whetstone, George. "Sir Phillip Sidney, his honorable life, his valiant death, and true vertues." In *Elegies for Sir Philip Sidney (1587)*. Edited by A. J. Colaianne and W. L. Godshalk. Delmar, N.Y.: Scholars' Facsimiles and Reprints, 1980.

Wilson, Thomas. *Wilson's Arte of Rhetorique*. 1553. Reprint, edited by G. H. Mair. Oxford: Clarendon Press, 1909.

Wither, George. *Abuses stript, and whipt*. London, 1613.

Wroth, Mary. *The Poems of Lady Mary Wroth*. Edited by Josephine A. Roberts. Baton Rouge: Louisiana State University Press, 1983.

Wyatt, Sir Thomas. *The Complete Poems*. Edited by R. A. Rebholz. New Haven: Yale University Press, 1978.

Zepheria. London, 1594.

Secondary and Background Works

Althusser, Louis. "Ideology and Ideological State Apparatuses." In *Lenin and Philosophy and Other Essays*, translated by Ben Brewster, 127–86. London: New Left Books, 1971.

Anderson, Judith H. *Biographical Truth: The Representation of Historical Persons in Tudor-Stuart Writing*. New Haven: Yale University Press, 1984.

———. *The Growth of Personal Voice: Piers Plowman and The Faerie Queene*. New Haven: Yale University Press, 1976.

Appiah, Anthony. "Tolerable Falsehoods: Agency and the Interests of Theory." In *Consequences of Theory*, edited by Jonathan Arac and Barbara Johnson, 63–90. Baltimore: Johns Hopkins University Press, 1991.

Arendt, Hannah. "What is Authority?" In *Between Past and Future: Eight Exercises in Political Thought*, 91–141. New York: Penguin Books, 1977.

Atkins, J. W. H. *English Literary Criticism: The Renascence*. New York: Barnes and Noble, 1947.

Attridge, Derek. *Well-Weighed Syllables: Elizabethan Verse in Classical Metres*. London: Cambridge University Press, 1974.

Axton, Marie. *The Queen's Two Bodies: Drama and the Elizabethan Succession*. London: Royal Historical Society, 1977.

Baker-Smith, Dominic. "'Great Expectation': Sidney's Death and the Poets." In *Sir Philip Sidney: 1586 and the Creation of a Legend*, edited by Jan van Dorsten, et al., 83–103. Leiden: E. J. Brill, 1986.

Balibar, Etienne, and Pierre Macherey. "On Literature as an Ideological Form." In *Untying the Text: A Post-Structuralist Reader*, edited by Robert Young, 79–99. London: Routledge and Kegan Paul, 1981.

Barbour, Reid. "'Wee, of th'adult'rate mixture not complaine': Thomas Carew and Poetic Hybridity." *John Donne Journal* 7 (1988): 91–113.

Barnes, Catherine. "The Hidden Persuader: The Complex Speaking Voice of Sidney's *Defence of Poetry*." *PMLA* 86 (1971): 422–27.

Barrell, John. *Poetry, language, and politics*. Manchester: Manchester University Press, 1988.

Barroll, Leeds. "A New History for Shakespeare and His Time." *Shakespeare Quarterly* 39 (1988): 441–64.

Bates, Catherine. *The Rhetoric of Courtship in Elizabethan Language and Literature*. Cambridge: Cambridge University Press, 1992.

Beilin, Elaine. *Redeeming Eve: Women Writers of the English Renaissance*. Princeton: Princeton University Press, 1987.

Bennett, A. L. "The Principal Rhetorical Conventions in the Renaissance Personal Elegy." *Studies in Philology* 51 (1954): 107–26.

Bergvall, Åke. *The "Enabling of Judgement": Sir Philip Sidney and the Education of the Reader*. Stockholm: Almquist, 1989.

———. "Reason in Luther, Calvin, and Sidney." *Sixteenth Century Journal* 23 (1992): 115–27.

Berman, Sandra. *The Sonnet Over Time: A Study in the Sonnets of Petrarch, Shakespeare, and Baudelaire*. Chapel Hill: University of North Carolina Press, 1988.

Bernardo, Aldo S. *Petrarch, Laura, and the Triumphs*. Albany: State University of New York Press, 1974.

Berry, Edward. "The Poet as Warrior in Sidney's *Defence of Poetry*." *Studies in English Literature 1500-1900* 29 (1989): 21–34.

Bieman, Elizabeth. *Plato Baptized: Toward the Interpretation of Spenser's Mimetic Fictions*. Toronto: University of Toronto Press, 1988.

Bloom, Harold. *The Anxiety of Influence: A Theory of Poetry*. New York: Oxford University Press, 1973.

Boose, Lynda E. "The Family in Shakespeare Studies." *Renaissance Quarterly* 40 (1987): 707–61.

Bos, Sander, et al. "Sidney's Funeral Portrayed." In *Sir Philip Sidney: 1586 and the Creation of a Legend*, edited by Jan van Dorsten, et al., 38–61. Leiden: E. J. Brill, 1986.

Boswell, Jackson, and H. R. Woudhuysen. "Some Unfamiliar Sidney Allusions." In *Sir Philip Sidney: 1586 and the Creation of a Legend,* edited by Jan van Dorsten, et al., 221–37. Leiden: E. J. Brill, 1986.

Bourdieu, Pierre. *Outline of a Theory of Practice.* 1972. Translated by Richard Nice. Cambridge: Cambridge University Press, 1978.

Braden, Gordon. "Beyond Frustration: Petrarchan Laurels in the Seventeenth Century." *Studies in English Literature 1500–1900* 26 (1986): 5–23.

Brink, Jean. "Framing Philosophy: Sidney and Daniel." In *Perspective as a Problem in the Art, History and Literature of Early Modern England*, edited by Mark Lussier and S. K. Heninger, 81–93. Lewiston, Ky.: Edwin Mellen Press, 1992.

———. "Who Fashioned Edmund Spenser?: The Textual History of Spenser's *Complaints*." *Studies in Philology* 88 (1991): 153–68.

Bullough, Geoffrey. Introduction to *Poems and Dramas of Fulke Greville*. 2 vols. New York: Oxford University Press, 1945.

Buxton, John. "The Mourning for Sidney." *Renaissance Studies* 3 (1989): 46–56.

———. *Sir Philip Sidney and the English Renaissance*. London: MacMillan, 1954.

Caldwell, Mark. "Sources and Analogues of the *Life of Sidney*." *Studies in Philology* 74 (1977): 279–300.

Campbell, Lily. *Divine Poetry and Drama in Sixteenth-Century England*. Cambridge: Cambridge University Press, 1959.

Campbell, Marion. "Unending Desire: Sidney's Reinvention of Petrarchan Form in *Astrophil and Stella*." In *Sir Philip Sidney and the Interpretation of Renaissance Culture,* edited by Gary F. Waller and Michael D. Moore, 84–94. London: Croom Helm, 1984.

Cartmell, Deborah. "'Beside the shore of silver streaming *Thamesis*': Spenser's *Ruines of Time*." *Spenser Studies* 6 (1985): 77–82.

Cheney, Donald. "Spenser's Fortieth Birthday and Related Fictions." *Spenser Studies* 4 (1983): 3–31.

Chew, Samuel. "The Iconography of *A Booke of Christian Prayers* (1578) Illustrated." *Huntington Library Quarterly* 8 (1945): 293–305.

Clark, Ira. "Samuel Daniel's 'Complaint of Rosamond.'" *Renaissance Quarterly* 23 (1970): 152–62.

Colaianne, A. J., and W. L. Godshalk. Introduction to *Elegies for Sir Philip Sidney (1587)*. Delmar, N.Y.: Scholars' Facsimiles and Reprints, 1980.

Cole, Howard C. *A Quest of Inquirie: Some Contexts of Tudor Literature*. New York: Bobbs-Merrill, 1973.

Colie, Rosalie. *Paradoxica Epidemica: The Renaissance Tradition of Paradox*. Princeton: Princeton University Press, 1966.

Collinson, Patrick. *The Elizabethan Puritan Movement*. Berkeley and Los Angeles: University of California Press, 1967.

Connell, Dorothy. *Sir Philip Sidney: The Maker's Mind*. Oxford: Clarendon Press, 1977.

Coogan, Robert. "Petrarch's *Trionfi* and the English Renaissance." *Studies in Philology* 67 (1970): 306–27.

Craft, William. *Labyrinth of Desire: Invention and Culture in the Work of Sir Philip Sidney*. Newark: University of Delaware Press, 1994.

Craig, D. H. "A Hybrid Growth: Sidney's Theory of Poetry in *An Apology for Poetry*." *English Literary Renaissance* 10 (1980): 183–201.

Craig, Joanne. "The Queen, Her Handmaid, and Spenser's Career." *English Studies in Canada* 12 (1986): 255–68.

Crane, Mary Thomas. "'Video et Taceo': Elizabeth I and the Rhetoric of Counsel." *Studies in English Literature 1500-1900* 28 (1988): 1–15.

Crewe, Jonathan. *Trials of Authorship: Anterior Forms and Poetic Reconstruction from Wyatt to Shakespeare*. Berkeley and Los Angeles: University of California Press, 1990.

Croll, Morris W. *The Works of Fulke Greville*. Philadelphia, 1903.

Cummings, Peter M. "Spenser's *Amoretti* as an Allegory of Love." *Texas Studies in Literature and Language* 12 (1970): 163–79.

Danielson, Dennis. "Sidney, Greville, and the Metaphysics of 'Naughtiness.'" *English Studies in Canada* 10 (1984): 265–77.

Dasenbrock, Reed Way. *Imitating the Italians: Wyatt, Spenser, Synge, Pound, Joyce*. Baltimore: Johns Hopkins University Press, 1991.

———. "The Petrarchan Context of Spenser's *Amoretti*." *PMLA* 100 (1985): 38–50.

Davies, Kathleen M. "Continuity and Change in Literary Advice on Marriage." In *Marriage and Society: Studies in the Social History of Marriage,* edited by R. B. Outhwaite, 58–80. London: Europa, 1981.

Day, J. F. R. "Death be very proud: Sidney, Subversion, and Elizabethan Heraldic Funerals." In *Tudor Political Culture,* edited by Dale Hoak. Cambridge: Cambridge University Press, 1995.

De Grazia, Margreta. "Lost Potential in Grammar and Nature: Sidney's *Astrophil and Stella*." *Studies in English Literature 1500-1900* 21 (1981): 33–35.

DeNeef, A. Leigh. "Of Dialogues and Historicisms." *South Atlantic Quarterly* 86 (1987): 497–517.

———. "'The Ruines of Time': Spenser's Apology for Poetry." *Studies in Philology* 76 (1979): 262–71.

———. *Spenser and the Motives of Metaphor*. Durham: Duke University Press, 1982.

Dobin, Howard. *Merlin's Disciples: Prophecy, Poetry and Power in Renaissance England*. Stanford: Stanford University Press, 1990.

Doherty, Mary Jane. *The Mistress-Knowledge: Sir Philip Sidney's* Defence of Poesie *and Literary Architectonics in the English Renaissance*. Nashville, Tenn.: Vanderbilt University Press, 1991.

Dollimore, Jonathan. *Radical Tragedy: Religion, Ideology, and Power in the Drama of Shakespeare and his Contemporaries*. Chicago: University of Chicago Press, 1984.

Donnelly, M. L. "The Rack of Fancy and the Trade of Love: Conventions of *Precieux* and *Libertin* in Amatory Lyrics by Suckling and Carew." In *Renaissance Discourses of Desire*, edited by Claude J. Summers and Ted-Larry Pebworth, 107–29. Columbia: University of Missouri Press, 1987.

Dubrow, Heather. *Echoes of Desire: English Petrarchism and its Counterdiscourses*. Ithaca: Cornell University Press, 1995.

———. *A Happier Eden: The Politics of Marriage in the Stuart Epithalamion*. Ithaca: Cornell University Press, 1990.

———. "A Mirror for Complaints: Shakespeare's *Lucrece* and Generic Tradition." In *Renaissance Genres: Essays on Theory, History, and Interpretation,* edited by Barbara K. Lewalski, 399–417. Cambridge: Harvard University Press, 1986.

Duncan-Jones, Katherine. "Sidney, Stella, and Lady Rich." In *Sir Philip Sidney: 1586 and the Creation of a Legend,* edited by Jan van Dorsten, et al., 170–92. Leiden: E. J. Brill, 1986.

———. *Sir Philip Sidney: Courtier Poet*. New Haven: Yale University Press, 1991.

———, ed. *Miscellaneous Prose of Sir Philip Sidney*. Oxford: Clarendon Press, 1973.

Dundas, Judith. "'The Heaven's Ornament': Spenser's Tribute to Sidney." *Etudes Anglaises* 42 (1989): 129–39.

Dunlop, Alexander. "The Unity of Spenser's Amoretti." In *Silent Poetry: Essays in Numerological Analysis,* edited by Alastair Fowler, 153–69. New York: Barnes and Noble, 1970.

Dusinberre, Juliet. *Shakespeare and the Nature of Woman*. London: MacMillan, 1975.

Dwyer, June. "Fulke Greville's Aesthetic: Another Perspective." *Studies in Philology* 78 (1981): 255–74.

Eccles, Mark. "Samuel Daniel in France and Italy." *Studies in Philology* 34 (1937): 148–67.

Ellrodt, Robert. *Neoplatonism in the Poetry of Spenser*. Geneva: E. Droz, 1960.

Empson, William. *Some Versions of Pastoral*. London: Chatto and Windus, 1935.

Esler, Anthony. *The Aspiring Mind of the Elizabethan Younger Generation*. Durham: Duke University Press, 1966.

Evans, Frank B. "The Concept of the Fall in Sidney's *Apologie*." *Renaissance Papers* (1969): 9–14.

Ezell, Margaret J. M. *The Patriarch's Wife: Literary Evidence and the History of the Family*. Chapel Hill: University of North Carolina Press, 1987.

Falco, Raphael. *Conceived Presences: Literary Genealogy in Renaissance England.* Amherst: University of Massachusetts Press, 1994.

———. "Instant Artifacts: Vernacular Elegies for Philip Sidney." *Studies in Philology* 89 (1992): 1–19.

Farrand, Margaret L. "Samuel Daniel and his 'Worthy Lord.'" *Modern Language Notes* 45 (1930): 23–24.

Ferguson, Arthur B. *Clio Unbound: Perception of the social and cultural past in Renaissance England.* Durham: Duke University Press, 1979.

———. "The Historical Thought of Samuel Daniel: A Study in Renaissance Ambivalence." *Journal of the History of Ideas* 32 (1971): 185–202.

Ferguson, Margaret. *Trials of Desire: Renaissance Defenses of Poetry.* New Haven: Yale University Press, 1983.

Ferry, Ann. *The Inward Language: Sonnets of Wyatt, Sidney, Shakespeare, Donne.* Chicago: University of Chicago Press, 1983.

Fienberg, Nona. "The Emergence of Stella in *Astrophil and Stella.*" *Studies in English Literature 1500-1900* 25 (1985): 5–19.

———. "Mary Wroth and the Invention of Female Poetic Subjectivity." In *Reading Mary Wroth: Representing Alternatives in Early Modern England,* edited by Naomi Miller and Gary Waller, 175–90. Knoxville: University of Tennessee Press, 1991.

Fineman, Joel. *Shakespeare's Perjured Eye: The Invention of Poetic Subjectivity in the Sonnets.* Berkeley and Los Angeles: University of California Press, 1986.

Fisken, Beth Wynne. "'To the Angell Spirit . . .': Mary Sidney's Entry into the World of Words." In *The Renaissance Englishwoman in Print: Counterbalancing the Canon,* edited by Anne M. Haselkorn and Betty Travitsky, 263–75. Amherst: University of Massachusetts Press, 1990.

Flynn, Dennis. "'Awry and Squint': The Dating of Donne's Holy Sonnets." *John Donne Journal* 7 (1988): 35–46.

Forster, Leonard. *The Icy Fire: Five Studies in European Petrarchism.* Cambridge: Cambridge University Press, 1969.

Foucault, Michel. *The History of Sexuality.* Translated by Robert Hurley. New York: Vintage Books, 1980.

———. "The Order of Discourse." In *Untying the Text: A Post-Structuralist Reader,* edited by Robert Young, 48–78. London: Routledge and Kegan Paul, 1981.

———. *Power/Knowledge: Selected Interviews and Other Writings 1972-1977.* Edited by Colin Gordon. Translated by Colin Gordon, et al. New York: Pantheon, 1988.

Freccero, John. "The Fig Tree and the Laurel: Petrarch's Poetics." *Diacritics* 5 (1975): 34–40.

Friedrich, Walter G. "The Stella of Astrophel." *ELH* 3 (1936): 114–39.

Gardner, Helen. Introduction to *The Divine Poems*, by John Donne. Oxford: Clarendon Press, 1978.

———. Introduction to *The Elegies and the Songs and Sonnets,* by John Donne. Oxford: Clarendon Press, 1956.

Giddens, Anthony. *Central Problems in Social Theory: Action, Structure, and Contradiction in Social Analysis.* Cambridge: Cambridge University Press, 1979.

Giesey, R. E. *The Royal Funeral Ceremony in Renaissance France*. Geneva: E. Droz, 1960.

Gill, R. B. "Moral History and Daniel's *The Civil Wars*." *Journal of English and Germanic Philology* 76 (1977): 334–45.

Goldberg, Jonathan. *Endlesse Worke: Spenser and the Structures of Discourse*. Baltimore: Johns Hopkins University Press, 1981.

Gouws, John. "Fact and Anecdote in Fulke Greville's Account of Sidney's Last Days." In *Sir Philip Sidney: 1586 and the Creation of a Legend,* edited by Jan van Dorsten, et al., 62–82 Leiden: E. J. Brill, 1986.

Greenblatt, Stephen. Introduction to *The Power of Forms in the English Renaissance*. Norman, Ok.: Pilgrim Books, 1982.

———. *Renaissance Self-Fashioning from More to Shakespeare*. Chicago: University of Chicago Press, 1980.

———. *Shakespearean Negotiations: The Circulation of Social Energy in Renaissance England.* Berkeley and Los Angeles: University of California Press, 1988.

———. *Sir Walter Ralegh: The Renaissance Man and His Roles*. New Haven: Yale University Press, 1973.

Greene, Roland. *Post-Petrarchism: Origin and Innovations of the Western Lyric Sequences*. Princeton: Princeton University Press, 1991.

Greene, Thomas M. *The Light in Troy: Imitation and Discovery in Renaissance Poetry*. New Haven: Yale University Press, 1982.

Grosart, Alexander B. Introduction to *The Complete Works in Verse and Prose of Samuel Daniel*. London, 1885.

Gross, Kenneth. *Spenserian Poetics: Idolatry, Iconoclasm, and Magic*. Ithaca: Cornell University Press, 1985.

Guibbory, Achsah. "Sexual Politics / Political Sex: Seventeenth-Century Love Poetry." In *Renaissance Discourses of Desire,* edited by Claude J. Summers and Ted-Larry Pebworth, 206–22. Columbia: University of Missouri Press, 1993.

Guillory, John. *Poetic Authority: Spenser, Milton, and Literary History*. New York: Columbia University Press, 1983.

Gunn, Thom. Introduction to *Selected Poems of Fulke Greville*. Chicago: University of Chicago Press, 1968.

Hager, Alan. *Dazzling Images: The Masks of Sir Philip Sidney*. Newark: University of Delaware Press, 1991.

———. "The Exemplary Mirage: Fabrication of Sir Philip Sidney's Biographical Image and the Sidney Reader." *ELH* 48 (1981): 1–16.

Haller, William. "Hail Wedded Love." *ELH* 13 (1946): 79–97.

———, and Malleville Haller. "The Puritan Art of Love." *Huntington Library Quarterly* 5 (1942): 235–72.

Hamilton, A. C. "Sidney and Agrippa." *Review of English Studies* 7 (1965): 151–57.

———. *Sir Philip Sidney: A Study of His Life and Works*. Cambridge: Cambridge University Press, 1977.

Hampton, Timothy. *Writing from History: The Rhetoric of Exemplarity in Renaissance Literature*. Ithaca: Cornell University Press, 1990.

Hannay, Margaret. *Philip's Phoenix: Mary Sidney, Countess of Pembroke*. New York: Oxford University Press, 1990.

———. "'This Moses and This Miriam': The Countess of Pembroke's Role in the Legend of Sir Philip Sidney." In *Sir Philip Sidney's Achievements,* edited by M. J. B. Allen, et al., 217–26. New York: AMS Press, 1990.

Hardison, O. B. "*Amoretti* and the Dolce Stil Nuovo." *English Literary Renaissance* 2 (1972): 208–16.

———. "The Two Voices of Sidney's *Apology for Poetry*." *English Literary Renaissance* 2 (1972): 83–99.

Harvey, Elizabeth D. *Ventriloquized Voices: Feminist Theory and English Renaissance Texts*. London: Routledge, 1992.

Hazard, Mary E. "Renaissance Aesthetic Values: 'Example' For Example." *Art Quarterly* 2 (1979): 1–36.

Hedley, Jane. *Power in Verse: Metaphor and Metonymy in the Renaissance Lyric*. University Park: Pennsylvania State University Press, 1988.

Helgerson, Richard C. "Barbarous Tongues: The Ideology of Poetic Form in Renaissance England." In *The Historical Renaissance: New Essays on Tudor and Stuart Literature and Culture,* edited by Heather Dubrow and Richard Strier, 273–92. Chicago: University of Chicago Press, 1988.

———. *The Elizabethan Prodigals*. Berkeley and Los Angeles: University of California Press, 1976.

———. *Self-Crowned Laureates: Spenser, Jonson, Milton, and the Literary System*. Berkeley and Los Angeles: University of California Press, 1983.

Heninger, S. K. *Touches of Sweet Harmony: Pythagorean Cosmology and Renissance Poetics*. San Marino: Huntington Library, 1974.

Herman, Peter C. "'Do as I Say, Not as I Do': the *Apology for Poetry* and Sir Philip Sidney's Letters to Edward Denney and Robert Sidney." *Sidney Newsletter* 10 (1989): 13–24.

———. *Squitter-wits and Muse Haters: Sidney, Spenser, Milton and Renaissance Antipoetic Sentiment*. Detroit: Wayne State University Press, 1996.

Hieatt, A. Kent. *Chaucer, Spenser, Milton: Mythopoeic Continuities and Transformations*. Montreal: McGill-Queens University Press, 1975.

———. "A Numerical Key for Spenser's *Amoretti* and Guyon in the House of Mammon." *Yearbook of English Studies* 3 (1973): 14–27.

Himelick, Raymond. Introduction to *Samuel Daniel's Musophilus: Containing a General Defense of All Learning*. West Lafayette, Ind.: Purdue University Press, 1965.

———. "Samuel Daniel, Montaigne and Seneca." *Notes and Queries* 3 (1956): 61–64.

Ho, Elaine Y. L. "Fulke Greville's *Caelica* and the Calvinist Self." *Studies in English Literature 1500-1900* 32 (1992): 35–57.

Holahan, Michael. "Wyatt, the Heart's Forest, and the Ancient Savings." *English Literary Renaissance* 23 (1993): 46–80.

Howard, Jean E. "The New Historicism in Renaissance Studies." *English Literary Renaissance* 16 (1986): 13–43.

Howell, Roger. *Sir Philip Sidney: The Shepherd Knight*. London: Hutchinson, 1968.

Hulse, Clark. *Metamorphic Verse: The Elizabethan Minor Epic*. Princeton: Princeton University Press, 1981.

———. "Samuel Daniel: The Poet as Literary Historian." *Studies in English Literature 1500-1900* 19 (1979): 55–69.

———. "Stella's Wit: Penelope Rich as Reader of Sidney's Sonnets." In *Rewriting the Renaissance: The Discourses of Sexual Difference in Early Modern England,* edited by Margaret Ferguson, et. al, 272–86. Chicago: University of Chicago Press, 1986.

Hunt, John. "Allusive Coherence in Sidney's *Apology for Poetry.*" *Studies in English Literature 1500-1900* 27 (1987): 1–16.

Hunter, G. K. *John Lyly: The Humanist as Courtier.* Cambridge: Harvard University Press, 1962.

———. "'Unity' and Numbers in Spenser's *Amoretti.*" *Yearbook of English Studies* 5 (1975): 39–45.

Jackson, MacD. P. "The Printer of the First Quarto of *Astrophil and Stella.*" *Studies in Bibliography* 31 (1978): 201–3.

Javitch, Daniel. *Poetry and Courtliness in Renaissance England.* Princeton: Princeton University Press, 1978.

John, Lisle Cecil. *The Elizabethan Sonnet Sequences: Studies in Conventional Conceits.* New York: Columbia University Press, 1938.

Johnson, William C. "Amor and Spenser's *Amoretti.*" *English Studies* 54 (1973): 217–26.

———. *Spenser's* Amoretti*: Analogies of Love.* London: Associated University Presses, 1990.

Jones, Ann Rosalind. "Designing Women: The Self as Spectacle in Mary Wroth and Veronica Franco." In *Reading Mary Wroth: Representing Alternatives in Early Modern England,* edited by Naomi Miller and Gary Waller, 135–53. Knoxville: University of Tennessee Press, 1991.

———, and Peter Stallybrass. "The Politics of *Astrophil and Stella.*" *Studies in English Literature* 24 (1984): 53–68.

Jones, Robert C. *These Valiant Dead: Renewing the Past in Shakespeare's Histories.* Iowa City: University of Iowa Press, 1991.

Judson, Alexander C. *The Life of Edmund Spenser.* Vol. 10 of *The Works of Edmund Spenser: A Variorum Edition,* edited by Edwin Greenlaw, et al. Baltimore: Johns Hopkins University Press, 1945.

Kahn, Victoria. *Rhetoric, Prudence, and Skepticism in the Renaissance.* Ithaca: Cornell University Press, 1985.

Kalstone, David. *Sidney's Poetry: Contexts and Interpretations.* Cambridge: Harvard University Press, 1965.

Kantorowicz, Ernst H. *The King's Two Bodies: A Study in Medieval Political Theology.* Princeton: Princeton University Press, 1957.

Kaske, Carol. "Spenser's *Amoretti* and *Epithalamion* of 1595: Structure, Genre, and Numerology." *English Literary Renaissance* 8 (1978): 271–95.

Kau, Joseph. "Delia's Gentle Lover and the Eternizing Conceit in Elizabethan Sonnets." *Anglia* 92 (1974): 334–48.

Kay, Dennis. *Melodious Tears: The English Funeral Elegy from Spenser to Milton.* Oxford: Clarendon Press, 1990.

King, John N. *English Reformation Literature: The Tudor Origins of the Protestant Tradition.* Princeton: Princeton University Press, 1982.

———. *Spenser's Poetry and the Reformation Tradition.* Princeton: Princeton University Press, 1990.

Kinney, Arthur F. *Humanist Poetics: Thought, Rhetoric, and Fiction in Sixteenth-Century England.* Amherst: University of Massachusetts Press, 1986.

———. *Markets of Bawdrie: The Dramatic Criticism of Stephen Gosson.* Salzburg: Institut für Englische Sprache und Literatur, 1974.

———. "Parody and its Implications in Sidney's *Defence of Poesie.*" *Studies in English Literature 1500-1900* 12 (1972): 1–19.

———. "Rhetoric at the Court of Elizabeth I." In *Sir Philip Sidney's Achievement,* edited by M. J. B. Allen, et al., 44–57. New York: AMS Press, 1990.

Klein, Lisa. "'Let us love, dear love, lyke as we ought': Protestant Marriage and the Revision of Petrarchan Loving in Spenser's *Amoretti.*" *Spenser Studies* 10 (1992): 109–37.

———. "The Petrarchism of Sir Thomas Wyatt Reconsidered." In *The Work of Dissimilitude: Essays from the Sixth Citadel Conference on Medieval and Renaissance Literature,* edited by David G. Allen and Robert H. White, 131–47. Newark: University of Delaware Press, 1992.

———. "Spenser's *Astrophel* and the Sidney Legend." *Sidney Newsletter and Journal* 12 (1993): 42–55.

Kuin, Roger. "The Middleburg Weekend: More Light on the Proposed Marriage Between Philip Sidney and Marie of Nassau." *Sidney Newsletter and Journal* 12 (1993): 3–13.

———. "Sir Philip Sidney: The Courtier and the Text." *English Literary Renaissance* 19 (1989): 249–71.

Lamb, Mary Ellen. "The Countess of Pembroke and the Art of Dying." In *Women in the Middle Ages and the Renaissance*, edited by Mary Beth Rose, 207–26. Syracuse: Syracuse University Press, 1986.

———. "The Countess of Pembroke's Patronage." *English Literary Renaissance* 12 (1982): 162–79.

———. "The Myth of the Countess of Pembroke: The Dramatic Circle." *Yearbook of English Studies* 11 (1981): 194–202.

Lanham, Richard. "*Astrophil and Stella*: Pure and Impure Persuasion." *English Literary Renaissance* 2 (1972): 100–115.

———. "Sidney: The Ornament of His Age." *Southern Review* (Adelaide) 2 (1967): 319–40.

Lavin, J. A. "The First Two Printers of Sidney's *Astrophil and Stella.*" *The Library,* 5th ser. 26 (1971): 249–55.

LeGoff, Jacques. *History and Memory.* Translated by Steven Rendall and Elizabeth Claman. New York: Columbia University Press, 1992.

———. "Mentalities: a history of ambiguities." Translated by David Denby. In *Constructing the Past: Essays in Historical Methodology,* edited by LeGoff and Pierre Nora, 166–80. Cambridge: Cambridge University Press, 1974. Reprint, 1985.

Levao, Ronald. *Renaissance Minds and Their Fictions.* Berkeley and Los Angeles: University of California Press, 1985.

Lever, J. W. *The Elizabethan Love Sonnet*. London: Methuen, 1956.

Levy, F. J. "Fulke Greville: The Courtier as Philosophic Poet." *Modern Language Quarterly* 33 (1972): 433–48.

———. "Hayward, Daniel, and the Beginnings of Politic History in England." *Huntington Library Quarterly* 53 (1987): 1–34.

———. *Tudor Historical Thought*. San Marino: The Huntington Library, 1967.

Lewalski, Barbara K. *Protestant Poetics and the Seventeenth Century Religious Lyric*. Princeton: Princeton University Press, 1979.

———. *Writing Women in Jacobean England*. Cambridge: Harvard University Press, 1993.

Lewis, C. S. *The Allegory of Love*. New York: Oxford University Press, 1958.

———. "Donne and Love Poetry in the Seventeenth Century." In *Seventeenth-Century Studies Presented to Sir Herbert Grierson*. Oxford: Clarendon Press, 1938.

———. *English Literature in the Sixteenth Century*. Oxford: Clarendon Press, 1954.

Litt, Gary L. "'Images of Life': A Study of Narrative and Structure in Fulke Greville's *Caelica*." *Studies in Philology* 69 (1972): 217–30.

Loades, David. *The Tudor Court*. London: B. T. Batsford, 1987.

Loewenstein, Joseph. "Echo's Ring: Orpheus and Spenser's Career." *English Literary Renaissance* 16 (1986): 287–302.

———. "Sidney's Truant Pen." *Modern Language Quarterly* 46 (1982): 128–42.

Low, Anthony. *The Reinvention of Love: Poetry, politics and culture from Sidney to Milton*. Cambridge: Cambridge University Press, 1993.

Lyons, John D. *Exemplum: The Rhetoric of Exemplarity in Early Modern France and Italy*. Princeton: Princeton University Press, 1989.

MacArthur, Janet H. *Critical Contexts of Sidney's* Astrophil and Stella *and Spenser's* Amoretti. *English Literary Studies* 46. Victoria, B.C.: University of Victoria Press, 1989.

———. "'A Sydney, Though Un-Named': Lady Mary Wroth and her Poetic Progenitors." *English Studies in Canada* 15 (1989): 12–20.

MacCaffrey, Wallace T. *Queen Elizabeth and the Making of Policy 1572-1588*. Princeton: Princeton University Press, 1981.

Malcolmson, Cristina. "Politics and Psychoanalysis: Sidney's Imagery of the Child." Unpublished essay.

Manley, Lawrence. *Convention 1500-1740*. Cambridge: Harvard University Press, 1980.

———. "Spenser and the City: The Minor Poems." *Modern Language Quarterly* 43 (1982): 203–27.

Marotti, Arthur. "'Love is not Love': Elizabethan Sonnet Sequences and the Social Order." *ELH* 49 (1982): 396–428.

———. *Manuscript, Print, and the English Renaissance Lyric*. Ithaca: Cornell University Press, 1995.

Martin, Christopher. "Between Duty and Selfness: Greville's *Life of Sidney*." *Mid-Hudson Language Studies* 9 (1986): 19–29.

———. "Sidney's *Defence*: The Art of Slander and the Slander of Art." *Sidney Newsletter* 9 (1988): 3–10.

Martines, Lauro. *Society and History in English Renaissance Verse*. Oxford: Basil Blackwell, 1985.

Martz, Louis. "The *Amoretti*: 'Mostly Goodly Temperature.'" In *Form and Convention in the Poetry of Edmund Spenser,* edited by William Nelson, 146–68. New York: Columbia University Press, 1961.

———. *The Poetry of Meditation*. New Haven: Yale University Press, 1954. Reprint, 1962.

Masten, Jeff. "'Shall I turne blabb?': Circulation, Gender, and Subjectivity in Mary Wroth's Sonnets." In *Reading Mary Wroth: Representing Alternatives in Early Modern England,* edited by Naomi Miller and Gary Waller, 67–87. Knoxville: University of Tennessee Press, 1991.

Matthews, G. M. "Sex and the Sonnet." *Essays in Criticism* 2 (1952): 119–37.

Matz, Robert. "Sidney's *Defence of Poesie*: The Politics of Pleasure." *English Literary Renaissance* 25 (1995): 131–47.

May, Steven W. *The Elizabethan Courtier Poets: The Poems and Their Contexts*. Columbia: University of Missouri Press, 1991.

Mazzotta, Guiseppe. "The *Canzoniere* and the Language of Self." *Studies in Philology* 75 (1978): 271–96.

McCoy, Richard. *The Rites of Knighthood: The Literature and Politics of Elizabethan Chivalry*. Berkeley and Los Angeles: University of California Press, 1989.

———. *Sir Philip Sidney: Rebellion in Arcadia*. Sussex: Harvester Press, 1979.

McIntyre, John P. "Sidney's Golden World." *College Literature* 14 (1962): 356–65.

McKeon, Richard. "Literary Criticism and the Concept of Imitation in Antiquity." In *Critics and Criticism,* edited by R. S. Crane, 147–75. Chicago: University of Chicago Press, 1952.

Michel, Lawrence. Introduction to *The Tragedy of Philotas,* by Samuel Daniel. New Haven: Yale University Press, 1949.

Miller, Anthony. "Sidney's *Apology for Poetry* and Plutarch's *Moralia*." *English Literary Renaissance* 17 (1987): 259–76.

Miller, David Lee. "Abandoning the Quest." *ELH* 46 (1979): 173–92.

———. *The Poem's Two Bodies: The Poetics of the 1590* Faerie Queene. Princeton: Princeton University Press, 1988.

———. "Spenser's Poetics: The Poem's Two Bodies." *PMLA* 101 (1986): 170–85.

Miller, Edwin H. "Samuel Daniel's Revisions in 'Delia.'" *Journal of English and Germanic Philology* 53 (1954): 58–68.

Miller, Jacqueline. "'Love doth hold my hand': Writing and Wooing in the Sonnets of Sidney and Spenser." *ELH* 46 (1979): 541–58.

———. *Poetic License: Authority and Authorship in Medieval and Renaissance Contexts*. New York: Oxford University Press, 1986.

———. "'What May Words Say': The Limits of Language in *Astrophil and Stella*." In *Sir Philip Sidney and the Interpretation of Renaissance Culture,* edited by Gary F. Waller and Michael D. Moore, 95–105. London: Croom Helm, 1984.

Miller, Naomi J. "Rewriting Lyric Fictions: The Role of the Lady in Lady Mary Wroth's *Pamphilia to Amphilanthus*." In *Reading Mary Wroth: Representing Alternatives in Early Modern England,* edited by Naomi Miller and Gary Waller, 295–310. Knoxville: University of Tennessee Press, 1991.

Miller, Paul Allen. "Sidney, Petrarch, and Ovid: Imitation as Subversion." *ELH* 58 (1991): 499–522.

Mommsen, Theodor E. "Petrarch and the Story of the Choice of Hercules." *Journal of the Warburg and Courtauld Institutes* 16 (1953): 178–92.

Montgomery, Robert. "The Poetics of Astrophil." In *Sir Philip Sidney's Achievement,* edited by M. J. B. Allen, et al., 145–56. New York: AMS Press, 1990.

———. *Symmetry and Sense: The Poetry of Sir Philip Sidney*. Austin: University of Texas Press, 1961.

Montrose, Louis Adrian. "Celebration and Insinuation: Sir Philip Sidney and the Motives of Elizabethan Courtship." *Renaissance Drama* 8 (1977): 3–35.

———. "'Eliza, Queene of shepheardes,' and the Pastoral of Power." *English Literary Renaissance* 10 (1980): 153–82.

———. "Of Gentlemen and Shepherds: The Politics of Elizabethan Pastoral Form." *ELH* 59 (1983): 415–59.

———. "'The perfect paterne of a Poete': The Poetics of Courtship in *The Shepheardes Calender.*" *Texas Studies in Literature and Language* 21 (1979): 34–67.

———. "Professing the Renaissance: The Poetics and Politics of Culture." In *The New Historicism,* edited by H. Aram Veeser, 15–36. New York: Routledge, 1989.

———. "Renaissance Literary Studies and the Subject of History." *English Literary Renaissance* 16 (1986): 5–12.

Murphy, William M. "Thomas Watson's *Hecatompathia* (1582) and the Elizabethan Sonnet Sequence." *Journal of English and Germanic Philology* 56 (1957): 418–28.

Myrick, Kenneth. *Sir Philip Sidney as a Literary Craftsman*. 1935. Reprint, Lincoln: University of Nebraska Press, 1965.

Neely, Carol Thomas. "Representing Women: Disjunctions, Divisions, Disappearances." Paper delivered at the Ohio Shakespeare Conference, Akron, Ohio, March 1989.

Nelson, Lowry. "The Matter of Rime: Sonnets of Sidney, Daniel, and Shakespeare." In *Poetic Traditions of the English Renaissance,* edited by Maynard Mack and George de Forest Lord, 123–42. New Haven: Yale University Press, 1982.

Nelson, William. *The Poetry of Edmund Spenser*. New York: Columbia University Press, 1963.

Neuse, Richard. "Book VI as Conclusion to *The Faerie Queene*." *ELH* 35 (1968): 329–53.

Nichols, John. *Progresses and Public Processions of Queen Elizabeth*. 2 vols. London, 1823. Reprint, New York: Burt Franklin, 1964.

Nora, Pierre. "Between Memroy and History: *Les Lieux de Mémoire*." Translated by Marc Roudebush. *Representations* 26 (1988): 7–25.

Norbrook, David. *Poetry and Politics in the English Renaissance*. London: Routledge and Kegan Paul, 1984.

O'Connell, Michael. "*Astrophel*: Spenser's Double Elegy." *Studies in English Literature* 11 (1971): 27–35.

———. *Mirror and Veil: The Historical Dimension of Spenser's* Faerie Queene. Chapel Hill: University of North Carolina Press, 1977.

Orgel, Stephen. "Sidney's Experiment in Pastoral: *The Lady of May*." *Journal of the Warburg and Courtauld Institutes* 26 (1963): 198–203.

Ortner, Sherry B. "Theory and Anthropology since the Sixties." *Comparative Studies in Society and History* 26 (1984): 126–66.

Osborn, James M. *Young Philip Sidney, 1572-1577*. New Haven: Yale University Press, 1972.

The Oxford Companion to English Literature. 5th ed. Edited by Margaret Drabble. New York: Oxford University Press, 1985.

Pagels, Elaine. *Adam, Eve, and the Serpent*. New York: Random House, 1988.

Patterson, Lee. *Negotiating the Past: The Historical Understanding of Medieval Literature*. Madison: University of Wisconsin Press, 1987.

Pechter, Edward. "New Historicism and its Discontents: Politicizing Renaissance Drama." *PMLA* 102 (1987): 292–303.

Peterson, Douglas. *The English Lyric from Wyatt to Donne: A History of the Plain and Eloquent Styles*. Princeton: Princeton University Press, 1967.

Peterson, Richard S. "'Who Ever Made Such Layes of Love as He?'" Response paper presented at the 28th International Congress on Medieval Studies, Kalamazoo, Michigan, May 1993.

Pigman III, G. W. *Grief and English Renaissance Elegy*. Cambridge: Cambridge University Press, 1985.

———. "Limping Examples: Exemplarity, the New Historicism, and Psychoanalysis." In *Creative Imitation: New Essays on Renaissance Literature in Honor of Thomas M. Greene,* edited by David Quint, et al., 281–95. Binghamton, N.Y.: Medieval and Renaissance Texts and Studies, 1992.

———. "Self, Subversion, and the New Historicism." *Huntington Library Quarterly* 52 (1989): 501–8.

———. "Versions of Imitation in the Renaissance." *Renaissance Quarterly* 33 (1980): 1–32.

Pitcher, John. "Samuel Daniel, the Hertfords, and A Question of Love." *Review of English Studies* 35 (1985): 449–62.

———. "Samuel Daniel's Letter to Sir Thomas Egerton." *Huntington Library Quarterly* 47 (1984): 55–61.

Prendergast, Maria Theresa Micaela. "The Unauthorized Orpheus of *Astrophil and Stella*." *Studies in English Literature 1500-1900* 35 (1995): 19–34.

Prescott, Ann Lake. "Evil Tongues and the Court of Saul: The Renaissance David as a Slandered Courtier." *Journal of Medieval and Renaissance Studies* 21 (1991): 163–86.

———. *French Poets and the English Renaissance: Studies in Fame and Transformation*. New Haven: Yale University Press, 1978.

———. "King David as a 'Right Poet': Sidney and the Psalmist." *English Literary Renaissance* 19 (1989): 131–51.

———. Letter to the Editor. *Sidney Newsletter and Journal* 12.1 (1992): 29–31.

———. "The Thirsty Deer and the Lord of Life: Some Contexts for *Amoretti* 67–70." *Spenser Studies* 7 (1986) 33–76.

Primeau, Ronald. "Daniel and the *Mirror* Tradition: Dramatic Irony in *The Complaint of Rosamond*." *Studies in English Literature* 15 (1975): 21–36.

Purcell, J. M. "Sidney's *Astrophil and Stella* and Greville's *Caelica*." *PMLA* 50 (1935): 413–22.

Quilligan, Maureen. "Lady Mary Wroth: Female Authority and the Family Romance." In *Unfolded Tales: Essays on Renaissance Romance,* edited by George M. Logan and Gordon Teskey, 257–80. Ithaca: Cornell University Press, 1989.

———. "Sidney and His Queen." In *The Historical Renaissance: New Essays on Tudor and Stuart Literature and Culture,* edited by Heather Dubrow and Richard Strier, 171–96. Chicago: University of Chicago Press, 1988.

Quint, David. *Origin and Originality in Renaissance Literature: Versions of the Source*. New Haven: Yale University Press, 1983.

Quitslund, Jon. "Sidney's Presence in Lyric Verse of the Later English Renaissance." In *Sir Philip Sidney and the Interpretation of Renaissance Culture,* edited by Gary Waller and Michael D. Moore, 110–23. London: Croom Helm, 1984.

Rackin, Phyllis. *Stages of History: Shakespeare's English Chronicles*. Ithaca: Cornell University Press, 1990.

Raitiere, Martin. *"Faire Bitts": Sir Philip Sidney and Renaissance Political Theory*. Pittsburg: Duquesne University Press, 1984.

———. "The Unity of Sidney's *Apology for Poetry*." *Studies in English Literature 1500-1900* 21 (1981): 37–57.

Rasmussen, Carl J. "'How Weak Be the Passions of Woefulness': Spenser's *Ruines of Time*." *Spenser Studies* 2 (1981): 159–81.

———. "'Quietnesse of Minde': *A Theatre for Worldlings* as a Protestant Poetics." *Spenser Studies* 1 (1980): 3–27.

Rebholz, R. A. *The Life of Fulke Greville, Lord Brooke*. Oxford: Clarendon Press, 1971.

Rees, D. G. "Italian and Italianate Poetry." In *Elizabethan Poetry,* edited by John Russell Brown and Bernard Harris, 53–69. New York: St. Martin's Press, 1960.

———. "Petrarch's 'Trionfo Della Morte' in English." *Italian Studies* 7 (1952): 82–96.

Rees, Joan. *Fulke Greville, Lord Brooke 1554-1629: A Critical Biography*. Berkeley and Los Angeles: University of California Press, 1971.

———. "Fulke Greville's Epitaph on Sidney." *Review of English Studies* 19 (1968): 47–51.

———. "Past and Present in the Sixteenth Century." *Trivium* (1985): 97–112.

———. *Samuel Daniel: A Critical and Biographical Study*. Liverpool: Liverpool University Press, 1964.

———. *Sir Philip Sidney and* Arcadia. London: Associated University Press, 1991.

Renwick, W. L., ed. *Complaints,* by Edmund Spenser. London, 1928.

Ringler, William A. "Sir Philip Sidney: The Myth and the Man." In *Sir Philip Sidney: 1586 and the Creation of a Legend,* edited by Jan van Dorsten, et al., 3–15. Leiden: E. J. Brill, 1986.

Roberts, David. "Fulke Greville's Aesthetic Reconsidered." *Studies in Philology* 74 (1977): 388–405.

Roberts, Josephine. *Architectonic Knowledge in the* New Arcadia*: Sidney's Use of the Heroic Journey*. Salzburg: Institut für Englische Sprache und Literatur, 1978.

———. Introduction to *The Poems of Lady Mary Wroth*. Baton Rouge: Louisiana State University Press, 1983.

Roche Jr., Thomas P. "Autobiographical Elements in Sidney's *Astrophil and Stella*." *Spenser Studies* 5 (1984): 209–29.

———. *The Kindly Flame: A Study of the Third and Fourth Books of Spenser's* Faerie Queene. Princeton: Princeton University Press, 1964.

———. *Petrarch and the English Sonnet Sequences*. New York: AMS, 1989.

———. Review of *The Yale Edition of the Shorter Poems of Edmund Spenser*. *Spenser Newsletter* 22.2 (1991): 7–11.

Rollins, Hyder Edward, ed. *The Phoenix Nest*. London, 1593. Reprint, Cambridge: Harvard University Press, 1931.

Rose, Mark. *Heroic Love: Studies in Sidney and Spenser*. Cambridge: Harvard University Press, 1968.

Rossky, William. "Imagination in the English Renaissance: Psychology and Poetic." *Studies in the Renaissance* 5 (1958): 49–73.

Rudenstine, Neil. *Sidney's Poetic Development*. Cambridge: Harvard University Press, 1967.

Ryding, Erik S. In *Harmony Framed: Musical Humanism, Thomas Campion, and the Two Daniels*. Kirksville, Mo.: Sixteenth Century Essays and Studies, 1993.

Sacks, Peter. "*Astrophel*." From *The English Elegy: Studies in the Genre from Spenser to Yeats*. Reprinted in *Edmund Spenser: Modern Critical Views*, edited by Harold Bloom, 239–49. New York: Chelsea, 1986.

"Samuel Daniel and Fulke Greville." *Times Literary Supplement*, 5 June 1930, p. 475.

Satterthwaite, Alfred W. *Spenser, Ronsard, and Du Bellay: A Renaissance Comparison*. Princeton: Princeton University Press, 1960.

Saunders, J. W. "The Stigma of Print: A Note on the Social Bases of Tudor Poetry." *Essays in Criticism* 1 (1951): 139–64.

Schmitz, Gotz. *The Fall of Women in Early English Narrative Verse*. Cambridge: Cambridge University Press, 1990.

Schoenfeldt, Michael C. *Prayer and Power: George Herbert and Renaissance Courtship*. Chicago: University of Chicago Press, 1991.

Scott, Janet. *Les Sonnets Élisabethains*. Paris, 1929.

Seronsy, Cecil. "The Doctrine of Cyclical Recurrence and Some Related Ideas in the Works of Samuel Daniel." *Studies in Philology* 54 (1957): 387–407.

———. *Samuel Daniel*. New York: Twayne Publishers, 1967.

Sharpe, Kevin. "Cavalier Critic? The Ethics and Politics of Thomas Carew's Poetry." In *Politics of Discourse: The Literature and History of Seventeenth-Century England*, edited by Kevin Sharpe and Steven N. Zwicker, 117–46. Berkeley and Los Angeles: University of California Press, 1987.

Shepherd, Geoffrey, ed. Introduction to *An Apology for Poetry*, by Sir Philip Sidney. London, 1965.

Shuger, Deborah. *Habits of Thought in the English Renaissance: Religion, Politics, and the Dominant Culture*. Berkeley and Los Angeles: University of California Press, 1990.

Sinfield, Alan. "Astrophil's Self-Deception." *Essays in Criticism* 28 (1978): 1–17.

———. "The Cultural Politics of the *Defense of Poetry.*" In *Sir Philip Sidney and the Interpretation of Reniassance Culture,* edited by Gary Waller and Michael D. Moore, 124–43. London: Croom Helm, 1984.

———. *Literature in Protestant England 1560-1660.* London: Croom Helm, 1983.

———. "Sidney and Astrophil." *Studies in English Literature 1500-1900* 20 (1980): 25–41.

Skretkowicz, Victor. "Building Sidney's Reputation: Texts and Editors of the *Arcadia.*" In *Sir Philip Sidney: 1586 and the Creation of a Legend,* edited by Jan Van Dorsten, et al., 111–24. Leiden: E. J. Brill, 1986.

Smith, Hallet. "The Art of Sir Thomas Wyatt." *Huntington Library Quarterly* 9 (1946): 323–55.

———. *Elizabethan Poetry: A Study in Conventions, Meaning and Expression.* Cambridge: Harvard University Press, 1952.

———. "English Metrical Psalms in the Sixteenth Century and Their Literary Significance." *Huntington Library Quarterly* 9 (1946): 249–71.

Spencer, Theodore. "The Poetry of Sir Philip Sidney." *ELH* 12 (1945): 251–78.

Spiller, Michael R. G. *The Development of the Sonnet: An Introduction.* London: Routledge, 1992.

Steinberg, Theodore L. "Spenser, Sidney, and the Myth of Astrophel." *Spenser Studies* 11 (1994): 187–201.

———. "Weeping for Sidney." *Sidney Newsletter and Journal* 11 (1991): 3–15.

Stone, Lawrence. *The Family, Sex, and Marriage in England 1500-1800.* New York: Harper & Row, 1977.

Strauss, Walter L. *Hendrik Goltzius: The Complete Engravings and Woodcuts.* 3 vols. New York: Abaris Books, 1977.

Strickland, Ronald. "Pageantry and Poetry as Discourse: The Production of Subjectivity in Sir Philip Sidney's Funeral." *ELH* 57 (1990): 19–36.

Strong, Roy. *Portraits of Queen Elizabeth I.* Oxford: Clarendon Press, 1963.

Struever, Nancy S. *The Language of History in the Renaissance: Rhetoric and Historical Consciousness in Florentine Literature.* Princeton: Princeton University Press, 1970.

Stull, William L. "'Why Are Not *Sonnets* Made of Thee?': A New Context for the 'Holy Sonnets' of Donne, Herbert, and Milton." *Modern Philology* 80 (1982): 129–35.

Summers, Joseph H. "'Sir Calidore and the Country Parson." In *Like Season'd Timber: New Essays on George Herbert,* edited by Edmund Miller and Robert DiYanni, 207–18. New York: Peter Lang, 1987.

Svensson, Lars-Haken. *Silent Art: Rhetorical and Thematic Patterns in Samuel Daniel's* Delia. Lund: CWK Gleerup, 1980.

Tennenhouse, Leonard. "Sir Walter Ralegh and the Literature of Clientage." In *Patronage in the Renaissance,* edited by Guy Fitch Lytle and Stephen Orgel, 235–58. Princeton: Princeton University Press, 1981.

Thomas, Brooke. *The New Historicism and Other Old-Fashioned Topics.* Princeton: Princeton University Press, 1991.

Thomson, Patricia. "The Literature of Patronage, 1580–1630." *Essays in Criticism* 2 (1952): 267–84.

———. *Sir Thomas Wyatt and His Background.* London: Routledge and Kegan Paul, 1964.

Todd, Margo. *Christian Humanism and the Puritan Social Order.* Cambridge: Cambridge University Press, 1987.

Todd, Richard. "Humanist Prosodic Theory, Dutch Synods, and the Poetics of the Sidney-Pembroke Psalter." *Huntington Library Quarterly* 52 (1989): 273–93.

Tourney, Leonard. "Spenser's *Astrophel*: Myth and the Critique of Values." *Essays in Literature* 3 (1976): 141–51.

Trexler, Richard C. *Public Life in Renaissance Florence.* New York: Academic Press, 1980.

Ulreich Jr., John C. "'The Poets Only Deliver': Sidney's Conception of *Mimesis*." *Studies in the Literary Imagination* 15 (1982): 67–84.

van Dorsten, Jan. "Literary Patronage in Elizabethan England: The Early Phase." In *Patronage in the Renaissance,* edited by Guy Fitch Lytle and Stephen Orgel, 191–206. Princeton: Princeton University Press, 1981.

———, et al., eds. *Sir Philip Sidney: 1586 and the Creation of a Legend.* Leiden: E. J. Brill, 1986.

Vickers, Nancy. "'The blazon of sweet beauty's best': Shakespeare's Lucrece." In *Shakespeare and the Question of Theory,* edited by Patricia Parker and Geoffrey Hartman, 95–115. New York: Methuen, 1985.

———. "Diana Described: Scattered Women and Scattered Rhyme." *Critical Inquiry* 8 (1981): 265–79.

Vovelle, Michel. *Ideologies and Mentalities.* Translated by Eamon O'Flaherty. Cambridge: Polity Press, 1990.

Wall, John N. *Transformations of the Word: Spenser, Herbert, Vaughan.* Athens: University of Georgia Press, 1988.

Wall, Wendy. *The Imprint of Gender: Authorship and Publication in the English Renaissance.* Ithaca: Cornell University Press, 1993.

Wallace, Malcolm. *The Life of Sir Philip Sidney.* Cambridge: Cambridge University Press, 1915.

Waller, Gary. "Acts of Reading: The Production of Meaning in *Astrophil and Stella.*" *Studies in the Literary Imagination* 15 (1982): 25–35.

———. *English Poetry of the Sixteenth Century.* London: Longman, 1986.

———. "Fulke Greville's Struggle with Calvinism." *Studia Neophilologica* 44 (1972): 295–314.

———. *Mary Sidney, Countess of Pembroke: A Critical Study of her Writings and Literary Milieu.* Elizabethan and Renaissance Studies 87. Salzburg: Institut für Englische Sprache und Literatur, 1979.

———. "The Rewriting of Petrarch: Sidney and the Languages of Sixteenth-Century Poetry." In *Sir Philip Sidney and the Interpretation of Renaissance Culture,* edited by Gary Waller and Michael D. Moore, 84–94. London: Croom Helm, 1984.

———. *The Sidney Family Romance: Mary Wroth, William Herbert, and the Early Modern Construction of Gender.* Detroit: Wayne State University Press, 1993.

———, ed. *The Triumph of Death and Other Unpublished and Uncollected Poems by Mary Sidney, Countess of Pembroke (1561–1621).* Salzburg: Institut für Englishe Sprache und Literatur, 1977.

———, and Michael D. Moore, eds. *Sir Philip Sidney and the Interpretation of Renaissance Culture*. London: Croom Helm, 1984.

Warkentin, Germaine. "Patrons and Profiteers: Thomas Newman and the 'Violent enlargement' of *Astrophil and Stella*." *The Book Collector* 34 (1985): 461–87.

Waswo, Richard. *The Fatal Mirror: Themes and Techniques in the Poetry of Fulke Greville*. Charlottesville: University Press of Virginia, 1972.

Watson, George. *The English Petrarchans: A Critical Bibliography of the "Canzionere."* London: Warburg Institute, 1967.

Webster, John. "'The Methode of a Poete': An Inquiry into Tudor Conceptions of Poetic Sequence." *English Literary Renaissance* 11 (1981): 22–43.

———. Introduction to *William Temple's Analysis of Sir Philip Sidney's* Apology for Poetry. Binghamton, N.Y.: Medieval and Renaissance Texts and Studies, 1984.

Weiner, Andrew. "Sidney, Protestantism, and Literary Critics: Reflections on Some Recent Criticism of *The Defence of Poetry*." In *Sir Philip Sidney's Achievements*, edited by M. J. B. Allen et al., 117–26. New York: AMS Press, 1990.

———. *Sir Philip Sidney and the Poetics of Protestantism: A Study of Contexts*. Minneapolis: University of Minnesota Press, 1978.

Welsford, Enid. *Fowre Hymns; Epithalamion: A Study of Edmund Spenser's Doctrine of Love*. New York: Barnes and Noble, 1967.

White, Hayden. *Metahistory: The Historical Imagination in Nineteenth-Century Europe*. Baltimore: Johns Hopkins University Press, 1973.

Williamson, C. F. "The Design of Daniel's *Delia*." *Review of English Studies* 19 (1968): 251–60.

Wilson, Christopher R. "*Astrophil and Stella*: A Tangled Editorial Web." *The Library* (6th ser.) 1 (1979): 336–46.

Wilson, Jean. *Entertainments for Elizabeth I*. Woodbridge, England: D. S. Brewer, 1980.

Wilson, Luke. "*Hamlet*: Equity, Intention, Performance." *Studies in the Literary Imagination* 24 (1991): 91–113.

———. "*Hamlet*, Hales v. Petit, and the Hysteresis of Action." *ELH* 60 (1993): 17–55.

Winters, Ivor. *Forms of Discovery: Critical and Historical Essays on the Forms of the Short Poem in English*. Chicago: Alan Swallow, 1967.

Wood, Chauncey. "Sin and the Sonnet: Sidney, St. Augustine, and Herbert's 'The Sinner.'" *George Herbert Journal* 15 (1992): 19–32.

Wooden, Warren W. Introduction to *The Life of the Renowned Sr Philip Sidney* by Fulke Greville. 1652. Delmar, N.Y.: Scholars' Facsimiles and Reprints, 1984.

Woolf, D. R. "Community, Law and State: Samuel Daniel's Historical Thought Revisited." *Journal of the History of Ideas* 49 (1988): 61–83.

Wrightson, Keith. *English Society 1580-1680*. New Brunswick: Rutgers University Press, 1982.

Young, Frances B. *Mary Sidney, Countess of Pembroke*. London: David Nutt, 1912.

Young, Richard B. "English Petrarke: A Study of Sidney's *Astrophil and Stella*." In *Three Studies in The Renaissance: Sidney, Jonson, Milton*. New Haven: Yale University Press, 1958.

Zim, Rivkah. *English Metrical Psalms: Poetry as Praise and Prayer, 1535-1601*. Cambridge: Cambridge University Press, 1987.

Zouch, Theodore. *Memoirs of the Life and Writings of Sir Philip Sidney*. York, 1808.

Index